Cambridge Studies in Modern Political Economies

Editors
SUZANNE BERGER, ALBERT HIRSCHMAN, AND CHARLES MAIER

Organizing interests in Western Europe: pluralism, corporatism, and the transformation of politics

Sponsored by the Joint Committee on Western Europe of
the Social Science Research Council and
the American Council of Learned Societies

Organizing interests in Western Europe

Pluralism, corporatism, and the transformation of politics

Edited by

SUZANNE BERGER

Department of Political Science
Massachusetts Institute of Technology

CAMBRIDGE UNIVERSITY PRESS

Cambridge
London   New York   New Rochelle
Melbourne   Sydney

Published by the Press Syndicate of the University of Cambridge
The Pitt Building, Trumpington Street, Cambridge CB2 1RP
32 East 57th Street, New York, NY 10022, USA
296 Beaconsfield Parade, Middle Park, Melbourne 3206, Australia

First published 1981
First paperback edition 1983

Printed in the United States of America
Typeset by The Composing Room of Michigan, Inc., Grand Rapids, Michigan
Printed and bound by The Book Press, Brattleboro, Vermont

Library of Congress Cataloging in Publication Data
Main entry under title:
Organizing interests in Western Europe.
(Cambridge studies in modern political economies)
"Sponsored by the Joint Committee on Western Europe
of the Social Science Research Council and the American
Council of Learned Societies."
Includes index.
1. Pressure groups–Europe–Addresses, essays,
lectures. I. Berger, Suzanne. II. Joint Committee
on Western Europe. III. Series.
JN94.A792P76   322.4'3'094   80–16378
ISBN 0 521 23174 4 hard covers
ISBN 0 521 27062 6 paperback

Contents

Contributors

SUZANNE BERGER
> *Department of Political Science, Massachusetts*
> *Institute of Technology, Cambridge, Massachusetts, U.S.A.*

GERALD D. FELDMAN
> *Department of History, University of California –*
> *Berkeley, Berkeley, California, U.S.A.*

GUDMUND HERNES
> *Department of Sociology, University of Bergen, Bergen, Norway*

JOHN T. S. KEELER
> *Department of Political Science, University of Washington, Seattle,*
> *Washington, U.S.A.*

JÜRGEN KOCKA
> *Department of History, University of Bielefeld, Bielefeld, West*
> *Germany*

JUAN J. LINZ
> *Departments of Sociology and Political Science,*
> *Yale University, New Haven, Connecticut, U.S.A.*

CHARLES S. MAIER
> *Department of History, Duke University, Durham, North*
> *Carolina, U.S.A.*

CLAUS OFFE
> *Department of Sociology, University of Bielefeld, Bielefeld, West*
> *Germany*

ALESSANDRO PIZZORNO
> *Department of Sociology, University of Milan, Italy, and Harvard*
> *University, Cambridge, Massachusetts, U.S.A.*

CHARLES F. SABEL
> *Program in Science, Technology and Society, Massachusetts*
> *Institute of Technology, Cambridge, Massachusetts, U.S.A.*

MICHELE SALVATI
    Department of Economics, University of Modena, Modena, Italy
PHILIPPE C. SCHMITTER
    Department of Political Science, University of Chicago, Chicago, Illinois, U.S.A.
ARNE SELVIK
    Institute of Industrial Economics, Bergen, Norway

Preface

This volume concludes the first phase of an ongoing investigation by the Joint Committee on Western Europe of the Social Science Research Council and the American Council of Learned Societies into the structures and tendencies of the contemporary societies of Western Europe. The chapters reflect the diverse perspectives on interest groups of a dozen scholars working out of very different disciplinary, national, and political traditions. They also reflect three years of common effort; in the four meetings in which these essays were discussed, the authors were obliged to reconsider both premises and conclusions in order to respond to the questioning and alternative formulations offered by other participants.

Had each essay been written without the pressure to answer the common set of questions that emerged during the meetings, it would have been quite different from that presented here. The sessions thus not only produced a collection of essays more integrated by common concerns than the volumes that usually result from such conferences, but they also showed the possibility and intellectual promise of a mode of collaborative research that permits scholars with very different perspectives to work together, without the benefit of a single research project within which each would have an assigned role and without the presence of a single intellectual leader whose conceptions would orient the group. In trying to proceed without these elements, which have supported previous international research collaboration, we have undoubtedly lost a certain unity of conception and integration of the final product. But we believe these costs are justified when the counterpart is to challenge each scholar to reconsider old assumptions and to raise new questions for research.

We are especially grateful to the organizations that understood that funds for travel and international meetings were essential for a half-

European, half-American group and therefore provided them: the Social Science Research Council, the German Marshall Fund of the United States, the Fundación Juan March (Madrid), and the Fritz Thyssen Stiftung (Cologne). Portions of two of the chapters appeared elsewhere: Chapter 3 (Berger) is reprinted with the permission of *Comparative Politics*; Chapter 4 (Hernes and Selvik) is reprinted with the permission of the publisher from Gudmund Hernes and Arne Selvik, "Local Corporatism," in Gene F. Summers and Arne Selvik, editors, *Nonmetropolitan Industrial Growth and Community Change* (Lexington, Massachusetts: Lexington Books, D. C. Heath & Co., 1979). Paul Levenson translated Chapter 11 (Salvati) from Italian. Finally, the participants feel particularly indebted to Robert A. Gates, Staff Associate of the Social Science Research Council, whose faith in the endeavor and unfailing support sustained the project from beginning to end.

Suzanne Berger

Cambridge, Mass.
January 1981

Introduction

SUZANNE BERGER

These essays on interest groups in Western Europe are the product of a collective endeavor to reconsider certain fundamental premises about state and society in advanced industrial capitalist countries. The group of scholars that constitutes the Social Science Research Council–American Council of Learned Societies Joint Committee on Western Europe began its work in 1975. Our discussions started from a number of unresolved issues that each of the members identified in his or her own work and field of inquiry. Although the scholars came from different countries and disciplines and were of very diverse methodological and political persuasions, we were all by the early seventies experiencing certain common difficulties in carrying out research with the paradigms at hand. These troubles plagued both those who had been working within the framework of assumptions dominant in American social science of the sixties and those working along lines suggested by Marxist social analysis.

Societal problems and the problems of social science

The catalyst for the recognition of these theoretical problems was undoubtedly the series of social, economic, and political shocks experienced by all advanced industrial capitalist nations from the end of the sixties. As a result of this unanticipated break in a postwar period characterized by economic growth, prosperity, and low levels of social tension, the fundamental assumptions on which Western industrial societies had lived for twenty-five years were suddenly called into question. The energy crisis, the end of rapid growth, inflation, high unemployment, and rising social conflict challenged common conceptions of how industrial societies operated and of how they were evolving. The inability of social science to illuminate these new realities suggested the weakness of current theories.

1

One possibility was that the explanatory power of the theories was limited to a specific and rather brief historical period: the postwar years. But another view was that we had all along been seriously mistaken in our analyses of the advanced industrial countries. As Gudmund Hernes put it at an early meeting of the committee: "We need to confront both a crisis in sociology and a sociology of crisis." In a statement of the group's task at the time of its founding, we wrote:

The old maps of state, society, and economy no longer work, and Western industrial societies feel themselves embarked without guideposts or compasses on journeys whose way stations and destinations are no longer familiar. The problem is a double one: the terrain has changed; and the maps, which had only a very rough and perhaps spurious fit with the old state of affairs, have not been redrawn to take account of the new shape of the landscape.[1]

The difficulties that individual scholars faced in their research reopened debate on three great themes: the characteristics of the societies of advanced industrial, capitalist countries; the nature and role of the state in these countries; and the course of the trajectory along which these societies are moving. The committee began general discussion of these issues and of alternative paradigms for conceptualizing them in 1975 and soon came to focus on interest groups.

There were several reasons that interest groups moved to the center of the group's concerns. First, theory on the nature and role of groups that mediate between society and state has been critical to the development of several of the social sciences. In American political science, for example, debate over interest groups, pluralism, and sovereignty marks the beginnings of the modern discipline. Not only the empirical bases of American political science but also its normative views of the political process were shaped by reflection on the role of groups in a democratic state. Madison and de Tocqueville stand at the heart of American political thought about how to protect and enlarge the sphere of individual freedom in a democratic society. For political scientists, then, any "return" to fundamental questions about state and society in industrial countries is bound to reopen the conceptualizations of interest groups at the core of their discipline.

Even in fields like economics in which group theory had not been central, there have been recent attempts to append some account of the presence and significance of organized interests to the basic models of the discipline. And the problems of integrating these patches into more systematic views have become more and more vexing. Given the centrality or, at least, the troublesomeness, of interest groups for the main puzzles of contemporary social science, it was hardly surprising that every member of the committee had carried out research on some aspect or another of interest groups. The group's discussions pushed members to consider the theoretical implications of the difficulties they had experienced in accounting for the results of empirical research with the old paradigms of their disciplines. These essays thus reflect new questions posed to research that was initiated or even substantially completed before the group was constituted.

It was, however, not only the theoretical centrality of groups that mediate between society and state that turned discussion to the representation of interests. It was also the apparent relevance of these groups for understanding major new problems of "ungovernability," inflation, and economic stagnation. As Philippe Schmitter explains in this volume, organized groups in industrial societies have recently been singled out as the principal source of the declining authority of government as well as of the increasingly heavy burden of demands placed on it (see Chapter 10). Even those who reject this account of the apparent breakdown in governmental authority have to explain how transformations in the groups that mediate between society and the state affect the capabilities of government and the nature and intensity of social demands on government.

Similarly, economists of both Keynesian and Marxist schools have had to introduce the role of organized interests into explanations of stagflation in the seventies. As Michele Salvati shows in analyzing the responses of French and Italian business and trade-union groups to widespread social unrest at the end of the sixties, the "same" groups in these two countries, facing the "same" problems and constraints responded very differently, with different consequences for subsequent growth rates and inflation (see Chapter 11). Other economists interpret the role of organized groups in the economic crisis of the seventies in another perspective from Salvati's.[2] But the significant fact is that virtually all (the monetarists excepted) these accounts of contemporary economic problems incorporate interest groups. Although not all the chapters in this volume analyze current issues, even those such as Feldman and Kocka who study interest groups in the nineteenth and early twentieth centuries raise questions about them that reflect contemporary concerns with the ways in which different modes of interest intermediation and organization contribute to political stability or instability and to economic growth or stagnation.

Intellectual antecedents

Nothing makes clearer how far-reaching the implications of the views of interest groups that emerge from this collection of essays are for understanding advanced industrial states than a comparison of this effort with one carried out twenty years ago – also under the aegis of the Social Science Research Council. At the first research planning meeting of the Committee on Comparative Politics of the Social Science Research Council in 1957, the group decided on an investigation of the ways in which interests are articulated, aggregated, transmitted to government, and translated into policy in various countries. In that project as in our own, the purpose of looking at interest groups was to approach broader issues about societal functioning and change. As Gabriel Almond wrote in a report on the committee's work, it turned to interest groups with

the expectation that the systematic examination of interest groups in their complex interrelations with public opinion, political parties and formal governmental institutions will enable us to differentiate more accurately between political systems as *wholes*. [It is] a search for a more complete and systematic conception of the political process as a whole. . . .[3]

The research carried out did indeed constitute an approach to politics and society as a whole, as the committee had intended, and not simply a collection of case studies of interest groups in countries at various stages of political and economic development. With respect at least to the advanced industrial capitalist societies, the general outlines of the theory of politics and society that surfaces in these studies may be briefly sketched out. This summary oversimplifies and perhaps also overstresses the elements of unity and theoretical coherence of this body of research. But it is precisely this consensus on a general theory of politics and society that stands in striking contrast to the partialness of the theories, the uncertainties, and the points of disagreement of this present collection of essays.

Society and interests

The view of civil society that emerges from the studies of the late fifties is one in which social structures and the economic system generate a set of demands and interests. These are essentially the same in all societies at the same stage of political and economic development. However different French farmers' associations may appear from American ones, the essential fact is that in both places they represent farmers. As from one industrial society to another the agricultural sector of the economy has broadly the same features, so too, farmers have broadly the same needs. As Henry Ehrmann put it in an essay that appeared in the same year as the first report of the Committee on Comparative Politics (1958),

The interests which groups defend in their respective countries are similar even where the political regime or the party system differ widely. The conflicts that arise between the various interests have an equal similarity, although the forms in which the conflicts are resolved will be shaped by the general socio-economic and political milieu.[4]

In this view, needs, demands, and interests are considered all as virtually synonymous. The number of interests in society is in principle unlimited and the relations among them are indeterminate. The theories of development that underpin this view of civil society identify some interests as systematically dominant: those that arise from the technologically advanced industrial segments of the economy as more powerful than those generated by backward sectors; those interests put forward by the modern strata of society as more weighty than those presented by traditional strata. But just as there is no systematic explanation of why certain interests emerge whereas others remain latent, so there is no general theory – as there is in Marxism – of the ranking, or relations of dominance and subordination, in the potentially infinite array of interests that industrial society generates. Indeed, the theories of pluralism that are integral to this perspective demonstrate why no single interest or set of interests can always triumph. Crosscutting cleavages in society, the overlapping memberships of groups, social mobility – all work to maintain a fluidity in the relations among various organized interests and to undermine the bases on which a situation of permanent domination could be constructed.

Interest groups form as spontaneous emanations of society. The boundaries between them correspond to what may be regarded as the "natural" divisions of society, that is, those generated by different roles in the economy and statuses in society. The claims that these groups make are, in Almond's terms, the "raw materials" or "unaggregated demands" which, at least in the Anglo-Saxon democracies that provide the model for the theory, are then "processed" or aggregated by political parties.[5] In "raw form," the interests present and organized in societies at the same stage of development are the same. Where the interest groups' system is not independent of the political party system, the demands expressed by a socioeconomic group may be quite different from those expressed by the same groups elsewhere, for the parties have distorted them. As Almond writes of France and Italy: "When parties control interest groups they inhibit the capacity of interest groups to formulate pragmatic specific demands; they impart a political ideological content to interest group activity."[6] But in the most highly developed systems, that is, the United States and Britain, the two stages of the political process remain distinct, and organized groups are autonomous expressions of the interests of society. Their demands can be conceived as the essentially unmediated demands of socioeconomic groups

themselves. The answer then to the questions of why different interests are present and organized in various societies and of why from
country to country the same groups may conceive their interests quite
differently lies in the greater or lesser autonomy of interest groups
from parties and not in the process of interest formation itself.

The various routes that Western nations followed to modernization
and industrialization, the specificities of national traditions and values, have not created different interests from society to society.
Rather, the interests of industrial societies at the same stage of development differ mainly insofar as conditions in some countries made
it possible for interests to emerge and organize freely and in other
countries to subordinate interest group formation to ideological politics, thereby deforming the expression of the pragmatic needs, the
"real" interests, of society.

Representation and the definition of interests

In this view of interests as the unmediated reflection of fundamental properties of socioeconomic structures, questions about
representation receded in importance. Previous traditions of social
inquiry had raised two broad questions: how to define interests and
how to structure relations within a group in order to produce a convergence between the purposes of members and organizational purposes. The literature on interest groups produced under the aegis of
the Committee on Comparative Politics paid relatively little attention
to these questions. First, the issue of what a group's interests are, of
how long-term and short-term objectives are reconciled, of how and
by whom needs and solutions are interpreted tended to disappear
from the structural-functionalist agenda, because the approach
stressed the extent to which socioeconomic structures constrained the
content of interest group demands, that is, determined interests.

But concurrently with the work of the Committee on Comparative
Politics, another set of scholars produced a theory of group formation
that did directly address the issue of the definition of collective goals
by voluntary associations. It accounted for the presence or absence of
organized interests by the rational calculations that a self-interested
individual would make about the utility of associating with others to
satisfy his or her own objectives. Whereas the perspective of the
Committee on Comparative Politics suggested that all significant social and economic interests were potentially organizable and tended
to treat unorganized "latent" interests as ones that had not *yet* organized, the second group of theorists distinguished between those
interests that could and those that could not be organized. The most
influential of this work was Mancur Olson's *The Logic of Collective*

Action, which systematically explored the conditions under which rational individuals would be most likely to form groups to pursue their utilities.[7] The analysis focused on the nature of the objectives of collective action (whether divisible or indivisible; whether they could be denied to nonmembers or had to be universally extended); the number and weight of potential members (many members with few personal resources, few with substantial resources great enough to procure the good without association); and the incentives organizations could distribute to make membership "profitable" to those who otherwise would more rationally enjoy the benefits provided by the organization as free riders.

In this model of group formation, the initial assumptions virtually disposed of representation as a problem: An individual would form and join only such organizations as served his or her own interest. Only where individual and collective goods coincided would groups be formed at all. Because individual utilities exist prior to and independent of group formation, because individuals choose groups to advance private aims, only by error or misguided passion could a person find himself in an organization that did not represent his own best interests.

The problem of representation in social theory was, however, not only one of group formation and the identification of collective interests. It was also the question of whether relationships of power within groups were (or could be) organized to produce outcomes that served the interests of members – and not mainly the power seeking of leaders or the needs of the bureaucracy or the interests of contending factions. The research on interest groups carried out under the aegis of the Committee on Comparative Politics tended to give an optimistic answer to such questions. The notion that the sociology of organizations inherently posed problems for representation was dismissed via an attack on Michels' "law of oligarchy." As Samuel J. Eldersveld put it in a 1958 review of the American literature on interest groups: "[W]e have tended to regurgitate the oligarchical model without empirical verification, and without recognizing that certain components in the oligarchical concept and certain alleged effects of oligarchy may not be applicable to the American scene."[8] Seymour Martin Lipset's study of the Typographical Union, which was carried out in the same period, was extremely important for the development of this line of thought, for it provided empirical evidence that, in some organizations at least, structures favored a competition among leaders, hence providing members with resources for controlling outcomes.[9]

But Lipset's book was followed by little other research on the societal or intraorganizational factors that make it more or less likely that organizations represent members and not chiefly the ambitions of leaders or the needs of bureaucrats. The studies of interest groups in various countries that the committee sponsored devoted relatively little attention to relations between leaders and followers or to conflicts within the group over objectives. The convergence between the interests of the members and the policies of the organization was more taken for granted than questioned. And this literature tended to assume an identity of interests between those in a socioeconomic category who belong to an interest group and others in the same broad category who are unorganized. The question of representation was reformulated as a problem for survey research. Almond, for example, proposed to compare the attitudes of the general public with the views of organized interests.[10] Thus surveys were to answer the questions of whom interest groups represented and of whether the interests defended by the organized were the same as those of the unorganized.

Interests and politics

The third pivot of this literature of the late fifties and sixties was the characterization of interest groups in terms of their specific functions within the political system. The central notion in this approach to comparative politics was that the differences in the politics of various societies may be understood as variations in the ways common functions are carried out. Of these functions, that of articulating and transmitting the specific demands of society into the political process was, in the most advanced societies, carried out by interest groups. In traditional societies, there exists the same need for channeling social demands into arenas of authoritative decision making, but other institutions (kinship ties or clientelism, for example) perform the functions that in modern societies are taken over by interest groups.

With respect to the industrial societies, the theoretical discussions in this literature focused primarily on distinguishing between the functions of interest groups and those of political parties. Various structural distinctions between these two types of political organization were noted – that parties run candidates for elections and interest groups do not; that constitutions formally sanction the existence of parties but not of interest groups; and others.[11] But the key to analyzing interest groups, this literature proclaimed, was not through the classification of structures but through differentiating the functions performed by parties and interest groups. The defining characteristic of interest groups is that they articulate the claims and needs of society and transmit them into the political process. In the most developed political systems the division of labor between interest groups, parties, and government is one in which interest groups transmit "pragmatic specific" demands to parties; parties aggregate these demands, integrate them into a general program, and mobilize support for them; and parliaments and bureaucracies enact them as policies and laws and implement them. As Ehrmann put it, "the political party stands between the special 'unaggregated' demands of the interest groups and the authoritative decision making of the parliament and bureaucracy."[12] The less developed the political system, the less differentiated these functions; but these accounts make clear that the process of political development brings about a specialization of functions in which the tasks of interest groups, parties, and government are progressively well specified.[13] This division of labor in the developed countries is a stable one and, moreover, one that is stabilizing for the political system.

However similar the functions of interest groups are in this perspective, their structures are recognized to be variable. Societies at different stages of economic and political development are likely to have very dissimilar forms of interest representation. But even societies with the same socioeconomic structures may well have interest groups that differ significantly. These variations are largely accounted for in this literature by regime characteristics that shape the channels of access through which groups press their claims. Differences in institutional arrangements, in policies, in political and bureaucratic personnel, in national traditions and political cultures may all affect the *forms* of interest representation. But the substance remains essentially the same under all guises.

This analysis of the formation of interest groups, of representation, and of the political functions of interest groups nourished a fruitful theoretical and empirical literature. But by the seventies, serious doubts were emerging about the adequacy of this conception of interests, as the general theory of society and politics out of which this approach had been developed came under attack. The research problems that led to such questioning are laid out in the individual chapters of this volume. Despite all their differences, they have in common a particular kind of break with the premises of the previous literature.

First, none of the present essays take interests as givens. Even those authors such as Offe and Schmitter who assign a very heavy weight to the economic and social determinants of interests find it necessary to build models of interest group formation and behavior that systematically incorporate variables other than socioeconomic ones. Taken together, the chapters suggest that the impact of national historical experience, the weight of intraorganizational factors in defining interests, and the role of the state in structuring relations among interests are so significant for group formation that one cannot analytically define the "real" interest of a group, which would be given by socioeconomic structures, and distinguish it from the "forms" of these interests, which would be determined by national specificities and politics. The central question that runs through the volume is *how* socioeconomic, historical, organizational, and political processes shape interest. And the issue of organizational forms, far from being a matter of tactical adaptation to circumstances, here is analyzed as part of the process of the definition of interests.

Once the question of why a particular group emerges to organize a particular segment of society again becomes an intellectual puzzle that cannot be resolved by simple reference to socioeconomic factors or by an assumed coincidence between individual and collective utilities, the issue of representation inevitably reemerges. The relations between leaders and members, between the organized and the unorganized, between the defense of short-term and long-term interests, between contending interpretations of group interests – all of these classic problems of representation surface as central themes in these chapters.

Second, the question of what interest groups *do* – of their functions within the social system – to return to the structural-functionalist vocabulary – is reopened in these chapters. The notion of a common function of interest groups – transmitting and articulating the demands of society into the political process – has largely disappeared and in its stead there is description of a variety of different roles that interest groups fill in contemporary societies. Many of these are roles the previous literature assigned to political parties or to government: socializing citizens, organizing consensus, making policy, implementing laws, and so forth. There is no longer any conception of a stable division of labor among parties, interest groups, and government, but rather specification of the circumstances under which various configurations emerge. Thus the question of the forms of interest representation in various countries is reformulated here as a question about the possible "trade-offs" among parties, pressure groups, and government and about the consequences of different divisions of labor among these institutions.

Finally, several of the authors in the volume raise the question of the impact of interest groups – and of different patterns of interest organization – on the political and economic well-being of contemporary societies. The literature of the fifties and early sixties tended to

suggest that as long as interest groups performed the task of representing specific, pragmatic demands, they stabilized the political system. Whenever they assumed more global tasks and elaborated broad
social programs (as they did when they fell under the sway of ideological parties), they were destabilizing elements. Several of the chapters
virtually reverse this hypothesis, pointing to the destabilizing consequences of pluralism and the paralysis of parties and parliaments,
faced with ever more complex problems of social regulation. They
explain the spread of corporatist patterns of representation as one
way of shifting some of the tasks of social coordination, conflict resolution, and policy formulation out of the party-parliamentary arena
into the domain of interest groups.

The origins of interest group formation

The common points of departure of the chapters in this volume are
the observation that societies contain an indefinite number of potential interests and the question of which interests organize in a given
society in a particular period. None of the contributions argue that
socioeconomic and market factors by themselves determine the composition, forms, or modes of operation of a system of representation.
Although all the authors accord significant weight to such factors,
each chapter relies on some other line(s) of explanation to account for
the fact that in societies with basically the same set of "raw" materials, different patterns of interest organization exist. The essays go
beyond the partial explanation that socioeconomic structures provide,
by analyzing the specificities of national historical experience, the role
of the state, and the instabilities inherent in the operation of a representational system. Individual chapters emphasize one or another of
these variables, but the overall sense of the volume is that
socioeconomic structures, history, politics, and organizational transformation provide complementary accounts of the process of interest
formation and not rival and mutually exclusive theories.

Social and economic determination of group formation

There is broad agreement among the authors on the ways in
which socioeconomic structures shape interests. First, the division of
labor and certain other "natural" social divisions – ethnic, religious,
generational, and so forth – create as many points of opportunity
around which groups may organize. These points of opportunity reflect the location and clustering of social, economic, and political resources, which are very unevenly distributed across society. As individuals or groups seek to maintain or improve their position relative

to others, they locate themselves with reference to these clusters of resources. The principal means of improving one's lot in this process is to exploit those resources of which one has the most or to which one has the easiest access. "Interests," then, are determined by the structures of industrial societies to the extent that their technologies, forms of ownership, labor markets, and social systems create particular clusters and distributions of resources that recur from society to society, making it equally rewarding in all these societies for groups to coalesce at the same locations on the social map.

This formulation, however, still leaves interests undetermined, in two ways, as Pizzorno argues here. First, socioeconomic location does not provide an unequivocal answer to an individual's (or group's) problem of identity. How does the man who owns a small farm and grows grapes in Corsica locate himself on the map of the distribution of resources and figure out which group he should join to advance his fortunes? Each of his coordinates suggests a different interpretation of his situation, that is, a possible and alternative formulation of his interests. How he defines himself will determine which group(s) he joins: specialized winegrowers' association or farmers' union or Corsican regionalist movement or national political party. Each of these organizations has a particular conception of the interest it defends, from which it derives a strategy. Thus the winegrowers' association argues that winegrowers' fortunes are determined by the market for wine, competition from Third World producers, the prices of inputs, distribution networks, and so forth. A winegrower has, therefore, more in common with another winegrower anywhere in France or the European community than with anyone else. And the right strategies for collective action are lobbying the bureaucracy and parliament in Paris and Brussels. The Corsican regionalist movement argues that every Corsican – winegrower or shopkeeper or worker or industrialist – has problems that stem from one and the same cause: living in a region with a peripheral and colonized position in the nation. Therefore a Corsican has more in common with another Corsican than with anyone in his own trade or class elsewhere in the country; and the only real solutions are regional development, political autonomy, and so forth. The contradictions between the conceptions of interest and the strategies of alliances promoted by these two organizations are so great that although the Corsican winegrower is a potential candidate for either association, he could hardly be an active participant in more than one.

The first issue, then, which socioeconomic structure leaves open, is identifying with which group one's fate and fortunes lie. But even when individuals decide which groups to form, the question of how that group's interests should be pursued remains: by the maximization of short-term objectives or sacrifice for long-term goals? by reformist or radical strategies? And who among the various rival interpreters of the group's interests knows best?

At this point the authors of the volume depart from the pluralist model, which the argument thus far presented might equally well support. Although there are an indefinite number of potential interests and a fundamental indeterminacy about how to identify them and how to advance them, still, some interests are less indeterminate than others. In industrial capitalist countries with liberal democratic governments, organizations representing labor and capital are not simply groups like any others. They are both less variable in their identification of interests and more powerful in relation to other groups. In such societies two kinds of resources are so important and their uneven distribution creates inequalities of power that are so consequential that they virtually determine the groups that organize to control them. These resources are economic – control of capital and labor – and citizenship – control of numbers and legitimacy. Greater access to these resources makes organizations of labor and capital potentially more powerful than any others. In contrast to the pluralists, then, the authors of this volume see associations of employers and of workers as occupying points of far greater strategic importance for most of the battles of industrial societies than those that any other interest groups can seize. Where the pluralists saw interest groups as competing in a political market no one of them could dominate, these essays suggest that – to the extent that groups and the relations of power among them are determined by socioeconomic structures – unions and organized capital are always likely to prevail. And to account for the fact that they do not – despite the enormous "natural" advantages bestowed by the socioeconomic system – the essays move to the explanations we now consider.

History and group formation

With respect to the previous literature, these essays reflect a far greater concern with history. The chapters of Maier, Pizzorno, and Schmitter develop general theories of the transformation of representational systems from the beginnings of industrialization to the present and distinguish several phases within this period. Their conceptualizations vary considerably, but each identifies an "initial" phase of estate representation in which interests coincide with the social system, a "liberal parenthesis" in which representation was organized on an individual basis and association was entirely voluntary, hence fragmented and unstable; then, finally a period from the end of the nineteenth century to the present, characterized by the presence of mass parties and by stable organized interest groups with multiple objectives, professional leaders, and bureaucracies. The most significant differences among the authors lie in their characterizations of the latter period, principally in the debate over whether the period as a whole is a pluralist one in which relationships among parties and organized interests change but within stable parameters (Pizzorno) or whether a fundamental discontinuity separates a period of a voluntaristic pluralist mode of association that ends around World War I from a corporatist pattern of interest formation that prevails in most of the advanced industrial societies today (Schmitter).

The essays stress not only the common trajectories of industrial societies but also the significance of the specificities of national experience for interest group formation. The great transformations that industrialization and democratization brought about in nineteenth-century Europe left in place societies which, although similar in socioeconomic systems and the access to full citizenship of all the male population, were still substantially different. As the chapters by Feldman, Kocka, and Maier indicate, the paths to modernity of European societies retained and reinforced important elements of the past; the pattern of incorporation and elimination – as well as the original stock of materials – varies considerably from country to country. In Germany, for example, the preservation of a powerful aristocratic landed elite, the vitality of feudal values, and the precocious flourishing of the bureaucracy created a template for interest organization very different from the one that shaped groups elsewhere. Thus as Kocka's chapter shows, the "feudal-bureaucratic" nexus in Germany not only shaped the forms of white-collar organization and aspirations, but, in fact, *created* a white-collar class, carving a social category with sharply defined boundaries out of a mass of socioeconomic materials that elsewhere produced white-collar groups that were broader and more porous.

The state and interest group formation

Among the specificities of national experience that have shaped interest group formation, one stands out in the essays as particularly important: the timing and characteristics of state intervention. The differences among national patterns of interest organization reflect significant variations in the substance of social and economic programs and in the sequence of adoption of policies. In response to new policies, groups organize to protect themselves against the state or against other groups. They organize as well to gain access to new advantages that require lobbying or even direct participation in decision making. The appearance of new groups in response to legislation or decrees stimulates further proliferation, as still other groups form in imitation of or reaction against the new organizations. The impact of state interventions on interest group formation can be observed not only at the level of national government but at local and regional levels as well, as Hernes and Selvik argue in their study of local corporatism in Norway. Finally, as Keeler shows in his research on how French agricultural legislation in the sixties fostered corporatism in farmers' associations, changes in policy may transform organizational patterns – despite all the inertia and resistance that old structures offer.

The literature on interest groups of the fifties and sixties had also stressed the impact of government on interest groups; the notion, there, however, was that different policies, personnel, and channels of access would affect organizational forms and strategies. In the essays, although the issue of "packaging" or forms is taken up, the claim is a stronger one: that the state has a significant part in shaping the content and definition of interests, and not only organizational tactics and strategies. Thus Offe, for example, defines two categories of interest groups: class organizations and "policy takers," the latter a set of groups stimulated into formation by their stake in decisions and policies of national government. Offe's examples of "policy takers" include associations of taxpayers, welfare clients, and local governments. In addition to the impact of the state through the content and sequence of its policies, the essays consider two other ways in which the state shapes interests: through the incentives that particular regime types provide for particular patterns of organization and through the authoritative attribution of public status to interest groups.

The relationship between regime type and interests is a key issue in the chapters by Schmitter and Berger. The former demonstrates the high correlation between Social Democratic governments and corporatist systems of interest intermediation in West Europe; the latter traces out the shifts in patterns of middle-class organization in France as the regime changed from a parliamentary to a presidential one and as the coalitions that underpinned the presidential system shifted their gravitational center.

Finally, the state molds interest by attributing public resources and powers to particular groups. The formal attribution of status to an interest group may give it legal rights to participation in lawmaking and implementation, to regulation of the behavior of its members, to public funds. Offe's contribution to this volume focuses on this legally sanctioned institutionalization of interest group authority, which he considers the determining characteristic of contemporary corporatism. On corporatism, there is substantial disagreement among the authors, as there is in the considerable literature that has appeared on this topic in the past decade. Both Pizzorno and Schmitter develop theories of corporatism very different from Offe's. They see the origins of corporatism in liberal democratic countries as deriving from changes in society or from internal transformation of the system of representation – corporatism from below. Thus Schmitter writes of "societal corporatism" as emerging "largely but not exclusively, as the result of interassociational demands and intraorganizational processes – from below, so to speak, rather than from a conscious effort by those in power to mold the type of interest intermediation system" (see Chapter 10). In contrast, Offe argues that the initiative and incentive for the establishment of corporatist arrangements lie with the state. But Schmitter and Pizzorno, too, recognize the importance of legal recognition and delegation of public functions to interest groups and acknowledge the stake, if not the primary role, of the state in promoting this type of representative system.

The mechanisms of change of representational systems

The formation and reformation of interests results, finally, from the operations of the representative system itself: This is the central theme in the contributions of Pizzorno and Sabel. Pizzorno analyzes how contradictions within the pluralist system provoke the emergence of new groups. In Pizzorno's terms, the pluralist system of representation is inherently unstable, that is, unable to prevent the eruption of new collective identities on the scene or the recurrent explosion of ideological passions. Pluralism leads to "a cyclical emergence of new collective identities"; as interests are aggregated, their organizations become progressively more bureaucratized, the split between the interests and perspectives of leaders and members widens, and the conditions for the dissolution of the group and its replacement by another are created (see Chapter 9). But after each wave of new entrants has passed, the system absorbs them, satisfying some of the demands, co-opting some of the leaders, and reasserting the need for expert decision making.

Sabel deals with the same issues in his analysis of how the bureaucratization of trade-union organizations and the struggles for power within them by rival factions create permanent incentives for the revival of ideology and the jettisoning of short-term pragmatic goals and accommodation to the system. It is precisely in the instabilities – of the representational system as a whole for Pizzorno, of oligarchy within particular groups for Sabel – that the hopes for representation lie. Only at moments of reformation, ideological commitment, and mobilization can followers check and control leaders, for in times of institutionalization and bureaucratization, the organization's professionals hold most of the cards. Schmitter, too, associates the stability of the organization of interest groups with their failure to represent members. And precisely because – in contrast to Pizzorno and Sabel – he sees contemporary interest group systems as relatively invulnerable to internal dissolution, his conclusions about participation and representation are quite pessimistic. Indeed, he rejects the term "interest representation" as embodying a misleading view of relations between members and their organizations and uses instead the term "interest intermediation" which includes not only the process by which interests are transmitted from the base into the political process but also that by which "interests are taught to, transmitted to, imposed upon members by associations themselves, independent of member preferences and authoritative commands" (Chapter 10).

In sum, once the essays go beyond socioeconomic structures to explain group formation by history or the impact of the state or by contradictions inherent in representative systems, the question of representation again becomes important. For if the content and strategies of groups are not tightly constrained by the utilities of individual members or by socioeconomic structures, then there are likely to be divergent interpretations of a group's interests and a gap between the interests of members and those of organizational professionals. The chapters are more or less pessimistic about representation, depending on the views taken on the stability of the institutionalization of interests. They reopen old questions about the prospects of participation and democracy in modern societies.

The functions of interest groups

The work of the Committee on Comparative Politics on interest groups started from a common conception of the political system, of the functions that had to be carried out to maintain stability, and of the division of labor among interest groups, political parties, and the government. In the present volume, there is no longer any agreement on how to conceptualize the political system – indeed, few of the authors would even pose the problem in those terms. Here the divisions and uncertainties of the authors stand in greatest contrast to the broad consensus of the scholars who wrote under the aegis of the Committee on Comparative Politics twenty years ago. The debate among the authors over the relations between civil society and the state – over how to define the political system and its functions – runs throughout the volume. One controversy we have already signaled: over the role of the state in promoting corporatism. But the absence of a common conception of the state in advanced industrial capitalist societies is most telling in the discussions of the functions carried out by interest groups. The model of the political system provided our predecessors with a complete specification of the functions that had to be performed in industrial societies. Without any such common framework, the authors of the present work converge only on the importance of certain functions in ensuring the stability and reproduction of the political and economic systems of advanced industrial capitalist countries, for example, on the centrality of the role that interest groups play in regulating conflict between labor and capital. But they do not agree on how to draw up the complete agenda of problems that industrial societies must solve.

The essays deal with two related but distinct issues about the functioning of interest groups in contemporary West European societies. They consider how the scope of interest group activities varies with changes in society and in government. And they analyze the "trade-offs" possible among interest groups, political parties, and government. The previous literature saw interest groups in advanced industrial societies as formulating social demands and channeling them into the political process. The research presented here, however, shows interest groups performing tasks that go far beyond anything that could be conceived in this way: not only expressing interests, but generating them and instilling them in members; not only transmitting demands into arenas of authoritative decision making, but participating in those arenas and implementing policy. Virtually every function that was once imagined to be the province of political parties or of government is in some of the most developed societies now being performed by interest groups.

Some of the authors in this volume (Maier, Hernes, Schmitter) account for what they see as the substantial enlargement of the range of activities of interest groups by transformations of society and the economy: by increasing social complexity, by shifts in capitalist economies that alter relations between labor and management, by growing international interdependence. Other chapters (Berger, Keeler, Offe, Salvati) stress more the role of politics. They relate shifts in the scope and content of the tasks carried out by interest groups primarily to changes in the state: to increasingly frequent and penetrative attempts to regulate society and economy, to the strength or weakness of parliamentary and party institutions, to the composition of the coalitions that underpin government and opposition, to bureaucratic capabilities. Thus Offe, for example, explains the development of corporatism (in his sense, interest groups exercising public authority) by the growing inability of political parties to propose coherent programs and the declining effectiveness of traditional bureaucratic techniques.

Both explanations that emphasize societal changes and those that privilege political variables raise the question of whether a long-term transformation of the functions of interest groups is in progress in advanced industrial societies. Schmitter does make such a case, arguing that the more voluntarist, fragmented, and unstable pluralist mode of representation corresponded to social and economic systems that have now been irreversibly altered. The reallocation of political functions among interest groups, parties, and government that is involved in corporatism reflects changes taking place in capitalist societies from the early twentieth century. Corporatism has spread more or less rapidly across the developed countries, depending on a variety of national facilitating conditions or obstacles. The trend is toward its establishment as the stable mode of interest intermediation in advanced industrial capitalist societies.

But the main thrust of the essays is against any such unilinear theory of the transformation of systems of interest representation. The case that Pizzorno and Sabel make for the instabilities of systems of representation suggests cyclical variations in the relationships among parties, interest groups, and the state. And the factors that they identify as vulnerabilities of corporatist arrangements – for example, the difficulties of legitimating the transfer of public authority to private groups – recur in other chapters as explanations of the breakdown of particular national experiments with extending the scope of interest group powers. These failures result not only from the internal contradictions of interest group functioning but also from the impossibility of severing interest group politics from politics *tout court*. This is the conclusion of Feldman's analysis of why business and labor in Weimar Germany were unable to negotiate the accommodations that would have preempted state intervention in industrial relations, as well as of Salvati's account of how the presence of the Communist party in France and Italy blocks the emergence of corporatism. Moreover, if the flourishing of corporatism depends on Social Democratic regimes, as Schmitter indicates, what changes might a spell of Center-Right government bring in interest representation, even in those countries in which corporatism has apparently dug its roots deepest?

All of this suggests that the division of functions among parties, interest groups, and governments is not a stable one. Some of the spheres in which interest groups have currently replaced parties or state authority are ones in which the specific weaknesses of interest groups are likely to be exposed. Interest groups that have exceeded their competence, if not their mandate, may well be pruned down to narrower tasks. However unpredictable, changes of government and regime inevitably alter the terms of the trade-offs among interests, parties, and the state. The entry of new problems into the political arena may allow parties and parliaments to recoup some of the ground lost to corporatism. And mounting pressure on the whole system from those who have been excluded from it may lead to mass mobilization and ideological confrontations which unsettle the division of labor among political institutions.

The impact of representational systems

Finally, the authors of this volume depart from work on interest groups of twenty years ago in their perspective on the relationship between interest group systems and political and economic stability. The earlier literature analyzed pluralism as a system of representation that supported political legitimacy and stability by fragmenting conflicts into specific, pragmatic, hence negotiable differences of interest. For the economy as well, the competition of various groups – whether conceived as a market or in Galbraith's terms as a system of countervailing powers – was imagined to increase the social product. Over the past decade, this optimism has been greatly eroded by reflections from all points on the political spectrum on the sources of the "ungovernability" of advanced industrial societies. The thrust of these arguments has been that the effective enfranchisement of previously excluded segments of society has increased political participation, multiplied the number of organizations competing in the pluralist system, and increased the volume of demand beyond any level that government can satisfy.[14] The dynamics of political systems in which parties regularly outbid each other in electoral promises feed a process of escalating interest group demands; and no effective equilibrating mechanisms come into play. Governments buy time with the ever softer currency of inflation and the potentially explosive recourse to unemployment.

The essays accept these conclusions, in part at least: They see pluralism as an unstable system of interest representation, with a destabilizing impact on politics and the economy. But here the analyses that point to these conclusions focus not on the volume of demands generated by pluralism, but on the impact of its operating modes on the legitimacy and effectiveness of the political system

(Chapter 9). Thus Schmitter hypothesizes that governability is "less a function of aggregate overload, of 'imbalance' between the sum total of societal demands and state capabilities, than of the discrete processes that identify, package, promote, and implement potential interest claims and commands" (Chapter 10).

The mechanisms of pluralism – intergroup competition and bargaining; voluntary membership, hence weak organizational control over members; multiple and overlapping organizational jurisdictions; the narrow definition of group goals; the exclusion from the system of those with too few resources to reach the organizational threshold – all of these allow a wide representation of interests and opinions, but at a price. The costs are of two kinds: those that diminish the political system's efficiency – its capacity for identifying and ranking problems and for making and implementing policy; and those that diminish its legitimacy – the extent to which its personnel and policies are perceived as operating for the public good and not only for private or sectoral or class advantage. The advantages of pluralism are thus most evident (and its characteristic dysfunctions are least damaging) in states that are very affluent and relatively noninterventionist, for in these cases the "waste" and friction of pluralist modes of representation matter less. Similarly, pluralism works well in political systems where consensus depends on common and deeply rooted political beliefs and not primarily on assessment of the system's performance and output. Although the delegitimating effects of pluralism may then erode confidence in particular interest organizations or particular representatives, the legitimacy of the state is not sapped (Chapter 9). In sum, pluralism may be reasonably compatible with political stability as long as it is not required to add to the state's capabilities or to its general popular acceptance.

Viewed from this perspective, democratization and higher levels of political participation make pluralism increasingly less workable not so much by adding to the load of demands to be processed as by changing the character of the issues at stake in politics. The new goods demanded may be of a kind that pluralist systems of interest representation have never provided. Some of the authors in the volume argue that insofar as these new demands require more social and economic coordination to augment the system's regulative capabilities, corporatism is more compatible with "governability" than pluralism (Chapter 10).

But it may be, as others argue, that what lies at the origin of the current crisis is an erosion of old political values and beliefs and that no measures to increase the efficiency of the system can compensate for this loss – indeed, that the effectiveness of the state cannot be increased precisely because of this decline in political legitimacy.[15] For those who identify the source of the "ungovernability" of advanced industrial states in this way, corporatism appears to be a solution that is irrelevant or perhaps even more destabilizing than pluralism. Irrelevant, because in countries where there are major challenges to the legitimacy of the political system, corporatism is largely absent. Corporatism flourishes in the Social Democratic regimes of Scandinavia and cannot get a foothold in France or Italy. (Indeed, as Salvati points out, in France once the legitimacy of the state had been reinforced by triumphant elections, it was quite possible to restore efficiency without any corporatism; whereas in Italy, in the absence of any such increment of political authority, it was impossible to make the system more effective – despite the considerable willingness of unions and employers to move to quasi-corporatist modes of bargaining.) Finally, corporatism may be destabilizing insofar as it is likely to generate conflicts that exacerbate problems of legitimacy. Precisely those features of corporatism that stabilize representation – the organizational monopolies, the clearly defined jurisdictions, the exercise of public authority by private groups, the possibilities for organizational control of members, the bureaucratization of interest groups – all widen the gap and harden the lines that separate the represented from the excluded. For the latter, the state appears as the appanage of particular interests and not the agent of the general interest. Part III of this volume groups a set of chapters that deal explicitly with these questions about the impact of systems of representation, but the debate on this issue runs throughout the volume.

The essays have been grouped in three parts: Part I, The Determinants of Interest Group Formation; Part II, The Functioning of Interest Groups; and Part III, State, Society, and Representation: The Changing Relationship. These divisions correspond to the discussion in this introductory chapter of interest group formation, of the functions of interest groups, and of the impact of systems of representation. But just as we have been forced here to move back and forth among these themes, so the authors too have found it impossible to separate out one set of questions about interest groups without at the same time providing implicit or explicit answers to the wider range of issues we have signaled. In this volume, then, the reader will not find a progression from one set of issues to the next, but a series of successive approaches to the same questions.

Notes

1 *Proposal for a Joint SSRC–ACLS Committee on Western Europe* (New York: Social Science Research Council, February 28, 1975), p. 4.

2 See Robert O. Keohane, "Economics, Inflation, and the Role of the State: Political Implications of the McCracken Report," *World Politics* 31(1) (1978).

3 Gabriel A. Almond, "A Comparative Study of Interest Groups and the Political Process," *American Political Science Review* 52 (1958):271. For an account of the meetings the Committee on Comparative Politics held on interest groups and a list of the publications generated by this activity, see Committee on Comparative Politics, *A Report on the Activities of the Committee, 1954–70* (New York: Social Science Research Council, March 1971). Mimeo.

4 Henry W. Ehrmann, "Preface," in *Interest Groups on Four Continents,* ed. H. W. Ehrmann (Pittsburgh: University of Pittsburgh Press, 1958), p. viii.

5 Almond, op. cit., p. 271.

6 Ibid., p. 276.

7 Mancur Olson, *The Logic of Collective Action* (Cambridge, Mass.: Harvard University Press, 1965).

8 Samuel J. Eldersveld, "American Interest Groups: A Survey of Research and Some Implications for Theory and Method," in Ehrmann, op. cit., p. 185.

9 Seymour Martin Lipset, Martin Trow, and James Coleman, *Union Democracy* (Garden City, New York: Anchor Books, 1962). The study was first published in 1956.

10 Almond, op. cit., pp. 273–4.

11 Harold D. Lasswell and Abraham Kaplan, *Power and Society* (New Haven: Yale University Press, 1950), p. 170.

12 Henry W. Ehrmann, "The Comparative Study of Interest Groups," in Ehrmann, op. cit., p. 4.

13 Almond, op. cit., p. 276.

14 See, for example, the analysis in Michel J. Crozier, Samuel P. Huntington, and Joji Watanuki, *The Crisis of Democracy,* Report on the Governability of Democracies to the Trilateral Commission (New York: New York University Press, 1975).

15 See John H. Goldthorpe, "The Current Inflation: Towards a Sociological Account," in *The Political Economy of Inflation,* eds. Fred Hirsch and John H. Goldthorpe (London: Martin Robertson, 1978).

Part I

The determinants of interest group formation

1

"Fictitious bonds... of wealth and law": on the theory and practice of interest representation

CHARLES S. MAIER

"The first requisite of a representative system is, that the representative body should represent the real public opinion of the nation," wrote Walter Bagehot one hundred and twenty years ago. "Nor is this so easy a matter as some imagine. There are nations which *have* no public opinion."[1] The statement was written to sound self-evident, but, in fact, representing "opinion" had not been considered the task of Parliament a century before Bagehot and it seems an antique aspiration a century after. In different ways, the eighteenth-century and the twentieth-century representative systems have assigned equal or higher priority to speaking for interests, although in the eighteenth century the interests were rarely organized in a formal sense, whereas in the contemporary world they are highly structured.

Likewise for Bagehot, Parliament was the uncontested representative organ:

The accordance of the opinion of Parliament with that of the country is the principal condition for the performance by Parliament of its great function of ruling the country. This can only be secured by the continuance in Parliament of many members representing no special interest, bound down to state the ideas of no particular class, themselves not markedly exhibiting the characteristics of any particular *status*, but able to form a judgment of what is good for the country as freely and impartially as other educated men.[2]

The focus on Parliament, with its alleged function of aggregating the nation's best judgments on the public welfare, also has an outmoded ring. Not merely has Parliament always been an arena for the interests that Bagehot felt encroaching, but it has become reduced to only one such arena, if still the preeminent one. Parapolitical bargaining networks link trade-union confederations, associations of industrialists and farmers, physicians and public service employees with each other and with agencies of the state designed to control and encour-

27

age their activities. It is these networks that form the focus of the chapters in this volume. This particular contribution attempts to understand under what conditions the present system of political and economic transactions arose and functioned, hence, too, what circumstances might well limit its effectiveness.

The transactions of the "state" with the organized interests of "civil society" are not construed here as a complete alternative to parliamentary or territorially based representation, but as a functional supplement. In some circumstances this supplement plays an extensive, even dominant role, in other situations only a secondary one. These circumstances need to be specified. Analysis is further complicated because the representation of organized interests has sometimes involved the growth of new institutions, such as joint labor-management forums, or has deputized spokesmen for private associations with quasi-public functions and status (recall Blue Cross, the National Recovery Administration, continental Chambers of Commerce, or the East India Company). In other cases, representation of emerging interests has proceeded by subtle transformation of older parliamentary parties or executive agencies so that they carry out new forms of brokerage (witness interwar ministries of commerce or labor, or late nineteenth-century conservative parties). Because this chapter considers the functions and tasks of interest representation and not merely the forms, both types of development require attention.

Institutions evolve in response to crisis or opportunity; hence the history of interest representation can be usefully organized in terms of successive challenges to parliamentary and parapolitical structures of representation (which, following increasingly common usage we will term "corporatist" here).[3] Hintze interpreted the rise of parliamentary representation as an outgrowth of the European system of estates.[4] It is just as revealing, however, to view the development as a response to the difficulties, in particular, which overtook the estatist system and not just as a general extension. In turn, the new interest groups and linkages between the state and economic life emerging in the late nineteenth century reflected an impatience with liberalism. They arose, that is, in response to the hesitation on the part of parliamentary notables or state bureaucrats to restricting the market's role in setting prices. The various European societies allowed far different scope for laissez-faire, but whatever the respective role allotted, it came under attack. If parliaments resisted infringing on the market, interest group mobilization could serve hard-pressed farmers and industrialists, or ambitious political leaders seizing their causes. Yet between an earlier age of estatist interests that waned during the course of the late eighteenth century and an era of "collective"[5] or interest group rivalry that arose toward the end of the nineteenth century lay an interval of relative parliamentary insulation from the needs and pleas of the marketplace. This era was the zenith of Bagehot's parliament and of his informed public opinion; to borrow a suggestive, if overdrawn image: the liberal parenthesis.[6]

Of course the schema is too rigid and must do injustice to the variety of European historical experiences. Nor is one stage of representation really eliminated; instead, it is overlaid by the newer development. Parliaments have thrived while adapting to organized interest representation; the intensity of market capitalism has probably increased, even if the market is far more structured by organized interests and state agencies; the liberal parenthesis has not really been closed – nonetheless, there is transformation enough to make the typology a useful starting point. Thus the historical portion of this chapter will attempt to outline the transitions that first widened and then began to close the scope of both parliamentary liberalism and the liberal market. From the historical material it will seek to isolate some general propositions about the conditions under which different forms of interest representation function. It can fittingly conclude with scrutiny of the contemporary situation: a moment when parliamentary and corporatist institutions appear in difficulty simultaneously.

From interest to party: the legitimation of the partial good

The legitimacy of any political system requires that citizens feel adequately represented. In turn, the test of adequacy involves both outcomes and procedures. It is not surprising that systems of representation should begin to lose legitimacy when results are chronically disappointing, when they fail to distribute the rewards of power or income anticipated in advance. But procedural criteria remain equally difficult to satisfy over the long run because of the lurking conflict between the representation of particular interests and any regime's commitment to pursue the general welfare. Interest groups, "private government," or "corporatist" trends have all been regarded with suspicion even when they have functioned effectively in allocating public benefits. This uneasiness is hardly novel. Viewed in historical perspective, all forms of corporate representation and party delegation have awakened distrust in their formative stages. Interest group representation just inherited the stigma attached to parties a century earlier. Parties had to overcome the suspicions raised by cabals and factions. The line between conspiracy and the legitimate representation of a partial interest remains a sensitive one. For most writers on politics the justification of any single group's claim to power or public resources remained pragmatic: Pluralist competition was sanctioned only as the price one paid for liberty. Liberalism, construed as a doctrine that stressed the emancipation of individual personality, may have a high ethical core; liberalism, construed as an accommodation of group rivalry, has been conceded (especially to labor) only piecemeal. (Between the Declaration of the Rights of Man and the 1884 French Law of Associations lay almost a century.) Much of today's uneasiness about "corporatism" just continues this longer term legacy of ambiguous acceptance.

The history of parties and interests is a complex one, intimately connected with the beginnings of a mercantile, "bourgeois" society in the late seventeenth and eighteenth centuries. As both J. A. W. Gunn and Albert Hirschman suggest, the idea of interest was refocused in the early modern era. From a concept referring to the utility of princes and states (raison d'état) it evolved into one evoking the advantages of subjects. This new "private sector" connotation originally awakened few concerns, for the alignment of particular interests with the public good was deemed theoretically and practically possible. The statesman, moreover, could exploit the interests of individuals and groups as a counterweight to invidious ambitions, vainglory, and other anticivic passions: Following interests meant acting rationally and predictably. Indeed the great distinction of nineteenth-century sociology between military societies dominated by warriors and priests and industrial societies, divested of aggressiveness and superstitious creeds, was adumbrated early on in the theory of interests.[7]

The ascendant concept of interest played a dual role in the political thinking of the eighteenth century. It promised a natural, even organic basis for governing wealthy modern societies; however, it also threatened corruption and factional manipulation. Like the classical types of government (rule by one man, by a few, or by the many), the new impulses of commerce and interest could bring about either beneficial or degenerate outcomes: humming trade or the South Sea Bubble, doux commerce or John Law.[8] Early eighteenth-century British writers such as Defoe and Davenant explained that the growth of commerce and the development of England's unique ability to muster public credit (hence to wage wars without the standing armies that elsewhere buttressed despotism) rested on sophisticated social covenants. Emphasis on the contractual bases for generating wealth undermined the earlier identification of civic virtue with yeoman landed property. Money itself, so Locke had argued, allowed wealth to be stored without decay and could thus justify unequal accumulation; in turn, government was erected to protect the holdings money allowed.[9] "Money has a younger sister," wrote Defoe. "Her Name in our Language is call'd CREDIT. . . . This is a coy Lass and wonderful chary of her self; yet a most necessary, useful, industrious Creature. . . ." Credit, he continued, depended not on a particular ministry, "but upon the Honour of the Publick Administration in *General*," and thus required and further nurtured social cohesion.[10]

On the other hand, outside Whig circles, money and credit remained problematic and subject to abuse ("See Britain sunk in lucre's sordid charms," Pope inveighed after the Bubble) – as they did for Montesquieu across the channel.[11] Nor were critics of a paper economy likely to be reassured by the Machiavellian cynicism of Bernard Mandeville in which self-interest, deceit, and vanity combined to produce a thriving hive economy: "Thus every part was full of Vice/ Yet the whole Mass a Paradise."[12] As Tory spokesmen found themselves excluded from power for a generation, they fulminated in opposition against faction, patronage, and commerce's disintegrating influences alike, as did Goldsmith (whose later hostile summary provides this paper's title):

> As nature's ties decay,
> As duty, love, and honour fail to sway,
> Fictitious bonds, the bonds of wealth and law,
> Still gather strength, and force unwilling awe.[13]

As a homeless opposition in Walpole's new England of supposed stockjobbing and clientelism, the Tories rediscovered the general interest. It was to be championed by Bolingbroke's patriot king and based on the virtuous cooperation of "the rich and great families." For the Tory critics Walpole's regime meant the same process of centralization that dismayed Boulainvilliers or Montesquieu in France, or later Justus Möser in Germany. It seemed only a petty difference that the British executive relied less on browbeating the aristocracy than on suborning them with patronage, placemen, and a general mercantile disintegration of the agrarian order.[14]

With the passing of Whig domination and George III's effort to free himself of the Newcastle network of parliamentary patronage, partisan positions were reversed. As a Whig opponent, Burke resumed many of Bolingbroke's indictments in 1770: If prerogative had declined, "influence" had replaced it. The ministry's effort to purchase its own majority (in contrast to the earlier Whig commerce in seats, which Burke naturally did not belabor) aimed at "sowing jealousies among the different orders of the state and of disjointing the natural strength of the kingdom." Burke, however, suggested not a patriot king, but reanimation of the defunct principle of party: party as "connection" among great families (a remedy that also echoed

Bolingbroke) and party "as a body of men united for promoting by their joint endeavors the national interest upon some particular principle in which they are all agreed." Party was intended to reinvigorate parliament as a control on the king by the people; at the same time parliament was to represent the nation's diverse interests. A good monarch could construct a government that would give tolerable satisfaction by choosing men with a following: "Here it is that the natural strength of the kingdom, the great peers, the leading landed gentlemen, the opulent merchants and manufacturers, the substantial yeomanry, must interpose."[15]

Burke's 1770 tract counterposed the interests of English society against the pretensions of the court; but it was equally plausible to plead the representation of interests against those who would democratize the Commons. By the 1790s, Whig as well as Tory conservatives were defending the oligarchical composition of Parliament in language similar to Montesquieu's earlier justification of the venality of offices. As William Paley argued, no matter how restricted the franchise, the House of Commons still contained "the greatest landlords and merchants, the heads of the army, the navy, and the law, the occupiers of the great offices of state. If the country is not safe in these hands in whose hands would it be?" From this view it was a logical step to the defense of "virtual representation." Since Parliament represented interests and not individuals, every man would find his stake defended, even if he himself enjoyed no suffrage. For Paley and Burke, England was governed by the crown and the estates, and the modern term for estates in a postfeudal society such as Britain's was interests.[16]

Interest representation was not merely practical representation and thus far different from the utopian notions that would soon agitate the continent; it also remained supposedly nondivisive. Unless taxes were to be vastly increased, interests would not become mutually conflicting. Moreover, they were not yet formally organized: They were not yet interest groups. Together the interests formed the constitution in its original sense; their respective strivings augmented national prosperity and did not undermine it. What were the guarantees of harmony? Mandeville's earlier tough-minded pluralism might appear too amoral. But Adam Smith reconciled the driving force of private aspirations with the common good through the more providential invisible hand; or as Montesquieu said, "Happy it is for men that they are in a situation in which though their passions prompt them to be wicked, it is, nevertheless, to their interest to be humane and virtuous."[17] For Burke, not the logic of economic competition but the historically molded national community ensured a similar regulating principle. Interests emerged as a natural exfoliation of an organic society, compatible with the general welfare as branches might be with a tree.

Such reassurances that private goals meshed with the public welfare came easily enough during a period of trade expansion and relative harmony at home. Despite Burke's overheated rhetoric, the issue before Britain in 1770 was which segment of a national oligarchy would rule, not of parliamentary legitimacy in general. Given the restricted limits of the political community and of public debate; given, too, the buoyancy of eighteenth-century empire, and the desire to co-opt the mercantile elite into the ruling coalition, the limited competition of factions after 1760 remained compatible with an overarching consensus. The older Tory condemnation of faction and party (and the Tory temptation to reject any political role save that of the landlords) was hardly necessary: Political managers had no need for such reactionary programs, at least not before the "subversive" democratic threats of the 1790s.

In the British context, interest and parties based on interest might be viewed as compatible with the general welfare of the governing classes. But as David Hume pointed out, new principles of division were emerging. "Parties from *principle,* especially abstract speculative principle are known only to modern times and are, perhaps, the most extraordinary and unaccountable phenomenon that has yet appeared in human affairs."[18] Representation was to be justified increasingly on the basis of intrinsic individual rights, less on the basis of collective needs.

This change was part of the crisis of political mobilization that shook the Atlantic world from the 1760s through the 1790s. If the elites of the British Empire had successfully domesticated the appeal to interests so that it was compatible with their oligarchic political regime, this regime now faced renewed assaults. Its critics sometimes proposed new, more subversive ideas of interest. Sometimes they tended to abandon the language of interest altogether as they sought more fundamental categories of representation. In the small urban arenas of American revolutionary politics, for example, the new claimants for representation merged the language of profession and interest with newer notions of majority rule. The "Mechanics" of Charleston and New York called for "the virtuous part of a free Republic . . . to Associate and Coalesce into one fraternal band," and even to impose binding instructions on legislative delegates. They conceded that political division was natural in a republic "while there exists a difference in the minds, interests, and sentiments of mankind."[19] American democrats, in short, adapted the inherited vocabulary of interest to convey a newer political division between majority and minority.

In differing degrees the oligarchic political systems of the late eighteenth century aroused criticism everywhere. Notions of interest – as expressed in terms of "estates" or "corporations" – came under attack in prerevolutionary France. Rousseauian discontent with the invidious distinctions of "civilization," with private opulence and *amour propre*, suggested that interests were identified with corruption. The French revolutionaries were more reluctant than Americans to accept the possibility that good citizens in a republic might remain permanently divided. Political virtue, the patriotic commitment of the participating citizen, replaced interest as the principle that supposedly aligned individual fulfillment with the needs of the whole. Nonetheless, by the period of the Directory, the hard-pressed Jacobins themselves argued for the naturalness of party divisions, differentiating party from "faction," which they condemned as subversive. Outside France, in the German or Italian states, or in Spain, it was often impatient royal reformers who assailed privilege; in Britain, radical critics condemned the hypocrisy of a "free Constitution" under which Pitt silenced their applause of France.[20]

Insofar as individuals or majorities demanded representation by virtue of principle or inherent rights, political association had to change its nature accordingly. "Interest" lost its utility as a criterion for representation for both conservatives and democrats. It no longer retained legitimacy enough to serve the conservatives as a political defense. And whereas democrats might cling to the language of interest as a transitional claim, they really were calling for a broader inclusion of citizens in general. Ironically, no sooner had diverse interests been accepted as safe for the polity, than political divisions surged over the frail channels they provided. For those seeking to manage a society without revolution, as in Britain, or to channel radical change into stable, representative forms, as in the United States, the ideological task became one of redomesticating the new, potentially inflammatory associations of "party" – in Madison's concept, "curing the mischiefs of faction."

In an age of emerging liberal individualism how could political managers substitute for the earlier ballast provided by the Burkean concept of interest so as to dampen civil strife or democratic "excesses"? How did one represent majorities without endangering minorities? Memories of religious intolerance and the example of Robespierre's republic remained vivid inducements to work out mechanisms for containing conflict. In the United States, federalism and the very geographical extent of the Republic, so Madison suggested, could dilute dangerous and even majoritarian factions. In other societies deference and property might reinforce stability. Deference presupposed a "natural aristocracy" equipped by wealth, leisure, and intellect to rule and gamble on an electorate capable of judging political talent.[21] Property became the critical testimony of this independent judgment. "Property is indeed a very imperfect test of intelligence; but it is one test," as Bagehot, one of its rearguard but perceptive defenders, summarized. "If it has been inherited it guarantees education; if acquired, it guarantees ability. Either way it assures of something."[22] In France the spokesmen for parliamentary liberalism also sought a middle-class ballast. The universality of interests that Burke had found in the House of Commons as a whole, the French Doctrinaires, such as Guizot and Royer-Collard, located in the middling strata, indeed in each middle-class man. The bourgeois voter incorporated the generality of nonaristocratic interests; and because he could not favor any one of his own multiple interests excessively without injuring the aggregate, political moderation would be assured. Whereas Bagehot would rely on different parliamentary constituencies to ensure representation of diverse interests,[23] the French "whigs" sought not to incorporate diversity but to average it out. "It is in the middle class that all interests can find their natural representation: those higher up have a need to dominate that has to be opposed; underneath there is ignorance, habit, dependence, and thus a complete lack of what is needed."[24]

In effect, though, turning to the middle class and to property for political defense meant turning toward party itself as a principle of stability. By the mid-nineteenth century the European parties generally were serving to keep rival leaders and dissenters within the governing elites from stirring up the explosive elements of urban society. They routinized conflict among the middle and upper classes, and they also offered a framework for future integration of the working classes. "The great fault of the present time is that men hate each other so damnably," Melbourne had complained after the great political battles of the early 1830s; but by the late 1840s, party competition had channeled these animosities. When Aberdeen explained to the queen, "The only permanent bond of Party, according to my notions, was the possession of office or the pursuit of it," he was obviously referring to a competition within safe limits.[25] "The distinguishing influence of free institutions consists in their giving birth to popular parties," an American commentator suggested,[26] while even in the post-1848 reaction a German commentator emphasized how important parties had become. "If opinion counts for more than interest for the man of today, the times do not deem it a reproach.... The party today has more political reality than the estates whose interests are definitely subordinate to party interest."[27]

Party, therefore, had become acceptable, and even convenient. What had originally threatened as an instrument for imposing ideological fanaticism had become by the mid-nineteenth century a conservative tool for managing political society. In effect, parties of opinion had come to represent interests; but living more familiarly with classes and parties, men could let the older language of interest lapse.

And yet no sooner was party, as the organizer of opinion, finally accepted as a device for order, than it began to alter under a new and urgent reintrusion of interest politics. Now with a difference, however. Interests were to be organized not just on the level of parliament as British Whig theory suggested, nor within the *juste milieu* of the bourgeois electorate, as French liberalism prescribed. Instead, interests would take form as associations on the level of civil society between Parliament and the middle-class voter. Burke and Bagehot believed that a parliament insulated from pressures from above and below could adequately aggregate society's implicit interests, without those interests organizing themselves; Guizot and Royer-Collard entrusted the 200,000 electors of the *monarchie censitaire* to give adequate vent to concrete interests. But by the last third of the nineteenth century those speaking for interests found neither solution sufficient. Instead, they appropriated the intermediate level of political "space" to ensure collective force and parliamentary leverage. They organized to exert permanent pressure.

The formal organization of interests, however, meant that no sooner had party become legitimate than it had to be itself transformed. Either the assemblies of notables that comprised the mid-nineteenth century parties had to undergo a major evolution into permanent mass electoral organizations, or they were fated to lose their impetus. Parties allegedly of ideas had to become parties of interests in a world of organizing interests. The whig zenith quickly became the whig sunset.

This is not to argue that mid-century parties had not spoken for interests, just that for a brief interval they had transmuted the language. Indeed, the very stress on public opinion had expressed a deep class interest. Only an ascendant bourgeoisie, which really wrote off the stake in society of the urban and rural working classes, could have claimed the reading public as the source of legitimacy. As Treitschke, unattractive *Realpolitiker* that he might be, wrote about Germany: "Political theory . . . can seldom actually cause a party to be formed unless it corresponds to the interest of a social force. The interests of the social classes, for instance, have much more a say in party doctrine than the parties themselves admit."[28]

Nonetheless, that did not mean that there was no real institutional basis for the liberal concept of a politics of "opinion." It is important to understand the factors that even briefly allowed for the triumph of parties of opinion before examining the new world of interest groups. In a Europe of restricted suffrage, regimes briefly rested on a peculiar interstitial class basis. As John Vincent has suggested, the Victorian equipoise did not really result from the fact that a cohesive middle class had become dominant and was yet unchallenged by labor. Rather, it reflected an interim situation in which the aristocracy had relinquished its former political monopoly even if it still filled leading offices. The balance of social forces varied enormously from country to country, but in each case a relative postaristocratic hiatus of power seemed to validate liberal theory.[29]

Consider first the factors mitigating mid-century antagonisms among elites. The major conflicts between representatives of manufacturing and champions of agriculture either lay behind (as in Britain after repeal of the corn laws) or they had not yet become so virulent as they would later, elsewhere (as in Germany between 1890 and 1900). In the countries that were undergoing less rapid industrialization, the economic conflicts between landlords and bourgeois never became so salient. Gentry and even grandees often championed the causes of liberalism and economic development, for example, Cavour in Piedmont or Szechenyi in Hungary. Antebellum plantation owners, Magyar magnates, and Orleanist notables, such as de Tocqueville, comprised an international reformist aristocracy, convinced that political community must be based on the literate classes. Their bourgeois allies felt that within this coalition they could chalk up enough of their own solid achievements, so that even when middle-class influence was set back they did not feel totally thwarted. Despite the frustrations of 1848, subsequent progress made toward bureaucratic rationalization and national unification was to reconcile important sectors of bourgeois opinion in central Europe. Progress toward breaking down caste barriers seemed assured. In Britain the advent of the public schools and the opening of the Conservative party to business interests meant the gentrification of the commercial elite. In France, the Orleanist monarchy and later the Second Empire diligently created their own notables and titled retainers. In general, all the great institutional reform movements of the 1860s involved an effort to strengthen national power by broad co-optation of bourgeois leadership. Post-Ausgleich Austria and Hungary, the Bismarckian North German Confederation and Empire (at least from 1867 to 1878),

Bonapartist France, Italy under the Old Right and thereafter under
the Left led by Depretis, Britain of the Second Reform Bill, even
post-Civil War America and Meiji Japan; each regime found it urgent
to admit select bourgeois circles that were previously outside the
traditional governing elites, even while seeking to prevent any democratic swamping of what remained a cohesive political cartel. The age
of public opinion, in short, corresponded to an era of middle-class
advance. Even more specifically it signified a period of limited reforms and national centralization carried out under aristocratic and
bourgeois coalitions.

Religious questions also strengthened mid-century middle-class
liberalism, just as they had helped to crystallize liberal doctrines in
the first place. The tenacity of the established church reinforced the
cohesiveness of liberal opposition in Austria, Spain, and even Britain.
Until the end of the *Kulturkampf* in Germany, the *Ralliement* in France,
and the advent of the Giolittian era in Italy (a period spanning 1878–
1905), Catholics in these countries tended to condemn participation in
the political system pure and simple or else they organized parties
that liberals could self-righteously denounce as subversive.

Thus the landed classes, the exclusion of Catholics from day-to-day
politics, the still insignificant level of working-class representation
cumulatively strengthened the liberal elements of the European regimes. National questions exerted a further major influence. Any state
that allegedly represented individuals and not collective interests depended on a clear sense of perimeter to preserve some threshold
sense of community. Atomism within required a national frontier
without. National identity provided the only cement for the liberal
idea of the state, and it was fitting that the period of liberal ascendancy should also be that of national consolidation. On the European
continent the success of liberal nationalism could be achieved only at
the expense of Habsburg power. Since the Congress of Vienna, and
Metternich's congress system, Vienna had sought to preserve its own
internal hegemony over the peoples of the Habsburg Empire by
mobilizing an international confederation of aristocratic elites. However, the attempts at restraining Magyar, Italian, Slav, and German
national movements led Austria into a decade of disastrous setbacks
between the Crimean War and the defeat to Prussia (1853–66). Opposition to Habsburg supranational claims had mobilized Spanish and
Neapolitan revolutionaries, Hungarian magnates, British liberals,
French Orleanists and Bonapartists, Italian patriots, and German National Liberals. Just as the reform forces at the French Estates General
of 1789 had begun by calling themselves "patriots," so the patriotic
forces arrayed against Vienna naturally aligned with liberalism. The

victory of European nationalism, at least until after the Ausgleich of 1867 and subsequent German unification was simultaneously a triumph for national communities with strong, if not always dominant liberal influence. By 1867, Austria was itself a nation-state, and with liberals in charge, to boot.

Liberal society, to be sure, remained an elitist system, even in the advanced parliamentary states. But the priorities that prevailed were those of individuals and families, or those of the possessing classes in general, not the middle ground of organized interests. Class interests were institutionalized in terms of restricted suffrage requirements and the parliamentary or party organization of public (middle-class) opinion. Private interests prevailed in private compacts. Those who counted for something dined, hunted, played, fought, or slept together. But those fruitful liaisons did not constitute interest group politics. County courts and assizes, race meets and regiments, political clubs, and even Masonic lodges (to reach down and include the earnest but less endowed) provided a matrix for politics, but they were not yet associations organized for special collective causes.

From party to interest group: representation in a mass society

Several long-term developments served to displace these patterns of cozy parliamentary, party, or bureaucratic rule. The intensification of international military competition after Crimea meant increased state responsibilities, as wars took place during 1854–5, 1859, 1864, 1866, 1870–1 (and in America, 1861–5), and alliances became permanent after 1879. Escalation of international competition, with its heavy fiscal demands, had accompanied severe institutional crises in the 1640s and 1650s, from 1680 to 1720, in the late eighteenth century – and was now again to exert a seismic influence in the latter nineteenth century. Liberalism was a call for cheap and minimal government. But in the Darwinian half-century to follow *The Origin of Species*, international competition came to be viewed as a relentless destiny, and liberalism was increasingly seen as an indulgence.

Indeed the very apex of liberalism, the 1850s and 1860s, brought the first indications of decline. The Bonapartist regime represented the outlines of a coming corporatism. This plebiscitarian experiment claimed legitimacy precisely as a reaction against liberal parliamentary fragmentation; it was a government of action installed to supersede a feckless regime of oratory. But any government that rejects the given representation of interests must seek a substitute; and French antiparliamentary forces, in any case, have avowedly searched for *le pays réel*. These "real" forces could be little else but the interests who had spokesmen or might be available for organization. In its cultivation of Catholics, its manipulation of bureaucrats, and its initial rewards for business the Second Empire worked toward the rudiments of a plebiscitarian corporatism. In the twofold search for support – the continuing dialogue with potential collective interests, and the periodic acclamation by the general mass of voters – lay much of the innovative character of Napoleon III's government. Bonapartism prefigured the end of the liberal parenthesis.

The advent of the "great depression" after 1873 tended even more specifically to undermine the prerequisites for parliamentary liberalism. This long phase of declining prices began with a severe trade recession, and then continued with a quarter-century compression of agricultural revenues. Monetary contraction in respect to real growth may have been one cause (triggered in turn by the absence of new gold sources and by deflationary public policies), but new wheat from the prairies, the pampas, and the steppe also played a major role. The response was a turn toward organization. French iron makers had formed the Comité des Forges as early as 1864 in the face of the Bonapartist move toward free trade. Le Travail National followed in 1870, while French agrarians also organized: large landowners in the Société des Agriculteurs (3,500 members in 1878 and 11,000 by 1894) – the conservative Rue d'Athènes – and "republican" peasants in Gambetta's Société Nationale de l'Encouragement de l'Agriculture (the Boulevard Saint-Germain).[30]

Tariff protection became the major inducement to organization, as tariffs provided a public subsidy that could overcome inertia and the disincentives to group formation. In 1876 hard-pressed German manufacturers constituted the Centralverband Deutscher Industrieller to seek tariff relief, while the major agrarian pressure group, the Junker dominated Bund der Landwirte, formed in 1893 as a demagogically effective response to Chancellor Caprivi's moderate policy of negotiating reciprocal trade treaties. Only Britain resisted – and barely – the wave of tariffs in Europe and America between 1879 and 1902. Following tariffs, the new groups often wrested other legislative concessions, as in France, where the agriculturalists won public organization of their *caisses de credit* and *mutuelles d'assurance*.[31]

Tariffs comprised only one expression of a broader competitive nationalism. Late nineteenth-century imperialism, with its search for military security and naval expansion, represented just one aspect of a major transition in Western bourgeois society. Government officials, spokesmen for middle-of-the-road parties, beleaguered liberals concerned about rivals on their left, industrialists enthused by a world of iron ships, organized a host of associations to lobby for military spending and planting the flag abroad. Some of this involved manipulation from above; however, veterans' leagues, nationalist student movements, provincial businessmen in search of participation and a meaningful cause, all involved a direct incursion of the middle-class public into political life. The new articulation of public opinion meant the supplementing or bypassing of parliaments; in turn it allowed neo-Bonapartist ("Caesarist") efforts by officials to deal directly with interests while it encouraged spokesmen for interest groups to secure direct access and voice. The middle-class public thus emerged with possibilities for more immediate influence, but was simultaneously fragmented into single-purpose constituences. The unified Victorian vision (idealized to be sure) of public opinion gave way to a more fragmented politics of partial interests – and patriotic passions.[32]

The proliferation of interest groups and the new politicking deeply affected contemporary observers, who sensed that a profound change in the forms and substance of representation was underway. From one viewpoint the new groupings were just extensions of the liberal impulse toward free association. This was the case for labor unions, which had been freed from common law restrictions on "combination" in Britain in 1824–5, granted the right to organize as private associations in the German states during the 1860s, and accorded similar liberty in France by the 1884 Law of Associations (and its further liberalization of 1901). But many of the new trade associations in Germany, France, and other countries with a tradition of public law were less manifestations of liberalism than delegations of state authority. France, Germany, Italy, and Spain each possessed regional chambers of commerce, established on the base of earlier guilds by Napoleonic decree, then exported to French-occupied Europe, and thereafter preserved by the Restoration regimes. These associations were augmented by national delegations in some cases (e.g., the Deutscher Handelstag). The national or regional organs in turn came to overlap with the trade associations recognized as public law bodies which different industries were generating.[33] By the end of the 1870s, state and private-sponsored marketing and lobbying organizations were thickly interwoven in a quasi-official legal space. Many moderate liberals felt that sanctioning these new groups was the means to effective representation. Waldeck–Rousseau, the *Progressiste* premier of the government of "republican defense" at the turn of the century viewed the 1901 Law of Associations as the true expression of French liberalism.[34] It promised a fabric of public participation more like England's and far more promising than rhetorical declarations of parliamentary sovereignty. Furthermore, Rudolf von Gneist had earlier praised German associational activity as his country's approach to *Selbstverwaltung:* the healthy, autonomous self-government that the English also enjoyed thanks to their medieval constitution. Otto von Gierke similarly saw the long tradition of *Genossenschaften* as the functional equivalent of the Western liberal tradition. Yet these theorists were simultaneously disturbed as well as reassured by the new interest groups. They interpreted the *Verbände* less as spontaneous expressions of autonomy than as disguised efforts at state organization, and Gneist himself warned in 1894 of the "dissolving of our parliaments into splintered occupation and property groups."[35]

Sociologists and political analysts commented on the emerging trend, not in isolation but as part of a new stress on group organization in general. The years of the great depression (1873–96) were simultaneously an era of post-liberal disillusion with parliamentary representation. The heroic work of national unification lay behind in Italy and Germany. In those countries, and in the America of James G. Blaine, the France of the Panama scandal, or the Spain of the *turno politico* and *caciquismo,* corruption and clientelism seemed to be the essence of popular government. As part of this jaundiced estimate, the notion came naturally that partial group interests, and not individual civic participation, formed the basis of public life. Such cynicism was hard on liberalism but creative for conservative political sociology. It fit in with a growing belief in irrationalism and an emphasis on the primitive, communal drives toward collective organization (Fustel de Coulanges, Taine, Barrès), with skepticism about democracy and a search for underlying drives for power by the manipulation of ideology on the part of elites (Mosca, Pareto).[36] Arthur Bentley's analysis of 1908, *The Process of Government* may have initiated formal American reflection on interest groups, but it logically belonged to a pattern of analysis a generation old in Europe.[37]

Revival of the Left after the 1890s, the growth of state intervention in the economy, and the wave of massive strikes that punctuated the first decade of the new century further stimulated group theories. Political and legal theorists now seized on the newer interest organizations to support antidemocratic impulses and lament what might be called "overloaded liberalism." Leon Duguit's political implications may have remained ambiguous even as he sought to deny the reality of the state as an abstract Roman law entity and substitute in its stead a web of reciprocal duties based on natural associations and groups.[38] Working along some of the same lines, the Italian jurist Santi Romano offered a sociological view of the state that emphasized "the increasing division of our society into classes and corporations." In contrast to the formalist equality guaranteed by the state under the *Code Civil,* the real relationships of society, such as those between employer and worker, "still require and probably shall always require inequality among individuals, the supremacy of some and the subordination of others."[39]

The thickening of interest groups thus seemed to suggest that the associations and conflicts of economic and social life were overflowing the juridical categories of the nineteenth-century state. Nor were pressure groups the only sign of this "lag" on the part of public and parliamentary institutions. The inner transformation of political parties also reflected the twofold thrust of the new development: on the one hand, the fragmentation of the citizenry into a welter of conflicting roles and partial interests; on the other, a more direct and democratic political mobilization. The electoral successes of the Gladstone liberals and Joseph Chamberlain's Birmingham caucus in the 1880s, the reorganization of the German Social Democrats after 1890, the formation of the French Radical Socialist party in 1901, meant that the major European factions were evolving from whiggish clubs into permanent electoral and patronage organizations with full-time staffs, affiliated newspapers, annual congresses, and continuing communication between local and national leadership.[40] At the same time, however, some of the new parties were being virtually captured by such homogeneous social classes that they were becoming largely interest groups in their own right, although designed to struggle in the parliamentary arena rather than in the marketplace. The European social democratic parties might be viewed in this light, even though they remained committed in theory to a total transformation of society, which transcended normal interest group aspirations. A clearer case was the identification of the German Conservative party with the militant rye-growing estate owners of East Elbia, who organized their own Agrarian League in 1893 as well as coming to dominate the older Prussian-based party. Furthermore, the Italian Nationalist Association of 1910 (and thereafter party) fell under the control of Ligurian iron and steel manufacturers, who depended on government contracts and found it useful to bankroll a press that trumpeted military preparedness and expansion.[41]

Both on the Left and the Right the distinction between parties and interest associations thus tended to erode step by step with the increasing activity of European governments in raising tariffs, increasing armaments, initiating early welfare measures, and generally intervening in the capitalist marketplace. Liberals who remembered and sometimes idealized the mid-century parties of notables contrasted the crassness and demogogy of populist imperialism with the earlier gentlemanly game of politics. Indeed the elegiac regrets started as early as the 1860s, and by the end of the century had deepened into a major sense of disorientation and lost mission.[42]

The ramifications of the great depression after 1873, the development of an "organized capitalism," the harsher international competition provided major impulses to the direct mediation of interests. But so too did the rise of working-class organizations. Despite major uprisings as late as 1898 in Milan, 1909 in Barcelona, and 1914 in various Italian Adriatic cities, by the end of the nineteenth century the specter of violent revolutionary upheaval was passing. Reformist Socialists recognized the difficulties of armed revolution; urban insurrection seemed an obsolete romanticism. And why place in jeopardy a Socialist organization that promised to become a majority party as the working class grew? In sum, the growth of social democracy, the related expansion of trade unions (and in the German and British cases the reciprocal permeation of labor's party and labor's interest groups), the encroachments of revisionism and reformism – all opened up the Left to the same new patterns of brokerage as were emerging on the Right.

This did not mean that the forces of the Right were uniformly willing to bargain with trade unionists and social democrats. Some moderates were, many entrepreneurs resisted, and conservative politicians often oscillated between efforts at confrontation and cooperation. At the least, however, organization on the Left produced employer counterorganization on the Right. National and regional employer federations in Germany, Italy, France, Britain, and the United States were constituted early in the twentieth century to counter new union pressure. Membership overlapped, of course, with the earlier business interest groups organized to control market competition.[43]

Just as political parties slowly won acceptance and then legitimacy, so, too, interest group brokerage gradually changed from a suspicious innovation to a convenient channel of representation. Parties had become acceptable when it was demonstrated that rather than serving as instruments for radicals and zealots, they actually contributed to channeling political passions, to facilitating political management. Parties might temper the winds of doctrine. Likewise the web of interest groups offered to dampen the distributive conflicts of industrial society; to pay off sullen and fractious farmers, to even out the business cycle for industry, to encourage working-class leaders to reap short-term benefits for their followers within capitalism, to allow religious communities (especially Catholics) to preserve their cultural identity in secular society.

World War I and the Great Depression illustrated how deep an inroad interest group representation had actually made. Economic mobilization in World War I created new ties between government and producer groups and lent business associations enhanced regulatory power. In France, for instance, the Comité des Forges took over the procurement of metals abroad. In Germany, private corporations and the armed forces jointly organized war companies for purchasing and allocation of raw materials. In Britain, the railroads were combined and controlled; cotton, jute, and insurance largely taken over. In the United States, a War Industries Board was finally established to regulate prices, allocate materials and war orders, and overcome the chaos of earlier procurement attempts. To avoid strikes, labor unions everywhere won new grievance procedures – the counterpart in the economy to the participation of Socialist party leaders in French and British cabinet coalitions. The role of the state in overseeing the new partnership between unions and industrial leaders similarly became more massive, especially when munitions ministries wrote clauses specifying labor relations into all their contracts with industrial suppliers.[44]

"State socialism" during the war prompted both business spokesmen and political reformers to envisage prolonging the system. Maitland familiarized English readers with the work of Gierke; Duguit's ideas crossed the channel; Mary Parker Follett waxed enthusiastic over "The New State" in America; Laski (along with Lippmann and Beard) discovered that U.S. wartime agencies were encouraging a new pluralism. On the Left, a syndicalist impulse could motivate the projects for guild socialism of G. D. H. Cole and others, whereas in Central Europe and Italy the "councils" that were observed carrying out the revolution in Russia might also serve to socialize the economy. Industrial leaders also celebrated the virtues of an industrial order that would overcome the earlier "wasteful" competition of laissez-faire capitalism. Walther Rathenau and Wichard Möllendorff in Germany and Etienne Clémentel in France outlined industrywide and regional economic councils that would continue the wartime work of allocating scarce raw materials, setting prices, and establishing output targets. With the regulation of the marketplace turned over to joint industry and labor boards, the tasks of political representation would supposedly become minimal. As the Haldane Committee on the Machinery of Government reported in 1918, effective administration required departments "to avail themselves of the advice and assistance of advisory boards so constituted as to make available the knowledge and experience of all sections of the community affected . . ."[45] Wartime institutions such as the Wool Control Board, with its representation of workers, manufacturers, and the state, suggested promising models. "For the first time in history," wrote the British historian of economic control in wartime, "the world began to have a vision of what human association, raised to its high-est degree, might accomplish."[46]

What prevailed after the Armistice, however, was the far more widespread businessmen's desire to shake off bureaucratic controls, raise their prices, buy and sell where they wished. The collective vision did not readily survive in the marketplace; and the schemes for planned economies in Britain, France, and Germany were never insti-tuted despite countless hours of discussion. Nonetheless, the balance of power between capital and labor could not be restored to the *status quo ante.* Individual entrepreneurs found it harder to rely on their own market power to set the terms of labor contracts. In France, Britain, and the United States, employers did recover ascendancy after major unsuccessful strikes in the postwar period. In Germany and Austria, where discredited regimes collapsed with defeat, only quasi-corporatist bargaining could achieve a *modus vivendi.* When right-wing forces tired of this compromise and recovered their strength, they resorted to dictatorship.

Still, even when dictatorship was attempted in the 1920s it had to be instituted in a careful relationship to given social and economic inter-ests. Mussolini, for example, had to reinforce the organization of industry to secure effective control, as he defined it. Mussolini, more-over, and Primo De Rivera in Spain both made significant attempts to deal with labor and to go beyond simply bludgeoning it into submis-sion. Because the Italian Fascist rise to power had required several years of brutality against working-class activists, Mussolini could not easily negotiate with Social Democrats and trade unions, as could Primo, who took power by virtue of a royal *pronunciamento.* Nonethe-less, for the decade of the twenties at least, Mussolini's partial en-couragement of Fascist syndicalism represented a notable effort on the part of his regime. It amounted to an authoritarian version of the more general attempt under Western capitalism to transform the rep-resentatives of interests into bureaucratic partners. In the nineteenth century, liberals had sought to discipline ascendant middle-class or working-class citizens by endowing them with parliamentary repre-sentation and responsibility. After 1918 anyone seeking to control the politicized marketplace, as well as the parliament, needed to co-opt the leadership of the collective economic forces into corporatist roles, simultaneously private and public.[47]

In the liberal states this process could take the form of in-stitutionalizing social compacts directly. To be sure, some form of pressure from working-class forces was usually a prerequisite. The revolutionary outbreaks in central Europe in 1918–19, the weakening of capitalist legitimacy due to the world economic crisis, and the subsequent left-wing electoral victories in some countries all helped redress the balance of social forces and stimulated new collective social contracts. The Stinnes–Legien agreement establishing union–industry collaboration during the German Revolution of 1918 (see Feldman's chapter, this volume), the Matignon Accords that ended the sitdown strikes immediately following the Popular Front victory in France, and the 1938 Saltsjöbaden agreement between Swedish unions and employers (LO and SAF) were salient examples of these economic constitutions. The provisions for collective bargaining provided first by the National Recovery Act of 1933, and then the Wagner Act of 1935, allowed American labor to seek decentralized functional equivalents.

Thus two major variants of interest representation emerged between the wars. In the democratic states, economic elites did not feel they could use the state to enforce their predominance in the marketplace. In the authoritarian regimes, elites were not prepared to desist from coercive remedies. Either they felt themselves insufficiently organized at the level of civil society to hold their own in the economic arena, or else they were after an earlier sort of socioeconomic domination that postwar conditions no longer allowed (short of repression). Still, even when these frightened or imperious elites supported authoritarian regimes, they had to accept some state recognition of labor's potential collective strength.

A discussion of the emergence of interest groups that opened by citing the search for agricultural and industrial protection thus must close with the issue of how European capitalism was to come to terms with organized labor. Certainly farmers, handicraft artisans, bankers, textile producers, chemical industries, insurance executives, wood producers, homeowners and taxpayers, retail shopkeepers, and so forth did not let any of their multifarious and active pressure groups lapse. The difficulties of agriculture remained to envenom much of interwar politics. Still, the treatment of organized labor became the salient issue of the interwar political economy. Industry and labor dominated public disputes because their respective claims seemed to subsume so many others. The unemployment that plagued Great Britain throughout the 1920s, that repeatedly afflicted Weimar Germany, that ravaged most economies in the early 1930s, called attention to labor in general more than industry branch by branch. It made the overall level of employment, not its composition, politically crucial. The framework of interest group conflict thus underwent a simplification. Even when they meant cruel repression, the experiences of World War II, moreover, brought at least a juridical recognition of labor as a corporate group, as in Vichy France or the occupied Netherlands. Thereafter, the initiatives of the Resistance coalitions confirmed the central role of labor in postwar political and social institutions. The neo-Keynesian political leaders of the years after 1945, convinced that the state must pursue high employment and growth, were responding to an agenda set by labor and naturally looked to unions as their major political interlocutors.[48]

This dialogue with labor completed, in a sense, the legitimization of interest group representation. For with the post-1945 era and the emergence of welfare states, organized labor did not appear as just another interest group. In the post-Fascist climate, the working class and its representatives had apparently earned a broader mandate. Class representatives though they might be, they still spoke in their own right for the public interest. The identification was attested to by an implicit change in underlying economic objectives. Deep into the depression the priority of national economic policies had remained maintenance of foreign-exchange stability, even when it entailed high unemployment. After the war, a full-employment "standard" silently replaced the earlier international discipline of the gold or gold-exchange standard. Accepting the primacy of full employment meant that a major priority of the working class had become that of society in general.

On the other hand, the spokesmen for capital learned that this compromise largely guaranteed the ownership and control they deemed essential. If labor and social democracy became more than a mere interest group, business had always been and remained more than a mere interest as well. Given the decentralized signals that a capitalist economy transmitted by falling exchange rates, inflationary price rises, and changes in discount rates, propertied interests did not need to organize explicitly to reap many of the benefits of collective action. Workers required unions to compete on equal terms in a capitalist marketplace; industrialists, financiers, investors could respond without association given the signals of the price system. Each side, therefore, retained a different trump after 1945. Labor was accepted as an organized interest with a claim to speak for the general welfare in light of the earlier catastrophes of mass unemployment, fascism, and war, and the force it had displayed in the Resistance. Business was an interest that needed less organization than labor under the ground rules of the capitalist marketplace which even labor accepted. Given that trade-off, social democracy – as has been mordantly suggested – became the highest stage of capitalism.[49] Significantly, too, the ideological affirmations of the 1950s and after centered less on liberalism than on pluralism – a concept that suggested collective social actors more than individuals. With the redefinition of welfare states as pluralist, the persisting conundrum of reconciling partial interests and the common good seemed to have found a satisfactory resolution. "Fictitious bonds of wealth and law" had evolved again into a happy Burkean consensus of great interests.

Strategies and dilemmas of interest representation

The historical development previously sketched suggests that interest group organization responded to the international rivalry, economic strains, and working-class political challenges that have accumulated since the end of the nineteenth century. But important questions remain both for systematic comparative history and contemporary analysis. First, why have some societies encouraged a denser and richer proliferation of interest groups than others? Second, how have interests operated within different political systems, and how are they likely to function during the present period of economic slow-down now that the euphoric pluralism of the postwar era has dissipated?

To crossbreed the ancient animal metaphors of politics and philosophy we can define two polar strategies – that of the hedgehog and the lion. The hedgehog's strategy aims at insulation or exemption for a constituency from unfavorable trends by making outsiders' intervention appear very costly. The leonine strategy is the more ambitious one of seeking hegemonic control over a wider political system or market arena. Today's National Rifle Association is a hedgehog; the AFL-CIO growls like a lion; the Swedish labor confederation, the LO, was until recently an even more convincing lion; national medical associations are somewhere in between. Some groups begin as hedgehogs but find themselves impelled to adopt ever more active interventions and end up behaving as lions.

Successful strategy depends in turn on the conditions set by the broader political organization of society. To measure these factors it helps to introduce the concept of corporatism, defined here as a partial devolution of public policymaking and enforcement on organized private interests. This process can be initiated by public officials to augment their own control over social and economic life. Alternatively, the process can be generated by interest group representatives themselves. In either case, the development of corporatist bargaining probably encourages an interest group to strive for the role of the lion rather than that of the hedgehog – unless it merely wishes to defend a nonzero-sum claim that does not require contesting scarce resources with other groups.

The emergence of interest groups does not make a corporatist out-

come inevitable. The United States, for example, has always generated many pressure groups, in part because the committee system of
the Congress and relative governmental decentralization offer multiple points of contact for vocal interests. On the other hand, the very
diffusion of authority that encourages interests to present their claims
has made experiments in corporatism brief and fragile. Philippe
Schmitter has suggested that, in general, early growth of associations
from the humus of civil society "upward" may forestall a later, more
cohesive corporatism and disciplined governance.[50] The search for
corporatist institutions in Italy in the early twentieth century, before
and during the Fascist era, was more intense than that in France
because Italian society had found it harder to generate effective
bourgeois interest associations. Those that had emerged remained
fragmented and unable to defend what the elites felt were their vital
interests during a period of democratic mobilization and radical challenges.

Obviously, not all societies entered the era of interest group formation with the same capacity for organization. Nor was this capacity
itself the result of any single line of development. Liberal or democratic regimes may nurture associations more than authoritarian ones.
Nonetheless, if democratic vigor requires associations (de Tocqueville's judgment), association does not depend solely on democracy.
The independence of city states and fragmented territories, the
ubiquity and vigor of guilds, persisted long enough in Germany so
that the transition from a pre-liberal to post-liberal proliferation of
interest groups was easy. As Jürgen Kocka and others, following Max
Weber, have emphasized, the prestige of officialdom remained strong
because of the bureaucracy's role in state building and its recruitment
from the nobility. Hence occupational groups recreated bureaucratic
organization and sought their own official relationship with the
state.[51] Although this behavior may have handicapped German
liberalism, it helped make Wilhelmian and Weimar society peculiarly
"modern" in the major role that interest groups easily assumed.
Elsewhere, traditions of religious or ethnic pluralism could encourage
the formation of interest associations, as in the Netherlands with its
accommodation of confessional differences by "pillarization" or *Ver-
zuiling*.[52] In terms of the outcome for liberal and tolerant governance
during the first half of the twentieth century, German and Dutch
legacies seem to have had opposed results. Both backgrounds, however, could produce high associational levels.

Beyond diverse national traditions, the structure of regimes sets
important parameters for interest group activity and corporatist
trends. Granted that the reconciliation of group demands must be a
basic task for any political system (Bentley's old postulate), modern

interest group bargaining is still only one of several possible alternatives. An older parliamentary politics sufficed as long as the voting elites could preserve an overriding gentlemen's consensus. Depretis's and Giolitti's *trasformismo*, Canovas's *turno politico*, the ritualistic debates between Disraeli and Gladstone, served that need. Two developments, however, threatened the coziness of parliamentary representation. The powerful ruler had to satisfy the economic and status requirements of his national elites, but he could do so by intervention from above, by bureaucratic negotiation with industrialists or agricultural associations. Strong executive authority might inhibit political parties but it often encouraged the formal constitution of groups out of latent interests. In fact, as executive regimes tended to lose their initial plebiscitory authority they had to cast about all the more widely to secure interest group support. Napoleon III after the Cobden Trade Treaty of 1860, Bismarck after 1876, de Gaulle after the explosion of 1968 (and his successors) all resorted to increasing logrolling tactics to minimize parliamentary gains.

If declining Caesarism encouraged interest representation outside of Parliament, so, too, did ascendant mass democracy. The weakening of old liberal or conservative elites meant the rise of new parties and the appearance, so frequently noted at the turn of the century, of a new political class. "Class" was a misleading term, for what united its members was less a station in life than a professional commitment to mobilize voting blocs either by crusades, chauvinism, or patronage. The new political leadership arose in parliaments that the *Honoratioren* were being forced to relinquish. No more than Caesarist executives did the new leaders have reason to turn back toward the old elites: Their task was to pulverize and then reassemble on the basis of interest, ideology, or ethnicity the constituencies earlier organized by deference. Thus the growth of interest representation was also a likely accompaniment where political assemblies underwent the transition to mass democracy. Where political elites remained cohesive enough to slow down this transition – in Italy until the period, 1900–15; in Spain until, 1898–1917 – interest group intervention lagged. At best interests remained organized on the basis of older regional "chambers," such as the Lliga in Catalonia or the Unione Industriale of Turin. Interest group intervention also lagged where the older elites might themselves patronize the transition to mass democracy, as in Great Britain.

To summarize, then, oligarchy and interest group representation should correlate negatively. Bonapartism, or at least Bonapartism under stress, and mass democracy alike provide a stimulus for the organization of interests.

How these interests will behave within the larger political system is a further question. Hedgehogs or lions? The choice, as noted, depends in good part on the strategy rewarded by the larger system of brokerage. Consider, for example, the case of France. If declining executive regimes encourage interest group organization, then interests should have been stronger during the 1860s and after 1968 in comparison to the respective earlier decades. If ascendant mass democracy also mobilizes interests, there should likewise have been organization during the period from 1877 to 1906 as the forces of democratic republicanism waged successive battles against older elites. On the other hand, the strategy and styles of interest representation should have been significantly different. The executive regimes sought nonparliamentary mediators for broad social forces; they encouraged an implicit corporatism. The Third Republic in its formative period, however, encouraged interests but hardly corporatism. Its parliamentary class depended on local voters and regionally based *notables* in departmental councils. As problems came to require national solutions and central allocations – starting with the tariffs, then encompassing wartime regulation and post-1914 fiscal dilemmas – the hedgehog disposition of interest groups was slowly modified. Nonetheless, in pre-1914 France, as in the United States before the New Deal, a national legislature with important committees responsive to differing interests, encouraged vigorous pressure groups but allowed a minimal encroachment of corporatist trends.

This brings us to a final set of questions. What logic carries a system of interest groups, or latent interests hitherto loosely organized, into a structure of corporatist bargaining? And thereafter, what forces will limit the corporatist trajectory and perhaps even reassert parliamentary authority? Is there an equilibrium mix of parliamentary and corporatist representation? It may be that corporatist organization must increase apace with the increased functions of government. Every centralization of an allocative task prompts a new search for consultation and codecision making. The crises involved in wartime provide just the clearest and most dramatic example of calling in delegations from industry and labor. At these points the organizations credentialed or sometimes actually called into being can no longer content themselves with a hedgehog posture; they must protect their interests by negotiating over a broad range of issues and cannot just pursue a search for enclaves. Once begun the process is contagious: Member organizations discover the advantages that quasi-public participation provides in securing internal discipline and broadening recruitment. Potential rival organizations seek equal privileges. The corporatist tendency would appear to be ineluctable.

In fact, the trend may not be monotonic or stable. No matter how efficient a system, the legitimacy of corporatism can still be questioned. For every celebration of "pluralism" there are reproaches of vested interests, *féodalités financières,* and other abuses of the popular will.[53] Moreover, recent developments suggest that several sorts of difficulty will arise to beset the corporatist system. Corporatist tendencies can either augment or confuse the cleavages within a polity. Since World War II corporatist trends have generally centered on industry–labor organizations that parallel the political party divisions between social democracy and Christian democracy (or other conservative parties). The centrality of incomes policy has encouraged this development; indeed Schmitter has correlated the progress of corporatism with the strength of social democracy. Lehmbruch, too, finds corporatist alignments reinforcing political coalitions and cleavages.[54] Nonetheless, this reinforcement is not the only possibility. Persisting religious and ethnic divisions can cut across class lines. Differences on nuclear policy can fracture the labor movement. Issues concerning inflation have in the past separated those concerned with protecting assets (lower middle-class savers) from those concerned with protecting income (higher income managers with "leverage," and sometimes wage earners concerned about a deflationary crunch on jobs).

These and other strains make it likely that the tendencies toward corporatism also have limits: There will probably be no corporatist euthanasia of the European constitutions. In contemporary Europe, corporatism may be most advanced where the working class is best organized; but as Peter Lange has recently pointed out, the corporatist temptation for working-class parties in the political wilderness of opposition is lower than for those long in power. Swedish social democracy can allow its affiliated unions to be deputized by the state because the Social Democrats themselves are virtually part of the Swedish constitutional order; but Italian Communists are more likely to use the market power of their affiliated workers to wrest a coalition role for the party than quasi-official "concerted action" on incomes policy.[55]

Yet assuming that the mix of parliamentary and corporatist representation is not likely to be radically shifted, is the representational system stable as a whole? From a pluralist perspective, interest group formation and brokerage should function well with no immanent tendencies toward breakdown. From a Marxist viewpoint, corporatist tendencies represent an adaptive response of capitalism, but one that is ultimately liable to succumb to underlying contradictions. Without subscribing to theories of inevitable breakdown, but recognizing that no institutional patchwork is immortal, we can at least discern the fault lines. These considerations suggest that the corporatism that divides economic groups along the same lines as parties may well magnify polarization and ideological conflict. The negotiations between labor and capital may indeed originate as a means of taking allocative disputes out of the parliamentary arena; however, the distributive conflicts may become acute enough to reintensify ideological confrontation and again strain all institutions. (The crisis of 1930 in Germany offers a classic example. The dispute between labor and industry negotiators over the costs of unemployment insurance grew into a conflict that destroyed the last democratic parliamentary coalition.)

On the other hand, the formation of corporatist alignments across party lines, whether around inflation, ethnic issues, or energy, is conducive to policy paralysis. It reflects not so much a disagreement between parties or classes but within them. It tends to yield ad hoc politics as one group after another wins an accommodation that cancels out the previous concession. Tendencies toward clientelism between particular bureaucratic agencies and diverse interests may well be intensified. The upshot may be a paralysis on socioeconomic issues reminiscent of ethnolinguistic fragmentation; pillarization becomes Balkanization.

In both cases the strains on political party or parliamentary representation resurface in corporatist bargaining systems. Interest group formation and mediation may temporarily shift the locus of brokerage, may cool down an overheated clash of forces. But if social groups are claiming more income than an economy generates, more "positional" goods than are logically available, conflict results in any case. Interest group mediation thus provides a political analog of price and wage indexation. If the social "partners" press for gains only from insecurity and out of fear they may be victimized, then corporatist bargaining, like indexation, can clarify the gains and losses at stake and reduce conflicts that arise from uncertainty. If, however, the given interests are asking for more than others are willing to cede, harsh struggle must attend any system of representation, parliamentary or corporatist.

Finally, there are two further difficulties in corporatist representation: the widening issues that must be brought in and the alienation of those who must be left out. On the morrow of World War II, labor strove for the social reforms loosely described as the welfare state. But the welfare state implied a dualist concept of the capitalist economy. Working-class representatives sought a guarantee that those left out of prosperity – the victims of unemployment, age, or disability – would be given support. In return, the organization of production itself would be left to management and capital. This division of function, however, seems less feasible in an age of rapid technological change and obsolescence, especially as Third World nations emerge as major industrial competitors. Aging of populations through the remainder of the twentieth century will make the earlier compartmentalization of welfare policy and production policy even less viable. Just to support redundant labor prevents reallocation of resources and limits industrial investment. No intelligent architecture of welfare seems really feasible without some degree of social investment control as well. Hence the splitting of functions accepted after 1945 may no longer make sense; at the least, it may not appear to make sense to a new generation of the European Left. The great social *Ausgleich* on which corporatist equilibrium has been constructed during the past generation – rendering welfare and high employment unto labor, rendering control of investment to management (and sometimes the state) – may be nearing its term. Renegotiation of the compromise may not be impossible, but it probably will not be easy.

The list of difficulties finally includes those left out. Every move toward the organization of corporate interests is simultaneously a step toward exclusion of those not subsumed in a state-supervised structure of bargaining. To credential unions is to consign nonunion labor to a marginal status of passive citizenship. These outsiders may benefit from welfare rights but do not participate in making allocative decisions. Whether this exclusion must lead to crisis is also impossible to predict. Marginalization of social groups is hard on those emarginated but not always fatal to those within the charmed circle: The handloom weavers suffered, rebelled . . . but lost.

Ultimately, the difficulties afflicting interest representation and conciliation do not seem to depend on the format or the locus of group bargaining. From the viewpoint of those with an interest in social stability, the "century of corporatism" has helped take Western society through two major transitions that might have been far more revolutionary than they actually became. As an issue of political party conflict, the reduction of the European peasantry contributed decisively to the weakening of interwar parliamentary liberalism. As an issue of interest group bargaining, the transition could be completed with far less damage. Likewise, the "integration" of much of the industrial working class into welfare states required the conversion of ideological confrontation into the lesser disputes resolved by interest group bargaining. The one-time farmers work in the city; the workers vacation in the country: The transformation testifies to the achievements of a postwar society that was increasingly "corporatized." Nevertheless, it is far from clear whether the forms of political and economic mediation produced this outcome or themselves emerged from other, deeper trends. It is impossible to assess postwar "success" or contemporary institutional vulnerability without knowing whether the decades after World War II represented an exceptional period of economic growth and collective social discipline or a more enduring transformation. That issue is crucial to historical evaluation and contemporary analysis, and it is still open.

Notes

1 Walter Bagehot, "The History of the Unreformed Parliament and Its Lessons (1860)," in *Essays on Parliamentary Reform* (London: K. Paul, Trench, 1883), p. 125.

2 Walter Bagehot, "Parliamentary Reform (1859)," in *Essays on Parliamentary Reform*, p. 104. The corollary of the Bagehot view was that "opinion" was a lofty and stable discernment of community needs. For Burke, in contrast, "opinion" had signified the volatile electoral preference that a true representative often had to override. See Hanna Fenichel Pitkin, *The Concept of Representation* (Berkeley and Los Angeles: University of California Press, 1967), pp. 176, 205–6.

3 The term increasingly used to summarize the linkage of public institutions and organized interests is "corporatism." For a recent clarifying discussion see Gerhard Lehmbruch, "Einige Entwicklungslinien und Probleme in der Korporatismus-Diskussion," unpublished paper prepared for the Arbeitskreis "Parteien-Parlamente-Wahlen," (Neuss: February 23–4, 1979); also Philippe Schmitter, "Modes of Interest Intermediation and Models of Societal Change in Western Europe," *Comparative Political Studies* 10(1) (1977):7–38. Schmitter's typology stresses the sources of corporatism; my own prior use of "corporatism" attempted to describe emerging tendencies (and not final structures) as of the 1920s. See Charles Maier, *Recasting Bourgeois Europe: Stabilization in France, Germany, and Italy in the Decade After World War I* (Princeton, N.J., Princeton University Press, 1975), pp. 9–15, 580–94. When I used the term "corporative pluralism" for the liberal states – cf. "Strukturen kapitalistischer Stabilität in den zwanziger Jahren," in *Organisierter Kapitalismus*, ed. Heinrich A. Winkler (Göttingen: Vandenhoeck und Ruprecht, 1974), pp. 195–213 – I was unaware of Stein Rokkan's prior usage in the chapter on Norway in *Political Oppositions in Western Democracies*, ed. Robert Dahl (New Haven: Yale University Press, 1966), pp. 105 ff.

4 Otto Hintze, "The Preconditions of Representative Government in the Context of World History," [1931] in *The Historical Essays of Otto Hintze*, ed. Felix Gilbert (New York: Oxford University Press, 1975), p. 353. On representative bodies see also Emile Lousse, "Assemblées d'états," in *L'Organisation corporative du Moyen Age à la fin de l'Ancien Régime: Etudes présentées à la Commission Internationale pour l'Histoire des Assemblées d'Etats*, Vol. 7 (Louvain: Bibliothèque de l'Université, 1943), pp. 231–66; and A. R. Myers, *Parliaments and Estates in Europe to 1789* (London: Thames and Hudson, 1975).

5 The term "collective" was employed first by Albert V. Dicey, *Lectures upon the Relation Between Law and Public Opinion in England During the Nineteenth Century* (London: Macmillan, 1905) to describe the infringements of laissez-faire. In the corporatist sense used here the concept was taken up by Samuel Beer, *British Politics in the Collectivist Age*, rev. ed. (New York: Knopf, 1969).

6 I have borrowed the term "liberal parenthesis" from Alessandro Pizzorno. See also the description of an "era of parties" between an age of corporations and an age of professionally based groups (c. 1789–1889) in François Olivier-Martin, "Le déclin et la

suppression des corps en France au XVIIIe siècle," in *L'Organisation corporative du Moyen Age à la fin de l'Ancien Régime*, Vol. 3 (Louvain: Bibliothèque de l'Université, 1937), p. 163.

7 J. A. W. Gunn, *Politics and the Public Interest in the Seventeenth Century* (London: Routledge and Kegan Paul, 1969); Albert O. Hirschman, *The Passions and the Interests* (Princeton, N.J.: Princeton University Press, 1977), pp. 32–42.

8 For the ambiguities see J. G. A. Pocock, *The Machiavellian Moment: Florentine Political Thought and the Atlantic Republican Tradition* (Princeton, N.J.: Princeton University Press, 1975), pp. 426–7, 436–61; on *doux commerce*, cf. Hirschman, *Passions and Interests*, pp. 59–63; and compare Montesquieu *The Spirit of the Laws*, 1748, Chap. 20, trans. Thomas Nugent (New York: Hafner Publishing, 1949), with the *Persian Letters*, 1721, cxlii. For early United States: Ralph Lerner, "Commerce and Character: The Anglo-American as New-Model Man," *William and Mary Quarterly*, 3rd ser. 36(1) (1979):3–26.

9 John Locke, *The Second Treatise of Government* (New York: The Liberal Arts Press, 1952), Chap. 5, paragraphs 47–50, and 124, 134, where Locke argued inequality was "practicable without compact, only by putting a value on gold and silver"; however, "preservation" of property required institution of government. Cf. C. B. Macpherson, *The Political Theory of Possessive Individualism: Hobbes to Locke* (London: Oxford University Press, 1964), pp. 203–21; and on Locke's stand against legislative adjustment of monetary values (because bullion supposedly registered prior natural rights) see Joyce Oldham Appleby, "Locke, Liberalism, and the Natural Law of Money," *Past and Present* 71(May 1976):43–69.

10 Defoe's *Review* [1706] cited in Pocock, *Machiavellian Moment*, p. 452.

11 Alexander Pope, *Moral Essays*, Epistle III, line 143; cited in Isaac Kramnick, *Bolingbroke and His Circle: The Politics of Nostalgia in the Age of Walpole* (Cambridge, Mass.: Harvard University Press, 1968). For Montesquieu, see note 8.

12 Bernard Mandeville, *The Fable of the Bees*, 1705, and with supporting text, 1714; cf. Thomas A. Horne, *The Social Thought of Bernard Mandeville* (New York: Columbia University Press, 1978). For specimens of modern Mandevillism see Edward Banfield, *Political Influence* (Glencoe: Free Press, 1961), pp. 324–41; and Ralf Dahrendorf, "In Praise of Thrasymachus," *Essays in the Theory of Society* (Stanford, Calif.: Stanford University Press, 1968).

13 Oliver Goldsmith, *The Traveler*, 1764, cited in Kramnick, *Bolingbroke*, p. 80.

14 Besides Kramnick see Bernard Bailyn, *The Origins of American Politics* (New York: Knopf, 1968), pp. 37 ff.; Caroline Robbins, *The Eighteenth-Century Commonwealthman* (Cambridge, Mass.: Harvard University Press, 1961), pp. 271 ff.; J. H. Plumb, *The Origins of Political Stability: England 1675–1725* (Boston: Houghton Mifflin, 1967), for the emergence of the Walpole regime; Franklin L. Ford, *Robe and Sword: The Regrouping of the French Aristocracy After Louis XIV* (Cambridge, Mass.: Harvard University Press, 1953), Chap. 12, on the *thèse nobiliaire;* and Klaus Epstein, *The Genesis of German Conservatism* (Princeton, N.J.: Princeton University Press, 1966), pp. 297–338 on Möser.

15 Edmund Burke, "Thoughts on the Causes of the Present Discontents," 1770, excerpted in *Burke's Politics*, eds. Ross. J. S. Hoffman and Paul Levack (New York: Knopf, 1959), p. 23. The British radicals understood the oligarchic nature of Burke's critique. See Ian R. Christie, *Wilkes, Wyvill and Reform* (London: Macmillan, 1962), pp. 42–3.

16 J. R. Pole, *Political Representation in England and the Origins of the American Republic* (Berkeley and Los Angeles: University of California Press, 1971), pp. 442–57, 526–31 (citation on p. 454). On Burke's abstract construction of interests, divorced from particular real groups, see Pitkin, *The Concept of Representation*, p. 174.

17 Montesquieu, *Spirit of the Laws*, XXI, Section 20; cited by Hirschman, *Passions and Interests*, p. 73.

18 David Hume, "Of Parties in General," in *David Hume's Political Essays*, ed. Charles W. Hendel (New York: The Liberal Arts Press, 1953), p. 81.

19 Pauline Maier, "The Charleston Mob and the Evolution of Popular Politics in Revolutionary South Carolina, 1765–1784," *Perspectives in American History* 4 (197):192–4.

20 For the Jacobin willingness to accept parties (once, of course, they had lost control), see Lynn Hunt, David Lansky, and Paul Hanson, "The Failure of the Liberal Republic in France, 1795–1799: The Road to Brumaire," *Journal of Modern History* 51 (4) (1979):734–59. On British opposition to Pitt see John Thelwall's *Tribune*, April 25 and May 23, 1795, cited in E. P. Thompson, *The Making of the English Working Class* (New York: Vintage Books, 1966), p. 159.

21 For Madison's view, *The Federalist Papers*, No. 10. On deference see J. G. A. Pocock, "The Classical Theory of Deference," and Richard W. Davis, "Deference and Aristocracy in the Time of the Great Reform Act," *American Historical Review*, 81 (3) (1976):516–23, 532–9; also David Cresap Moore, *The Politics of Deference: A Study of the Mid-Nineteenth Century English Political System* (Hassocks, Eng.: Harvester Press, 1976).

22 Walter Bagehot, "Parliamentary Reform" [1859] in *Essays on Parliamentary Reform*, p. 40.

23 Bagehot, "Parliamentary Reform," pp. 101–2.

24 Royer-Collard cited in Dominique Bagge, *Le conflit des idées politiques en France sous la Restauration* (Paris: Presses Universitaires de France, 1952), pp. 110–13.

25 Melbourne and Aberdeen cited in Norman Gash, *Reaction and Reconstruction in English Politics, 1832–1852* (Oxford: Clarendon Press, 1965), pp. 126, 128.

26 Frederick Grimke, *The Nature and Tendency of Free Institutions* [1848], cited by Richard Hofstadter, *The Idea of a Party System* (Berkeley and Los Angeles: University of California Press, 1970), p. 265.

27 Ludwig August von Rochau, *Grundsätze der Realpolitik*, ed. Hans-Ulrich Wehler (Frankfurt/M.: Ullstein, 1972), pp. 94–5. For another testimony of German interest in parties in the wake of 1848, see Wilhelm Wachsmuth, *Geschichte der politischen Parteien alter und neuer Zeit*, 3 vols. (Braunschweig: Schwetscke und Sohn, 1853–6). And for the rich fabric of associations in pre-1848 Germany, which, if not strictly speaking political, still helped articulate middle-class opinion, see Otto Dann, "Die Anfänge politischer Vereinsbildung in Deutschland," in *Soziale Bewegung und politische Verfassung. Beiträge zur Geschichte der modernen Welt*, eds. U. Engelhardt, V. Sellin, H. Stücke (Stuttgart: Klett Verlag, 1976), pp. 197–232.

28 Heinrich von Treitschke, *Parteien und Fraktionen* [1871], cited in Theodor Schieder, "The Theory of the Political Party in Early German Liberalism," in *The State and Society in Our Times*, trans. C. A. M. Syme (London: Nelson, 1962), p. 96.

29 John Vincent, *The Formation of the British Liberal Party, 1857-68* (Harmondsworth: Penguin Books, 1972), pp. 12–13.

30 See Pierre Barral, *Les agrariens français de Méline à Pisani* (Paris: Colin, 1968), pp. 105–28; also Michel Augé-Laribé, *La politique agricole de la France de 1880 à 1940* (Paris: Presses Universitaires de France, 1950), pp. 72–80, 219–20, 237–40.

31 In addition to those mentioned see on tariffs, Peter A. Gourevitch, "International Trade, Domestic Coalitions, and Liberty: The Crisis of 1873–1896," *Journal of Interdisciplinary History* 8 (2) (1977):281–313; Eugene O. Golob, *The Méline Tariff: French Agriculture and Nationalist Economic Policy* (New York: Columbia University Press, 1944); Alexander Gerschenkron, *Bread and Democracy in Germany* (Berkeley and Los Angeles: University of California Press, 1943), Part I; Hans Rosenberg, *Grosse Depression und Bismarckszeit* (Berlin: De Gruyter, 1967); Benjamin H. Brown, *The Tariff Reform Movement in Britain, 1884–1895* (New York: Columbia University Press, 1943); Ivo Lambi, *Free Trade and Protection in Germany, 1868–1879* (Wiesbaden: Steiner, 1963). For the emergence and manipulation of interest groups in this period, including the exploitation of the tariff issue, see also Sanford Elwitt, *The Making of the Third Republic: Class and Politics in France, 1868–1884* (Baton Rouge: Louisiana State University Press, 1975), pp. 230–72; Giampiero Carocci, *Agostino Depretis e la politica interna italiana dal 1876 al 1887* (Turin: Einaudi, 1956), especially pp. 408–9; Helmut Böhme, "Big Business Pressure Groups and Bismarck's Turn to Protectionism, 1873–79," *The Historical Journal* 10(1973):218–36; Hartmut Kaelble, *Industrielle Interessenpolitik in der wilhelminischen Gesellschaft* (Berlin: De Gruyter, 1967); Dirk Stegman, *Die Erben Bismarcks. Parteien und Verbände in der Spätphase des Wilhelminischen Deutschlands* (Cologne and Berlin: Kiepenheuer und Witsch, 1970); Hans-Jürgen Puhle, "Parlament, Parteien und Interessenverbände 1890–1914," in *Das kaiserliche Deutschland*, ed. Michael Stürmer (Düsseldorf: Droste, 1970), 340–77, and the same author's two volumes: *Agrarische Interessenpolitik und preuss-ischer Konservatismus im Wilhelminischen Reich (1893–1914)* (Hanover: Verlag für Literatur und Zeitgeschehen, 1967), and *Politische Agrarbewegungen in kapitalistischen Indus-triegesellschaften: Deutschland, USA und Frankreich im 20. Jahrhundert* (Göttingen: Vandenhoeck und Ruprecht, 1975); also the essays included in *Interessenverbände in Deutschland*, ed. Heinz Josef Varain (Cologne: Kiepenheuer und Witsch, 1973), pp. 139–161.

32 The issue of the social causes of imperialism goes back at least to John Hobson, *Imperialism: A Study* (London: John Nisbet, 1902), but the major historiographical statements have centered on Germany. See Eckart Kehr, *Schlachtflottenbau und Parteipolitik* (Berlin: Ebering, 1930); Hans-Ulrich Wehler, *Bismarck und der Imperialismus* (Cologne: Kiepenheuer und Witsch, 1969); and for a partial counterstatement, Geoff Eley, who may overstate their analysis of manipulation from above, see Geoff Eley, "Die 'Kehrites' und das Kaiserreich: Bemerkungen zu einer aktuellen Kontroverse," *Geschichte und Gesellschaft* 4(1)(1978):91–107; also Eley, "Reshaping the Right: Radical Nationalism and the German Navy League, 1898–1908," *The Historical Journal* 21 (2) (1978): 327–54.

33 Cf. Dieter Schäfer, "Der deutsche Handelstag auf dem Weg zum wirtschaftlichen Verband," in *Interessenverbände*, ed. Varain, pp. 120–38; also Heinrich A. Winkler, *Pluralismus oder Protektionismus? Verfassungspolitische Probleme des Verbandswesens im deutschen Kaiserreich* (Wiesbaden: Steiner, 1972), pp. 5 ff.

34 See Pierre Sorlin, *Waldeck–Rousseau* (Paris: Colin, 1966). pp. 208 fn., 236–64.

35 Gneist and Gierke cited in Winkler, *Pluralismus oder Protektionismus?* p. 28–9. For Gneist and Gierke see also Heinrich Heffter, *Die deutsche Selbstverwaltung im 19. Jahrhundert* (Stuttgart: Koehler, 1950) pp. 372–403, 525–30; and, in general, Otto von Gierke, *Das deutsche Genossenschaftsrecht*, 4 vols. (Berlin: Weidman, 1868–1913).

36 Cf. Claude Digeon, *La crise allemande de la société française (1870–1914)* (Paris: Presses Universitaires de France, 1959), pp. 215–52, 403–49; Gaetano Mosca, *Elementi di scienza politica* [1896, 1923], published in English as *The Ruling Class*, trans. H. D. Kahn and ed. A. Livingstone (New York and London: McGraw-Hill Book Co., 1939); Vilfredo Pareto, *Les systèmes socialistes* [1902] (Geneva: Droz, 1965).

37 Arthur Bentley, *The Process of Government*, ed. Peter H. Odegard (Cambridge, Mass.: Harvard University Press, 1967): "All phenomena of government are phenomena of groups pressing one another, forming one another, and pushing out new groups and group representatives (the organs or agencies of government) to mediate the adjustments. . . . The interest is nothing other than the group activity itself." (pp. 269, 271.)

38 Leon Duguit, *Le droit social, le droit individuel et les transformations de l'état* (Paris: Alcan, 1908).

39 Santi Romano, "Lo Stato moderno e la sua crisi," in *Scritti minori*, Vol. 1 (Milan: Giuffrè, 1950), pp. 311–25; the passage here cited by Paolo Ungari, *Alfredo Rocco e l'ideologia giuridica del fascismo* (Brescia: Morcelliana, 1963), p. 37.

40 For the comment this aroused see M. Ostrogorsky, *La démocratie et l'organisation* *des partis politiques,* 2 vols. (Paris: Calmann-Lévy, 1903); Max Weber, *Wirtschaft und Gesellschaft,* 5th ed. (Tübingen: 1972), pp. 837–51; "Politics as a Vocation," in Hans Gerth and C. Wright Mills, *From Max Weber* (New York: Oxford University Press, 1958), pp. 99–112; and Robert Michels, *Political Parties,* trans. E. and C. Paul [1915] (New York: Dover, 1959).

41 On the Nationalists: Richard Webster, *Industrial Imperialism in Italy, 1908–1915* (Berkeley and Los Angeles: University of California Press, 1975); Franco Gaeta, *Nazionalismo italiano* (Naples: Edizioni Scientifiche Italiane, 1965); and Ungari, *Alfredo Rocco,* especially Chap. 5. On the agrarians see the Puhle citations in note 31. A contemporary judgment on the capture of the parties, although overstressed, in Emil Lederer, "Die ökonomische Element und die politischen Ideen im modernen Parteiwesen," *Zeitschrift für Politik,* 5(4)(1912).

42 Revealing in this regard were the Liberals' efforts to define the middle classes they allegedly represented. On this, and on the relationship to interest groups, see James J. Sheehan, *German Liberalism in the Nineteenth Century* (Chicago and London: University of Chicago Press, 1978), pp. 169–77, 248–57; and cf. Dan S. White's chapter on "National Liberalism in the Context of European Politics," in *The Splintered Party* (Cambridge, Mass.: Harvard University Press, 1976), pp. 199–222.

43 Etienne Villey, *L'Organisation professionnelle des employeurs dans l'industrie française* (Paris: Alcan, 1923); Mario Abrate, *La lotta sindacale nella industrializzazione in Italia* (Milan: Angeli, 1967); Anthony L. Cardoza, "Agrarian Elites and the Origins of Italian Fascism: The Province of Bologna, 1901–1922," dissertation, Princeton University, 1975; and the German sources cited in note 31 and Fritz Tanzler, *Die deutschen Arbeitgeberverbände 1904–1929* (Berlin, 1929).

44 See William Oualid and Charles Picquenard, *Salaires et tariffes, conventions collectives et grèves: la politique du ministère de l'armament* (Paris: Presses Universitaires de France, and New Haven: Yale University Press, 1928); Henri Flu, *Les comptoirs metallurgiques d'après-guerre (1919–1922)* (Lyon: Thèse, 1924) with background on the war; E. M. H. Lloyd, *Experiments in State Control at the War Office and the Ministry of Food* (Oxford: Clarendon Press, 1924); W. F. Bruck, "Die Kriegsunternehmung. Versuch einer Systematik," *Archiv für Sozialwissenschaft und Sozialpolitik* 48(3) (1921):547–95; the material in Gerald Feldman, *Army, Industry, and Labor in Germany, 1914–1918* (Princeton, N.J.: Princeton University Press, 1966); Paul A. C. Koistinen, "The 'Industrial-Military Complex' in Historical Perspective: World War I," *Business History Review,* 41(4) (1967):378–403.

45 Cited in A. H. Birch, *Representation* (London: Pall Mall Press, 1971), p. 103. For the plans cited see G. D. H. Cole, *Workshop Organization* (Oxford: Clarendon Press, 1923); Arthur Gleason, *What the Workers Want* (New York: Harcourt, Brace and Howe, 1920), pp. 169 ff., 185 ff.; Walther Rathenau, *Von kommenden Dingen* (Berlin: Fischer, 1917) and *Die neue Wirtschaft* (Berlin: Fischer, 1918); Wichard von Moellendorff, *Der Aufbau der Gemeinwirtschaft* (Jena: Diederichs, 1919); Etienne Clementel articles in *Journée Industrielle* (April 1919), cited by Maier, *Recasting Bourgeois Europe,* pp. 74–6.

46 Lloyd, *Experiments in State Control,* p. 1. For the general problems of wartime controls see pp. 259 ff. For a useful discussion of emerging pluralist theory among British and American writers before, during, and after World War I, which traces the filiation from Gierke and Duguit to Maitland, Figgis, Laski, Lippmann, Beard et al., see Paul F. Bourke, "The Pluralist Reading of James Madison's Tenth *Federalist,*" *Perspectives in American History* 9 (1975):271–95.

47 On Mussolini's labor policy see Adrian Lyttelton, *The Seizure of Power: Fascism in Italy 1919–1929* (London: Weidenfeld and Nicolson, 1973), pp. 217ff. and 315ff.; Renzo De Felice, *Mussolini il fascista, L'organizzazione dello stato fascista 1925–1929,* Vol. 2 (Turin:

Einaudi, 1968); Gaetano Salvemini, *Under the Axe of Fascism* (New York: Viking Press, 1936); and other sources cited in Maier, *Recasting Bourgeois Europe*, pp. 556–78. National Socialist policies in Germany involved far less of an effort to establish a corporativist façade; syndicalist spokesmen met defeat within the circles of the regime far earlier (witness the slaying of Gregor Strasser on June 30, 1934); and the Labor Front represented a more naked and centralized search for control and domination. See Gerhard Schulz, *Die Anfänge des totalitaren Massnahmenstaates* (Frankfurt/Main: Ullstein, 1974), Chaps. I.3 and V (originally published as Part II of K. D. Bracher, G. Schulz, and W. Sauer, *Die nationalsozialistische Machtergreifung* (Cologne: Westdeutscher Verlag, 1960); and T. W. Mason, *Arbeiterklasse und Volksgemeinschaft. Dokumente und Materielen zur deutschen Arbeiterpolitik 1936–1939* (Opladen: Westdeutscher Verlag, 1975).

48 See Jacques Julliard, "La Charte du Travail," in *Le Gouvernement de Vichy 1940–1942*, eds. René Rémond and Janine Bourdin. Colloque de la Fondation Nationale des Sciences Politiques (Paris: A. Colin, 1972); also John P. Windmuller, *Labor Relations in the Netherlands* (Ithaca, N.Y.: Cornell University Press, 1969), pp. 83–120; and, in general, Leo Panitch, "The Development of Corporatism in Liberal Democracies," *Comparative Political Studies* 10(1) (1977):61–90.

49 Cf. Alan Wolfe, "Has Social Democracy a Future?" *Comparative Politics* (October 1978):100–125; and on the systemic political–economy advantages for business, see Offe, Chapter 5 of this volume, and Charles Lindblom, *Politics and Markets* (New York: Basic Books, 1977).

50 Philippe Schmitter, "Modes of Interest Intermediation and Models of Societal Change in Western Europe," *Comparative Political Studies* 10(1) (1977):7–38.

51 See Kocka, Chapter 2 of this volume; also his influential *Unternehmensverwaltung und Angestelltenschaft am Beispiel Siemens 1847–1914* (Stuttgart: Klett, 1969). Cf. Winkler, *Pluralismus oder Protektionismus?* p. 32.

52 See Arend Lijphart, *The Politics of Accommodation: Pluralism and Democracy in the Netherlands* (Berkeley, Cal.: University of California Press, 1968).

53 On the continuing lesser legitimacy of corporatist arrangements see Hans Daalder and Galen A. Irwin, "Interests and Institutions in the Netherlands: An Assessment by the People and by Parliament," in *Interest Groups in International Perspective*, ed. Robert Presthus, *The Annals*, 413(1974):58–71.

54 Gerhard Lehmbruch, "Liberal Corporatism and Party Government," *Comparative Political Studies* 10(1) (1977):91–126; also Schmitter, "Interest Intermediation and Regime Governability in Contemporary Western Europe and North America," Chapter 10 of this volume.

55 Peter Lange, "Sindacati, partiti, stato e liberal-corporativismo," *Il Mulino*, (266) (November–December 1979):943–72.

2

Class formation, interest articulation, and public policy: the origins of the German white-collar class in the late nineteenth and early twentieth centuries

JÜRGEN KOCKA

This chapter deals with three major issues of interest group analysis. First, it explores in some detail the mechanisms leading to the formation of interest groups (associations). The interplay of social class and group formation, political interventions into the social structure, and older historical traditions of preindustrial origins determines interest group formation in this case. The stress is on national specificities and international comparison.

Next, it explores one important effect of interest groups: their impact on class and group formation (social structuration). It will be shown that lines of social differentiation, tension, and conflict are defined and redefined, reinforced or weakened through processes in which interest groups play a major role.

Third, the chapter suggests how surviving preindustrial structures and traditions of corporate and bureaucratic type facilitate and shape, even at an advanced stage of industrialization, the rise of modern corporatism. Eighteenth-century bureaucratic and corporate traditions maintained their vitality in Germany, although liberal sociopolitical reforms, the rise of the marketplace, and capitalist industrialization largely destroyed the old corporatist-absolutist world. In contrast to Britain and the United States, in Germany surviving traditions and structures helped to develop and legitimize new types of quasi-corporate and partly bureaucratic organization, gradually supplementing and superseding the market from the late nineteenth century. Interest groups are central to this process of transformation which continues today.

White-collar and blue-collar workers

The distinction between blue-collar (wage) workers and white-collar (salaried) employees has a ubiquitous character and can be observed in all capitalist–industrial systems.[1] In all such societies those employed in dependent positions (self-employed persons are not treated in this paper) fall into two broad categories: manual and nonmanual, blue collar and white collar, *ouvriers* and *employés*, *Arbeiter* and *Angestellte*, and this distinction is regarded as socially and politically relevant.

What are the common characteristics of white-collar employees that distinguish them from blue-collar workers? White-collar workers perform selling, administrative, work-preparing, controlling, and coordinating functions in contrast to production proper. These functions are mostly performed at some distance from the places of production, in special departments (offices) and institutions (commercial establishments, banks, administrative bureaus, etc.). White-collar workers are exclusively or primarily engaged in nonmanual work that treats information and not things. Frequently this type of work is less routinized and more difficult to quantify than manual work. This is why it is often harder to control by the employer. Work in offices and stores by and large is less noisy, cleaner, and physically less demanding than manual work in agriculture and industry, which implies differences in the work milieu and work culture of *Arbeiter* and *Angestellte*. The collective organization, mechanization, and automization of white-collar jobs began later and have remained less complete than in blue-collar work. Even in highly mechanized offices, mechanized processes do not integrate and determine the movements, rhythms, and work of office employees as thoroughly as in the case of workers in highly mechanized production units.

On the average, white-collar employees have career chances that are at least slightly better than those of blue-collar workers, because there is more continuity between the lower and middle (sometimes even higher) positions and qualifications in the office sector and because the office sector is vertically more differentiated than the production sector.

White-collar employees receive salaries, not wages; this means their earnings are more calculable over longer periods of time, less tied to short-range changes in the individual's measured achievements, less dependent on short-term market variations, and more compatible with seniority criteria than piece rates, hourly, daily, or weekly wages. On the average, white-collar employees earn more and are better qualified than blue-collar workers.[2] Frequently white-collar employees have more job security and shorter working hours than blue-collar wage workers (although especially in this respect differentials have tended to diminish).

Everywhere distinctions of this kind have contributed to the higher social recognition that white-collar positions enjoy, *ceteris paribus*, over blue-collar positions, although national and historical variations on these matters have been considerable. Everywhere these distinctions have had consequences for social and political life outside the workplace. The white-collar/blue-collar distinction ("collar line") has stratified consumption and living patterns, friendship and marriage patterns, political discourse and social identification, organizational and political behavior, and so on. Here again, variations between time periods and societies have been pronounced, and generalization is risky.[3]

The purpose of this chapter is not to explain these differences between white-collar employees and blue-collar workers in terms of the structural characteristics and functional requirements of the societies in which such differences can be observed or to attempt another sociological theory of the white-collar/blue-collar difference or of the salaried employee in general.[4] Rather, I would like to caution against hasty sociological generalizations by stressing that many differences between white-collar and blue-collar workers are subject to national and historical variations. The sharpness and the shape of the "collar line" are deeply conditioned by historical processes in which the interplay between class structuration, interest group formation, and government policy has been of central importance. The discussion will be limited to employees in the private sector and focus on lower and middle ranks, excluding managerial employees.

White-collar workers as "private civil servants"

Blue-collar/white-collar differences as previously sketched were already visible in German enterprises in the first phase of German industrialization, from the 1840s to the 1870s.[5] Within the factories, entrepreneurs clearly distinguished between salaried persons and wage earners with respect to type and amount of payment, job security, and early welfare benefits. White-collar and blue-collar workers differed in general status and in attitudes to the firm. Outside the workplace and the enterprises, the distinction between blue collar and white collar remained rather vague and irrelevant up to the 1880s, although both in law and in popular sociological treatises and in the self-images of those concerned the distinction between manual and nonmanual employees was not totally absent. There was little *practical* incentive or reason to distinguish between *Angestellte* and *Arbeiter*. The concepts used for a sociological map of nonmanual groups were primarily sectoral, distinguishing between occupations or groupings of occupations (such as *Handlungsgehilfe*, commercial clerks, engineers, bookkeepers, bank employees, etc.). There would have been little purpose in lumping these categories together – as the concept *Angestellte* would later do – and differentiating them from another category of employees, that is, *Arbeiter*. In fact, the concept *Angestellte* was as yet hardly used in its later meaning; early substitutes such as *Privatbeamte* (private civil servants) were not much more common either (although they existed), and this state of the sociopolitical terminology probably reflects both the special way that those concerned thought of themselves and the way contemporaries envisioned the structure of their social environment. Organizations with socioeconomic purposes and with socioeconomic recruitment criteria representing nonmanual groups to the extent that they existed at all were organizations of single occupations or occupational groupings: mainly associations of commercial employees (including those in retailing and wholesaling and even those with jobs in manufacturing enterprises) and professional associations of engineers (including salaried employees and self-employed engineers as well).[6]

Preliminary comparisons[7] with other countries seem to show that the distinction between nonmanual salaried employees and manual wage workers was rather pronounced and emphasized in Germany. From visitors' reports, educational literature, description of social relations within factories, publications of employees' associations, and other such sources, a comparison between Germany and the United States can be drawn that suggests that the status superiority of nonmanual or manual work was clearer in the former than in the latter. An average office employee claimed and got social recognition superior to a manual worker even when this manual worker was highly skilled and better paid; corresponding differences in life-styles and dress patterns were more pronounced on the German than on the American side. This is hardly surprising if one compares the Old World and its feudal past,[8] its traditional disregard for manual work and its sharper sense of status differences with the "new nation" of the United States characterized by labor shortages, a rather egalitarian culture, and no feudal traditions on which to base a special claim for the superiority of nonmanual work.[9] But even if one considers Britain and France, one observes a particular emphasis on the white-collar/blue-collar line in Germany, even in that early time.[10] Neither in the United States nor in Britain did technicians, supervisory persons, clerks, or bank employees conceive of themselves as *Privatbeamte* ("private civil servants"), thus expressing that they used public civil servants as a normative reference group,[11] as a model for self-identification. But this is how many German private-salaried employees conceived of themselves and how they were seen and labeled by others until the early twentieth century. Because of a strong unbroken bureaucratic tradition – bureaucratization preceded industrialization in Germany but not in Britain or the United States – there was in most German states a powerful, highly esteemed civil service at least from the late eighteenth century, whose status, security, and proximity to authority impressed large parts of the public and especially the salary earners outside the public sphere. As the terminology indicates, they modeled their self-image, social claims, ideals, and behavior after this bureaucratic model. To a large extent this was wishful thinking, but, in the mind of the salaried persons, as in the mind of contemporary observers, it contributed to a sharpening of the line between *Angestellte* and *Arbeiter*, who in this social model were defined as a contrasting group with a different position in the system of authority.[12] Similarly, some groups of salaried employees, those in wholesaling and retailing, called themselves *Handlungsgehilfen* and continued to perceive themselves as belonging to a specific corporate group (*Stand*), the *Handelsstand*. Specific claims for dignity and social recognition, a particular stress on general and commercial education as a basis for social claims and privileges, and strong attempts to differentiate themselves from other employees, especially from manual workers, resulted from this traditional self-identification.

Consequently, these employees resented all tendencies at the workplace and in society at large that threatened traditional differences between themselves and those below. In Germany, corporate traditions had not been challenged and weakened by a revolution from below, and in spite of partial modernization in other spheres, they continued to affect the claims and expectations of large groups of the population. The demands of commercial employees' associations are a case in point; these associations had partly originated in guild-type brotherhoods of the eighteenth century, continued into the nineteenth, and slowly changed into voluntary associations and organized interest groups.[13]

Images, conceptions, and attitudes – which derived from older traditions – influenced behavior, social relations, and institutions and were reinforced by them in turn, especially when this served the interest of the powerful. Within German manufacturing companies of the second third of the century, for instance, the line between (monthly) salaries and (hourly, daily) wages seems to have been drawn much more sharply than in American counterparts. Salaried persons (including the salesperson, the ordinary office clerk, and mostly the foreman) were privileged over manual workers (including the most skilled ones) in terms of job security, work hours, fringe benefits, and industrial relations in general. By granting such differential treatment, management met the expectations of those concerned and contributed to the sharpening of the major dividing line within the labor force. Correspondingly, the specific corporate (*Ständisch*) expectations of commercial employees were partly met and reinforced by the living-in system still common in Germany in the late nineteenth century and also by specific provisions of commercial law which granted protection against sudden dismissal and similar advantages to commercial employees but not to wage workers and other employees. This stands in sharp contrast to the United States, France, and Britain.

Formation of a white-collar class

It should be kept in mind, however, that by the 1880s, in spite of the differentiations previously stressed, the dividing line between blue collar and white collar remained fragmented and vague, peripheral to public opinion, and politically rather irrelevant. The pair of concepts *Arbeiter/Angestellte* was not yet fully developed; nor did the different white-collar groups perceive themselves to have enough in common in order to develop a common consciousness, common organization, and common actions that would cut across occupational lines and distinguish sharply between themselves and blue collars; nor did the white-collar/blue-collar line figure much in the writings of contemporary social scientists or in the decisions of politicians.

By the 1910s and 1920s the picture had radically changed. Not only had the number of salaried employees grown quickly in these decades: At the beginning of World War I there were roughly two million of them in contrast to about fourteen million wage workers.[14] Also, the concept *Angestellte* was by then fully established, lumping together different groups of salaried employees across occupational and professional lines and sharply distinguishing them from those below (mainly blue-collar wage workers) and from all self-employed groups. The first books on the *Angestellten* problem had been published, whereas previously the literature had dealt with individual salaried groups (like commercial employees) only. Publications of associations and the vocational literature show that members of single white-collar groups occupationally defined, such as technicians or clerks, increasingly conceived of themselves not only as members of a specific occupational group, but also as members of a stratum *Angestellte* in contrast to *Arbeiter*. Public debate inside and outside the parliament dealt with the *Angestellten* in general and what was called *Angestelltenfrage*. The associations of different white-collar occupations began to join hands and work together, and something like a white-collar movement developed with very different white-collar groups. Of course, the various types of white-collar workers continued to differ in many ways and maintained specific occupational or sectoral identities. Nevertheless, the concept *Angestellte* now began to refer to a real social group with common features and interests. These latter were manifest in the self-consciousness of members; were exhibited in their contacts and relations; and influenced their actions. This social group became recognized as such by contemporary observers and by members of other groups as well.[15]

What had happened?

1. Technological change and economic modernization created, also in the nonmanual sphere, new jobs and restructured old ones that could no longer be described in terms of traditional occupational classifications. The old-fashioned concept *Handlungsgehilfe* (commercial employee) with traditional connotations and status claims was very inadequate as a label for new, very routinized and specialized office jobs with few educational and training requirements. In addition, those having such jobs would easily move from the office of a large manufacturing corporation to an insurance company and to a lawyer's office. Defining oneself and being defined as *Angestellter* in general was a reaction to such changes in the occupational structure which tended to empty the content of the traditional occupational structure.[16] Such changes of occupational structure must have happened in other industrial systems of similar maturity, too. Because in other countries such as the United States a similar sharpening of the blue-collar/white-collar line did not take place at the time,[17] factors other than occupational structure must have been more important in accounting for what happened in Germany.

2. Formation of the *Angestellten* as a social group or "class" with common features, interests, and associations was a reaction to the formation of the blue-collar class. Group formation and interest articulation in one sector of the social structure led to group formation and interest articulation in other sectors as well. This mechanism was manifold and complex: So long as labor unions had recruited their members primarily on occupational or craft bases, the inclusion of salaried employees had been neither a real possibility nor had it been a problem. It had not led the salaried employees to identify themselves as nonlabor and to organize on this basis. Organizing the printers in a printers' union or the toolmakers in a toolmakers' union meant little for the technician or the bookkeeper in the same factory or for the retail clerks elsewhere.[18] But the situation changed when industrial unions gained ground from the 1890s on and when the or-

ganization of workers was fostered by stressing the common interests of all workers as a class against capital and bourgeois society. When unions did not restrict themselves to organizing cabinet makers or toolmakers but tried to organize all workers of the metalworking industries, the issue arose, implicitly or explicitly, of whether or not a technician or a bookkeeper in these industries was a worker and eligible for the union. This was a *practical situation* that served to remind salaried employees of those rather vague self-images described in the preceding section. This practical situation helped make them more conscious of these self-definitions, made these self-definitions more explicit, and developed among white-collar salaried employees a feeling of communality based on not being a worker. Only a negligible minority decided the other way round. No salaried persons seem to have joined industrial unions. Indeed, the workers did not expect them to do so. Only a very small portion of commercial employees joined an organization (Zentralverband der Handlungsgehilfen) that cooperated with blue-collar unions within the Social Democratic Federation of Labor, the *Generalkommission*. Up to 1933 there were no German unions that included blue-collar and white-collar workers within one and the same organization.[19]

This tendency toward a clearer delineation and structuration of the white-collar class due to the formation of the blue-collar working class had a particular political and ideological dimension which contributed to the specific meaning and "loading" of the blue-collar/white-collar difference in Germany. Largely because of the authoritarian structure of the German social and political system that had never been radically transformed by a successful revolution and that retained powerful preindustrial and prebourgeois elites and traditions, the German labor movement developed in fundamental opposition to the status quo. It adopted Socialist objectives and stressed global social and political aims. Due to increased prosecution in the seventies and eighties, it adopted a specific brand of Marxism as its official ideology. Its international orientation ran counter to the nationalism of Germany with its belated process of unification from above. Partly in practice and largely in theory, the German labor movement was clearly distinguished from American "business unionism," but also from the craft orientation of British unions which stressed common class characteristics of *all* workers, general social reform, and political action much less than their German counterpart. The specific features of the German labor movement (and of the German working class) can largely be explained as a reaction to the repressiveness and specific archaisms of the German social and political structure that retained many of its premodern traits while developing a most modern industrial–capitalist economy.[20]

This specific radicalism and massive character, the class consciousness, and the emphasis on politics of the German labor movement provoked or facilitated a very pointed and politicized antiproletarian and anti-Socialist rejection by most of the middle and upper classes. Antiproletarianism and antisocialism were sentiments that were in part at least stimulated to integrate a society riddled with frictions and tensions. In this highly charged and polarized situation the traditionally vague inclination of salaried groups to define themselves apart from the workers got a new political impetus and an unprecedented sharpness. The traditional claim for superiority that had been accentuated by older – bureaucratic and corporate (*ständisch*) – traditions acquired a new role within a postcorporate class society. Not being a worker and not belonging to the proletariat thus became a political issue, in addition to the status issue that it had been in the past. Consequently, some of the new white-collar associations were founded on the politicized notion of not being a worker. This is especially true for the most powerful employees' association of the German Empire, the Deutschnationaler Handlungsgehilfen-Verband (German National Union of Commercial Employees), which was founded in 1893 on an antiproletarian and anti-Socialist, nationalistic and anti-Semitic platform.[21]

3. Political determinants of the formation of the white-collar class in reaction to the blue-collar movement produced patterns of organization in Germany that differed significantly from those in other industrial societies. Without a mass-based, class-conscious labor movement, American society in the same period lacked a decisive stimulus for white-collar/blue-collar differentiation, and consequently this "collar line" remained more blurred and less relevant socially and politically in the United States. In Great Britain as well, the different orientations of the labor movement and the different reactions to it of the middle classes meant that the white-collar/blue-collar line did not become such a determining social and political cleavage. Both in the United States and in Britain the *internal* differences within the salaried categories remained stronger than in Germany, although such differences did not altogether disappear on the German side either, and the transformation of "white collars" from a statistical or analytical category into a group did not proceed as far as in Germany. Even language reflects this national difference: *White-collar employees* is a more artificial, abstract, and less common term than is *Angestellte* in Germany.[22]

But this is only part of the story. Yet another factor accounts for the formation of a white-collar class in Wilhelmine Germany. Due to increasing state intervention in society and the economy, the organization of interests along the emergent lines of social differentiation both influenced government policy and in turn contributed to the crystallization and hardening of those lines of differentiation.

The public insurance system that Bismarck created as an instrument of social integration became the central problem with respect to which the definition of *Angestellte* in contrast to *Arbeiter* developed. It was the most important of the *issues* that caused white-collar salaried employees to organize: First, the public accident, health, and pension insurance legislation of the 1880s had to define which categories of persons would be covered. The lawmakers, unaware of the long-range consequences their actions would have for social stratification, included all workers (*Arbeiter*) but only those salaried employees (*Angestellte*) earning less than a specified income per year (2,000 marks around 1890). This provision led to some early court cases in which judges had to decide whether a specific person making more than 2,000 marks a year was an *Arbeiter* or an *Angestellter*, because in the first case he or she would be subject to the obligatory insurance system, but not in the second case. From these legal debates and legal definitions the concept of *Angestellte* developed its contours.[23]

In addition, the public insurance system contributed in another way to the formation of the German white-collar class. The laws first provided for identical treatment of blue-collar workers and the large majority of white-collar salaried employees. The payments to and the benefits from these insurance schemes were scaled according to wage levels, length of membership, and some other criteria, but not differentiated along the white-collar/blue-collar line. These laws provided for self-governing bodies in which those who were subject to public insurance determined the administration of these schemes through elected representatives. But some of the laws (especially the health insurance law) provided that employees' groups that wished to set up voluntary insurance schemes of their own could do so instead of coming under the public schemes as long as certain minimum requirements were fulfilled and public supervision was accepted. By choosing this alternative, groups of employees would have the chance to decide in favor of higher payments and benefits, to modify conditions, and to control the administration of the schemes themselves.

Not surprisingly, some groups of salaried employees felt sufficiently different and superior to the mass of the workers (and sufficiently wealthy too) to choose this alternative. The first foremen's association was founded with mainly this purpose in 1884, on a national level, following the Deutscher Techniker-Verband in 1882 (the first organization of technicians and engineers working for the socioeconomic interests of its members – in contrast to the strictly professional Verein Deutscher Ingenieure).[24] The first attempt to organize salaried employees from different occupations and sectors resulted from the same conditions: The Deutscher Privatbeamten-Verein was founded in 1881; it included bookkeepers, engineers, firemen, bank employees, office workers employed by local communities without civil service status, and others and provided for an insurance scheme imitating as much as possible the retirement benefits of civil servants.[25] In all these cases, traditional claims for superiority and separate treatment were mobilized by the threat of being handled by new government programs in the same way as and together with those who were regarded as different and inferior. Traditional claims were sharpened and became the basis for interest articulation and common action. Resulting organizations needed definitions of those who should be eligible; they brought people together for common purposes, thus contributing to their growing cohesion. The decisive step on this path was the mobilization for the separate public white-collar insurance law (*Angestelltenversicherungsgesetz* – AVG), which was enacted in 1911. With respect to the general old-age pension scheme (1889) covering all wage workers and most white-collar workers (up to 2,000 marks per year), a specific white-collar opposition developed in the 1890s, especially after 1901. The majority of employees' associations (under the lead of three commercial employees' associations but including associations of technicians, foremen, general office employees, bank employees, etc.) agitated in favor of taking all *Angestellte* out of the (by then) well-established Bismarckian general insurance scheme and establishing a specific insurance system for *Angestellte*, which would be more adequate for their special needs. By this they allegedly differed from blue-collar workers. They demanded an insurance system modeled as much as possible after the pension schemes of civil servants: After all, they perceived themselves as *Privatbeamte*. They were ready to pay a slightly higher premium, wanted higher benefits, and required specific conditions (retirement at 65 instead of at 70; pensions to be paid when they could no longer pursue their specific occupations, whereas workers received pensions only after they were incapable of any type of work). In the course of ten years of agitation in favor of this AVG, which would provide a privileged position for all white-collar employees, new ideologies and rhetoric were developed to justify the differences and superiority of white-collar employees. The employee associations grew; associations of different occupations came together and formed loose federations in order to pressure in favor of this law or – in the case of a small minority – against it. In these years a common identity of *Angestellte* across occupational lines crystallized

in spite of many continuing differences. At the same time, the separation between white-collar workers and blue-collar workers became
manifest. The concepts of *Privatbeamte* and *Angestellte* became fully
accepted, and the meaning they carried became popular within a
context of interest politics – through local committees, gatherings,
publications, and pressures on candidates in election campaigns and
then on the parliamentary parties.

In 1911 this white-collar insurance law was enacted, although benefits remained far lower than those of civil servants, for financial reasons. Why did these claims for legal privilege succeed? Largely because these demands eventually received support from different
middle-class parties and the government, which hoped by satisfying
them to retain this quickly growing mass of salaried employees outside the strong Socialist camp, as supporters of the status quo or of
moderate middle-class reforms. The AVG was an important part of
what was then called *Mittelstandspolitik*, and finally even most Social
Democrats voted for the law to avoid jeopardizing the chance that in
the future they might win votes from these groups (which had voted
thus far for non-Socialist parties overwhelmingly).

The law had to define who belonged to *Angestellte* and who did
not, because this had become a very practical question. All attempts
to find a general definition on the basis of the arguments that had
been put forward in order to justify the claim for privileged treatment
failed. Whether *geistige Arbeit* (intellectual work); higher positions
between workers and management; proximity to the employer; authority; nonroutinized, individual work; personal responsibility; or
educational superiority was used as a criterion, each referred to only
some of those who would later be circumscribed and legally
privileged as *Angestellte*. Politics partly determined who would be an
Angestellte and who would not. For example, the draft of the law
presented by the government did not include ordinary office workers
in the category *Angestellte*, but when the draft came out of the
Reichstag committee, office workers were included and belonged to
those subject to the new law, except when they performed only low-
level or "mechanical" services. In 1924 all were included. The law also
included all retail clerks among those subject to privileged treatment
under the AVG – quite in contrast to the public statistics that until
then had counted them as workers. Retail clerks had been recruited,
together with wholesale commercial employees and others, by the
powerful commercial employees' associations, on the basis of quasi-
corporate recruitment criteria including all those with commercial occupations and education. These associations strongly influenced the
decision making process; they successfully tried to get all their mem-

bers in. In other words, the exact location of the line of differentiation between *Arbeiter* and *Angestellte* resulted from a political compromise. It is not surprising that the law simply enumerated the groups subject to its provisions without any general definition or justification.[26]

It would be difficult to overestimate the importance of this law for defining the difference between white-collar and blue-collar workers in the following years and decades. From now on the legal issue was whether or not an employee qualified as white collar. This was not only an academic but also a practical question: How should jobs that fell in between the clear-cut cases be classified? In practice, these cases were increasingly resolved by treating as *Angestellte* all those who were subject to the *Angestelltenversicherungsgesetz* (AVG).[27] Labor and social legislation enacted in later years frequently differentiated between *Arbeiter* and *Angestellte* by incorporating the definition of 1911 (slightly revised and enlarged in later years). The Auxiliary Service Law (*Hilfsdienstgesetz*) of 1916 and the Works' Committee Law (*Betriebsrätegesetz*) of 1920 made employee representation plans obligatory within most enterprises, except small ones. Against little opposition, they provided for blue-collar committees and white-collar committees to be elected separately by the corresponding groups and for separate representation. Again, the definition of 1911 was applied.[28] Other examples could be given for later years. The more laws differentiated in this way, the more relevant the blue-collar/white-collar line became for real-life chances.

Formation of interest groups in Germany in contrast to other Western countries

There were no similar developments in the United States, Britain, or France.[29] On the one hand, those traditional claims for differentiation (sketched in an earlier section) were nonexistent or weaker in these countries, in which older bureaucratic and corporate (*ständische*) traditions played a much smaller role. Thus the demand for legal recognition of traditional, but vague, differentials on the side of white-collar workers was less pronounced and was hard to legitimize. In the last analysis this difference results from the different patterns of modernization in Germany and the Western countries from the late eighteenth century: the role of bureaucracies and bureaucratic models, the impact or lack of revolutionary breaks, the early or late industrialization, the variable strength of older corporate traditions, and so forth.

On the other hand, the character and role of the national labor movements were different. It was previously argued that the specific character and massive challenge posed by the German labor movement – which itself must be explained in terms of the German modernization pattern – induced and accelerated the formation of the white-collar employees' class. In fact, without this proletarian and socialist challenge, the strange law of 1911 would not have been enacted, because it found decisive support from those who feared a major shift of salaried workers into the socialist camp and tried to prevent that.

Finally, Germany pioneered government interventions of a welfare state type. Again, the particular intensity of class tensions and other domestic political instabilities seem to have been responsible for this early development of government interventionism. This is part of Germany's move toward "organized capitalism," which occurred earlier than elsewhere.[30] The early development of social legislation stimulated social groups to organize on the basis of lines of differentiation, which in consequence became more precise and impermeable. The process of interest articulation and interest group formation resulted in influencing political decisions and outputs, which in turn reinforced those lines of social structuration.

The specific definition of the concept *Angestellte* was a result of a political process in a specific historical situation. Subsequent attempts to theorize on the nature of *Angestellte* and to explain it in general sociological terms thus ran into grave difficulties when they proceeded to abstract from the particular historical situation in which this concept had developed. Most sociological literature on *Angestellte*, at least in Germany, seems to support this conclusion.

Due to the processes analyzed as well as other factors not discussed here (e.g., education, the relative strength or weakness of other lines of social differentiation and conflict, such as ethnicity), the white-collar/blue-collar distinction in Germany was stressed, defined, and loaded with relevance more than in other Western countries. At least until 1933, partly even in the present, the white-collar/blue-collar line counts more in Germany than elsewhere in social and labor legislation,[31] industrial relations, union structures, political behavior, collective mentalities, public symbolism, political language, and in other respects. Due to its legal status, the white-collar/blue-collar line in Germany gained a particular capacity for resisting those economic and social changes which might have undermined the differences between these two groups and leveled the white-collar/blue-collar distinction in the following decades. More than in other countries this distinction survived the erosion of its own origins. This partly explains why white-collar employees' frustration and protest were so

strong and important when finally, around 1930, the differentials between themselves and the wage workers were threatened and eroded
by economic crisis and political change. But to pursue this subject
would require us to link our argument to an analysis of the social
conditions that facilitated the rise of fascism.[32]

Conclusions

In the context of this volume four more general results that this chapter suggests should be stressed:

1. The social and economic interests, tensions, and conflicts alone
cannot explain the formation of interest groups; the impact of the
political system plays a major role in determining the timing, shape,
and intensity of interest group formation. Pre-1914 Germany was not
yet a parliamentary democracy but an authoritarian system: There
was a powerful, rather uncontrolled bureaucracy, a strong military,
and influential landed elites. Yet there was partial democratization as
indicated by the general suffrage on the national level and by the
protection of basic liberal rights, at least in principle. This combination of partial democratization and authoritarian rule proved to be
favorable for the rise of interest groups and other aspects of modern
corporatism. One can hypothesize that both a strictly authoritarian
alternative and a full-fledged parliamentary democracy with strong
parties would have been more of an obstacle to the rise of an elaborate
system of interest groups at this early time. Preindustrial structures
and traditions of a bureaucratic and feudal corporatism remained
strong in Germany from the eighteenth century. They proved to
facilitate the rise of modern corporatism in the late nineteenth and
early twentieth centuries. In this respect, Germany seems to have
differed from Great Britain and the United States. This partly explains
why Germany was an early pioneer in developing strong interest
groups, direct relations between the interest groups and the bureaucracy, and other aspects of modern corporatism.

2. The rise of organized interests and formalized movements in one
sector of the society initiates or accelerates the rise of organized interests and formalized movements in another, thus demonstrating the
working of a "spillover effect." State interventions for some classes
and groups generate the necessity of state interventions for others.
The impact of organized labor and labor insurance legislation on the
structuration and organization of the German white-collar class demonstrate this.

3. The criteria of recruitment to and the boundaries of interest
groups are not fully determined by the socioeconomic structure and

the occupational system out of which they emerge. German interest group formation has tended to result in rather comprehensive groups in contrast to functionally or occupationally more specific groups that would have been conceivable and which have been more frequent in other countries. Preindustrial structures and traditions of a corporate and a bureaucratic type were stressed as the main factors explaining this trend toward comprehensiveness in Germany. What was analyzed here was salaried employees who organized as "commercial employees" or even as *Angestellte*, although they might have organized as retail clerks or bookkeepers as well; in fact, this is what happened in late nineteenth-century United States. One could easily demonstrate the same pattern with respect to the self-employed lower-middle classes, the working-class movement, and the professional organizations in Germany. It seems plausible to assume that this relatively high degree of comprehensiveness was partly a cause and partly a consequence of the relatively abstract and generalized character of these interest groups' aims and policies.

4. The interest groups can be analyzed as elements in the complex process of class and group formation. They both reflect and determine such processes. They are manifestations of class and group patterns, but they also react back on those patterns by reinforcing and sometimes redefining them. Interest groups, too, serve as vehicles for transmitting government interventions which, intentionally or not, contribute to shaping the emerging and changing system of classes and groups. Certainly this is not true for all interest groups. For a closer study of this relationship it would be necessary to investigate the relationship between interest groups and members and how much and in what ways they influence their social identification.

Notes

1 In fact most of the aspects of the white-collar/blue-collar distinction can be found in noncapitalist industrial societies too, and some of them also in preindustrial societies, as soon as they have developed a minimum of functional differentiation and division of labor. Reasoning in this chapter is restricted exclusively to industrial societies of a capitalist structure.

2 It should be stressed, however, that such comparisons of average earnings, average levels of qualification, and so on *presuppose* the distinction between *Arbeiter* and *Angestellte* but do not constitute or explain it. In addition, there is a broad range of overlapping: Some categories of skilled wage workers earn more and have more schooling than some categories of unskilled salaried employees.

3 From the broad literature on these general blue-collar/white-collar differences cf. E. Lederer, *Die Privatangestellten in der modernen Wirtschaftsentwicklung* (Tübingen: Mohr (Paul Siebeck) 1912); E. Lederer and J. Marschak, "Der neue Mittelstand," *Grundriß der Sozialökonomik*, IX, 1 (Tübingen: Mohr, 1926), pp. 120–41; F. Croner, *Die Angestellten in der*

modernen Gesellschaft (Frankfurt: Humboldt-Verlag, 1954); H. Steiner, *Soziale Struktur-veränderungen im modernen Kapitalismus. Zur Klassenanalyse der Angestellten in Westdeutschland* (Berlin: Dietz, 1967); D. Lockwood, *The Blackcoated Worker* (London: Allen and Unwin, 1958); C. Wright Mills, *White Collar* (New York: Oxford University Press, 1951); R. Girod, *Etudes sociologiques sur les couches salariées* (Paris: Rìvière, 1961); M. Crozier, *The World of the Office Worker* (New York: Schocken Books, 1973), trans. from *Le Monde des employés de bureau* (Paris: Seuil, 1965); E. F. Vogel, *Japan's New Middle Class* (Berkeley: University of California Press, 1963); A. Giddens, *The Class Structure of the Advanced Societies* (New York: Barnes and Noble, 1973), Chap. 10; *White Collar Trade Unions. Comparative Developments in Industrial Societies* ed. A. Sturmthal (Urbana, Ill.: University of Illinois Press, 1967). Many comparative studies of stratification and mobility presuppose the white-collar/blue-collar line as an ubiquitous and rather constant socially relevant line of distinction. Cf. for example, S. M. Lipset/R. Bendix, *Social Mobility in Industrial Society* (Berkeley: University of California Press, 1959); S. Thernstrom, *The Other Bostonians* (Cambridge, Mass.: Harvard University Press, 1973).

    4 There have been many attempts of this kind, especially in the German literature. In addition to Lederer, Croner, and Steiner quoted in note 3, cf., for example: F. Croner, *Soziologie der Angestellten* (Köln and Berlin: Kiepenheuer and Wisch, 1962); M. Kadritzke, *Angestellte – Die geduldigen Arbeiter. Zur Soziologie und sozialen Bewegung der Angestellten* (Frankfurt: Europäische Verlagsanstalt, 1975), pp. 13–138 (with the older literature, criticized from a Marxist point of view). In fact, if it were the purpose of this chapter to explain the white-collar/blue-collar distinction in general sociological terms, the limitation to *capitalist*–industrial systems could prove harmful because that distinction is certainly not specific to capitalist–industrial systems. Consequently, it cannot be sufficiently explained in terms of mechanisms specific to capitalist–industrial systems.

    5 Cf. for the following section (details, evidence, and literature): J. Kocka, "Industrielle Angestelltenschaft in frühindustrieller Zeit," *Untersuchungen zur Geschichte der frühen Industrialisierung vornehmlich im Wirtschaftsraum Berlin/Brandenburg*, ed. O. Büsch (Berlin: Colloquium Verlag, 1970), pp. 315–67.

    6 For the early history of associations of commercial employees, cf. F. Mantel, *Die Angestelltenbewegung in Deutschland* (Leipzig: Gloeckner, 1921); P. Lange, *Die soziale Bewegung der kaufmännischen Angestellten* (Berlin: Grebel, 1920); with respect to the Verein Deutscher Ingenieure (VDI) founded in 1856, cf. G. Hortleder, *Das Gesellschaftsbild des Ingenieurs*, 2nd ed. (Frankfurt: Suhrkamp, 1970); K.-H. Manegold, "Technology Academized: Education and Training of the Engineer in the 19th century," *The Dynamics of Science and Technology*, eds. W. Krohn et al. (Dordrecht and Boston: Kluwer, 1978), pp. 137–58.

    7 This section follows J. Kocka, *Angestellte zwischen Faschismus und Demokratie. Zur politischen Sozialgeschichte der Angestellten: USA 1890–1940 im internationalen Vergleich* (Göttingen: Vandenhoek and Ruprecht, 1977), pp. 79–187; English language edition Sage Publications, London: 1979.

    8 For the relationship among authority, privilege, and the standing of nonmanual work in feudal society, cf. W. Mager in *Theorien in der Praxis des Historikers* (*Geschichte und Gesellschaft*, Special Issue 3), ed. J. Kocka (Göttingen: Vandenhoek and Ruprecht, 1977), pp. 48–51.

    9 Cf. S. M. Lipset, *The First New Nation* (Garden City, N.Y.: Doubleday, 1967).

    10 Some evidence and literature can be found in Kocka, *Angestellte*, pp. 319–28.

    11 For this concept, cf. W. G. Runciman, *Relative Deprivation and Social Justice* (Berkeley: University of California Press, 1966), pp. 11–12.

    12 As a representative voice for this kind of ideology, cf. the booklet by the functionary of a white-collar employees association: H. Potthoff, *Die Organisation des*

Privatbeamtenstandes (Berlin: Siemenroth, 1904). This kind of ideology has found its way into later sociological treatises that analyze *Angestellte* in terms of a "theory" of delegation of power. Cf. the books by Croner in notes 3 and 4.

13 Cf. Gewerkschaftsbund der Angestellten (ed.), *Epochen der Angestelltenbewegung 1774–1930* (Hamburg: Sieben Stäbe-Verlag, 1930).

14 This growth has often been documented. The best book on this topic is M. Dittrich, *Die Entstehung der Angestelltenschaft* (Stuttgart: Kohlhammer, 1939).

15 Cf. the first pioneering book on the white-collar problem, E. Lederer, *Die Privatangestellten in der modernen Wirtschaftsentwicklung*, (Tübingen: Mohr (Paul Siebeck), 1912); further on, Lederer, *Die Entwicklungstendenzen in den Organisationen der Angestellten* (Heidelberg: Carl Winter, 1914); H. Potthoff, "Der Begriff des 'Angestellten'" *Arbeitsrecht* 1(1914):97–107.

16 These phenomena were recognized by association representatives and lawmakers who referred to them in order to justify demands for common treatment of different types of *Angestellte* by social legislation. Cf. *Stenographische Berichte über die Verhandlungen des Reichstags*, 108 (1888):66 and 203 (1905):5012.

17 Cf. Kocka, *Angestellte*, Chaps. 2, 3.

18 A special problem existed in the case of foremen: Should they be eligible for unions organizing their craft in this specific enterprise or should they be regarded as a part of management? This problem has not yet been studied for the nineteenth and early twentieth centuries, but mainly it seems that foremen were not included in German labor unions.

19 It was under National Socialist dictatorship that (compulsory) associations organized *Arbeiter* and *Angestellte* together. At the present the majority of West German unionized white-collar employees belong to industrial unions, that is, to associations in which blue-collar workers are usually in the majority.

20 Cf. M. Weber, "Der Nationalstaat und die Volkswirtschaftspolitik," 1895, ibid., *Gesammelte politische Schriften*, 2nd ed. (Tübingen: Mohr, 1958), pp. 1–25; O. Hintze, "Das Verfassungsleben der heutigen Kulturstaaten," 1914, ibid., *Staat und Verfassung*, 2nd ed. (Göttingen: Vandenhoek and Ruprecht, 1962), p. 422; H.-U. Wehler, *Das Deutsche Kaiserreich 1871–1918*, 3rd ed. (Göttingen: Vandenhoek and Ruprecht, 1977); F. Stern, *The Failure of Illiberalism: Essays on the Political Culture of Modern Germany* (New York: Knopf, 1972), Pt. I.

21 Cf. H. Irwahn, *Bilder aus der Urgeschichte des DHV* (Hamburg: 1920), pp. 26 ff.; I. Hamel, *Völkischer Verband und nationale Gewerkschaft. Die Politik des deutschnationalen Handlungsgehilfen-Verbandes 1893–1933* (Frankfurt: Europäische Verlags-Anstalt, 1966); L. E. Jones, "Between the Fronts: The German National Union of Commercial Employees from 1828–1833, *Journal of Modern History* 48(1976):402–82.

22 Cf. Crozier, *The World*, p. 7.

23 Cf. J. Kocka, "Angestellte," *Geschichtliche Grundbegriffe. Historisches Lexikon zur politisch-sozialen Sprache Deutschland*, eds. O. Brunner et al. Vol. 1 (Stuttgart: Klett, 1972), pp. 110–28, especially 116–27.

24 Bund technischer Angestellter und Beamter (ed.), *25 Jahre Technikergewerkschaft. 10 Jahre Bund technischer Angestellter und Beamter* (Berlin: 1929), pp. 13–5; *Deutscher Werkmeister-Verband 1884–1909. Festschrift*, 2nd ed. (Düsseldorf: 1910), p. 88.

25 Cf. "Privat-Beamten-Zeitung," *Magdeburg*, 16(1900):68.

26 Cf. Kocka, *Unternehmensverwaltung und Angestelltenschaft am Beispiel Siemens 1847–1914* (Stuttgart: Klett, 1969), pp. 513–44.

27 Cf. *Internationales Handwörterbuch des Gewerkschaftswesens*, Vol. 1, (Berlin: Werk und Wirtschaft Verlagsaktiengesellschaft, 1932), p. 50.

28 Cf. G. D. Feldman, *Industry and Labor in Germany 1914–1918* (Princeton, N.J.: Princeton University Press, 1966).

29 There had been a similar law in Austria a few years earlier (1900) that partly influenced the German legislation.

30 Cf. *Organisierter Kapitalismus. Voraussetzungen und Anfänge,* ed. H. A. Winkler (Göttingen: Vandenhoek and Ruprecht, 1974), especially pp. 19–57 (article by J. Kocka and H. U. Wehler).

31 L. François, *La Distinction entre employés et ouvriers en droit allemand, belge, français et italien* (Liège: Faculté de Droit, 1963).

32 Cf. H. Speier, *Angestellte vor dem Nationalsozialismus. Ein Beitrag zum Verständnis der deutschen Sozialstruktur 1918–1933* (Göttingen: Vandenhoek and Ruprecht, 1977).

3

Regime and interest representation: the French traditional middle classes

SUZANNE BERGER

After decades of economic and social transformation, differentiation, and decline, the French traditional middle classes at the end of the seventies are both more dependent on the state for their survival and more powerful politically than at any other time in the postwar period. Organizations representing shopkeepers and artisans have obtained far more from the state in the past ten years than they did even during the heyday of Poujadism. That this should be the case is doubly puzzling: These social categories have been in rapid decline for the past twenty years; at the same time, successive governments of the Fifth Republic have announced that the first priority of economic policy is modernization and industrialization of France.

Understanding why organizations that defend a shrinking part of France have been so successful requires accounting for the character of the traditional middle classes and of the organizations that represent them. The central fact is that the cohesion and power of the traditional middle classes depend on a certain common relation to the state more than on common economic interests. Over the past twenty years, changes in the relationship to the political system, and only secondarily, changes in the economic and social situation of small independent property holders, have determined the prospects for middle-class organization. The waning and waxing power of organizations of the independent middle class and the flourishing of different organizational types in the Fourth and Fifth Republics reflect above all shifts in the organization of national power and in the politics of the groups that have controlled the state. These changes at the level of national politics provide the explanatory thread that allows us to pull into a clear pattern the diverse and ambiguous organizational efforts of the French middle classes. The path that leads from the Poujade movement in the middle fifties to Gérard Nicoud's CID–

UNATI in the seventies, Jean Royer's spectacular tenure as minister of commerce at the end of the Pompidou presidency and failure as a presidential candidate, to an association of small and medium businessmen (UNICER) and a recently organized peak-level federation of all organizations of the middle classes, from farmers to cadres (GIR), covers a course laid out by the transformation of the French state from the last years of the Fourth Republic into the third decade of the Fifth.[1]

As Arno Mayer has argued in his analysis of the lower-middle classes, there is no adequate economic definition of the *petite bourgeoisie:*

More decisively even than the proletariat or the bourgeoisie, the lower middle class demonstrates that although the relations of production are a necessary determinant of class, they do not constitute a sufficient one ... [T]he place and movement of class in economy, society, and polity are a function not exclusively of shared economic interest, but also of ideological configurations and political relations, notably in conjonctures of dynamic conflict.[2]

Even if one focuses on small independent property holders and excludes members of the liberal professions and salaried groups, such as teachers, technicians, and civil servants, all of whom belong to the middle classes in the broad sense, still no core set of economic relationships can be singled out as defining the traditional middle class. Rather, the class of small independent property owners – farmers, shopkeepers, artisans, small businessmen – is circumscribed economically by various overlapping and converging elements: small firm size, higher labor–capital ratios, particular market relations, lower productivity, family ownership, personalistic management styles, familistic business strategies.

The social groups that fall within these boundaries have been declining over the past thirty years but still represent a substantial part of the active population. In commerce, the number of small shops has been falling since the fifties: rapidly toward the end of the sixties, then leveling off in the seventies. By 1973 small independent commerce still represented three-quarters of all French distribution.[3] For artisans, although the smallest units in France have declined, those employing six to nine workers have increased; indeed, in the building trades the numbers went up by a third in the period 1962–70.[4] As a result, in 1970 artisans still composed 10 percent of the active work force in France and in 1972 had a volume of trade three times that of the automobile industry.[5] The active farm population fell from 20.3 percent of the work force in 1954 to 8.5 percent in 1974.[6] But the countryside is still dominated by small and medium family farms; despite rural exodus, the proportion of farms under five hectares fell only from 35 to 31 percent of all farms.[7] In industry, although the tiniest industrial units, plants with fewer than ten workers, have declined from 39 percent of all plants in 1936 to 25 percent in 1954 to 20 percent in 1966, there has been remarkable stability in the small-to-medium firms employing fewer than one hundred employees: In 1926 firms with eleven to twenty workers accounted for 10 percent of the industrial work force and in 1966, for 8 percent of the industrial work force. Plants employing twenty-one to one hundred workers had 28 percent of the work force in 1926 and the same percentage in 1966.[8]

Groups as diverse as these can hardly be said to have common economic interests, let alone to constitute a class. What stabilizes and hardens the distinctions between these groups and others in society are political decisions and social perceptions and values. Political crystallization of interest and value creates out of an economic domain with rather weak elements of cohesion a class with stable contours and considerable potential for collective action. Politics not only firms up the boundaries of the class; it determines membership. In the first and most obvious sense, some of the members of the traditional middle class are there only because of political protection – subsidies, legislative restrictions on competition, special treatment – without which they would not have survived. Next, what appear to be economic differences between members of the traditional middle classes and the modern capitalist class often have political, not economic, origins. Where traditional firms have lower labor costs, for example, the causes may lie not only or primarily in lower productivity, but also in such factors as the absence of unionization in smaller companies, the state's willingness to overlook violations of social security, minimum wage, and working conditions' legislation, and the relative docility of workers who accept jobs in such plants. The extent of unionization, the enforcement of industrial regulations, and the availability of a secondary labor force willing to take bad jobs at bad wages are all factors determined as much by societal and political forces as by economic ones. Finally, even owners of firms with the "same" mode of production may not fall into the same class, because of the values, attitudes, and perceptions that other groups in society have of the traditional middle classes and that are rendered authoritative by the state. For example, the owners of large firms, no matter how labor intensive or unprofitable or "traditional" in management style, will in virtually all analyses, political or economic, be lumped together with the capitalists of large modern firms and not with small shopkeepers.

Different norms, institutions, and modes of state intervention have been developed to regulate the activities of the small independent property holders, on one hand, and those of the large capitalist sector, on the other. For example, the 1967 decree requiring firms to create profit-sharing schemes for workers applies only to companies with more than one hundred employees; the 1968 law recognizing the right to establish a union section is binding only on those with over fifty workers; special credits granted in the wake of the May–June 1968 events were extended to firms with a volume of trade under 20 million francs; and so forth.[9] By these and other such rules, differences that the simple play of economic forces might have distributed over a continuum are by political decision clustered into distinct and discontinuous segments. In similar fashion, the state intervenes in the countryside in ways that recognize, reinforce, and recreate a distinctive status for the peasantry. Politically, the peasantry shifts in and out of the traditional middle classes: Many of the considerations that dictate special protection from the state for the commercial, artisanal, and industrial small holders extend to include small peasant proprietors; on the other hand, the policies developed for agricultural property reflect a conception of the countryside as a special world apart. Historically, peasant organizations have oriented their strategies and programs in order to capitalize on this conception of the distinctiveness and unity of the peasant class. For this reason, we will exclude peasant associations from the following discussion, although in fact the transformations of peasant organizations have covered much the same course as those of the commercial, artisanal, and industrial middle classes.

In sum, the distinguishing economic characteristics of small independent property owners are inextricably bound up with politics; and the coherence and unity of the disparate groups that form the traditional middle class are above all political creations. The traditional middle class owes its collective existence in part to objective similarities in the economic interests of the members, but mainly to their common perceptions of having the same situation in society and with respect to the state and to the state's establishing rules that identify them as a political and social entity.

This tight dependence of the class of small independent property holders on the state for collective identification has made the organizations of the middle class extremely sensitive to changes in politics: in the regime, in the distribution of power within government, in policy and broad governmental objectives, and in the balance of forces that contend for national power. The principal strengths and weaknesses of the traditional middle class, insofar as they determine possibilities for mobilization and organization, derive from their political situation. First, significant elements within the class need political protection in order merely to survive. Next, the middle classes have been unable to formulate a positive and coherent program of demands. Even those organizations of the middle class that behave least like broad mass protest movements and most like classic interest groups have programs characterized by a sweeping attack on the system on one hand and a buckshot scattering of demands on the other. These organizations seem most in their element when conducting an all-out attack on the state; and even in their moments of maximum collaboration with the bureaucracy in the elaboration and administration of programs seem unable to articulate their demands in a fashion coherent enough to provide the basis for state action. However different a Léon Gingembre – who has spent the past thirty years as president of the CGPME operating in parliamentary and bureaucratic arenas – from a Gérard Nicoud – whose talents have been best deployed before large crowds of aroused shopkeepers and before the besieged offices of tax collectors – the former's positive program is not much more developed than the latter's.

These two elements of weakness – the need for protection for survival, the incapacity to elaborate a program – coexist with two elements of strength. First, there is the formidable potential of mobilization against the state. Aside from the May–June 1968 strikes, the groups that have been the most disruptive in the Fifth Republic have come from the traditional middle classes: small peasant proprietors in the early sixties, then shopkeepers and artisans in the seventies. The threat of mobilization by these groups has won them substantial concessions from the government. The second element of strength is the centrality of the traditional middle class for the political and economic projects of groups in the modern sector. Without rehearsing here arguments made at length elsewhere, the issue is that the traditional economic sector provides a critical flexibility to the modern economy through its use and absorption of labor.[10] Groups from the modern sector also rely heavily – and increasingly, as the subsequent argument will suggest – on the political support of the traditional middle classes. The various ways in which the modern capitalist sector and the elites in the parties of the governmental majority use the traditional groups to bolster their positions are as many sources of leverage for the independent middle class.

But how these assets can be used rests critically on the balance of power in national politics. This rapid survey of the characteristic strengths and weaknesses of traditional middle-class organization suggests that they derive from particular relationships to the political system. How they can be exploited – and how they can be compensated for – depends on political configurations and conjunctures that the middle class discovers but does not determine.

As Harry Eckstein and others have observed, the structures of national politics, the framework within which policy is made, and the nature and timing of policies are among the principal determinants of the structure, demands, and behavior of all interest groups.[11] Philippe Schmitter, at the conclusion of an essay that explores how societal and economic changes affect interest group formation and behavior, suggests that the state may also have a significant impact on the pattern of interest intermediation, via the "indirect and often unintended impact of public policy [on] the timing, form, internal structure, area of representation, mode of action and type of leadership of associations," the cooperation of representatives of interest groups and bureaucrats in the administration of public programs, and the "attempt to create encapsulated segments of associational privilege and policy protection."[12]

In the case of the French traditional middle classes, however, the notion implicit in Mayer, Eckstein, and Schmitter (despite all the important differences among them) of politics intervening to mold essentially "the same" socioeconomic forces into distinctive national patterns does not go far enough in spelling out the basic indeterminacy of economic and social forces and the determining weight of politics. The point is not only that interest groups of the French traditional middle classes are significantly different from those of Italy or any other country but that within France itself, the structures, behavior, and goals of these groups have varied considerably over time. This variability, as the subsequent discussion will attempt to show, has coincided with changes in national politics. Great formative events and broad structural differences in political development have undoubtedly established the particular contours of interest group formation in France and constrained subsequent evolution in ways that make systematic comparisons between France and other advanced industrial societies possible. Yet within these contours, the range of variation – in patterns of mobilization, in organizational type, in goals, in cooperation with the state or violent resistance to it – remains significant.

From the parliamentary to the presidential republic

With the passage from the Fourth to the Fifth Republic, a massive transfer of power took place, out of parliamentary arenas into bureaucratic ones. These shifts in the locus and personnel of decision making had profound consequences for virtually all French interest groups, for although some groups operated far more easily than before in the relatively closed circles where bureaucrats and interest group leaders hammered out deals, other groups that had depended heavily on the numbers they represented and on their political skills in parliamentary institutions found themselves disadvantaged by the new distribution of power. In the case of peasant organizations, for example, the influence of the general farm organization, the Fédéra-tion National des Syndicats d'Exploitants Agricoles (FNSEA), de-clined in the early days of the Fifth Republic, whereas the associations of specialized producers acquired new strength. The latters' limited objectives, their use of experts trained in the same elite schools as government experts, and their capacity to deliver support for gov-ernment policy were all strengths in battles fought out in bureaucratic arenas. The general farm organization had a global approach, as the representative of all French agriculture, with its leaders skilled in deal-ings with politicians, not technocrats, and a capacity to deliver votes – all key assets in Parliament, but less valuable once the locus of decision moved into the bureaucracy.[13]

Shopkeepers' and artisans' organizations experienced an even more radical transformation in the passage from the Fourth to Fifth republics. The Poujadist movement, which had won two and a half million votes (9.2 percent of registered votes) and fifty-two deputies in the last legislative elections of the Fourth Republic, disappeared in the Fifth, and interest group organizations took its place.[14] The Union de Défense des Commerçants et Artisans (UDCA), organized in 1953 by Pierre Poujade, the owner of a small bookstore-stationery shop in the backward department of the Lot, started with a defined clientele and with a single demand: to stop the state from collecting more taxes from shopkeepers and artisans. But from the outset, Poujade rejected the classic modes of interest group organization and negotiation with politicians and bureaucrats and launched the movement on a course of action more like that of a political party than of a pressure group. As Bourne describes the evolution of the movement, from a simple antitax program in 1953 to the broad demands of 1956 for maintaining the French colonies in Africa and convening the States-General, "One can hardly call it a 'shift to politics,' since the initial attitude was decisive, and spontaneously revealed a global project."[15]

First, the structures the movement developed as it spread across France through the mid-fifties were those of a mass organization. In Poujade's view, the only way to force the state to meet the demands of the traditional middle classes was to organize as the workers had: "We have suffered the consequences of mass movements; we have responded with a mass movement," in Poujade's phrase.[16] Mass mobilization of shopkeepers and artisans to protest the descent of tax inspectors in small towns all over France, huge rallies for Poujade's speeches during triumphal national tours, the promotion of a "cult of personality" around Poujade, his authoritarian control over the movement – all these stood in sharp contrast to the modes of operation of the Confédération Générale des Petites et Moyennes Entreprises, which had been the principal spokesman for middle-class interests in the Fourth Republic. Organized in 1944 and presided over from that date until 1978 by Léon Gingembre, the CGPME had a program of demands virtually identical to the one the Poujadists started to push in the fifties. The differences between the two organizations lay not in the policies they advocated for the middle classes but in their approach to politics. Gingembre's activities consisted largely of negotiating with party politicians and with bureaucrats; Poujade refused all efforts at operating within the Parisian network of ministerial–interest group relations.

Not only the mass character of the UDCA but the extension of its program beyond the corporatist interests of the traditional middle classes and the widening of its audience beyond the shopkeepers and artisans that had been the original clientele revealed the movement's basic tendency: to behave like a political party in the defense of middle-class interests. By early 1955 the movement had spread to virtually all of France, and the only areas of weakness were the big cities. Poujade started to reach out to new groups, organizing a peasant movement (Union de Défense des Paysans) in the spring of 1955, followed in the same year by rather less successful gestures in the direction of intellectuals, the liberal professions, and employees.[17] At the same time, the focus of the movement shifted from the specific grievances of segments of the middle class to a call for changing the whole system or, rather, in Poujade's sense, rescuing republican institutions from the hands of those sold out to trusts, foreign interests, and corruption, and returning Parliament to its original mission of defending the common people.

In this massive assault on the Parliament and the deputies, the Poujade movement in a curious sense reaffirmed the legitimacy of the very institutions it attacked. For the Poujadists saw Parliament as the institution in which political decisions ought to be made and accepted the function of the deputies as policy makers. When the Poujadists refused to get enmeshed in negotiations with bureaucrats and politicians, it was not only because they thought that, like Gingembre before them, they would end up co-opted and impotent. It was also because deputies ought to make the laws, and interest groups ought to check up on them, not replace them. On these grounds, the Poujadists refused to offer any concrete solutions to the problems they raised. As Poujade argued, "Why don't you suggest a program, say all the do-nothings and well-fed of the regime. But if I, a stationer, and you, a blacksmith, have to invent a program, what's the use of that mob of parasites that we feed by the sweat of our brow?"[18]

If the current deputies could not be forced to change their ways and to yield to the demands of the people, the solution was to turn them out – *sortons les sortants!* – and elect others who would. The Parliament and deputies have been corrupted and subverted; put in honest representatives of the real people and restore the system. Unlike the traditional Right, the Poujadists did not seek to get rid of Parliament, deputies, and the republican system, but to use them for their own ends. When Poujade finally concluded that the effort to bring Parliament around by pressuring the deputies had been unsuccessful, the decision to replace the "bad" deputies with "good" ones was a logical one. Even when the new ones – fifty-two elected on Poujadist lists in 1956 – behaved much like the old ones and, in particular, proved unwilling to accept direction from Poujade, the movement still focused its energies and resources on influencing decisions in parliamentary arenas.

With the advent of the Fifth Republic and the massive electoral victories of the Gaullists, the UDCA electorate evaporated and the Poujade movement virtually disappeared except from the chambers of commerce. The defense of the traditional middle classes reverted to the old "professional" organizations that were, by experience, structure, and instinct, better suited to operating in the new arenas of power than they had been to competing with the Poujadists. Both the politics and the policies of the first years of the Fifth Republic were, however, highly unfavorable for the traditional middle classes. The electoral strength of the Gaullists was so great, and their penetration of white- and blue-collar electorates so substantial, that the notables and traditional middle classes were far less important to the new regime than they had been to the parties and governments of the Fourth Republic. At the same time, the economic policies of the new government launched modernizing programs that threatened to undermine and destroy the traditional economic sector.

No measure better exemplifies these new policies than the 1960 Fontanet circular forbidding manufacturers to refuse sale to retailers who were undercutting the prices of the small shops. Under the pressure of traditional commerce, industrialists had been refusing merchandise to stores such as the Centres Leclerc that were trading on large volumes and low prices. With the removal of this barrier to competition, a rationalization of the tax system that was easier to implement in large modern stores than in the small shops, and the noninterventionist stance of the administration at all the points –

building permits, despecialization of commercial licenses, urban land use planning, and so forth – at which the state could have regulated commercial development, the way was open for a rapid expansion of supermarkets. The number of small shops declined by 20,000 from 1966 to 1971, whereas in the same period 1,887 supermarkets and 143 *hypermarchés* (giant supermarkets) were created.[19]

In sum, given the weakened position of the traditional middle classes in the coalition of social forces that supported the government in the first decade of the Fifth Republic and the government's commitment to modernizing strategies in the economy, it is hardly surprising that the CGPME had few successes to bring home to its constituencies. Despite the organization's long familiarity with ministerial corridors and its willingness to play the rules of the new game, the political balance was weighted too heavily against the traditional economic sector to make an effective defense possible.

The Fifth Republic, second phase

The events of May–June 1968 announced a transformation in the politics of the regime and with it the rising power of the traditional middle classes. Three political changes were critical in this respect. First, the social tranquillity of the first decade of the regime disappeared, and unrest and social instability became the continuing preoccupation of government. The most serious cause for concern was, of course, the groups that exploded in the spring of 1968 – labor and students. But even after protest from these sectors was subdued, the issue of social unrest and political disruption did not disappear. In the wake of 1968, a wave of protest developed, from groups like the shopkeepers that had been silent and acquiescent in the past. The government's willingness to make major concessions after 1968 to the traditional middle classes would derive in part from the need to quiet them down and in part from the regime's growing dependence on them, as other groups in the population began to "rock the boat."

The second change that increased the political leverage of the middle classes was the growing strength of the Left and the polarization of politics. As the majority's margins of victory narrowed, it would become more and more important to bring out all the potential electorate of the Right. The new centrality of the traditional middle classes to the government – even though they were unlikely to shift to the Left – was bound to increase their influence. Finally, the competition among parties of the governmental majority, especially after 1974, made the traditional middle classes the object of intense bidding and hence also served to increase their potential power. Social unrest, the new strength of the Left, increased competition within the Right – each of these could be seen in germ in 1968, and yet it would take another decade for the possibilities to ripen enough so that a transformation of the regime would come to seem possible. Despite the shrinking numbers of small shopkeepers, artisans, and peasants, these groups would make major gains in the second decade of the Fifth Republic, for each of the basic lines of change in the political system increased the opportunities for middle-class organization.

In 1969, after a decade of political impotence in the face of a growing economic threat from large modern commerce, a violent protest by shopkeepers and artisans broke out in southeastern France, led by Gérard Nicoud, a small-town cafe owner, and clustering under the banner of organizations that would come to be known as the CID-UNATI.[20] The CID-UNATI was a true child of the Fifth Republic. The shopkeepers and artisans had finally discovered about the system what the peasants and students had learned before them: Where political bargaining goes on in closed bureaucratic arenas, the only way for groups excluded from the negotiating table to have their demands recognized is to take to the streets. With the decline of Parliament in the Fifth Republic and the atrophy of channels of party political representation, the paths to power ran through the ministries and, to a lesser extent, through the Gaullist party. Some groups are better able to defend themselves than others in such a system, and, as 1968 was to demonstrate, the groups that were unable to find channels through which their interests could be advanced resorted to violent protest. The lesson was, as the peasants had found in the early sixties, that violence paid and that its rewards were directly proportional to the weakness of the regime. Gérard Nicoud explained:

Why were we forced to illegality? Of all French social classes, we were the only one that until 1969 had expressed its discontent only with pious wishes or legal protest. The result as of January 1, 1969: NOTHING, absolutely NOTHING. Now, looking around us, we could see others were using more direct arguments. Farmers blocked the roads, and the government gave in. Truckers, the same. Employees, when they struck, locked in the bosses and used wildcat strikes. Even the National Police, supposedly the guarantor of legality, threatens to march on the Matignon and throw the minister out the window!

And everywhere, public authorities yield and sanction these acts of force. . . . the method obviously is a profitable one. May 1968 was to reveal to us the path we had to take. Not only did the government, though well aware of our serious problems, do nothing for us, but, terrified by the wave that threatened to carry it off, it leaned on us for support; flattering us, invoking "the Flag," "the Republic." . . . What a disillusion! All we got were more supermarkets.... Finally, no one can deny the evidence if they compare what our social class obtained up to 1969 and the results since 1969 [i.e., since CID-UNATI violence].... Whose fault is it that concertation takes place in the street? Above all, the Executive.[21]

Starting in April 1969 with an attack on a tax office in La Tour du Pin (Isère), Nicoud and his troops moved on to tax strikes, sit-ins in tax offices, kidnappings of tax inspectors, pitched battles between shopkeeper–demonstrators and the police, and, a year later, a rally in Paris, which 40,000 attended. By 1971 the CID–UNATI won 43 percent of the seats in elections for the *chambres de métiers* (the parapublic chamber of artisans); the next year, it took over 40 percent of the vote in elections for delegates to pension funds for artisans, shopkeepers, and industrialists; participation in the 1972 election rose to a record 50 percent (previous elections had drawn 20 to 30 percent of those eligible to vote.)[22]

As Nicoud had foreseen, mobilization paid off. The militants who had been arrested and given prison sentences, including Nicoud himself, were amnestied by Parliament. The amnesty, which had been strongly opposed by the Chaban-Delmas government, was accepted by Messmer; for the prospect of the 1973 legislative elections made high levels of shopkeeper protest unacceptable. From 1972 on, legislation designed to satisfy the demands of the shopkeepers and artisans poured out of Parliament.

The culmination of this wave of political solicitude for the traditional middle classes was the nomination of Jean Royer, an independent conservative who was mayor of Tours, as minister of commerce and artisanry in April 1973 and the passage of the "Royer law" (*loi d'orientation pour le commerce et l'artisanat*), which went far beyond any of the CID-UNATI's demands in arming small shopkeepers and artisans against competition from the modern sector. "*C'est la providence des boutiques*," in the phrase Napoleon used in 1812 to describe the new National Guard. The law regulated commercial competition by forbidding loss-leaders and false advertising; it reformed the social security regimes for independents and established special funds for property owners who were "the victims of urbanization"; it gave the chambers of commerce new authority to set up commercial centers; it established a system of "preapprenticeship" – over loud protests by the unions and the Left – to enable firms to employ children in the last two years of school on a part-time basis; it announced plans for a reform of the *patente*. Above all, the law established departmental commissions for "commercial urbanism" to rule on any proposed opening or enlargement that involved stores over 1,000 square meters in cities with over 50,000 inhabitants, over 750 square meters in towns from 500 to 50,000 inhabitants, and over 400 square meters in the smallest communes. In these commissions would sit equal numbers of local elected officials and representatives of shopkeepers and artisans. For the first time in the history of the French Republic, authority to limit entry into trade was delegated to a corporatist body.

In this extraordinary series of concessions, the politicians recognized and acceded to the core of Nicoud's demands: that the traditional middle classes be given that share of power of which they had been deprived by inability to gain access into the privileged arenas of political decision. Turning the right to regulate commercial development over into the hands of the "professionals," the Royer law confirmed the success of Nicoud's interest group strategy. Unlike the Poujadists who had refused to offer concrete policy proposals or to be drawn into negotiations with the bureaucracy, the CID-UNATI always described itself in terms of a long catalog of specific demands. Limiting its constituency to shopkeepers and artisans and its demands to measures affecting their direct interests, CID–UNATI never started down the path that had led the Poujadists into the 1956 legislative elections. Most of Nicoud's account of the movement and of his own philosophy is a detailed discussion of tax reforms, proposals to improve pension and sickness funds for the independents, schemes to compensate owners of firms that fail because of "unfair" competition, and so forth.[23]

Far from seeking to change the rulers – "the experience of Pierre Poujade only buried our problems for twenty years"[24] – the CID-UNATI only wanted the rulers to grant them their due in the system. Nicoud reflecting on what the CID-UNATI might have done in 1968 had it existed then, remarks: "All I can say is that the fate of the pensioners would have come before that of the government or whatever party. Real syndicalism must stay out of all political considerations and serve the interests it represents…"[25] The refrain of the CID-UNATI is always the same: If they won't listen to our pacific, reasonable requests, then we will force them to heed. "If instead of ignoring us, indeed condemning us, the State had held out a hand to help the thousands among us to adapt, to modernize in a word, if they had given us a chance, then anger would never have exploded."[26]

The pattern of support for the CID-UNATI confirms that it was above all perceived by its constituency as anti-state and not as partisan. A survey of shopkeepers and artisans in 1973 found in answer to the question "Are you personally favorable or opposed to the CID–UNATI of M. Gérard Nicoud?" that 22 percent described themselves as "very favorable."[27] The biggest differences were between supporters of parties in and out of government, not between Left and Right: 26 percent of the Communist electors, 30 percent of the non-Communist Left electors, and 28 percent of the *reformateur* electors were "very favorable," whereas the figure fell to 15 percent of the majority electors.

With the Royer law in place, the number of new supermarkets declined sharply: 30 percent fewer supermarket openings in 1974 than in the preceding year. The small shopkeepers (*commerçants indépendants*) and artisans had succeeded in obtaining almost all the seats reserved for "the professionals," and among the local elected officials who sat on the commissions, many were themselves from the traditional middle classes. More authorizations were denied (238) than accepted (222).[28] In 1975 the reform of the *patente* and its replacement by the "professional tax" satisfied the last major outstanding demand of the CID-UNATI. With the implementation of the new tax, artisans paid 53 percent less than they would have with the old tax; shopkeepers with fewer than three employees, 62 percent less than they would have paid with the patente. Indeed, 29 percent of the artisans and 39 percent of the shopkeepers paid a tax that was less than 25 percent of the *patente!*[29] To appreciate how great a triumph these results represented for traditional middle-class organization, one must bear in mind that the groups whose support was being so avidly courted were declining and that the measures taken in their favor clearly ran counter to the interests of powerful groups in the modern sector. Equally important, as the minister of finance (Giscard d'Estaing), who opposed the Royer bill, had foreseen from the outset, these concessions to the traditional sector would contribute to the rising rate of inflation, which was to become the government's principal preoccupation.

From Fifth to Sixth Republic?

If waves of middle-class organization and protest responded primarily to changes in the economic and social situation of these groups, hence to relative levels of satisfaction of their demands, there should have been a return to the "normalcy" of the 1958–68 period once Royer and the reformed tax system had produced their results. In fact, the CID-UNATI did enter into decline; a third of its members did not renew their memberships at the end of 1974; although still strong in the *chambres de métiers* and the *chambres de commerce*, the CID-UNATI had peaked by 1974 and seemed unable to expand its influence.[30] Nicoud cast about for new themes and targets: a philosophy announced at the 1974 national congress of fighting planning in the name of man against the machine, a demand that shopkeepers be given more power in the *chambres de commerce*, a violent attack on a Leclerc supermarket in La Rochelle. The CID-UNATI was clearly on the way downhill.

But the phase that opened in 1974 with the election of Valéry Giscard d'Estaing as president has not seen the disappearance of middle-class mobilization but only its transfer out of interest group organization into forms that in their broad appeal and political reach suggest Poujade's movement more than Nicoud's. The first step in this direction was the presidential campaign of Jean Royer, whose law had established his claim to represent the traditional classes. Royer presented himself as a candidate above party, who would unite the French around the core virtues of "Unity, Effort, and Equilibrium." The familiar themes of the conservative Right reappeared: for a strong state, but a decentralized one; for protecting the family, against abortion; for the state to act as arbiter in the economy, against planning. He presented his candidacy as a response to a crisis of morality that was undermining French society. His official campaign poster showed a smiling family in a garden and the slogan: "Vote Jean Royer; he will give a heart to France." His campaign manager, paraphrasing Camus, described Royer as carrying forward the task of the age: to halt the disintegration of society. Put in more direct terms, Royer's campaign manager in eastern France, Yvonne Garrette, arguing with the president of a local shopkeepers association, said: "Look at the people around Royer; they're people like us – for the family unit – traditional – *la bonne France, quoi*! Moreover, voting for Royer is like voting for ourselves, because the greater the vote for Royer, the more whoever's elected will have to count with the middle classes."[31]

The campaign was a failure. Royer received only 3.2 percent of the vote, far from the 7 percent that political analysts had predicted or the 10 percent his supporters confidently expected. Yet despite the strange qualities of the candidate and the dismal electoral returns, the Royer campaign was no bizarre accident but, instead, showed the direction in which the politics of the traditional middle classes would move as the contest between Left and Right became a closer one and conflict between the parties of the governmental majority became more acute.

The current politicization of middle-class organization and shift from interest group to more directly political forms of action is nowhere clearer than in the case of Léon Gingembre, who for almost thirty years had led the CGPME along the first course and then, in 1975, announced the formation of an organization of owners and of small and medium business (Union des Chefs d'Entreprise, UN-

ICER). Although the CGPME would continue to defend the professional interests of its constituents, UNICER was to defend the small businessman's place in the nation against the attacks of the denigrators of free enterprise and freedom *tout court*. Gingembre received 140,000 letters approving the declaration to the president in which he had announced the new line, and UNICER rapidly acquired 25,000 members.

As Gingembre describes his decision to organize UNICER, the decisive fact was that Giscard d'Estaing, elected by a narrow margin, spent his first year in office trying to woo the Left electorate and neglecting the "silent majority," the traditional middle classes. In France, Gingembre argues, there are two big forces: The unions and the big industries, engaged in a game of tennis in which the people in between – the independents, the small and medium-sized businesses – are constantly hit by the ball until they finally invade the field and attack the umpire.[32] In this vivid image, the umpire is the state; and UNICER's role is to force the state to reckon with the prospects of defection of the traditional middle classes on whom it has always relied. It is not because our clientele will vote Left, argues Gingembre, that the state must heed us, but because the majority will lose unless our class actively works for its reelection. Afraid of the *programme commun*, the small industrialists may give up on politics or surrender to the Left too soon.

Moving to exploit the same changes in the regime, presidents of five organizations representing middle-class categories founded Groupes Initiative et Responsabilité (GIR) in early 1977.[33] The statement of principles announced that the founding parties had discovered, beneath the diversity of their professional interests, common elements that united them: "the choice of liberty, a pleasure in risk, the sense of effort and the exercise of responsibility and initiative." And on the basis of these values, the GIR would confront the political parties – "that alas reject the aspirations of those unsatisfied with more or less empty theories, since they daily face the cruel reality of facts" – with a vast middle-class movement.[34]

Royer, UNICER, GIR thus abandoned the specific demands that characterized CID-UNATI programs and reached out to a wider audience in a political language suggesting broad claims on the state. Like the Poujadists in the last years of the Fourth Republic, these groups responded to the instability of the regime with an attempt to aggregate and politicize diverse middle-class interests in a broad-based movement. And like the Poujadists in the Fifth Republic, these movements would virtually disappear after 1978, once the collapse of the Union of the Left and the strengthening of Giscard d'Estaing's control over the majority had again consolidated the regime.

The first of the conclusions that emerge from the apparent political opportunism and organizational volatility of the interest groups representing the traditional middle classes is that the economic and social demands of these strata can be expressed in a variety of different types of organizations. Because the range of organizational variation extends from groups that push their claims in violent and illegal opposition to the state to groups that collaborate in essentially corporatist arrangements, the issue of which organizational type predominates at any time is a highly consequential one for other actors in the system and for the prospects of stability or transformation. Although a Poujade and a Gingembre may well defend interests that are "objectively" the same, this fact may at crucial junctures matter less than the differences in the ways in which each organizes the defense of these interests.

Second, although the interest groups of the traditional middle classes are not the only ones that change in response to shifts in politics, still, their organizations seem strikingly more volatile than are the organizations of either labor or capital. The latter are more stable and more insulated from political fluctuations because their organizational strength depends on strategic position in the economy, hence on control over economic resources, whereas the traditional middle-class organizations depend much more heavily on their leverage over political resources. To the extent that the power of the organizations representing labor and capital derives from the critical functions their members carry out in the economy, the situation of these organizations is cushioned against political shifts, barring of course the kind of radical regime changes that would, for example, suppress unions or nationalize capital. In contrast, political changes of far lesser magnitude than regime transformation have deep consequences for the patterns of mobilization and for the chances of political influence of the middle-class groups.

Finally, the history of the instability of traditional middle-class organizations in France reflects the members' tenuous attachment to the group and a remarkable fickleness with respect to leaders. However much the lack of long-term organizational commitment and the incapacity to conceive collective objectives of the traditional middle classes suggest the image of the politically passive peasants that Marx likened to "potatoes in a sack," the analogy is misleading. For the middle classes, unlike the peasants of the *18th Brumaire*, are not willing to remedy their organizational incapacity by turning themselves over into the hands of strong leaders. On the contrary, the history of these movements in contemporary France is marked by the extraordinary "ingratitude" of these classes, even to organizations and leaders that have brought home the political bacon. Where a labor union would likely be strengthened by a successful strike or contract negotiations, the middle-class interest groups in France have usually declined after their greatest moments of triumph, as did, for example, the CID-UNATI after the passage of the protectionist legislation of the seventies. This suggests a highly instrumental commitment that leaves little room for the development of strong organizations or leaders. It also suggests why mobilization of the traditional middle classes, despite their declining members, remains a permanent temptation – and danger – in European politics. In nations in which the other major socioeconomic groups are securely moored by long-acquired organizational loyalties and disciplines, the traditional middle classes are still *disponible*. However unorganizable over the long term, these groups remain candidates for surges of collective action whose consequences are the more disruptive for coinciding with the historic moments of greatest political instability.

Notes

1 Pierre Poujade's movement was the Union de Défense des Commerçants et Artisans (UDCA); Nicoud's, a merger of the Comité d'Information et de Défense (CID) with the Union Nationale des Travailleurs Indépendants (UNATI); Léon Gingembre, president of the Confédération générale des Petites et Moyennes Entreprises (CGPME), launched in 1975 a Union des Chefs et Responsables d'Entreprise (UNICER); Groupes Initiatives et Responsabilités (GIR) was formed in 1977.

2 Arno J. Mayer, "The Lower Middle Class as an Historical Problem," *Journal of Modern History* 48(September 1975):425.

3 Speech by Yvon Bourges, minister of commerce, reported in *Le Monde*, February 15, 1973.

4 Claude Quin, *Classes sociales et union du peuple de France* (Paris: Editions Sociales, 1976), pp. 118–19.

5 "L'Artisanat et le secteur des métiers," from *Revue économique de la Banque nationale de Paris*, April 1973, reprinted in *Problèmes économiques* 13 (June 1973):4.

6 Quin, op. cit., p. 35.

7 *Recensement général agricole* (1955, 1970), cited in F. Clavaud et al., *Quelle agriculture pour la France?* (Paris: Editions Sociales, 1974), annexes.

8 Michel Didier and Edouard Malinvaud, "La concentration de l'industrie s'est-elle accentuée depuis le début du siècle?" *Economie et statistique*, (2) (June 1969):7.

9 Examples are taken from Bernard Brizay, *Le Patronat: histoire, structure, stratégie du CNPF* (Paris: Editions du Seuil, 1975), pp. 290–3.

10 See Suzanne Berger, "Uso politico e sopravvivenza dei ceti in declino," in *Il caso italiano*, eds. F. Cavazza and S. Graubard (Milan: Garzanti, 1974), and Chap. 4 in S. Berger and M. Piore, *Dualism and Discontinuity in Industrial Societies* (New York: Cambridge University Press, 1980).

11 Harry Eckstein, *Pressure Group Politics* (Stanford: Stanford University Press, 1960), Chap. 1.

12 Philippe C. Schmitter, "Modes of Interest Intermediation and Models of Societal Change in Western Europe," *Comparative Political Studies* 10 (1) (April 1977):35.

13 This argument is developed more fully in Berger, *The French Political System* (New York: Random House, 1974), Chap. 4.

14 On the Poujade movement, see the brilliant analysis by Stanley Hoffmann, *Le Mouvement Poujade* (Paris: Colin, Cahiers de la Fondation Nationale des Sciences Politiques, No. 81, 1956). An interesting recent treatment of the movement is Dominique Bourne, *Petits bourgeois en révolte? Le mouvement Poujade* (Paris: Flammarion, 1977). George Lefranc in *Les Organisations patronales en France* (Paris: Payot, 1976), gives brief histories of the UDCA as well as the CID-UNATI and CGPME.

15 Bourne, op. cit., p. 7.

16 Cited in Hoffmann, op. cit., p. 40. For a comparison of the organization with that of the traditional pressure groups of the middle classes, see Hoffmann, op. cit., pp. 261–82.

17 On the fortunes of Poujadism in the countryside, see Jean-Michel Royer, "De Dorgères à Poujade," in *Les Paysans et la politique*, eds. J. Fauvet and H. Mendras (Paris: Colin, Cahiers de la Fondation Nationale des Sciences Politiques, No. 94, 1958).

18 Cited in Bourne, op. cit., p. 131.

19 *Le Monde*, December 19, 1972.

20 On the Comité d'information et de Défense-Union Nationale des Travailleurs Indépendents (CID-UNATI), see Lefranc, op. cit., pp. 234–9; Gérard Nicoud, *Les Dernières libertés . . . menottes aux mains* (Paris: Denoël, 1972); André Bonnet, "Un nouveau groupe de pression: Le CID-UNATI," *Revue politique et parlementaire*, 843/5(June–July 1973).

21 Nicoud, op. cit., pp. 82–83.

22 *Le Monde*, November 28–29, 1972; December 16, 1972.

23 Nicoud, op. cit.

24 Nicoud at meeting, Palais des Sports, quoted in *Le Monde*, September 28, 1972.

25 Nicoud, op. cit., p. 83.

26 Ibid., p. 80.

27 "Les Petits commerçants et artisans," results of a SOFRES survey carried out between January 30 and February 13, 1973, on a sample of 1,000.

28 These statistics are drawn from *Libre-Service Actualités*, "Atlas des super et hyper," cited in *Le Monde*, January 3, 1975.

29 Data from a survey by the Ministry of Economy and Finance, reported in *Le Monde*, January 21, 1977.

30 *Le Monde*, October 15, 1974; January 23, 1975.

31 Quotes are from Madame Garrette's electioneering, the week before the first round of the 1974 presidential election.

32 Interview with Léon Gingembre, April 15, 1976.

33 The founding presidents are Michel Débatisse, FNSEA; Léon Gingembre, CGPME; Francis Combe, Assemblée permanente des chambres de métiers; Yvan Charpentié, Confédération générale des cadres; Jacques Monier, Confédération des syndicats médicaux français.

34 *Le Monde*, February 13–4, 1977; March 3, 1977.

4

Local corporatism

GUDMUND HERNES AND ARNE SELVIK

Corporatism increasingly has become the focus of social research.[1] Loosely defined, it describes a system of interest intermediation between organized groups and the state apparatus, particularly in the economic area. This can take many forms, for example, representation on public committees or consultation on proposed new legislation.

Rokkan has argued that the multifarious interaction of government agencies and interest organizations – what he calls "corporate pluralism" – supplements and, to some extent, supplants territorial representation through the electoral process – what he calls "numerical democracy."[2] His thesis is that votes count in regular elections and determine *who* will be the members of representative bodies. But organized interest groups, with their permanent and full-time staffs, manned by experts on par with those found in specialized state agencies, continuously provide the more important input to political decisions, and hence to a large extent determine *what* the content of public policy will be. "Votes count, but resources decide."

Originally corporatism was considered a system for the political representation of economic interests. In contrast to Marxist theory, which bases its "vertical" theory on the conflicting interests of workers and capitalists generated in the labor market and in the authority relations of production, corporatism sought to reduce this conflict through horizontal interest representation encompassing both employers and employees in the different sectors of the economy. Several corporatist theorists of various political persuasions envisioned a central body composed of representatives from the organized interests in the different sectors. Its purpose was partly to coordinate economic decisions in the various branches of the economy, partly to

103

resolve their conflicting claims on the factors of production, and partly to set levels of remuneration for workers and employers in the various sectors.

Viewed this way, a corporate system could partly supplement and partly replace the market as the automatic regulator of decentralized economic decisions. Increased monetization and extended markets led to an increasing division of labor but also had the potential for more far-reaching economic repercussions, which might widen and amplify local or sectoral crises. Manufacturing not only produced more and more differentiated goods but also groups lodged in different economic positions that became carriers of different and potentially conflicting economic interests. Hence the market was not only a mechanism for decentralized coordination; it was also a major source of social conflict. This called for the organization of conflict resolution. By joint action between the affected interests and political authorities, the free determination of prices could be modified (for example, by public guarantees of minimum prices), free entry into the market could be limited (so as to prevent overcapacity or price wars), free establishment of firms could be confined (so as to secure balanced growth), and free access to commercial activities could be regulated (so as to reduce wide fluctuations in income). In this perspective, corporatism can be considered a way of systematically modifying the free operation of the market by incorporating into the public decision-making apparatus those groups that are affected by the unhampered operation of the market. These are groups that to a large extent organize in response to their market conditions.

Virtually all the literature on corporatism focuses on interest intermediation at the national level. The main thesis of this chapter is that corporate systems are now rapidly growing at the local level, at least in the Scandinavian countries. Are the same causal processes at work here as at the national level? What are the consequences of this development likely to be? To approach these questions we will present preliminary results of research on this development in Norway.

Theories of growth of corporatism: the effects of market conditions

Schmitter defines corporatism as a system of interest representation in which the constituent units are organized into a limited number of singular, compulsory, noncompetitive, hierarchically ordered and functionally differentiated categories, recognized or licensed (if not created) by the state and granted a deliberate representational monopoly within their respective categories in exchange for observing certain controls on their selection of leaders and articulation of demands and supports.[3] Drawing on Manoilesco, Schmitter also distinguishes between *societal* corporatism, organized from below, with autonomous and penetrative organizations, and *state* corporatism, organized from above, with dependent and penetrated organizations. In the former case, the characteristics of the formal definition are more fuzzy than in the latter, because, for example, the noncompetitive aspect is less strictly enforced and is the result of voluntary agreements among associations. Examples of societal corporatism are found in Switzerland, the Netherlands, and Scandinavia; examples of state corporatism in Portugal, Spain, Brazil, Peru, Mexico, and Greece.

Societal corporatism is found imbedded in political systems with relatively autonomous, multilayered territorial units; open, competitive electoral processes and party systems; ideologically varied, coalitionally based executive authorities – even with highly "layered" or "pillared" political subcultures. State corporatism tends to be associated with political systems in which the territorial subunits are tightly subordinated to central bureaucratic power; elections are nonexistent or plebiscitary; party systems are dominated or monopolized by a weak single party; executive authorities are ideologically exclusive or more narrowly recruited and are such that political subcultures based on class, ethnicity, language, or regionalism are repressed. Societal corporatism appears to be the concomitant, if not ineluctable, component of the postliberal, advanced capitalist, organized democratic welfare state; state corporatism seems to be a defining element of, if not structural necessity for, the antiliberal, delayed capitalist, authoritarian, neomercantilist state.[4]

Because our empirical focus is on Norway, our concern in this chapter will be on societal corporatism.

In *Modern Capitalism* Shonfield views the expansion of the state as a way of correcting deficiencies of the market. The modern state finds itself simultaneously trying to accomplish several important goals: to foster full employment, to promote economic growth, to regulate working conditions, to smooth out business cycles, to cover individual and social risks, to resolve labor conflicts, and to prevent inflation. Governments attempt to attain these goals through bargaining with and between organized groups about their future behavior in order to move economic conditions along the desired or agreed-on path.[5]

The first six of the items on the list are also goals of public policy at the *local* level. Municipalities try to secure full employment within their boundaries, sometimes by subsidies, or even by running businesses themselves. In Norway there have been many examples of the latter during the recent recession. Many have also adopted growth-promoting policies. This is partly done by investments in infrastructure, such as communication facilities, as well as by erecting factory halls and plants to induce firms to locate production units there. This is also a form of subsidy, in part funded by the national government, the so-called *SIVA-anlegg* (industrial parks). Communes have, in addition, improved their educational systems in order to increase the skills of the local labor force. Furthermore, institutional reforms have taken the form of establishing new positions, the most important of which is the so-called *tiltakssjef,* which roughly can be translated "director of initiatives." His chief task is to attract new industry and to advance the working conditions of older establishments. With respect to working conditions, local ordinances have been adopted to change them. Many municipalities have also tried to reduce the impact of the recent downturn in business cycles by temporary measures and appropriations or exemptions from standard rules. Some parts of the social security system are financed at the local level, with considerable variations between municipalities. For example, the support for the disabled (*uføretrygd*) is national, but the larger urban communities in particular appropriate additional funds. The same holds for pension and health programs. Finally, municipal authorities have on occasions tried to mediate in local labor disputes, even though mostly informally.

Schmitter (1974) and Solvang (1974) have emphasized that the growth of corporatist structures, such as public committees with interest group representation, has been characterized by spurts in response to economic crises. No doubt the same tendency has been observed at the community level during the recent slump, for many more initiatives in the political arena have been taken, by local authorities, business, and trade unions. Often they operate as a team, directing their efforts toward the national government. This shows up in the response to a question asked of all members of Parliament in the spring of 1977.[6] The question ran: "Has there during the last few years been any tendency toward more joint initiatives from communities, in which local politicians, administrators, trade union officials, business executives or organizations operate together?" The responses in Table 4.1 indicate a marked shift, which three-quarters of the representatives note.

In a questionnaire mailed to the chief executives of 800 of the largest corporations in Norway (response rate 72 percent), we find that a substantial number have directed joint initiatives toward public authorities at different levels. Most of these initiatives are directed toward municipal authorities (at the time of the questionnaire, there were 444 municipalities). Next come the ministries, then such public agencies as the Customs Service, Labor Agency, Postal Service, and so forth. Contacts on district level between municipality and the na-

Table 4.1. *Response to a question about increases in joint initiatives from the local level, asked of Norwegian members of Parliament, spring 1977 (in %)*

A marked tendency toward more joint initiatives	25.2
A certain tendency	51.0
No change	22.6
Rather few such initiatives	0.6
No answer	0.6
Total	100.0

For members of Parliament, N = 155.

Table 4.2. *"Have employee representatives participated in promoting the interests of your firm or (detailed) industry by contacts with the authorities during the last five years?" (replies of industrialists)*

	Several times	Once	Never	No contact/ no answer
Municipality	21.7	8.0	58.7	11.6
Ministry	14.4	10.0	59.4	16.2
Subordinate Authority	13.7	5.5	60.9	19.9
District	12.1	4.1	64.9	18.9
Parliament	7.3	3.7	67.3	21.7

tional state (Norway is divided into nineteen such districts) are next to last; and there is least contact with the Parliament, one of many indicators that the "numerical channel" and the legislature have declined in importance in overall decision making in society (see Table 4.2).

Tables 4.3 and 4.4 show a clear tendency for firms to have more *frequent* contacts with authorities at different levels and to judge these contacts more *important*. For our purposes, the most significant fact is that this is especially important on the municipal level. More than a quarter of the firms interact with municipal authorities almost every month, whereas less than one-sixth do so with ministries, one-tenth with district authorities, and less than one percent with the Parliament.

Executives spend more time now than before on interaction with public authorities, and more of this interaction is directed toward the administrative staffs rather than toward elected officials or politicians.

In sum, contacts between business and the authorities have increased in frequency and importance and are expected to increase further. The interface is broadest and the intensity highest at the local

Table 4.3. *"Have contacts with public authorities become* more *or* less *frequent* over the last five years?" *(replies of industrialists)*

	More frequent	As before	Less frequent	No contact/ no answer	Don't know
Municipality	44.3	37.0	3.0	12.8	2.8
Ministry	33.5	29.2	3.0	30.8	3.6
Subordinate Authority	27.0	35.9	1.2	32.6	3.0
District	24.9	36.5	2.0	32.4	4.3
Parliament	9.6	19.4	1.4	66.4	3.2

Table 4.4. *"Have the contacts with public authorities become* more *or* less *important* over the last five years?" *(replies of industrialists)*

	More important	As before	Less important	No contact/ no answer	Don't know
Municipality	45.9	33.5	2.5	14.6	3.6
Ministry	39.0	24.0	2.1	30.5	4.4
Subordinate Authority	32.2	29.5	1.2	32.7	4.1
District	30.4	29.9	2.1	33.2	4.3
Parliament	12.6	19.6	1.2	62.2	4.3

or municipal level, and more interaction is directed toward the administrative staffs than toward elected bodies or officials.

The mirror image of these tendencies at the municipal level is given in Table 4.5. It is based on a questionnaire sent to the mayor and the municipal manager (or highest administrative officer) in all 444 Norwegian municipalities (the response rates were 81 and 86 percent, respectively).[7] The table shows that about 40 percent have monthly or more frequent contacts with firms, that such contacts in the majority of cases have become more frequent over the last five years, and that three-quarters judge them more important. The mayor appears to be situated more centrally in the communication network than the highest administrative official. The apparent discrepancy between where contacts from business originate and where they are registered in the political system can probably be accounted for by two factors. First, contacts with the municipal administration are spread over more agencies and persons. Second, there are considerable variations between municipalities in their economic structure. The effects of these variations cannot be further explored here, however.

But it is worth noting that politicians to a greater extent than manag-

Table 4.5. *Municipal contact with business*

	Contact	Mayor (%)	Municipal manager (%)
How frequently have you had con-tact with firms about establishing or preserving employment opportunities in the municipality during the last year?	Daily	0.6	0.3
	Weekly	10.5	7.3
	Monthly	31.4	29.0
	A few times	55.5	57.3
	Never	2.0	6.2
	Total	100.0	100.0
Have such contacts become more or less frequent during the last five years?	More frequent	57.0	49.7
	As before	38.8	41.8
	Less frequent	3.9	5.0
	No contact	0.3	3.5
	Total	100.0	100.0
Have such contacts become more or less important for the munici-pality during the last five years?	More important	75.2	64.2
	As before	22.9	30.2
	Less important	1.5	2.6
	No contact	0.3	2.9
	Total	100.0	100.0

Table 4.6. *"Does the initiative for contacts with firms mostly come from the municipality or from the firm?"*

	Mayors (%)	Municipal managers (%)
Municipality mostly	27.6	16.8
Firms mostly	20.9	39.4
Evenly divided	51.5	43.8
Total	100.0	100.0

For mayors, $N = 360$; for municipal managers, $N = 383$.

ers *initiate* contacts with firms and that the latter to a larger extent are *recipients* of communications (see Table 4.6). Administrators define their own role as more passive than that of politicians. Again, there are considerable variations between municipalities depending on social structure, political composition, and administrative resources. But the main trend in itself is important: The administrative apparatus of the municipalities to a large extent exercises its authority by taking a stand on requests and proposals. Overall, we find the same tendency as has been reported in many studies of corporatism

Table 4.7. *"How do you view more organized cooperation between the municipality and organizations in the local economic and work life (trade unions, agricultural and fishery organizations, industry and trade associations, and the like)?*

	Mayors (%)	Municipal managers (%)
Of very great importance for the municipality	24.6	15.7
Of fairly great importance	34.0	26.1
Of some importance	29.7	43.2
Of little importance	4.2	6.7
Hard to say	7.4	8.3
Total	100.1	100.0

For mayors, $N = 360$; for municipal managers, $N = 375$.

at the national level: that more initiatives from the outside go to administrative officials than to elected representatives.

A final question is of interest in this context. Mayors and municipal managers were asked how they viewed more *organized* cooperation between the municipality and interest organizations in the local community, such as trade unions, agricultural and fishery groups, industry and trade associations, and the like. Table 4.7 shows both groups are in favor of more such contacts of a corporatist nature, and mayors more so than municipal managers. In sum, therefore, the contacts with individual firms have increased more in frequency and importance at the municipal than at the national level, workers more often participate in joint initiatives, and more structured contacts with local interest organizations is generally deemed to be appropriate. In short, our data indicate that it may be more appropriate to talk of "municipal monopoly capital" than of "state monopoly capital."

In other words, there are more reactions in the political arena to turbulence created by the market. There are several reasons for this.[8] The operation of the market is based on the principles of self-interest and competition. But if competition hurts the interests of a firm, it need not restrict its activities to market-oriented action. Firms are political actors, whose returns, conditions of expansion, and possibilities for survival are to a great extent decided within the political system. Self-interest does not stop at the boundaries of the market. Particularly when a firm is threatened by loss or bankruptcy, its executives are likely to look for political solutions to economic problems. This is reinforced by what could be called the "political self-confidence" of trade and industry, which has increased. Second, several forms of public support for entrepreneurial and industrial activity have been established, ranging from special state banks to funds for industrial conversion or financial support for relocation. There is both demand for and supply of public support. Next, workers have much at stake. A large fraction of the labor force has invested income, time, and effort in homes, cottages, boats, and so forth, that is, in capital goods or durables that are mortgaged and require a stable flow of income. When these investments are threatened by adverse market conditions, the reaction is political. Not surprisingly, the closest cooperation between labor and capital is found in firms that are in difficulties. Finally, many municipalities and local governments depend on regular tax revenues to meet their increasing commitments to education, care for the aged, welfare measures, development of infrastructure, and so forth. When the sources of revenue are put in jeopardy, municipal authorities are likely to turn to the state to assist the firms that provide its tax basis. In short, the national state is willing to do more, and in crises there are more firms in trouble and workers with personal investments and municipalities with greater commitments to be met. "They all have more at stake, and in difficulties it is therefore natural that they stick together."[9]

Expansion of public authority and institutional innovations

The developments previously described have largely the character of *ad hoc reactions to market conditions producing temporary coalitions for political action*. Nevertheless, the *aggregate* of such actions, which is growing and increasingly becoming a regular part of everyday political life, should be considered a definite corporatist trend emanating from local communities.

The development of local corporatism is, however, not only a reaction to variable economic conditions but also to changes in political structure. Over the last ten to fifteen years a wide array of new legislation has been passed that more strictly regulates the conditions under which business may be run. Politics affects profits in new ways. Hence business leaders and industrial organizations have to follow politics more closely, to influence the laws that are enacted and, once they are adopted, to shape the implementation of the new legislation. Much of this legislation leaves more discretionary power to administrative agencies in the public sector. Because this implies that policy decisions are not entirely determined by the legislation itself, it becomes relatively more important to keep a sharp eye on their contents and to do so on a more or less continuous basis. Two quotations illustrate this point, the first pertaining to corporatist development at the national level. The managing director of the Norwegian Mercantile Association in 1974 argued:

> Our firms are no longer primarily interested in their particular product group, but concentrate more on the common objectives of the industry. This is a result of recent developments and a question of the government's intentions. Trade associations must have a policy for trade and retailing. . . . If the government wants to regulate trade, it will first have to learn what trade is all about, which we can teach them better than anyone else. In this I make no distinctions between conservative and socialist governments. . .[10]

The year before, the assistant manager of the Norwegian Industrial Association argued for strengthening local member organizations, primarily because industry would increasingly be affected by the government's new planning system:

> As regards public planning, industry has realized that this activity is of vital importance for the conditions the industry needs to operate at the community, country or national level. Public planning concerns land use, changes in or expansion of the educational system, and a number of public activities essential to the environment in which firms and people have to operate. Industry realizes more and more that its interests must be incorporated . . . in the public planning process. Those who do not make their demands and points of view felt won't be heard . . .
>
> During the sixties the government attempted to develop legislation for an administrative organization to carry out major physical and economic planning – for example, the new building legislation, which lays down guidelines for regional and local planning. The bill was proposed by the government in the fall of 1964 and passed by the Parliament the following spring. This legislation is the basis for physical planning and zoning: regional plans and municipal plans are essential aspects. §20 of the law states: "The municipality shall as early as possible seek cooperation with public authorities, organizations, etc. which have an interest in the planning." So if industry is to assert itself in this planning, it needs organs or organizations which can coordinate the interests of industry, formulate them, and present them to the government . . .
>
> The Industrial Association will give high priority to developing local industrial organizations which can serve as opposite numbers to the governmental planning agencies. The Norwegian Industrial Association should coordinate industry's efforts on a national level, and certain means should be given to local and regional organs. But the Association cannot carry out the day-to-day work at every point in the country. Industry needs first to organize at the district level, and modes of work must be developed to ensure coordination and articulation of industry's interests. The next step is to ensure that contacts with the district authorities are established to enable us to promote our interests in the best possible way.[11]

In short, there seems to be an increasing need to manage the uncertainty created by the *expansion* of the public sector and *discretionary* power at the local level – the regulated want to regulate the regulators. This is perceived not only centrally in the leadership of the National Industrial Association, as illustrated by the following quotation from the chairman of the Industrial Association in the district of Vestfold:

I have definitely noticed a new understanding of the fact that industry has to work in close cooperation with local authorities. Until now we have been too concerned with the internal workings of the firm. We have been ill-prepared to handle "external" problems, such as land use, communications, housing, etc. I believe that the involvement by many of the industrial leaders in this district in these areas will affect the working conditions in firms as well as their modes of operation. By gaining insight, knowledge and personal contacts with a broader social and political milieu, we will be able to solve the "external" problems of firms in simpler and better ways. By investing time on these problems today, we will secure the interests of industry in the general plans that set the framework for industrial development in the years ahead. Put another way, it is preventive work for industry today to participate actively in the planning process at the district level.[12]

The Industrial Association in Vestfold district introduced a new institution: It took the initiative for establishing the public position of "industrial consultant" at the district level and proposed an "industrial advisory board" with representatives from the district Industry Association, the district Trade Union Council, and the district authorities. The board, which clearly has a corporatist structure, was established in 1973.

In sum, the sequence of development seems to have been, first, the extension of public authority and discretionary power for economic planning and development at the district and municipal level and, then, the reaction of industrial organizations to the expansion of local public authority by an internal organizational development to strengthen their capacity to exert influence and to establish public positions and advisory boards with industrial representation.[13] Hence not only fluctuating or changing market conditions are behind the growth in local corporatism. Another important impetus comes from expansion of local public authority and discretionary power.

This development has had two sequels. First, local initiative has been followed up at the national level. The Norwegian Industrial Association set up a special committee to suggest a general system for industrial consultants. Its point of departure was the system in the agricultural sector, which for a long time has used public agronomists as consultants, at both the district and municipal level. This arrangement came to serve as a model for the proposals of the special committee of the Norwegian Industrial Association. One may speak of *cross-sectoral political learning* in this context, that is, of institutional development as a learning process.[14] The proposals of the special committee were relayed by the Industrial Association to the national government, which in 1977 appointed industrial consultants in four districts, as an experiment.

The development was also pursued "from below," and four other districts have hired industrial consultants of their own, so that with the original one in the district of Vestfold, nine now function. Partly through a national experimental program and partly through diffusion by imitation, industrial consultants appeared in almost half the country's districts.

In five of the districts where the new positions have been set up, "industrial councils" were established in an advisory capacity for the industrial consultant, with representation from the District Industry Association and the district organization of the trade unions. These bodies are clear corporatist creations, for interest aggregation and articulation takes place within sectoral public bodies. This is a system likely to grow in the next few years. Examples of other such corporatist organs at the district level could also be given, in the agricultural as well as in the industrial areas.

The system of industrial consultants is now being expanded to encompass *municipalities* as well as *districts*. In 1977 funds were appropriated by the Parliament for the establishment of industrial consultants in three municipalities in each of five districts. Their main function is to provide information and guidance, particularly for smaller firms, about legislation, regulations, and funds available through public banks and financial institutions. Also for these lower level industrial consultants, advisory boards have been set up, with representation from both trade unions and the Industrial Association in the district. The district industrial consultant sits on this board to facilitate districtwide coordination.

Corporatist structures in the form of public agencies or boards with political representation from economic sectors have existed for some time for agriculture and fisheries. Some also have been found in the industrial sector (like the municipal *tiltaksnemnd*), and they are now rapidly expanding.

Detailed proposals have also been suggested about the form and function of representative corporatist bodies at the municipal level. In a recent issue of the leading journal of planners in Norway, *Plan og Arbeid*, an official in the Department of Development (*Utbyggingsavdelingen*) in the District of Troms, Finn-Steinar Heimly, presents a comprehensive design for such bodies.[15] His point of departure is that industry and municipalities have common interests in a stable and expanding business community and labor market. Industry desires to have a varied supply of services in the local community in order to attract and keep employees. Municipalities want a stable tax base and have a long-term interest in community development. Nonetheless, problems often arise. Business frequently argues that local politicians and administrators do not understand the need for swift action. Industry feels it has little support for the investment in plants and equipment that growth requires. Especially on zoning and infrastructure questions, industry feels it is up against a paralyzed decision-making apparatus.

The municipalities in Troms fall into two broad classes: *pressure areas* and *peripheral* ones. The former face economic, technical, and administrative capacity problems in planning and developing sites for industry and housing. The latter often find that the sites they have developed remain unused. Politicians and administrators feel there is little understanding of the fact that long-term planning is necessary to prepare new areas.

To solve these problems Heimly suggests further development and expansion of a model that already exists in the industrial councils in some communities. He suggests the name "Trade Council" (*Nareringsraad*) for this body, the same name as that suggested for a national corporate representative body in the thirties by both socialist and bourgeois politicians. The functions of this body should be to facilitate exchange and consultations between municipal authorities and industrial representatives; to increase mutual understanding; to mediate contacts with such bodies as the district, the state, financial institutions, and the like; and to discuss long-term policy on planning, zoning, labor supply, services, and so forth. There is every reason to expect that representative corporate bodies on the municipal level approaching this model will be created, but probably with considerable variations in the formal structure.

The driving forces behind this expansion have been changing market conditions, expansion of local authority and discretionary power, particularly over planning, and cross-sectoral learning. *Local reactions to changing market conditions have largely taken the form of ad hoc activities and coalition formation, whereas the reaction to expanding public authority at the local level has been institutional innovations.* The particularistic reactions to market conditions are probably due to the fact that their impact affects firms differentially. In contrast, new laws and regulations represent permanently altered conditions and regular decision making, which requires continuous attention if specific interests are routinely to be taken into account. Hence they call for changes in institutional arrangements and interest representation on a stable basis.

The extent to which firms or their employees act directly in the political system, or act through interest organizations, should be considered a variable or, rather, two variables, for direct and indirect action may be combined in different amounts. Considerable sectoral variations are possible because industries with well-developed national organizations will direct more efforts toward the national political system, whereas those with weak organizations are more likely to attempt local initiatives. Likewise, large monopolies or oligopolistic branches are more likely not to bother using interest organizations as intermediaries in interacting with public authorities.

Consequences of local corporatism

First, it is striking that the business community, by making demands for industrial consultants, representative boards, and the like, in effect is *arguing for an expansion of state power*. This, however, is a state power that the business community hopes to use to further its sectoral interests, possibly in cooperation with the trade-union movement.

Second, political decisions in the economic area at the local level become *more visible*. But different sectoral agencies sometimes act at cross-purposes. Hence there is a built-in tendency toward expanding boards with sectoral representation, or toward the creation of new bodies on which several sectors can be represented and bargain to resolve differences. In other words, it may lead to increased demands for corporatist participation in local administration so that corporatism to some extent feeds on itself.[16] Some have suggested that removing many important economic decisions from democratically elected bodies will make decisions more technocratic and depoliticized and lead to greater voter apathy. Whether participation or apathy is the more likely remains to be seen.

Third, the fact that specialists on industrial policy, such as the industrial consultants and their advisory boards, become situated at the local level creates a *potential source of conflict with the central administrative apparatus of the state*. They may represent a *counterexpertise* to public officials and policy makers in the industrial sector at the national level.

It is customary to distinguish between territorial representation through the electoral channel and functional representation through public committees encompassing spokesmen for organized interest groups at the national level. The new system of industrial consultants and their advisory boards at the district level provides a merger or *fusion of territorial and functional representation*. Local economic interests are given a better political foundation through new public programs, positions, and agencies at the district and municipal level.

This may result in greater pressure for the use of *more selective economic incentives.* The new experts on local economic conditions will have few difficulties in producing arguments and mobilizing wide local political backing for special supports, subsidies, differential taxes, or compensation for general taxes for particular industries in their districts in order to maintain employment or aid depressed areas. Such national government intervention in a selective and discriminate fashion to assist certain regions or industries has been called "neo-mercantilist." And the development of local corporatist structures no doubt will be an impetus toward more neo-mercantilist measures, particularly because the assistance given to one district provides an incentive for countervailing relief in others. In one word, we may expect a happy marriage between local corporatism and neo-mercantilism.

Hence we may anticipate that the *central administrative apparatus* to an increasing extent will have to *defend the market.* As Berreljord has stated,[16] we may observe an apparent ideological paradox: that the bureaucrats become the advocates for economic efficiency and impersonal operation of competition and the price mechanism. No doubt this may increase the potential for conflict between local and national levels of policy making, as local bureaucrats and politicians are likely to demand protection from market forces when they hurt local industries and employment. State officials may have to protect the market against local capitalists and their political allies.

Finally, we are likely to find *increasing competition between local communities* that vie for the location of plants from the same firms. They are caught in the prisoner's dilemma: All municipalities are forced to invest in industrial parks, and so on, which leads to overcapacity and little comparative advantage. All invest more, but their relative position remains roughly the same. This phenomenon could be called *"market inversion,"* because it is political units that contend and economic organizations that can choose. In the questionnaire sent to all mayors in Norway, they were asked: "How strong is the competition with other municipalities about firms (factories, plants, hotels, etc.) for locating their establishment in your community?" The responses are given in Table 4.8 (missing cases included).

The table shows 60 percent of the mayors and municipal managers reporting this competition and that about a quarter of them find it severe. Further analysis to identify the characteristics of communities that face the greatest competition is in progress. As direct and indirect subventions have to be funded in large part by local taxpayers, a

Table 4.8. *Competition with other municipalities for the location of firms*

	Mayors (%)	Municipal managers (%)
Severe competition	27.8	23.8
Fairly severe	31.9	37.4
Fairly little	26.9	19.9
Insignificant	13.5	18.9
Total	100.0	100.0

For mayors, $N = 360$; for municipal managers, $N = 366$.

paradoxical result may be to put already established firms in a less favorable position. Older cohorts of companies may have to support infant industry. So although local corporatist structures encourage neo-mercantilist policies from the national government against which its officials have to defend the operation of the market or free competition, local communities have to compete in a political market and woo firms with special favors to make themselves economically attractive.

Conclusion

In this chapter we have argued that most of the literature on corporatism focuses on the national level, but in several countries there is a trend toward corporatist structures at the local level. In Norway this is now the most rapidly expanding part of the corporatist system. This has come about partly as a result of changing market conditions, often expressed politically in ad hoc coalitions of business executives, trade unionists, and local officials. These ad hoc actions generate clear patterns – partly because one coalition learns from or imitates the behavior of others. But in part it is also due to new legislation aimed at regulating economic activity and placing more discretionary power at the local level. This has provided an incentive for institutional innovations to influence the use of the new authority. The response has, on the one hand, been an offensive to strengthen the local branches of industry associations, so that they can cope with the new challenges and opportunities and, on the other, the establishment of new public boards with functional or corporatist representation. This has several important current and potential consequences, ranging from growth of neo-mercantilist policies to increased community competition for industrial establishments. Further analysis is needed, not only to map differences between countries but also to be able to identify the processes that cause variations in local adaptations.

Notes

1 See, for example, Stein Rokkan, "Numerical Democracy and Corporate Pluralism" in *Political Oppositions in Western Democracies,* ed. Robert A. Dahl (New Haven: Yale University Press, 1966); and Frederick B. Pike and Thomas Stritch, *The New Corporatism* (Notre Dame: University of Notre Dame Press, 1974).

2 Rokkan, op. cit.

3 Philippe Schmitter, "Still a Century of Corporatism?" in Pike and Stritch (eds.) op. cit. p. 93.

4 Schmitter, ibid., p. 105.

5 Andrew Shonfield, *Modern Capitalism* (New York: Oxford University Press, 1965), p. 231.

6 The questionnaires referred to in this chapter are among those administered in connection with the Study of the Distribution of Power in Norway. This study is commissioned by the Prime Minister's Office and funded by appropriations directly from the Norwegian Parliament. It is directed by Gudmund Hernes.

7 Torodd Strand has been in charge of this survey of the municipalities for the power study and the questions we quote were included in the survey.

8 Gudmund Hernes, "Markedet som domstol" ("The Market as a Court of Law") *Norges Industri* 20 (1976).

9 Ibid. p. 22.

10 Interview in *NHST,* December 1974.

11 *Norges Industri* 21 (1973):15.

12 *Norges Industri* 21 (1974):6–8.

13 Cf. Ole Berrelfjord and Gudmund Hernes, "Markedsforvitring og statsbygging" ("The Withering Away of the Market and Statebuilding"), *Sosialøkonomen* 7 (1974):3–16.

14 Ibid.

15 Finn-Steinar Heimly, "Kommuneses tilrettelegging for naeringslivet" ("Municipal Facilitation of Business Activity"), *Plan og Argeid* 2 (1979):101–3.

16 Berrelfjord and Hernes, op. cit.

Part II

The functioning of interest groups

5

The attribution of public status to interest groups: observations on the West German case

CLAUS OFFE

Like all social phenomena, interest groups can be analyzed from three theoretical perspectives. Either we start with the *individual social actor* and explore his or her intentions, values, and expectations in joining the organization and his or her actual chances of influencing its policies and utilizing the resources and achievements of the organization. Or we start with the *organization* itself, the generation of its resources, its growth, its internal bureaucratization and differentiation, and its relations to other organizations. Or finally, we can focus on the global social system and start by asking what role it assigns to interest organizations, what legal or other constraints it imposes on the pursuit of certain interests, and what links it establishes between particular interest organizations and other elements of the social structure. Speaking loosely and metaphorically, one could say that these three perspectives look on interest organizations from "below," from "within," and from "above."

Three dimensions of the analysis of interest organization

It is only when we combine these three dimensions of organized forms of interest representation that we can arrive at a sufficiently complex explanation of their operation. When we ask such questions as: What factors lead to the formation of an interest group? What determines its relative influence and power in the political process? How can the specific articulation and definition of those demands be understood that an interest organization puts forward as being in "the interest" of those represented by the organization? we immediately encounter the need to proceed on three levels of analysis simultaneously. These are (1) the level of will, consciousness, sense of collective identity, and values of the *constituent* members of the inter-

123

est group; (2) the level of the socioeconomic *"opportunity structure"* of the society within which an interest group emerges and acts; and (3) the institutional forms and practices that are provided to the interest group by the *political system* and that confer a particular *status* as its basis of operation.

One of the biases of pluralist political theory results directly from its failure to take into account the relevance of the second and third elements of interest organizations. Pluralist theory tends to explain the existence, strength, and particular articulation of interest organizations by reference to properties of the constituent *elements* of the organization: their values, their willingness to sacrifice resources for the pursuit of their interest, their numbers, and so on. That this type of explanation leads at best to a very limited understanding of the dynamics of interest representation becomes evident as soon as we realize that an identical number of interested individuals with identical degrees of determination to defend and promote their interest may produce vastly different organizational manifestations and practices, depending on the strategic location of the groups' members within the social structure and depending on the political-institutional status their organization does or does not enjoy. The concrete shape and content of organized interest representation is always a result of interest *plus* opportunity *plus* institutional status. To employ structuralist language, we can also say that interest representation is determined by ideological, economic, and political parameters.

Such categorization of "factors" and "dimension" should not, however, prevent us from expecting – and exploring – the empirical connections among these three types of parameters. All three of the elements that together determine the shape and content of the system of interest representation do not operate with the same relative weight and importance. Historical changes in the system of interest representation (which would become manifest in a differentiation of organized interests, changes in the nature of conflict and cooperation, changes in the level of militancy, etc.) can be explained by changes on the level of values and ideologies in one period, changes of strategic positions and social power of groups in a second period, and changes on the level of political institutionalization of interest groups in still another period. In other words, *there exists some historical variability of the relative importance of ideological, economic, and political parameters* as they jointly determine the shape and content of interest organizations such as unions, trade and employers' associations, and professional associations. *Policies* that provide status to interest groups, assign certain semipublic or public functions to them, and regulate the type and scope of their activities are, under conditions of advanced capitalist social and economic structures, far more important factors affecting ongoing change in the system of interest representation than factors that have to do with changes of either *ideological* orientations or *socioeconomic* opportunity structures. Interest representation, for a number of reasons to be explored, tends to become predominantly a matter of "political design," and thus in part a dependent rather than independent variable of public policy making.

Two types of political rationality

In a highly schematic fashion, the changing relationship between the system of interest representation and public policy making can be represented as the shift from one type of political rationality to another one. Under conditions where the formation and activity of organized interest groups is not regulated by specifically attributed collective status given to the organization and its members, policy makers do not have much control over the intensity and content of specific demands that are being made in the political process nor over the number and identity of organized collectivities by which such demands are being made. At best, *political parties* are able to perform a reconciling function, thus overarching the specific conflicts of interest between organized groups and providing some pro- grammatic directives and priorities to policy makers. Under such conditions of low institutionalization of interest groups – conditions that come closest to the liberal-pluralist model of the political process – articulations of interest and demand have to be accepted as given from the point of view of the policy maker. His or her objective – and his or her standard of political rationality – would be to serve as many of the specific demand inputs as possible, given the limitations of fiscal and other resources, so as to satisfy a maximum of special inter- ests. This requires, in turn, increasing the efficiency and effectiveness of the governmental use of resources, maximizing predictive capacities, measuring cost/benefit ratios, employing sophisticated methods of policy and budgetary planning, using social indicators, and so forth. Because demand inputs have to be treated as given, the only thing that can and must be rationalized by a "good" policy maker is the efficiency and effectiveness of outputs. The working of civil society itself is considered as given – both in the sense that it can be taken for granted and that it is neither feasible nor legitimate to attempt to interfere with its internal dynamic. The political problem is one of compensating for market failures, resolving conflict, supervis- ing rules, and fine tuning. To be sure, there is a considerable range of conflict over the extent and nature of such policies which may be more or less "interventionist"; but they converge on the notion of the separation between the political and the socioeconomic spheres of social life, which is the underlying notion without which the very term "intervention" does not make any sense.

This type of political rationality, which we would associate with "active" interventionist policies aiming at optimal and comprehensive satisfaction of manifest (as well as some anticipated) interest is, however, not the only conceivable type of political rationality. If political parties fail to aggregate and reconcile, on the basis of their respective programmatic orientations, major segments of the electorate, and/or if policy makers find it difficult or impossible to accommodate significant interests due to the lack of sufficient fiscal and institutional resources at their disposal, the inverse type of political rationality is likely to take over. This one follows the imperative of keeping output constant, that is, at levels that are considered reasonable or affordable, while channeling demand inputs in a way that appears compatible with available resources. The variable to be manipulated and balanced, in this case, is not policy outputs, but *the system of interest representation and the modes of resolution of conflict.* It is this standard of political rationality that inspires "the search for the stable ordered society, for a system where competition, class conflict and political disunity [are] structurally rendered impossible" (Harris, 1972:66). The standard of a "good" policy here, to put it in the simplest terms, is not to satisfy demands but to shape and channel demands so as to make them satisfiable.

A parallel alternative of standards of political rationality can be found in the field of economic policy making. Just as the policy-making doctrine of "active interventionism" considers "interest" as the variable that is to be taken for granted and attempts to respond through effective policies, for Keynesian economic policy, the strategic point of intervention is the *demand* side of markets. Again, the standard of rationality is to make "adequate" responses to problems that are accepted as they emerge. The configuration of macroeconomic conditions that raises serious doubts about the validity of this standard of political rationality are such phenomena as stagflation and the "dualization" of the economic structure. Stagflation renders demand management unpractical as an instrument of economic steering, for it exposes the Keynesian policy makers to contradictory imperatives: Expand demand and state indebtedness in order to fight stagnation and reduce it in order to achieve monetary stability. They necessitate the shift to an alternative type of rational economic policy making, the shift to the *supply side* of the economy. Here the effort is to *structure* problems so as to make them manageable. Quantity and skill level of the work force, energy and raw materials, the price level at which labor power and natural resources are available, and the level and rate of technical change are the foci of economic policies that no longer merely respond to problems but that try to change the nature of problems so as to make future responses possible.

Both in the case of political rationality and economic policy, the common characteristic of the respective second alternative is to establish institutional parameters and/or physical and economic parameters that guarantee that the problems that have to be dealt with do not exceed the scope of the available resources and strategies of problem solving.

The distinction between the two modes of political rationality can be conveniently made in terms of "conjunctural" versus "structural" policies. Conjunctural policies would seek to maximize the adequacy of policy *responses* to problems as they emerge and appear on the agenda; the concomitant expectation is that such problems and demands will remain within a range of manageability defined by existing capacities of state action and their continuing improvement. Structural policies, in contrast, become the predominant mode of intervention as soon as this expectation is no longer supported by experience. They are adopted in response to conditions of economic and institutional crisis. In response to such crises, the physical and economic parameters of production and the institutional parameters of interest representation, which together constitute the nature of the problem, become subject to redesign. The shift is from policy output and economic demand management to the shaping of political input and economic supply – from "state intervention" to "politicization."

This chapter argues that the transition from "conjunctural" to "structural" modes of political strategies has been a dominant trend in advanced capitalist nations since the late sixties. It concentrates on strategies of institutional change concerning political inputs and explores the strategic significance and consequences of such changes. Using materials from the Federal Republic of Germany, this chapter considers (1) whether changes in the structure of interest representation can actually be explained by the intention to influence the volume and nature of political problems that appear on the political agenda and (2) whether the strategy of elimination of "problem overload" by institutionalizing filter mechanisms designed to reduce the magnitude of problems to manageable proportions is actually a workable and successful strategy or whether it generates its own specific failures and contradictions. We should be careful, however, not to mistake a conceptual distinction for an evolutionary sequence. It would be far too simplistic and quite inaccurate to work with a historical periodization of this kind, arguing, in effect, that there was a time when instrumental rationality was the dominant mode and that, at the end of this period, there was an unequivocal shift toward the rationalization of inputs and the supply side of markets. Although it may turn out to be justified to describe a particular historical period or configuration of political forces as being dominated by either of the two types of political rationality, it may well be more fruitful to study the simultaneity and interaction of the two. At what point and for what reasons does the orientation of policy makers toward problem solving and the achievement of stated goals turn into an orientation toward regulating the institutional setting that leads to the emergence of goals and problems? To what extent does the achievement of goals presuppose the creation of a new balance of supportive forces and the construction of new channels through which demands and political opposition are channeled? Our theme, then, is to explore the mechanisms by which new issues, new items on the agenda of the state apparatus, and new imperatives of intervention lead to changes in the system of interest representation, or how functional changes of public policy affect the institutional framework of politics. Growing state interventionism and increasing political institutionalization through corporatist forms of "functional representation," although conceptually distinct and even opposite modes of political rationalization, are nevertheless empirically connected developments.[1]

Reordering the system of interest representation – a new political issue

Although a harmonious and often euphoric view of a social and political order characterized by group processes prevailed throughout the fifties, a much more disenchanted attitude toward group processes has become prominent since the mid-sixties. What was discovered then, and has become part of the academic as well as nonacademic political discourse, was the propensity of a political order based on the uninhibited interplay of organized interest group forces to reproduce and even to exacerbate exactly those "anarchic" and disruptive tendencies that seemingly had been overcome in the transition from "competitive" to "organized" capitalism. More specifically, it came to be suspected that the bargaining power and political influence of organized interests undermined responsible parliamentary government based on political parties, caused an intolerably high rate of inflation and/or fiscal strain, and interfered with attempts at long-term and comprehensive social and economic planning. In addition, it appeared that conflict among the most powerful interest groups was settled, quite frequently, at the expense of social categories that are poorly organized (e.g., consumers, independent middle classes) and hence economically and/or politically vulnerable. These and similar concerns underlie various attempts to reorganize the relationship among interest groups and the relationship between interest groups and the state. In all cases the rationale has been to impose a certain measure of self-restraint, discipline, and responsibility on interest groups and to make the interaction between organized interests, on the one hand, and the legislative and executive branches of government, on the other, more predictable and cooperative. In short, the dynamics of "organized capitalism" were themselves seen in need of reorganization.

There can be little doubt that this wave of postpluralist realism concerning the urgency of institutional changes in the framework of interest representation and the conduct of politics reflects new policy problems confronting the capitalist state. In spite of vast differences in kind and degree between the problems of the first German republic in the mid-twenties and those of the second republic in the mid-sixties, in both cases, the question arose of the compatibility of serious economic policy problems, on the one side, and of the dynamics of uncoordinated interest group pluralism, on the other. The conflict was one *not of contradictory demands* but of political and economic demands, on the one side, and *systemic requirements*, on the other. Certain "excessive" demands generated by interest group pluralism appeared to transcend the limits of tolerance of the economic order.

To be sure, in the history of the Federal Republic there has always been a tradition of political commentary and analysis that is highly critical of the role played by organized interests (cf., e.g., Eschenburg, 1955; W. Weber, 1970). In sharp distinction to current contributions, however, the critical argument of this literature was not functionalist, but normative, appealing to such values as the bureaucratic ethos, the rule of law, the preservation of constitutional authority, and the separation of powers. What these authors were calling for was not institutional *innovation* in the system of interest representation but, rather, stricter adherence to *existing* constitutional norms that would protect the political system against illegitimate forms of influence and control that subverted state authority. Although this normative argument has never been fully abandoned in the academic and political literature, it figures only as an ideological façade for models and recommendations derived from functionalist arguments (Böckenförde, 1976; Bethusy-Huc 1976; Kevenhörster, 1976). That is, the focus of concern, the notion of what is threatened has shifted from constitutional *norms* to the requirements of sociopolitical *stability* and the effective performance of public policy which by the more recent authors is held to make institutional changes of the system of interest representation an urgent imperative.

The broad literature on planning and public policy making that has been produced in the Federal Republic since the late sixties started by exploring the organizational, informational, and budgetary requirements for effective and efficient policy making, thus trying to provide the necessary knowledge for the conduct of "active reform policies," which were the programmatic base of the early years of the Social Democratic administration after 1969. Their belief in the desirability of innovative (rather than merely responsive), highly coordinated (rather than fragmented), and long-term policy strategies led their proponents to realize that such rationalizations *within* the state apparatus were insufficient to improve the reform capacity of the state. They realized that under conditions of party competition and interest group pluralism, such reformist activism would face insurmountable political difficulties: lack of consensus, short-term mobilization, and increased level of conflict (for an English summary of this theoretical and empirical literature, cf. Mayntz and Scharpf, 1975). Strategies that would facilitate the creation of consensus and the absorption of conflict, including institutional devices to secure coordination not only among the various agencies of the state apparatus but also among state and *private* actors and organizations were increasingly held to be the most crucial prerequisites of active reformism (Hauff and Scharpf, 1975).

The need to achieve a "new social order" by "reforming democracy" had already been the substance of a political program by which Chancellor Ludwig Erhard, the leader of the last postwar administration without Social Democratic participation, tried to inaugurate a new form of politics for the Federal Republic in May 1965 – one and a half years before he had to quit office as a direct consequence of the first major recession that affected the West German political economy since World War II. This program, which, more precisely, for its lack of precision, should be called a vision of political order advertised under the title of a "societal formation" (*Formierte Gesellschaft*), was directly deduced from normative social theories of authors such as Eric Voegelin and Goetz Briefs. Basically, the theory consists in a grandiose developmental scheme specifying three stages in the development of nontotalitarian industrial societies. The first of these stages is "capitalism," characterized by extreme inequalities of wealth and power and the resulting high level of class conflict. The second phase, generally reached by European nations after World War I, is liberal-pluralist democracy, which is basically a transitory stage: It solves the structural problems of the old "capitalist" order by allowing for the development of powerful mass organizations (such as unions and recognized Social Democratic parties) and by providing a mechanism for equalizing power differentials based on economic power. At the same time, however, liberal-pluralist democracy introduces centrifugal tendencies that reach dangerous proportions the more the ongoing process of industrialization transforms the political economy into a highly complex and interdependent whole. The pluralist dissolution of values, disciplines, and traditions – the "end of ideology" – renders this precarious system even more vulnerable. Hence the need for a transition to a third stage: Its rationale is the adaptation of politics to the requirements of the advanced industrial "technostructure" and overcoming the disruptive impact of liberal-pluralist democracy. Shortsighted, narrow-minded, irresponsible, and illegitimate mass organizations must be curbed. Most important, distributional and social policy demands must be reconciled with the imperatives of economic modernization, growth, and competitiveness.[2]

This diagnosis leads to the following dilemma: In an advanced industrial economy, interest organizations have the power to interfere with public policy making in highly dysfunctional ways; hence, the need to *"keep them out."* At the same time, however, such representative organizations are absolutely indispensable for public policy, because they have a monopoly of information relevant for public policy and, most important, a substantial measure of control over their respective constituencies. Therefore they must be made *integral components* of the mechanisms through which public policy is formulated. Their potential positive function is as significant as their potential for obstruction. The trick, from this perspective, is to utilize the first while avoiding exposing public policy to the second. Any conceivable solution to this problem would imply more than what is required to solve the problem of neutrality and the enforcement of rule-of-law norms. In the latter case, the solution would consist in strengthening the demarcation line between private powers and public policy, although leaving the nature of organized interest representation itself unaffected. In the first case, any solution would be insufficient that does not change the internal structure and composition of the system of interest representation so that their indispensable potential for cooperation is maximized, and their potential for the "selfish" and "irresponsible" pursuit of particularistic interests is eliminated.

The new political *problematique* that has occupied the center of the stage since the mid-sixties is characterized by the growing sense of the failure of the purposive-instrumental type of rationality and the increasingly perceived need to "rationalize" the polity in terms of what Anderson calls a new "design." Because the claims and interests articulated within the framework of liberal-democratic institutions can no longer be reconciled with the basic prerequisites of capitalist stability and growth, these institutions themselves are at issue. The pervasive shift is from *conflict over group interest* to *conflict over ground rules,* from the definition of claims to the definition of legitimate claimants, from politics to metapolitics. This shift takes place in the conservative as well as in the Social Democratic camp, even though in different variants. The conservatives propose the restoration of "order" and call for the abolition of state interventionism; the Social Democrats understand that reformist interventionism presupposes for its success and continuity new arrangements over orderly cooperation and relatively conflict-free modes of interest representation. Both variants imply changes in the mode of interest representation, new regulations for the conduct of group and class conflict. Both are forced to design these regulations not according to some normative conception of a good and just political order but by pragmatic reference to functional requirements, limits of tolerance, and economic mechanisms. Modern conservatives find themselves forced to acknowledge the irrevocable reality of mass democracy, the welfare state, and collective representation of the working class in wage and other negotiations, although their ideologies of an organicist order or a world of free competition may leave no place for such phenomena. Social Democrats, on the other side, find themselves forced realistically to recognize the nontransformability of essential premises of the capitalist political economy, in spite of the socialist visions of their individual or collective past.

On both the conservative and the Social Democratic side, the question is thus raised not so much of the desirable goals and the most effective/efficient-purposive rational courses of action to accomplish them but of the appropriate ground rules, structural arrangements, and institutional designs that would be the most appropriate environment of public policy. The policy area of monetary stability is a good case in point: The controversial debate that goes on among policy makers on the left and on the right is no longer about the undesirability of inflation (on which they agree) or about the best state policies to control it (on which the options seem to be exhausted) but on how the relative power position of actors *outside* the public policy-making system (e.g., unions and highly concentrated industries) can be altered in a way that appears to be more conducive to a lasting success.

Instances of institutional design

In the West German case, a partial list of institutional changes and proposals for such changes would include the following items in chronological order.

1. In the early sixties, the programmatic notion of a *formierte Gesellschaft* was launched by conservative politicians and intellectuals. The term *formierte Gesellschaft*, as just described, carries the connotation of growth, predictability, and unity. It was used to describe the projected social and economic order to follow the "end of the postwar period" of reconstruction.

2. In 1964, a Council of Economic Advisers (*Sachverstaendigenrat*) was instituted which has since reported annually on the course and further prospects of the economy.

3. In 1967, a coalition government of Christian and Social Democrats passed legislation creating the *Konzertierte Aktion*, a highly informal mode of discussion and negotiation that provides an opportunity for state bureaucrats, employers, unions, and some other interest organizations to exchange views on current economic issues on the basis of policy goals suggested by the government.

4. In the course of the period 1965 to 1969, an explosive growth took place in the frequency with which committees of the *Bundestag* resorted to parliamentary hearings (*Anhoerungen*). In the same period, consultations between government officials and interest group representatives became established as a routine practice during the preparatory stage of legislation.

5. In 1972, a "code of honor" (*Verhaltensregeln*) for the members of Parliament was adopted, regulating the extent and manner in which deputies were supposed to disclose their relations to interest groups.

6. At the same time, all interest groups were required to register with the chairman of the Bundestag and to indicate their substantive area of interest and the number of members they represented.

7. In 1971, the Federation of German Unions (DGB) proposed legislation introducing an Economic and Social Council (BWSR) into the constitutional order. This new institution was intended to have far-reaching powers in the legislative process. Its proponents recommended the legislation because it would have the potential of concentrating all major government interest group interaction in one institution, thus making such interaction more visible and transparent.

8. In 1969, after the Social Democratic/Liberal coalition government came into office, various pieces of reform legislation, most notably the Urban Renewal Act (*Staedtebaufoerderungsgesetz*), assigned a legal status to certain interest groups and prescribed the involvement of such groups in the planning and implementation of policies. Similarly, various Social Democratic proposals for an "active industrial policy" (*Strukturpolitik*) and "investment steering" (*Investitionslenkung*) would create joint decision-making bodies (e.g., "*Branchenausschuesse*") composed of delegates of industry, unions, and state agencies and authorized to consider and recommend investment decisions. A similar model of "tripartite" decision making was recently adopted and institutionalized in the area of health policy, in which the problem of the "explosion" of health services costs is now being attacked by state-supervised and state-initiated intergroup negotiations.

9. In 1975, the Christian Democratic party (CDU) proclaimed in its electoral platform that "the democratic state is called upon to establish a framework regulating both the internal organization and the external activities of social groups." The promise to introduce such a framework was accompanied by complaints over the "irresponsible" behavior of such organizations in the past. The control of their allegedly enormous power and the need for its more balanced use in favor of hitherto unrepresented groups amounts to, according to the CDU platform, a solution of the "*Neue Soziale Frage*" ("new social question" – "*soziale Frage*" being the traditional Catholic and liberal term for class conflict). Although this notion of uncontrolled interest group power clearly was aimed at the "irresponsible," "inflation-causing" behavior of unions, the general thrust of the argument is not too different from a declaration in a Social Democratic policy document (OR 85) adopted in 1975, which promised "to resist vigorously any attempt at group-egotistic blackmail" – an appeal that, among other things, reflected the experience of a paralyzing air traffic control assistants' strike and several incidents in which employer organizations boycotted vocational training programs. The issue of illegitimate and uncontrolled interest group power was raised by both major parties during the 1976 campaign, in the course of which highly emotional terms such as *Unternehmerstaat, Gewerkschaftsstaat, Filzokratie*, all of them suggesting particularistic practices of corruption and patronage and illegitimate uses of power, became part of the common political vocabulary.

10. This issue has turned out to be neither superficial nor ephemeral, as can be seen from the continuing (and highly technical) political and academic debate on the desirability and the specific terms of a

Verbaendegesetz (Association Act), which was proposed by the Christian Democrats with the aim of imposing (cf. Dettling, 1976) constraints of "common interest orientation" (*Gemeinwohlbindung*) on interest organizations. It is of some interest to observe that the legal term *Gemeinwohlbindung* so far has been exclusively used to refer to the use of private property; the extension of this criterion to organizations implies the view that organization today is as much a source of social power as private property has long been recognized to be; hence it needs to be subjected to analogous limitations.

The relations between interest organizations and the state, and the restructuring of these relations through political means, have been issues in all these institutional changes and legislative proposals. Diverse as they are in significance and political context, a few generalizations emerge. First, all political parties represented in the Bundestag have recognized and accepted the problem of state interest group relations. Minor indications of reluctance on the part of the SPD[3] notwithstanding, the issue can today be considered a nonpartisan one. Second, such institutionalization, or assignment of political status to interest groups, is always two-sided in its effects.[4] Any attribution of status means that, on the one side, groups gain advantages and privileges although, on the other side, they have to accept certain constraints and restrictive obligations. In a typical case, access to government decision-making positions is facilitated through the political recognition of an interest group, but the organization in question becomes subject to more or less formalized obligations, for example, to behave responsibly and predictably and to refrain from any nonnegotiable demands or nonacceptable tactics.

Third, *none* of the changes mentioned or suggested plans for the political reorganization of state interest group relations were inspired by motives foreign to the liberal-pluralist doctrine of representative democracy that today constitutes the creed of political elites of advanced capitalist societies. Such changes are neither proposed by reference to Catholic doctrines or authoritarian images of society as an organically ordered whole nor inspired by Socialist aims of overcoming exploitation and oppression by the introduction of new mechanisms of popular control of political and social power.[5] The underlying motives are, rather, of a pragmatic and "functionalist" nature: to facilitate the resolution of distributive conflict, to obtain more reliable and predictive knowledge needed by policy makers, to relieve the state bureaucracy from the veto power of shortsighted interest groups, to combat inflation, recession, and fiscal crisis more effectively, and so forth. Such "nonideological," highly pragmatic reasoning on which programs for interest group institutionalization are based is both the strength and weakness of such programs. It is a source of strength because no principled political opposition is likely to be raised against proposals for more interest group institutionalization. At the same time, it is a source of weakness because no one is able to justify and legitimate – other than on an ad hoc basis – what groups are for what reasons entitled to what kind of status. As Anderson observes, "It is extremely hard in democratic theory to find grounds for investing the interests of capital and labor [or, for that matter, any other group] with the authority to make what are in effect public decisions. This is the flaw in any corporate theory of representation." (Anderson, 1977:14)

Fourth, regardless of whether institutionalization operates primarily through the attribution of privilege or the imposition of constraints (the two being, in effect, two sides of the same coin), we can conveniently categorize instances of institutionalization as belonging to one of three political approaches: Either the mode of interest representation vis-à-vis *legislation* (sometimes including participation in the administration and interpretation of legal norms in the court system) or the role of interest groups in policy *implementation* or the process of interest group *organization* itself (i.e., the relation between the organization and its members) is regulated.

Neo-corporatism – the dependent variable

In recent contributions by Anderson, Ionescu, Lehmbruch, Panitch, Ruin, Schmitter, Winkler, and others, the term *corporatism* (sometimes used in conjunction with qualifiers such as *neo*, *liberal*, or *societal*) has been used as an analytical concept to describe global changes in the political structure of advanced capitalist societies. *Corporatism* is a concept that does not describe a situation, but rather an "axis" of development. In other words, political systems can be more or less corporatist, more or less advanced in the process of corporatization, depending on the extent to which public status is attributed to organized interest groups. This process is relatively advanced when many interest groups have a publicly attributed status in all or most of the relevant dimensions of institutionalization, and it is relatively undeveloped where none or only few groups are institutionally defined in only a few of the dimensions. Empirically, approximation to the "ideal type" of corporatism thus depends on the number of *groups* affected and the number of *dimensions* in which they are affected. To begin with the latter, corporatization increases with:

1. The extent to which the *resources* of an interest organization are supplied by the state. This can take the form of direct subsidies or tax

exemptions, forced membership, privileged access to state-controlled mass communication, and so forth.

2. The extent to which the *range of representation* is defined through political decision. Examples include a public definition of the range of substantive areas in which an interest organization may operate and/ or of the potential membership (e.g., by number, by region, by individual position and status, etc.).

3. The extent to which *internal relations* between rank-and-file members and executive members of the organization are regulated.

4. The extent to which interest organizations are licensed, recognized, and invited to assume, together with a specified set of other participants, a role in *legislation, the judicial system, policy planning,* and *implementation,* or even are granted the right of *Selbstverwaltung* (*self-administration*).

We can label these four dimensions of the concept of corporatism *resource status, representation status, organization status,* and *procedural status.* In all cases, by status we mean the specifically attributed *formal* status of a group (as opposed to relations of informal cooperation between political and other segments of the elite, clientelistic relations, and status resulting from ad hoc tactical considerations of various groups or branches of the state apparatus); formal status is based on legal statute and formally adopted procedural rules that give the interest group some claim on a specific status. In other words, a group that has status in any of the four dimensions ceases to be exclusively determined in its actions and accomplishments by the interests, ideologies, need perceptions, and so forth of its members, plus the relative strength it enjoys in relation to other groups with whom it is engaged in competition or alliance. In pluralist political theory, only those two factors determine behavioral outputs. Consequently, pluralist theory is rendered obsolete by the emergence in the real world of the third of those three factors that we have distinguished in the first section of this paper, namely, specific political status. The attribution of positive political status to, for example, an organization of political refugees, a sports association, or an association of automobilists results directly in an incomplete determination of the organization's behavior by constituent members (because now the organization has resources to spend that do *not* flow from the willingness of members to contribute to a common objective; it has commitments to honor that are the price for political subsidy and hence are irreducible to the membership level); nor can the manifest behavior be explained by reference to the relative strength of conflicting groups or allies.

Positive political status allows an organization to enjoy partial immunity from its members as well as from other organizations. Not all instances of corporatization imply, however, the attribution of *positive* status. Equally common is the attribution of *negative* status as part of the dynamics that occur along the corporatism axis. For instance, subsidies may be taken away from an interest group; its representational status may be reduced by a restrictive redefinition of the substantive areas in which organizational activities are allowed to take place; and organization rules may be altered so as to make the achievement of internal consensus more complicated and time consuming. Also, corporatist institutionalization does not mean that, in reference to one particular interest organization, *all* status definitions must be either in the negative or the positive direction. We frequently find "mixed cases" in which, as a consequence of its institutionalization, an organization gains in procedural status but loses in resource status, or gains in resource status but loses in representation status, and so forth.

The second major component of the corporatism concept refers to *groups* that are affected by status attribution.

1. *"Market" participants:* This category includes all organized collectivities representing the supply or demand sides of either labor markets or goods and services markets. Here we find unions and employer organizations, investors, and consumers (as organized by branch of industry, region, size of firm, etc.). The chief reason they associate is to influence state policies that bear on the relative market position of their members. These organized collectivities are able to influence the state by directly making demands on policy makers, and their actions may have destabilizing effects on the social and political order. And although their influence varies greatly according to their class position, they are able to affect state policy making significantly – either by demands, by negative sanctions, or by side effects of their operation that are more or less unintended, such as inflation, but that nonetheless have direct implications for the stability of the social and political order.

2. *"Policy takers":* This is another category of interest groups in addition to organized collectivities of market participants, whose members are *directly affected by* state policies. They are participants in a political "market" in which taxation, subsidies, transfer payments, group privileges, and so forth are exchanged for political support and opposition. Coalitions of urban and regional governments are the most obvious and probably the most significant example of this category vis-à-vis the central state. Other examples are associations of taxpayers, welfare recipients, students, public hospitals, and automobile associations. The common denominator of all these groups

is that they are affected by policy decisions made on the level of the central state.

This distinction between organized interest groups that are in fact class organizations (at least to the extent that they comprise either the supply or the demand side of the labor market) or organizations of class fractions, on the one side, and organized interest groups representing collectivities that are specifically affected by state policies, on the other, raises a serious problem, which is brought up again and again in the corporatism literature.[6] The dilemma is this: either to transcend the limitations of the pluralism paradigm and base the analysis on categories of class and class conflict or to maintain the basic idea of pluralism, namely, the notion of structural differentiation of industrial society and the mechanism of collective action that leads to a multiplicity of interest organizations, which increasing state intervention stimulates. The first interpretation of corporatism has the advantage of taking into account the aspect of repressive discipline imposed by corporatist arrangements specifically on the unions, suggesting that such arrangements can primarily be understood as the outcome of a ruling class strategy to co-opt, integrate, and discipline working-class organizations and to create conditions that typically lead to a high degree of internal bureaucratization and hence to the containment of economic and political struggles. The shortcoming of this interpretation lies in its failure to come to grips with the phenomenon of corporatization of nonclass organizations (e.g., taxpayers, students, city governments, doctors, etc.), to which we have referred as "policy takers."

The alternative conceptual framework, however, is no less deficient. Although recognizing that corporatization affects groups far beyond the limits of class organizations, it fails to account for the impact of corporatist arrangements on the terms and institutional channels of class conflict and for the fact that such arrangements are typically advocated and promoted where the economic and political power of working-class organizations has grown beyond what the ruling class is willing to accept in the interest of continued and balanced capitalist accumulation.

The phenomenon of corporatist developments thus seems, in view of this theoretical dilemma, to require a *dual* or *combined explanation* that relies exclusively neither on the social class nor on the pluralist group paradigm. In such an explanation the state would pursue quite different objectives when granting the right to functional representation to unions, on the one hand, and to any "pluralist" interest group (e.g., doctors) on the other. We hypothesize that despite apparent similarity in the two cases, the underlying function that corporatization serves in the two cases is quite different. For working-class organizations, what is to be achieved is restraint, discipline, responsibility, and the greater predictability of conflict behavior that results from bureaucratization. In the case of ordinary pluralist interest groups, which are granted a public law status and the right to "self-administration," the dominant motive is the delegation, devolution, and transfer of political issues and demands into an arena in which they do not directly affect the stability of (central) government and the cohesion of its supporting party or party coalition but, on the contrary, help to reduce "overloaded" agenda. To be sure, *every* instance of the institutionalization of functional representation involves an exchange: The organized group gives something up and gains something in return. However, the political reason for instituting such arrangements may well be to reduce power in one case (i.e., loss of power in the case of working-class organizations) and, in the next one, to grant autonomy (i.e., the right to "self-government" or privileged access to the institutions of government granted to pluralist groups for the sake of devolution). We would expect, then, that corporatization means quite different "terms of trade" for the different collectivities affected by it and that the trade-off of losses and gains differs depending on whether "restraint" or "delegation" is the prime motive. This two-sidedness of corporatism is essential: It implies restrictions imposed on the power base of groups as well as a gain in autonomy. It means "etatisation" of group politics in one case and "contracting out" of state power to private groups in another case. The question is what the balance of losses and gains, or discipline and autonomy, looks like in the case of particular groups and class organizations. Before we turn to this question, we have to look into the thorny problem of a functional explanation of the rise of corporatist arrangements.

Only after we understand the *functions* performed and the specific benefits achieved by interest group institutionalization can we explain why it is precisely corporatism – and not, say, the socialization of the means of production, the restoration of market forces uninhibited by monopolization and state intervention, or other solutions – that seems to be so attractive as a solution to the problems just mentioned in advanced capitalist economic and political systems.

In the next section I shall try to give two tentative answers to why it is precisely corporatism that becomes broadly considered and accepted as an effective and efficient solution to problems that we typically find in these systems. One answer deals with political institutions of the liberal democratic state, the other with class forces and their relative social power. In the final section of this chapter I shall explore the possibility that corporatism, in spite of its apparent virtues as a solution to some systemic problems of the political economy, turns out to be a mixed blessing, which may not only heal major institutional defects but also generates new patterns of political conflict.

In a developed corporatist system, a second circuit is added to the machinery of the democratic representative polity. The institutional order of which periodic elections, political parties, and parliamentary government are the main elements is supplemented by a political arrangement consisting of major organized interest groups, their relative procedural status, and bodies of consultation and reconciliation. The characteristic feature of modern corporatism, in contrast to authoritarian models of corporatism (cf. Mayer-Tasch, 1971), is the *coexistence* of the two circuits with only a limited substitution of functional for territorial representation. The advantage of corporatist modes of interest representation over democratic representative ones resides in the potential of the former for *depoliticizing conflict*, that is, in restricting both the scope of the participants in conflict and the scope of strategies and tactics that are permitted in the pursuit of conflicting interests. The explanation of such a shift would be that more traditional arrangements generate more conflict than can be processed. Traditional channels of the democratic policy lead to "overparticipation" or an "overload" of unresolved issues. The major reason for the attractiveness of corporatist rearrangements of political decision making is its presumably greater capacity to deal with conflict.

In order to support this argument, it is essential to demonstrate that the hypothesized "need" for depoliticization has actually become manifest in the political institutions of the democratic representative "circuit." The following sketchy observations on the West German political system may serve to make it plausible that such a need exists. These observations concentrate (1) on the functions performed by political parties and (2) on dilemmas of bureaucratic policy making and policy implementation.

Political parties

Political parties, according to democratic representative theory, are to perform the dual function of aggregating votes, thereby providing the major channel for political participation to citizens, and designing comprehensive programmatic policy alternatives to be executed once the party has achieved sufficient electoral success to occupy government positions. There is considerable agreement among political scientists that parties today are much more successful in performing the first function – attracting voter support – than the second function – designing coherent policy alternatives. This is certainly true in the West German case. Whereas the voters vote for political parties, or even the government personnel representing political parties, political parties seem no longer to be the main authors of programmatic policy decisions. Such policy decisions (e.g., on tax reform, nuclear energy, economic policies, education reform, etc.) tend to result not from intraparty deliberations and consensus building but, rather, from interparty negotiations involving the parties in coalition.[7] Or else the proposals emerge from and are advocated by clearly identifiable segments, wings, and factions within the party and fail to get approval of the party as a whole. In fact, there is presently not one major issue of domestic policy making on which one party opposes another party more strongly than factions oppose each other within one and the same party. It is hardly an exaggeration to argue that the party as a political institution has ceased to perform the function of formulating and securing agreement on programmatic policy guidelines. More often than not, such decisions emerge from levels either superior (coalition government) or inferior (faction) to the party level.[8] This condition might well be explained as the paradoxical effect of the secular transformation of "class parties" into "mass integration parties" (Volksparteien). The more diffuse and heterogeneous the electoral basis of a party, and the more it attenuates its theoretical and ideological identity in order to become acceptable to as many groups and strata within the electorate as possible, the less it can decide on clear-cut policy options and alternatives. The erosion of the identity of political parties is also reflected in the changes in the organizational structure of the Christian Democrats and the Social Democrats that result from an increase in the strength of interest group wings and fractions within parties. Both the Social Committees (Sozialausschuesse) and the Economic Council (Wirtschaftsrat) of the CDU, as well as the Committee for Labor Questions (Arbeitsgemeinschaft fuer Arbeitnehmerfragen) and the Young Socialists (Jungsozialisten) within the SPD, have become major centers of intraparty conflict (as well as channels for intraparty political careers). The dissolution of party identities, originally hailed as a healthy sign of the "end of ideology" and the victory of the "catch-all-party" model, seems to have resulted in the growing inability of political parties to perform a major function. The burden of building a programmatic consensus on policies is shifted to the level of coalition governments.

This condition of often unresolvable intraparty conflict, plus the concomitant instability of governing party coalitions, generates the need for simpler, more reliable and predictable ways of reaching policy agreements. Governments depend on more direct supportive relations to major organized interests, and thus supplementary corporatist relations (as well as more plebiscitarian practices of government conduct) are the solution to a problem emerging from the disorganization of political parties. Somewhat contrary to Lehmbruch's notion of an alternative mode of consensus building being "increasingly required for economic steering," I would argue that it is not any specific characteristic of the policy area in question (i.e., economic steering) that gives rise to corporatist structures but the failure of political parties to perform as agents of the "formation of political will of the people" (a task that the West German Constitution assigns to political parties) and the "functional gap in consensus-building" that results.

Bureaucratic policy making and policy implementation
There is still another gap that corporatist modes of interest representation are more likely to close than any other political arrangement. This gap becomes visible when we look at the policy "techniques" through which a government can control certain critical variables in its environment, that is, national and international society. To summarize what I have elaborated elsewhere (Offe, 1975:Chap. 3), there are three basic alternatives, or policy methods, that can be applied to attain such control, and they appear to be used in a certain sequence and cumulatively, due to inherent limitations. The first of these methods of political control is the application of positive and/or negative incentives that are intended to modify courses of action citizens choose to follow. Hypothetical consequences (monetary rewards, punishment, etc.) are attached to specified kinds of action or inaction, so as to induce individual actors to produce the desired aggregate outcome. The limitation of this method of political control becomes manifest whenever actors do *not* respond to such incentives, especially if there are actors who are strategically placed to ignore incentives; an example of the latter occurs when a business firm does not react positively to tax exemptions and other benefits *and* when the failure to react is due to the expectation that a higher dose of incentives will, as a consequence, be offered by government. Sooner or later the exclusive use of this method becomes too costly in fiscal terms (or otherwise impractical as far as detailed surveillance of behavior and administration of sanctions are concerned).

The additional method of political control that is likely to be put into practice then is transformation of the production and distribution of certain goods and services into "public goods," increasing state spending for investment and consumption infrastructure, nationalization of certain vital industries, and so forth. The underlying theory in this second method of political control is that a framework of conditions is created that individual actors *cannot* escape even if they want to. Reliance on this method of political control, however, eventually stirs up significant political opposition to the regulations involved in producing and distributing these goods and services publicly and to the taxes required to finance them, which are interferences with individual freedom of choice and action. The objection is raised that such politically supplied goods and services cannot meet standards of efficiency and effectiveness. Active reformist policies of capitalist states have always encountered such resistance – be it in the area of welfare policies, socialized medicine, nationalized industries, education policies, and so forth.

The impasse of political techniques that are politically feasible but economically ineffective (namely, control by parametric incentives) and political techniques that might achieve the desired ends but are uncertain in their effectiveness and impractical because of political resistance (namely, the state production and distribution of "public goods") constitutes a favorable condition for corporatist rearrangements of the political structure. This third political technique rests on the premise that (1) the return to purely parametrical types of control is not tolerable and (2) the government cannot possibly acquire sufficient directive capacity to enable it to design and implement policies over the political resistance that interventionist programs are especially likely to provoke. What remains is the political method of absorbing potentially obstructive political resistance by granting "voice" options to those who are, due to the use of the second method, deprived of some of their "exit" options in order to prevent them from exerting their veto power on policies. The price for cooperation is to delegate parts of the policy-making power to those who might object to more "etatist" approaches to the solution of social and economic problems. Therefore procedural status is attributed to groups whose resistance could become critical to the implementation of policies.

In the areas of economic, labor market, education, and social policies the establishment of tripartite bodies (consisting of labor, capital, and state representatives) has become a widely used instrument of policy making. It leaves an often considerable range of discretion about public policy to intergroup negotiations. The resort to the method of tripartism suggests itself, as many observers have noted, because of its anticipated conflict-reducing effects. This effect can be the combined outcome of three separable mechanisms. First, the formal admission of corporate groups to the process of public policy formation favors the production of decisions that minimize the probability that social power will be used in order to obstruct or resist public policy, because the actual power of labor and capital, respectively, are already "registered" and taken into account in the process of its formation. Second, to the extent that interest organizations do control the attitudes and behavior of their members (which is, as we shall see, more likely in the case of labor than in that of business organizations), this organizational discipline can be used to prevent opposition from groups within the organization's membership. In this way the authority of the group's leadership is, so to speak, added to that of the state. Thus it functions as a mechanism of extended governmental control. Third, in case a policy meets or creates conflict and opposition, in spite of these safety mechanisms, the government alone is not to blame: All the actors that have participated in the process of making the decision in question would be held responsible. This makes such opposition less likely than otherwise, for any "relevant" opposing group would have to attack not only the government but also its own leadership. Combined, these three mechanisms can be expected to reduce the likelihood and intensity of conflict over public policy, and thus to depoliticize public life.

The fact that such corporatist policy-making bodies often provide equal rights and equal numbers of representatives to labor and capital does not contradict the conclusion that a partial privatization of political power takes place. For in these bodies, the use of political power becomes a group privilege (1) as far as common interests of all participating groups are concerned, which may well differ from a politically defined "common interest" and (2) as far as equal votes of labor and capital by no means balance differences of market power that prevail, due to structural as well as conjunctural reasons, between the demand and supply sides of the labor market. As soon as we have left the realm of those political institutions for which democratic representative political theory can provide legitimation (as we certainly have if we consider, say, the tripartite managing board of the West German labor market agency [*Verwaltungsrat der Bundesanstalt fuer Arbeit*]), a 50:50 proportion of votes for labor and capital is by no means more justifiable than is either 10:90 or 90:10. The only virtue of the 50:50 formula is that of creating the appearance that things are open and not decided in advance on the level of procedural rules, thereby relieving the state that has instituted such "balance" from objections of either of the two sides.

To summarize the argument, corporatist structures are the solution to situations in which parametrical methods of political control have become insufficient for economic reasons and interventionist methods have become impractical for political ones. In such situations, parademocratic political structures serve to contain and depoliticize conflict in a fragile reconciliation of the functionally required and the politically feasible.

Differential impact of corporatization on the organizations of labor and capital

Thus far, the analysis has led us to the identification of two "gaps," or instances of malfunctioning of the institutions of democratic representative government, which are serious enough to explain the resort to corporatist political structures: One is the erosion of party identities, the other is the typical impasse in bureaucratic design and implementation of policies. Explaining corporatist tendencies from institutional defects, however, is at best an intermediary step toward a theory of corporatism. It raises the questions: (1) Why do political parties, at least in the West German case, seem increasingly unable to catalyze the "political will of the people"? and (2) Why, in turn, has bureaucratic policy-making capacity declined?

Instead of speculating about causes of political decay, I prefer, rather, to explore some of the consequences of corporatist changes in the political structure. Here my argument will be that corporatist transformation not only compensates for the functional deficiencies of democratic institutions by depoliticizing conflict in terms of groups, issues, and tactics but also that it does so in an *asymmetrical* way. First, I want to demonstrate that organizations of labor and capital, although affected by exactly the *same* forms of institutionalization (i.e., attribution of political status, which provides them with the license to participate directly and jointly in the process of policy formation), are inhibited to a greatly *differing* extent in their freedom to pursue their respective interests, and, second, I argue that current proposals for interest group institutionalization are specifically *designed* so as to impose much more far-reaching restrictions on labor than on capital.

The social power of both capital and labor rests on ultimate sanctions of economic obstruction or withdrawal. Capital can threaten to discontinue its purchases of capital goods and labor power; and labor, to withhold labor power. The power of economic obstruction distinguishes labor and capital from traditional middle-class interests and interest groups, such as farmers and shopkeepers. Because very often there are too many of them in the first place, withdrawal of their contributions to the economic process would not help to improve their economic situation but would simply accelerate an economic process against which members of the traditional middle class indeed are trying to defend themselves. It is for this *economic* reason that if the traditional middle class is to win at all, it must withdraw *political* resources (votes) or become politically active (as in demonstrations, etc.), which is why the old middle class defies definition and analysis in economic terms (cf. Berger, Chapter 3, this volume).

Although the social power of both labor and capital rests on the possibility of withdrawing something, their organizations play a different role in mobilizing these sanctions. Whereas capital can bring its obstructive power to bear even *if it is not* organized as an interest group, the withdrawal of labor power can function as an instrument of power only if it is practiced *collectively*, that is, if it is organized in at least a rudimentary way. If a firm decides not to invest and/or not to employ workers, its decision is made autonomously on the level of the individual accumulating unit and in accordance with calculations of individual profitability. If workers decide to strike, they need some mechanism of aggregation and coordination; individual attempts to exercise their "negative" market power would be, in all but the most exceptional cases, negligible in effect and therefore counterproductive from the viewpoint of the individual actor.

Moreover, workers' interests are normally divided not only between different strata and segments of the working class but, as it were, within the individual worker. In contrast to business firms, workers do not have an unequivocal standard of "rationality" by which they can "optimize" among conflicting ends. Workers are always simultaneously interested in wages, continuity of employment, and working conditions. As long as they live in capitalist market societies according to the rules of which labor is treated as *if it were* a commodity, those three ends or interests remain to some extent mutually exclusive. The "optimal" mix of those conflicting ends cannot be calculated by individuals but only collectively by an organization. *Organization* thus provides both the quantitative aggregation of the *means* of power and the qualitative definition of the *ends* to which power is to be applied. This dual role is reflected in the importance working-class organizations have always attributed to such nonindividualistic principles as "solidarity" and "discipline." In other words, workers' organizations – in contrast to business organizations – are effective only to the extent that they manage to suspend partially the ties of their members to the environment of individualistic monetary incentives.

Neither of these principles is of major significance in the internal operation of employers' and investors' associations. Such organizations do not generate power that does not already exist, nor do they formulate ends that do not derive directly from the ends that are already defined and consciously pursued at the level of the individual member firms. What the organization does is provide services to member firms (which in this way may achieve a substantial cost reduction relative to a situation in which they would have to provide such services themselves) and to formulate and defend in the political arena those *individual* interests (relating to taxes, tariffs, regulation of industrial relations, etc.) that are *common* to all or most member firms. In contrast to unions, employers and investors associations do not create power and definitions of interest as the result of an organized process of mobilization and internal discourse among members; they merely state power positions that are already established and interest definitions that are already decided on.[9] Interest *organization* is thus much more essential to the defense and promotion of labor interests than to capital interests, because capital, mergers, monopolies, cartels, and so forth are the decisive instruments of enhancing social power. Conversely, restrictive political regulation of the forms of association and organizational activities must have a stronger impact on labor organizations than on employers'/investors' organizations.

Given that the power of labor and capital resides in their potential for obstruction, and given the unfeasibility of *eliminating* the power of either by political means, interest organizations must be subjected to constitutional forms and responsibility, so the argument runs (cf. Boeckenfoerde, 1976:475; Teubner, 1977). To the extent that such institutionalization is inspired by principles of democratic representation and aims at democratizing relations between the organization and its individual members, the group's participation in public policy making will gain in legitimacy.

It is obvious, however, that internal democratization cannot provide the same measure of legitimacy to interest organizations as it is able to provide, according to democratic representative theory, to governments, because it is not the entire people but functionally defined organization members who "legitimize" organization policies. Moreover, as becomes evident from a recent legislative proposal written by a committee of the Liberal party (FDP), the principle of internal "democratization" has very different meanings for labor and capital. Its (latent) function is not to confer greater legitimacy on corporatist elements within the political structure but to make it more difficult for labor in particular to mobilize power through organization. Although the proposal never specifically mentions unions but is rather intended to apply to "all politically significant associations," the organizational rules it imposes on such organizations would have quite selective impacts for organizations defending and promoting *workers'* interests as a result of the differences between labor and capital previously discussed. For instance, section 6 of the proposed law requires all interest organizations to "limit clearly" in their statutes those interests on which the organization wishes to represent its members. Because capital organizations are generally not instrumental in *articulating* those interests but simply in stating and transmitting them, it is much easier for them to comply with this specific requirement than it is for labor organizations, whose first task is to formulate a unified interest, the specifics of which cannot be stated in advance. If a union were forced to do so, this would limit its range of legitimate issues and activities – including those that might well be considered to bear on the defense of workers' interests. Similarly, the absence of a "calculus of optimization" in the case of unions that could be used to reconcile conflicting goals makes intra- or interorganization competition, disunity, and rivalry much more likely in labor unions than in business organizations. Here the question is to what extent unions achieve, in spite of such divisions, some measure of unity. Such unity is less likely to be achieved if the law prescribes the extensive protection of minorities (section 14), if it guarantees to nonmembers a legal claim to membership, taking partially away from the organization the right to deny admission (section 10), if it punishes acts of an interest organization designed "to discriminate against competing interest organizations" (section 22), if it requires state agencies to "give equal treatment to competing organizations with parallel goals" and to "maintain pluralism" among them (sections 4, 23), and finally if it entitles members to sue organizations in court for "partisan one-sidedness in representation or information of members" (section 25). Although these rules are meant to apply equally to labor and capital organizations, their impact will be highly asymmetrical, causing increased divisions and fragmention only within the former.[10]

Other proposals, too, for interest group institutionalization are quite explicit about the aim of taming "radical" and "irresponsible" inclinations within organizations to which political status is attributed, especially unions.

Yet another reason for the class bias of corporatist interest group institutionalization must be discussed. We have argued before that organization and leadership are of particular importance to the defense and promotion of working-class interests because they provide the only means of uniting and reconciling the social power of labor that otherwise would remain atomized in means and fragmented in ends. If this is true, any constraints imposed on the leadership and the forms in which organizational activities are conducted will have direct consequences for the type of demands that are being made as well as the intensity and unity by which they can be supported. Control of institutional form means at least partial control of political content and demands – in the case of labor, but not in the case of capital. Contrary to labor unions, capital organizations do not have any substantial control over the actions that their *members* choose to pursue. The attribution of political status to employers'/investors' groups therefore does not justify any expectation that the behavior of *member units* of such organizations will thereafter be under any greater political control than before such status was attributed. The traffic runs in one direction, because the viewpoint of organized capital can be transmitted to the political system but the spokesmen of these groups can make no binding commitments[11] and seem to have no more than a highly informal and unreliable influence on the behavior of their member units. In contrast, institutionalization in the case of unions means an exchange transaction in which cooperation is traded for formal participation in policy decision or moderation is achieved as a consequence of imposed "democratic" organization rules. No such "return" can be safely expected from government interaction with investor interest groups. Paradoxically, the political power of investors depends to some extent on the condition of *power-lessness* of their interest organizations, which have, neither de lege nor de facto, more than marginal control over members' investment decisions. What the government can do, then, in order to secure the willingness of investors to cooperate, is to design policies that are most conducive to profits – which remain the only channel by which investors are to be "controlled" – and win the support of organized labor for such policies (cf. Boeckenfoerde, 1976:480, 483). Only with this important qualification can we speak of corporatism as implying a "shift from a supportive to a directive role for the state in the economy" (Winkler, 1976:103).

Alternative patterns of political conflict

In what direction and within which limits will corporatist changes in political structure affect the intensity of social and political conflict and its content? In order to explore these interconnections, I shall sketch three alternative cases, one stable and two unstable.

Stable corporatism
Stable corporatism is a condition in which corporatist political structures succeed in providing an interest group consensus unchal-

lenged by radical or "immoderate" demands or tactics of conflict. The viability of this solution depends on how the political system manages to deal with the basic theoretical (as well as highly practical) deficiency of corporatist arrangements, namely, that no legitimizing principle can be provided for this particular fusion of private power and political authority. Why should *these* interest groups, in particular, be admitted to policy-making positions (instead of other groups)? Why should they be licensed to decide on *these* issues (as opposed to any wider or narrower agenda)? Or why should they follow *these* (rather than any other) procedural rules? Answers to these kinds of questions are, if given at all, at best pragmatic and hence debatable. Even if questions of justification of a particular institutional arrangement are usually of concern mainly to intellectuals, and of little concern to most people most of the time, will this indifference continue when significant material advantages are at issue? The ongoing debate on industrial codetermination as well as on macro- and sectoral codetermination in West Germany demonstrates that there are hardly any generally agreed-on principles about which group deserves what political status. Consequently, neither a "solution" nor the programmatic acceptance of given routines is in sight; but continued conflict is more probable. At the very least, corporatism, in order to be stable, must not only continually *generate* consensus; it must first of all *presuppose* consensus, that is, a solid and undisputed acceptance of a certain mode of interest representation and accommodation.

This requires, first, a certain tradition and organization of labor unions, which results in their willingness to accept the rules of "social partnership" (*Sozialpartnerschaft*), so "countries with a conflict-oriented labor movement are not well suited for liberal corporatism" (Lehmbruch, 1977:115). Apart from political traditions of the national working class, the attitude of "social partnership" seems to be reinforced by the organizational doctrine of a "unitary" union (*Einheitsgewerkschaft*), as opposed to organization by partisan affiliation or organization by trade; this type of organization is favorable to the maintenance of a highly "cooperative" attitude, because West German "unitary" unions are quite fragmented internally but lack the centralized political mechanisms to resolve their internal factional disputes (cf. Bergmann et al., 1975; Boeckenfoerde, 1976:483). Second, this condition of undisputed acceptance can be maintained if those oppositional forces that are unwilling to comply with the rules of corporatist political structures are deprived of some of their political and civil rights. Finally, corporatist arrangements could win de facto acceptance if the goals of prosperity and growth are accomplished to an extent that makes the quest for – and the conflict over – principles legitimizing such arrangements irrelevant. Although economic crisis, as Winkler maintains, is a precipitating factor in corporatist arrangements, it seems unlikely that prosperity will resolve or even obscure the issue of legitimacy.

Without engaging in social prophecy, all we can say is that if corporatist political structures develop and stabilize, this most probably will be due to specific national traditions and forms of organization of the labor movement and/or to a high level of political repression and/or to a condition of uninterrupted economic prosperity.

Increase in noninstitutional political conflict

The standard liberal warning against corporatist arrangements (or at least their extension) is that subjecting interest groups to overly rigid status obligations might reduce their "integrating capacity" and hence undermine their ability to influence and discipline rank-and-file members, who would rather engage in conventional and unpredictable modes of conflict (cf. Scharpf 1978:37). This argument clearly focuses primarily on the unions because, as we have seen, other interest organizations do not have any significant measure of control or influence over their constituencies. A wave of unexpected unofficial strikes that broke out in Germany in September 1969 is often cited in evidence to support this claim. These strikes were disapproved of by unions and partly directed against union leadership. Another recent phenomenon that is often interpreted as indicative of serious deficiencies in the "integrating power" of interest groups (and political parties) is a dramatic increase of militant citizen groups and single-purpose movements focusing on urban, environmental, educational, and other issues (*Buergerinitiativen*) and occasionally using violent tactics. Thus the second scenario would be one of polarization between highly institutionalized modes of representation of "core" interests and highly amorphous social movements of "marginal" segments of the social structure. This pattern of conflict appears most likely to emerge where core interests are not only highly institutionalized but also have interacted in a way that suggests the disappearance of conflict and outright class collaboration.

In such situations, the archetypal image of the "traitor" tends to be projected on unions, Social Democratic and Communist parties, or parliamentary government as such. This image in turn provides justification for focusing on particularistic identities and causes as being the only thing left that is worth struggling for. For instance, there has hardly ever been a more sudden increase in noninstitutional political conflict in postwar Germany than in December 1966, when the Christian Democrats and the Social Democrats formed a "grand coalition" government. The current large antinuclear energy movement in West Germany received broad support when cases of collaboration between union officials and nuclear energy industry bordering on corruption became public.

Two important consequences follow from the polarization between institutional and noninstitutional conflict. The first is that such movements may well be able to undermine the feeble legitimacy of political institutions, to disseminate feelings of suspicion and cynicism, and sometimes even to interfere with the functioning of political institutions. The second is that such "marginal" militancy, without any tradition, theoretical foundations, or organizations, will be unable to establish the coherence and continuity that would be needed in order to create a serious alternative to what it perceives as the solid alliance in power of the corruptor and the corrupted. Taken together, these two aspects suggest the scenario of a standoff confrontation, unproductive of major social changes except for an escalation of repression and violence.

Balancing the class bias of corporatism

This third scenario includes developments that result from the two unresolved tensions inherent in any corporatist system. One, as we have seen, is the class bias of corporatist arrangements, the depoliticizing effect of which favors capital organizations and discriminates against labor organizations. The other inherent tension is the polarizing effect that leads to a joint increase of both institutionalization of conflict *and* noninstitutional conflict.

These tensions could precipitate a process in which, in order to maintain the loyalty and allegiance of their rank-and-file members, union leaders would insist on demands and strive for accomplishments that are impossible to achieve *unless* the inherent bias of corporatism is overcome. This would require equalizing the participatory status of labor and capital within the framework of economic policy-making institutions so as to make agreements binding on investors to the same extent as they already have been accepted as binding by unions in the past. More specifically, it would mean that economic programs on which agreement has been achieved in tripartite policy-making bodies can be put into effect irrespective of whether or not investors, who are represented at the bargaining table by their respective interest organization, find it individually profitable to comply with such programs. This, of course, would imply doing away with a key element of the property right of investors, namely, the right *not* to invest, which is the source of the social power of private capital. Because unions, by accepting the status obligations assigned to them and by participating in tripartite policy making, *do* in fact give up some of the right to struggle more militantly for more far-reaching demands, an analogous "sacrifice" of employers'/ investors' interest groups could hardly be considered disproportionate. It would, however, shake the economic system at its foundations.

The idea of developing and using forms of functional representation to expand working-class power has a long tradition in the European labor movement. For instance, the concept of "functional democracy," according to which factory councils and workers' cooperatives were to play a strategic role in securing Socialist power and overcoming bourgeois hegemony in the Parliament and administration, was central to the programmatic thinking of Austro-Marxism (cf. Adler, 1926:151–8) and has been taken up by some Euro-Communists. Even if not thought of as an instrument of Socialist transformation, the possibility has been raised that, contrary to the intentions of its inventors, the political status attributed to unions within the policy-making apparatus of the state might become usable not as a means of containing the working class but to enhance its power. Esping-Andersen et al. argued in a recent article:

> Corporatism is an internally contradictory mode of incorporating the working class. The premise of a corporatist strategy is that the inclusion of . . . working class organization . . . in formal state planning processes will reduce working class opposition to state policies without requiring massive concessions to popular demands. . . . If [however, the working class] leadership maintains close ties to the working class and remains a legitimate instrument of real working class organizations . . . [this will] undermine the planning function of corporatism and brings class struggle into the administrative heart of the state apparatus itself. (Esping-Andersen et al., 1976:197; cf. Jessop, 1978:10)

As is the case with the two other scenarios, it is not difficult to find indications in present West Germany that lend some plausibility to the expectation that things will develop along these lines. For instance, union models of "co-determination beyond plant level" (*überbetriebliche Mitbestimmung*) have since 1971 been a demand in the trade-union (DGB) program that was given highest priority by union leadership. Union leaders and intellectuals close to the unions argue that wage restraints must be compensated for by institutional gains, because otherwise the legitimacy of unions would suffer in the eyes of rank-and-file members. After the Federation of German Employers Associations (BDA) had filed legal complaints over a recent codetermination act with the Supreme Court, the unions for the first time used their option of strategic nonparticipation and refused to continue to cooperate in the "concerted action." And one conservative opposition leader warned in Parliament that concerted action was in danger of being inadvertently transformed into an instrument of macro-codetermination. The issue may no longer be participation as such but, rather, the equalization of the extent to which parties will be constrained by decisions reached within corporatist policy-making bodies.

How likely an outcome this is may well be questioned, especially in view of the present condition of high unemployment, which generally tends to force unions to adopt defensive and cooperative strategies. One also must question the prospects for either of the two alternative scenarios. Which of them, if any, will be realized is certainly beyond the responsibility of the social scientist to predict.

Acknowledgments

Apart from the members of the Committee on Western Europe, I have received stimulating comments and criticisms on two earlier drafts of this paper from Rolf Heinze, Stephan Leibfried, Leo Panitch, and Jack Winkler.

Notes

1 An early example of the relation between new "output objectives" of public policy on the one side and new "input arrangements" on the other is, in German history, found in the coincidence of Bismarck's social security legislation and simultaneous legislation outlawing the activity of the Social Democrats. Less well known than this often-analyzed parallelism is that Bismarck's social policy innovations coincided with the creation of a corporatist constitutional body, the Preussischer Volkswirtschaftsrat (1881-7), which formed one major element of what Wehler describes as "authoritarian interest group syndicalism" (Wehler, 1975:90). This "National Economic Council" was the earliest corporatist experiment in modern German constitutional history, and it is interesting to note that most of its activity concerned consensus building among industrial, commercial, and agricultural interests on the new social policy (Dotzenrath, 1932:4). New policy programs, the adoption and implementation of new state functions, seem to require new participants (or nonparticipants) in the political process and new institutional forms of interest intermediation.

2 For a critical analysis of the short-lived "Formierte Gesellschaft" campaign of 1965, see Opitz, 1965. Erhard's programmatic statement can be found in his speech "Programm für Deutschland," Protokolle des 13. Bundesparteitages der CDU, Bonn, 1965. Although the concept of "societal formation" has been dropped from the Christian Democratic party program, the idea that the major task required of the party is to implement a "policy of order" (*Ordnungspolitik*) for the transition from the pluralist to a postpluralist stage of industrial society, including the developmental scheme already mentioned, certainly has not. Among the most recent documents proving this point, see the two volumes by W. Dettling (ed.). For a lucid analysis of parallel American and British ideas developing in the late fifties, see Draper (1961), who seems to be one of the first authors to apply the term "neo-corporatism."

3 The issue of granting (or reducing) political status to organized groups is of course a particularly sensitive one to the SPD. Proposals for an alteration of the political design of liberal democracy are most likely to affect the power position of the trade unions

negatively. But friendly and cooperative relations with the unions are traditionally considered a major political asset by Social Democratic and Labor parties. Therefore the only kind of institutional changes to be seriously and openly considered by a Social Democratic administration are those that involve at least apparent status gains for the unions.

4 For an illustration of the two-sided *noblesse oblige effects* of political status attribution, we might consider the extreme cases. Even in the case where a group is attributed the absolute *negative* political status of illegality or prohibition, its (at least temporarily effective) gains resulting therefrom consist in the solidarity and support obtained from other groups and organizations as well as in new tactical opportunities resulting from "going underground." This consequence, incidentally, is reflected in the usual second thoughts reactionary regimes are having regarding their own calls for "outlawing" Communist parties. Inversely, even the attribution of the most *privileged* political status to interest groups does regularly force them to at least use more moderate and more broadly acceptable language in stating and pursuing their interests.

5 Many of the recent students of neo-corporatist phenomena and developments seem to agree on the point that the corporatist status of interest organizations is "new" because of the "nonideological" nature of the legitimations offered to justify such transformations. Moreover, as Harris has demonstrated for the British case, the incorporation of interest groups into the state apparatus and the constitutional reliance on the principle of "functional" – rather than "territorial" – representation has always been among the constitutional aims of both Socialist and conservative movements. What is new about *neo*-corporatism is its "nonideological" origin and its peaceful coexistence with parliamentary doctrines and practices.

6 For instance, Panitch, arguing from a class theoretical perspective, insists in his discussion of corporatism that it is a political form that "is not so general as to encompass... any interest-group state relation," but that is rather specific to the "associations of business and labor" (Panitch, 1978:2,3). He then ends by narrowing the concept of corporatism by describing it as "a political form designed to integrate the organized working class in the capitalist state (Panitch, 1978:44). Similarly, Bob Jessop argues that "it is the involvement of organized labor that is distinctive about corporatism" (Jessop, 1978:15). In sharp contrast and not without considerable plausibility, Schmitter develops the concept of corporatism in view "of highly organized and specialized representatives of class, sectoral, regional, sexual and generational interests," which form "complexes of specialized associations often bypassing, if not boycotting, more traditional and more general partisan and legislative structures of articulation and aggregation" (1977:7–8).

7 Sometimes they even appear to be the outcome of what has been called a latent all-party coalition, to which German politicians often appeal by the standard phrase "solidarity of all democrats" (*Solidaritaet aller Demokraten*).

8 One could even argue that programmatic alternatives and innovations do increasingly originate from sources outside the formally constituted national political system. Such sources include, in the West German case, the Protestant church, organized science, and extraparliamentary single-issue movements; also the imitation of foreign examples appears often to play an important innovative function.

9 For similar arguments emphasizing the different nature of labor and capital interest organizations, cf. Preuss (1969:170 ff.) and Ehrlich (1966:272).

10 For the more limited argument that politically imposed "democratization" may well be considered as being contrary to the interests of group members, see Foehr (1976:50) and Mueller (1977:40). Further proposals for democratizing internal structures of interest groups are summarized in Teubner (1977:24–5).

11 *Knowing* that they are not binding for their constituencies anyway, employers' and investors' organizations can – and frequently do – make public commitments of the most popular sort. For interesting historical evidence supporting the argument (1) that big industry does not really need interest organizations in order to be politically successful and (2) that their interest organizations are unable to impose a binding discipline on employers and investors, see Abromeit (1977).

Bibliography

Abromeit, H., "Interessendurchsetzung in der Krise." *Aus Politik und Zeitgeschichte* (supplement to *Das Parlament*) 11 (1977):15–37.

Adler, M., *Politische oder soziale Demokratie* (Berlin: Lamb, 1926).

Anderson, C. W., "Political Design and the Representation of Interests." *Comparative Political Studies* 10(1977):127–52.

Beer, S., *British Politics in the Collectivist Age*. New York: Random House, 1969.

Bergmann, J., et al. *Gewerkschaften in der Bundesrepublik*. Gewerkschaftliche Lohnpolitik zwischen Mitgliederinteressen und oekonomischen Systemzwaengen. Frankfurt/M.: EVA, 1975.

Gräfin von Bethusy-Huc, V., "Vorschläge zur Kontrolle des Verbandseinflusses im parlamentarischen Regierungssystem." *Macht der Verbaende – Ohnmacht der Demokratie*: Beitraege zur Theorie und Politik der Verbaende, ed. W. Dettling. Muenchen: Olzog, 1976, pp. 221–36.

Boeckenfoerde, E. W., "Die politische Funktion wirtschaftlich-sozialer Verbaende und Interessentraeger in der sozialstaatlichen Demokratie." *Der Staat* 15(1976):457–83.

Dettling, W., ed. *Macht der Verbaende – Ohnmacht der Demokratie?* Beitraege zur Theorie und Politik der Verbaende. Muenchen: Olzog, 1976.

Dettling, W., et al. *Die Neue Soziale Frage und die Zukunft der Demokratie*. Bonn: Eichholz, 1976.

Dotzenrath, F. J., *Wirtschaftsraete und die Versuche zu ihrer Verwirklichung in Preussen-Deutschland*. Diss: Koeln, 1932.

Draper, H., "Neo-Corporatists and Neo-Reformers." *New Politics* 1(1961):81–106.

Ehrlich, S., *Die Macht der Minderheit*. Wien: Europa, 1966.
"On Functional Representation," *Sprache und Politik*. Festschrift fuer Dolf Sternberger zum sechzigsten Geburtstag, eds. C. J. Friedrich/B. Reifenberg Heidelberg: Schneider, 1968, pp. 326–39.

Enquete-Kommission Verfassungsreform des Deutschen Bundestages. *Beratungen und Empfehlungen zur Verfassungsreform*, 2 vols., Bonn, 1977.

Eschenburg, T., *Herrschaft der Verbaende?* Stuttgart: Kohlhammer, 1955.

Esping-Andersen, G., et al. "Modes of Class Struggle and the Capitalist State." *Kapitalistate* 4/5(1976):186–220.

Foehr, H., "Innere Demokratie in den Verbaenden." *Freiheit in der sozialen Demokratie*. Materialien zum 4. rechtspolitischen Kongress der SPD, Berlin, 1976.

Freie Demokratische Partei. *Entwurf eines Verbaendegesetzes*. Released Bonn, April 26, 1977.

Goldthorpe, J., "Industrial Relations in Great Britain: A Critique of Reformism." *Politics and Society* 4(1974).

Harris, N., *Competition and the Corporate Society*. London: Methuen, 1972.

Hauff, V., and Scharpf, F. W., *Modernisierung der Volkswirtschaft: Technologiepolitik als Strukturpolitik*. Frankfurt/M.: EVA, 1975.

Ionescu, G., *Centripetal Politics: Government and the New Centers of Power*. London: Hart-Davis, 1975.

158   CLAUS OFFE

Jessop, B., "Corporatism, Fascism and Social Democracy." Unpublished paper, 1978.

Kevenhoerster, P., "Kollektive Gueter und organisierte Interessen – Zur Steuerungskapazitaet politischer Institutionen gegenueber organisierten Sozialinteressen," *Macht der Verbaende – Ohnmacht der Demokratie?* Beitraege zur Theorie und Politik der Verbaende, ed. W. Dettling. Muenchen: Olzog, 1976, pp. 189–220.

Lehmbruch, G., "Liberal Corporatism and Party Government," Paper for the IPSA Congress. Edinburgh, 1976. Revised version in *Comparative Political Studies* 10 (1977):91–126.

Lowi, T., *The End of Liberalism.* New York: W. W. Norton, 1969.

Maier, C., *Recasting Bourgeois Europe.* Princeton, N.J.: Princeton University Press, 1975.

Mayer-Tasch, P. C. *Korporativismus und Autoritarismus.* Frankfurt: Athenaeum, 1971.

Mayntz, R., and Scharpf, F. W., *Policy Making in the German Federal Bureaucracy.* Amsterdam: Elsevier, 1976.

Mueller, E., "Das Unbehagen an den Verbaenden." *Aus Politik und Zeitgeschichte* 8(1977):36–44.

Naphtali, F., *Wirtschaftsdemokratie.* Berlin: Verlagsgesellschaft des Allgemeinèn deutschen gewerkschaftsbundes gmbH, 1928.

Nocken, U., "Corporatism and Pluralism in Modern German History." *Industrielle Gesellschaft und politisches System,* eds. D. Stegmann et al. Beitraege zur politischen Sozialgeschichte. Festschrift fuer Fritz Fischer zum siebzigsten Geburtstag. Bonn: Verlag Neue Gesellschaft, 1978, pp. 37–56.

Offe, C., *Berufsbildungsreform: Eine Fallstudie ueber Reformpolitik.* Frankfurt/M.: Suhrkamp, 1975.

Offe, C., and Wiesenthal, H., "The Two Logics of Collective Action – Theoretical Notes on Social Class and the Political Form of Interest Representation." Forthcoming in: *Political Power and Social Theory* 1(1979).

Opitz, R., "Der grosse Plan der CDU: Die 'formierte Gesellschaft.'" *Blaetter fuer deutsche und internationale Politik* (9) (1965).

Panitch, L., "The Development of Corporatism in Liberal Democracies." *Comparative Political Studies* 10(1977):61–90.

"Corporatism in Canada?" Unpubl. paper, April 1978.

Preuss, U. K., *Zum staatsrechtlichen Begriff des Oeffentlichen.* Stuttgart: Klett, 1969.

Ruin, O., "Participatory Democracy and Corporatism: The Case of Sweden." *Scandinavian Political Studies* 9(1974):171–86.

Scharpf, F. W., *Die Funktionsfähigkeit der Gewerkschaften als Problem einer Verbändegesetzgebung.* Berlin: International Institute of Management, discussion paper 21, 1978.

Schmitter, P. C., "Models of Interest Intermediation and Models of Social Change in Western Europe," *Comparative Political Studies* 10(1977):2–38.

Shonfield, A., *Modern Capitalism – The Changing Balance of Public and Private Power.* London: Oxford University Press, 1965.

Teubner, G., "Verbaendedemokratie durch Recht?" *Aus Politik und Zeitgeschichte* 8 (1977).

Organisationsdemokratie und Verbandsverfassung. Rechtsmodelle für politisch relevante Verbände. Tübingen: Siebeck-Mohr, 1978.

Weber, W., *Spannungen und Kräfte im westdeutschen Verfassungssystem.* Berlin: Duncker and Humblot, 1970.

Wehler, H. U., *Das deutsche Kaiserreich 1871 bis 1918.* Göttingen: Vandenhoeck and Ruprecht, 1975.

Winkler, J. T., "Corporatism." *European Journal of Sociology* 17(1976):100–36.

6

German interest group alliances in war and inflation, 1914–1923

GERALD D. FELDMAN

The subject of this chapter provides historians of modern Germany with a particularly useful opportunity to remind their colleagues in the allied social sciences and, indeed, in their own field, that the widespread and continuing fascination with modern German history can be focused on problems other than those bearing on the origins and history of the Third Reich. Especially now that it has become clear that 1945 was not the caesura it was presumed to be, the long-term structural development of Germany's polity and society has become an even more promising object of social scientific investigation because of its continuing relevance to contemporary problems of social and political organization and governance. The fundamental reason for the richness and suggestiveness of the German experience – a condition that certainly must go a long way toward explaining the remarkable German contributions to the social sciences at the end of the last century and in the early part of the present century – has long been recognized. Thorstein Veblen early in the century and Ralf Dahrendorf more recently have emphasized the incongruities, disharmonies, and asymmetries that arose from the manner in which Germany developed into the most advanced industrial society in Europe without shedding its preindustrial sociopolitical order and value system.[1] In an analysis of particular pertinence to this chapter, Wolfram Fischer has pointed out that Germany developed a highly articulated system of interest groups and interest group politics to accompany its industrialization, although it failed to form with equal alacrity the fully developed system of political parties and parliamentary institutions that he views as its logical and desirable counterpart. Thus, the interest groups tended to preempt the functions of political parties and parliamentary institutions.[2]

German history in the modern period, as noted by these authors, has been characterized by a remarkable superimposition of cleavages arising from rapidly advancing industrialization on preindustrial cleavages of a confessional, regional, socioeconomic, and political nature. The superimposition of "modern" and "premodern" cleavages multiplied the difficulties of successful intermediation and exacerbated already severe problems of governance arising from the problematic manner in which German national unification was achieved and the failure to make the transition to parliamentary government.[3] Ending the analysis here, however, simply revives, on a more sophisticated level, the danger of turning German history into another kind of study of the aberrant, of a "faulted nation,"[4] in which an Anglo-American norm serves as a model for and the measure of some presumed necessary harmony between industrial development, on the one hand, and sociopolitical development, on the other. Working with this framework as a point of departure has been extraordinarily useful to students of German history in their efforts to break through old historicist arguments of German conservative historians that Germany was "unique" and had to be judged on its own terms rather than on those of "Western" models.[5] It also brought German historiography closer to the other social sciences, which in the fifties and early sixties were working with models of modernization, pluralism, and consensus politics.

Nevertheless, if historians of Germany are to follow Marc Bloch's injunction that "we can truly understand the past only if we read it by the light of the present,"[6] then they must at least reconsider judging the German experience only in terms of the Anglo-Saxon, pluralist, consensus models. This reconsideration is not suggested for the old historicist reasons but rather because it seems that German experience is more relevant to the development of industrialized and industrializing societies than had been previously supposed. To judge German history by the Anglo-American models today can lead one to conclude that either the "aberrations" have relocated themselves or they never were such extraordinary "aberrations" at all. On the one hand, England now appears to be paying every available penalty for "taking the lead." One could make the discomforting argument that the economic superannuation demarcated by the climacteric of the 1890s was inevitably accompanied by a relative retardation in England's institutional development and a long-term reduction in the effectiveness and functionality of those democratic and parliamentary institutions we are prone to laud so effusively. On the other hand, the United States can no longer boast the relatively uncrowded institutional terrain or benefit from the various safety valves that apparently rendered its social, political, and economic dysfunctionalities bearable and affordable in earlier times. America has more than made up for the time lost in its bureaucratization. The combination of world responsibility and relative loss of self-sufficiency have combined with secular developments in the American economy to reduce socioeconomic and political space and leeway. The American landscape is now crowded with a host of competing interest groups and organizations, and the nation suffers from crises of confidence and authority in both representative and executive institutions.[7] The "Americanization" of Europe is being followed by the "Europeanization" of America, although perhaps both processes have been going on concurrently for some time.

There is a tacit assumption in most of the historiography on the Weimar Republic that parliamentary ineffectiveness in the face of competing interest group demands was the specific result of some combination of Germany's weak democratic traditions and the peculiarly difficult endogenous and exogenous pressures under which Weimar democracy labored. It should now be apparent, however, that stronger democratic traditions do not forever ensure the potency of democratic institutions or the integration and control of interest group pressures once countries like England or the United States have developed expensive and bureaucratized welfare states that face destabilizing internal and external pressures of their own. The specific vulnerabilities of any society's democratic institutions should not be confused with those more general problems of democratic governance, which high economic growth and fantasies about the "end of ideology" had veiled so well. In short, a case can be made for the reexamination of national histories from the perspective of secular trends in the patterns of governance of advanced industrial societies operating within a capitalist framework.

Late Imperial and Weimar Germany, therefore, with their strong bureaucratic tradition and apparatus; their capitalism so luxuriantly and inchoately "organized" into a crowded mélange of firms, concerns, trusts, cartels, trade associations, peak associations, trade unions, and so on; their oscillations between a chaotic pluralism unsuccessfully integrated by executive and parliamentary institutions; and various mixtures of societal and state corporatism would seem to be much more a harbinger of twentieth-century advanced industrial societies than was previously imagined.[8] Thus, if we reconsider Wolfram Fischer's discussion of interest group development in Wilhelmine Germany already mentioned, one may question, as does Jürgen Kocka, whether Fischer is not missing the point in arguing that the tendencies toward the expansion of interest group functions stood in contradiction to its retarded parliamentarization. As Kocka notes, it was the precise intention of its backward constitution to encourage interest groups to usurp the functions of parties and parliaments.[9] It is possible to go further, however, and argue that the "backwardness" of the German constitution permitted Germany the "great leap forward" into modern interest group politics and interest group–state "wheeling and dealing" so common today and so often conducted at the expense of parties and parliaments. Indeed, from the present perspective, the Wilhelmine and Weimar proclivity to promote collaboration between interest groups and government and corporatist tendencies would suggest, leaving the question of political rights aside, that they were very "forward looking" indeed.

From these perspectives, the part played by interest groups in the protracted crisis of war and inflation that lasted from 1914 to 1923 is of particular interest. Because of their high state of development compared to their counterparts elsewhere and because the interest group "game" had received relatively greater encouragement in Germany than elsewhere, the German interest groups were fated to play a particularly important role in the crisis. The importance of interest groups can, however, be overemphasized. The German experience is useful not only as a particularly extreme illustration of interest group action in crisis but also as a reminder of the limits of interest group capabilities and the limitations of any analysis of historical or contemporary governance that focuses too exclusively on the role of interest groups. The real problem is where interest groups fit into a system of governance that includes bureaucratic and parliamentary institutions, and the German case, because of the rather extreme and explicit role played by interest groups and interest group alliances there, may be particularly illuminating. Interest group development, therefore, forms part of a general complex of phenomena and changes catalyzed by World War I in Germany and elsewhere in the industrial world. Germany was the leading industrialized contender in the war, most hard hit by its demands and privations and most affected by its consequences because of defeat. For these reasons, the continuity between wartime and postwar experience in Germany was also most pronounced. This chapter, therefore, will be divided into two parts. The first will consider tendencies arising out of the wartime experience, which will serve as the background for the second section dealing with the alliance of organized industry and organized labor in the early Weimar Republic.

Wartime tendencies

The first major trend during World War I was the vast expansion of the powers and functions of government and bureaucracy under conditions that required the development of "crisis management" methods and techniques. It was not enough to expand bureaucratic agencies and to create new ones; it was also necessary to involve society in new ways through the subcontracting of public functions to private corporate groups with the organization and expertise required for the economic war effort. The co-optation of these groups involved more than giving orders and engaging in state surveillance to make sure the various tasks were accomplished. It also required eliciting cooperation through concession and compromise. This was particularly true in the case of organized labor, which had been denied official recognition before the war but was now absolutely essential in the economic mobilization. Particularly after the decision to go over to "total war" in the fall of 1916, the government demanded that industry and labor compromise their differences, at least for the duration, and became the arbiter of their conflicts. In sum, the government presided over the organization and management of the economy and was compelled to employ the assistance of interest groups toward this end and thereby to integrate them into the structure of governance.[10]

A fundamental problem as this process developed was whether "crisis management" was to be nothing more than what the term implied, that is, a series of ad hoc, temporary measures, or whether the management of the wartime crisis was to mark the beginning of new and permanent forms of organization and socioeconomic management and planning. These alternatives were not simply implicit in the situation. They were openly articulated and literally embodied in the persons of Lt. Col. Josef Koeth, the head of the powerful Raw Materials Section of the Prussian War Ministry, and his antipode, the technocratic and corporatist ideologist, Wichard von Moellendorff, an engineer who, with his mentor, the industrialist Walther Rathenau, had helped to found the Raw Materials Section and had then played a key role in major aspects of organizing the war economy. Koeth was the practitioner of war economics par excellence: "War economy does not mean to run the economy in wartime in such a way as to create the least economic damage. War economy means rather to run it in such a way that one wins the war."[11] Koeth hated long-term programs, refused to think beyond immediate emergencies, distrusted planning and planners, and insisted on modest production targets designed to achieve rapid results. In economics this meant ruthless allocation policies without thought of future consequences. In matters of social policy, it meant satisfying industry's demands for high profits in a manner that did not provoke public uproar and labor's demands for high wages and other benefits to keep the workers quiet and working. Koeth elevated opportunism and decisionism to principles of governance.

For Moellendorff, in contrast, the war economy provided an unparalleled opportunity to create a German *Gemeinwirtschaft* under
which German capitalism would be organized in the spirit of Prussian
discipline and self-sacrifice and under which corporate groups would
administer a planned economy in the service of the national welfare.[12] In economics, this meant allocation policies designed to promote the rationalization of the economy, whereas in social relations it
meant restraints on profits and wages. Not suprisingly, the German
war economy was run in the style of Koeth, but the vision of
Moellendorff was shared by a powerful and ambitious group of
younger bureaucrats in the ministries who hoped someday to preside
over a corporatively administered economy guided by principles of
national interest and welfare. Germany's government and bureaucracy emerged from the war badly scarred by its failures; the most
serious of course was the loss of the war itself. This led to a crisis of
authority and loss of legitimacy, which culminated in the overthrow
of the imperial regime.[13] Throughout the war and subsequently, the
regime was accused of being too weak, too bureaucratic, and too
incompetent to deal with the crises it faced, and there were constant
demands for truly effective dictatorial agencies and strong men who
would get things done by putting the right experts in the right places.
Koeth and Moellendorff emerged as symbolic alternatives to traditional bureaucratic forms of governance for many of those seeking
more effective means of managing the crises.

Just as the extension of state powers served both to threaten its
authority and legitimacy by "overloading" it and to provoke schemes
for making it dictatorial, so – to turn to the second wartime trend – the
parliamentary institutions of Germany became at once more powerful
and less adequate to the tasks they faced.[14] In the initial phase of the
war, the government sought to use parliament as an instrument of
plebiscital acclamation for the war effort through the so-called
Burgfrieden under which the parties were expected to vote for war
credits, and for the duration set aside criticisms of the government
and partisan conflicts. By 1916–17 the *Burgfrieden* had given way to a
bitter debate over war aims, severe criticisms of the government by
the right and left, and growing polarization between advocates of
reform and reaction. The actual performance of parliament was of a
mixed nature. To some extent, the Reichstag continued to function as
a potential agency of plebiscital acclamation by supporting the more
dynamic and forceful element of the government, the military,
against civil authorities in the matter of unrestricted submarine war-
fare in October 1916 and then in 1918 in connection with the Treaty of
Brest-Litovsk. However, parliamentary debate became an increas-

ingly accurate representation of the various discontents in the country and the parliament refused to follow the demands of the military for the mobilization of the civilian population of the country on terms unfavorable to labor. The Reichstag transformed the Auxiliary Service Law of December 1916 in a manner that registered the growing power of labor and the need to pacify it, the stalemate between industry and labor, and the incapacity of the government to impose discipline on either side.[15] Under the law, both the government and the industrialists were compelled to grant more recognition to labor than ever before and to give labor unions a major role in the socioeconomic functions of the war economy. Because the government was unable and unwilling to control profits, the Reichstag failed to restrict the free movement of labor as much as the military wished and encouraged high wage demands. The left-wing moderate bourgeois coalition that passed this bill increasingly organized and functioned as a bloc during the next two years and became the basis of the later Weimar coalition, a coalition that strongly advocated progressive social and political legislation.

The Reichstag's performance during the war was hardly distinguished, but it must be remembered that it was not constitutionally empowered to form its own government. The Reichstag clearly had the power and ability to pass major pieces of social and economic legislation if given the opportunity, but the experience of the Auxiliary Service Law also left a legacy of fear in governmental and industrial circles about giving it such opportunities – first, because the legislation turned out to be a mishmash of competing interest group demands and, second, because of excessive concessions to the trade unions. On the one hand, the Reichstag was feared and criticized for its lack of expertise and subordination to special interests. On the other hand, it was feared because it might perform what could reasonably be conceived as its function, namely, to respond to and represent the discontents and desires of the majority of the German people.

The third major wartime trend was the great increase in the centralization, membership, functions, and power of interest groups in the industrial sector, as well as elaboration of their already complex relationship with the government and parliament.[16] However highly developed and articulated for their time, the German industrial interest groups before the war presented a somewhat diffused and complicated picture that reflected the disparities of size, power, and development within the industrial structure. There were two peak associations (*Spitzenverbände*): the Central Association of German Industrialists, which represented heavy industry and the large firms in machine building and textiles, as well as the major trade associations of the latter industries; and the Federation of German Industrialists, which represented a variety of medium-sized and small firms in machine building and textiles, but also in various light industries. By and large, the Central Association was dominated by the heavy industrialists, and its members tended to be organized in powerful branch associations (*Fachgruppen*), such as the Association of German Iron and Steel Industrialists and the Association of German Machine Builders. Its lobbying techniques reflected the peculiar weight of the industrialists dominating the organization, individuals who had close contact with one another and the authority to make direct contact with highly placed persons in Berlin and elsewhere. Its methods were highly personalistic, although this did not exclude employing highly organized methods of subsidizing parties and the press.

Before the war, tensions within the Central Association were growing because of the differences between heavy industry – which was protectionist and favored continuation of the old alliance with the agrarian Junkers on the foundations of protectionism, imperialism, and sociopolitical reaction – and the manufacturing interests – which resented the pricing policies of the heavy industrial cartels and syndicates and were more moderate in their sociopolitical views. The manufacturing interests in the Central Association did not rebel because they could see little to gain by joining the Federation of German Industrialists, which was much less powerful and whose strength rested up on regional associations (*Landesverbände*) composed of industrialists who neither as individuals nor as firm representatives had the "clout" of their competitors in the Central Association. Before the war, it was possible to detect certain tendencies toward collaboration between the two peak associations, especially in the creation of a single national employer association in 1913. Alarm over the increased power of the trade unions and growing government and Reichstag interference in business matters increased the desire of industrialists to unite forces and to strengthen the voice of industry as a whole through unified and disciplined organizations. The barriers to effective unity, however, were very great. On the substantive level, there was the problem of reconciling the conflicts of heavy industry and its primary consumers in manufacturing. On the organizational level, there was the problem of overcoming the overwhelming influence and power of the representatives of large firms and concerns, which made it virtually impossible for the functionaries of peak associations and trade associations to win over and represent small and medium-sized business.

When these pre-war tendencies are kept in mind, the complex

consequences of war for industrial interest group organization and development become more intelligible. The war strengthened the cause of organization and organizational unity. The government used existing cartels, syndicates, trade associations, and peak associations in the allocation of raw materials, the granting of contracts, the fixing of prices, and the control of exports and imports. War committees were set up for each industry, usually under the leadership of trade association functionaries, and participation in the war economy virtually required membership in the organizations. Thus, membership became more inclusive because it was directly or indirectly imposed by the government, and the war economy, as noted earlier, came to rest on industrial self-government performed under government auspices with varying degrees of governmental surveillance. It was a truly happy time for peak association, trade association, and syndicate functionaries, who presided over growing staffs with the tasks of servicing and managing growing memberships. Similarly, the government urged the various industrial peak associations to unite and argued that industrial unity and organization would be necessary when peace came to ensure a smooth transition to a peacetime economy and to "fight the economic war after the war."

Generally speaking, the industrialists were pleased by the increased inclusiveness of their organizations and supported the cause of unity within the business community, although not always for the same reasons as the government. They understandably feared that government surveillance and control would be permanent, that true industrial self-government would be replaced by a controlled and planned economy as advocated by Moellendorff, and that a left-wing–dominated Reichstag would make the wartime gains and increased power of the trade unions permanent. Thus, they viewed industrial organization and unity as the best defense against such dangers, and this motive more than any other drove the industrialists to make the most of government encouragement to move in the direction of unifying their peak associations during the war. Plans were laid for the creation of one peak association to represent all industry; branch trade associations were established for industries that did not have them (e.g., the electrotechnical industry); and, superficially at least, reform of the Central Association was undertaken to satisfy the wishes of manufacturing interests. The nature of wartime requirements was such as to encourage centralization and branch organization, and this promoted the interests of the producer industries and the kinds of organizational structures and lobbying techniques used by heavy industry and the Central Association. Thus, if German industry was more organized than ever before, it was also more dominated by heavy industry and big business. The degree to which industrial interest groups could become truly representative of the general interests of their membership as distinct from the special interests of their dominant members remained very unclear.

At the same time, the new and unaccustomed demands on the industrial interest groups and the problems they anticipated in the reconversion and postwar economy forced them to confront new problems of self-definition and to develop a greater degree of ideological self-consciousness, thus exaggerating traditional industrialist postures. As might be expected, the key role played by industry in the war effort and its unquestionable accomplishments strengthened the productionist ideology of the industrialists, who now could truly view themselves as the *crème de la crème* of the "producing estates." Their traditional espousal of "production policy" against "consumption policy" now seemed more vindicated than ever before. Also vindicated was the contempt they had long harbored for the bureaucracy, whose preindustrial ethos demanded that state service be accorded a prestige and status not given in equal measure to those possessing technical skill, commercial acumen, and managerial competence. Leading industrialists continually demanded new "unbureaucratic" agencies with dictatorial powers, headed by persons who would heed the advice of advisory councils composed of expert businessmen. The failure of such agencies, which invariably had to pay heed to a variety of interests and needs, only strengthened industrialist criticisms of the government for its inability to rely on the objective advice of those in a position to know. These experiences, in turn, encouraged an increasingly shrill incantation of what was rapidly becoming a gospel of industrial self-government free of bureaucratic and, of course, parliamentary interference and controls. During the last year of the war, this desire to regain autonomy and run the economy according to the lights of the business community became so desperate that it provided an important ground for the desertion of the imperial regime by many of the leading industrialists.

This loss of confidence in the monarchy, which culminated in the agreement between organized industry and organized labor that was being formed even before the revolution, was certainly made easier by the fact that the wartime situation had also provoked the trade union leaders to confront problems of self-definition and ideology in new ways. The co-optation of the trade unions into the war economy and their integration into interest group politics through the Auxiliary Service Law strengthened enormously the reformist tendencies of the Socialist Free Trade Unions and made them more open and overt than ever before. The unions were quite pleased by government recognition and employment of their services, and were gratified by the Auxiliary Service Law and other legislation. They hoped that the government and the Reichstag would continue and extend these practices after the war. The most important goal of the trade unions, however, was employer recognition and voluntary collaboration in a partnership of *Arbeitsgemeinschaft* to reconstruct the economy and to restore Germany's economic position in the world. Although Marxist ideology made it easy enough for the Socialist trade union leaders to declare that the workers were "producers," the Marxism behind the rhetorical question of the trade union leader, Emil Kloth, "Are the unions representatives of the consumers or the producers?" was very slight indeed. In an article filled with praise of Fordism, thinly veiled imperialism, and emphasis upon the need to ensure Germany's economic future, Kloth declared that the German unions would have to assume a major role in the forthcoming effort to restore Germany's position in world markets. In the process, they would "finally prove themselves as representatives of the producers." Kloth and many of his colleagues felt that they, too, were members of the "producing estates" and deserved full partnership in the interest group game.[17]

Although there was much employer resistance to granting the unions such partnership, there was also a growing recognition on the part of leading industrialists and high civilian and military officials that trade union help was needed in the demobilization and reconversion. These persons understood the relatively unideological posture of the trade unionists and recognized that, without trade union help, the increasingly radicalized masses might have fallen under the sway of less amenable leadership and might have undermined the war effort. Many of these leading industrialists came to this judgment because they had learned that it was easier to work with "reasonable" trade unionists than to work with bureaucrats and parliamentary politicians.

By the end of the war, therefore, a paradoxical situation existed in Germany. On the one hand, class conflict and polarization had increased because of the social and political stalemate and the economic privations imposed by the war. On the other hand, the government's loss of authority was driving industrialists and trade unionists together in a remarkable effort to save what could be saved from the debacle through an assertion of the primacy of economics over politics. The alliance between industry and labor at the end of the war had the purpose of saving the German economy from the bureaucracy, parliament, and revolution. As such, it constituted a good deal more than an ad hoc arrangement between two interest groups mutually to accommodate one another with regard to their special interests. It was a deliberate effort on the part of the two leading interest conglomerations of the nation to play a central role in the actual functions of governance.

The Weimar alliance of industry and labor

The alliance between organized industry and labor at the end of the war was certified by the so-called Stinnes–Legien Agreement of November 15, 1918 – an agreement between Hugo Stinnes, the great industrialist, and Carl Legien, the head of the Free Trade Unions. It was embodied in the Central Working Community of German Employers and Employees (*Zentralarbeitsgemeinschaft* – ZAG).[18] In considering this agreement and alliance, we should, for analytical purposes, distinguish its three basic characteristics, however much they may have overlapped.

The first of these are the "bread and butter" issues that the agreement settled between labor and management, some of which were forced on the employers by the revolutionary situation and especially by the revolution itself: recognition of the trade unions as representatives of the workers, right to organize, return of the soldiers to their places of work, joint regulation of labor exchanges, creation of worker committees in the factories, negotiation of collective wage agreements, no employer support to "yellow unions," introduction of the eight-hour day in all industries. The most contested of these terms were those concerned with the yellow unions and the eight-hour day in all industries. The employers resisted their acceptance until the outbreak of the revolution made it necessary, and even then with a verbal agreement from the trade unions that they would recognize the rights of "yellow unions" that survived without employer support and a secret written agreement which made the future of the eight-hour day in Germany contingent on its internationalization. Manifestly, more than "bread and butter" was involved in these arrangements. In contrast to Russia, Germany had organizations or at least individuals that could come together to manage even a revolutionary crisis and to make compromises that registered changes in the existing power relationships. This political component was openly discussed and recognized, for the industrial leaders making the agreement frankly stated that the trade unions were the one group in society that had the power to contain the revolutionary situation and that no confidence could be placed in the weak German middle class (*Bürgertum*). The trade union leaders felt dependent upon the expertise of the industrialists and were fearful of extension of the revolution. Consequently, they sought to maximize gains in terms of their traditional goals but, in the case of Legien at least, took the view that voluntary commitments were superior to those imposed on the employers. They accepted Stinnes's argument that a day might come again when the employers would hold the upper hand and should therefore be bound by voluntary commitments.

The second major characteristic of the agreement was the explicit goal of circumventing the bureaucracy and parliament and having the demobilization and reconversion dictated by the interest groups. Naturally, the interest groups did not have the executive authority of enforcing agencies at their disposal, and therefore they demanded that a new demobilization office be set up under Lt. Col. Koeth with dictatorial socioeconomic powers. At the same time, a central committee based on parity between labor and management would be set up to serve as a *Zentralarbeitsgemeinschaft*, and *Arbeitsgemeinschaften* would be created for all the major industries. The policies of the demobilization office would be determined in collaboration with the ZAG, decreed by the former, and implemented on the basis of the greatest possible industrial self-administration by the *Arbeitsgemeinschaften*. In this way, the Reich Economics Office and the parliament would be circumvented and the greatest possible economic freedom be restored as rapidly as possible.

Intimately related to the circumvention of the traditional bureaucracy and parliament was the final characteristic of the agreement, the provisions for institutionalizing these structures on a long-term basis "for the solution of all economic, social and legal questions touching upon industrial life with the proper regard to all interests concerned."[19] Germany was not alone in producing schemes for labor–management collaboration on a long-term basis during this period. The Whitley Councils in England and various joint industry–labor boards in England,[20] France, Italy, and the United States also involved such goals, but they were unpretentious, short lived, and did not carry with them the idea, let alone the ideology, of interest group alliance and coalition that dominated the ZAG. There is nothing mysterious about why such an experiment should go further in Germany and have such an explicit character. On the one hand, the emergency was more severe and the imperatives for "concerted action" on the part of the two sides were greater. On the other hand, and more important in explaining this particular form of alliance and its intensity, was the precedent for such coalitions and alliances of interest groups in Bismarckian and Wilhelmine Germany. The *Arbeitsgemeinschaft* between industry and labor literally replaced the old alliance of industry and agriculture, which had played such a powerful role in supporting the protectionism, imperialism, and reaction advocated by the extreme right in the empire. The basis for such policies and the political system they were meant to shore up had disappeared, but the idea of a "cartel of productive estates" protecting one another's interests with the pretension of thereby serving the national welfare had not disappeared. In other words, the ZAG reflected the historically conditioned German proclivity to literalize the power of the dominant and best organized socioeconomic groups through the creation of more or less formal alliances to influence or even usurp the functions of governance.[21]

The ZAG was a failure, although a complicated failure, and this is no place to retell its complex history.[22] As an institution, it lasted until 1924 – that is, until the stabilization – and there were important movements to revive it in 1926 and again during the early phase of the Great Depression. Because one of the major reasons for the collapse of the Weimar Republic was the failure of industry and labor to reconcile their differences, the ZAG's history is of more than minor significance. First of all, it did not succeed in carrying through the complex organization of industrial *Arbeitsgemeinschaften* fast enough to play its intended role in the demobilization and reconversion or thoroughly enough to become a true foundation for the organization of the industrial sector of the economy. Consequently, a second source of failure was that the bureaucracy and parliament were in a position to recover their lost initiative and act without much reference to the ZAG. Third, the actual status of the ZAG became confused or undermined by the appearance of competing or related organizational ideas, such as the factory councils and the plans for a network of branch, regional, and other forms of councils culminating in a Reich Economics Council which found expression in the Weimar constitution itself. Although the ZAG was the agency called on to name the members of many of these bodies, its substantive role was diminished by them. Fourth, both the industrial and the labor leaders in the ZAG found themselves faced with opposition within their own ranks against various aspects of the Stinnes–Legien Agreement. This opposition presented itself not only in verbal protests but also in actual refusals to participate or withdrawals from the ZAG. Fifth, collaboration in the ZAG was further undermined by divisions over broader political issues, such as the Kapp Putsch of March 1920 and the trade union general strike against it, an event that tested whether the primacy of economics over politics represented by the ZAG could be carried to the point of neutrality toward the fate of Weimar's political democracy. Finally, the ZAG formally collapsed because consensus could not be achieved on the substantive questions of how the burdens of a lost war were to be distributed, and the employers took advantage of the termination of the Ruhr occupation and the stabilization to abrogate the eight-hour day and to reduce wages.

Given these difficulties, the remarkable thing is that the ZAG held together as long as it did, but the reasons for its continued existence, aside from a certain measure of inertia, can be enumerated. At the top of the list must come that desire for order and fear of radicalism, revolution, and anarchy that had made the ZAG possible in the first place. Both sides were anxious to maintain high employment, secure food subsidies and other vital necessities for the workers, and encourage high productivity, particularly to overcome the postwar energy crisis caused by low coal production. The ZAG partners, therefore, could collaborate in propaganda for high productivity, encouraging employers to be generous to workers in troubled areas and, above all, applying pressure on the government to give contracts and to cover the costs of food supplements and the like. To a great extent, these activities were made possible by inflation, which greased the arrangements and compromises aimed at crisis management. Thus it was no accident that the ZAG collapsed with the stabilization. Insofar as both sides could agree that measures conducive to inflation were justified in that they prevented revolution or that responsible economic management was impossible anyway because of reparations, they could jointly legitimize measures whose costs were either passed on to other consumers or covered by the printing press.

Interestingly and significantly, the one area in which the ZAG was able to live up to its goals of imposing its will on the government and parties was in those aspects of the inflationary economy connected with exports, where a complex network of control boards was necessary to ensure that goods were sold at sufficiently high prices and for foreign currency so that Germany could maximize her export advantages. In the summer of 1919 the ZAG forced the government to maintain a centralized system of export controls against the wishes of special regional and commercial interests, and industry and labor collaborated very effectively on these boards. Obviously, however, the system made sense only as long as the inflation continued and only insofar as German domestic wages and prices remained below world market prices. Once the rationale for these organizations disappeared, the employers lost interest in them, whereas the labor representatives were placed in the ludicrous position of desperately holding on to increasingly obsolete institutions because they had once provided a modicum of codetermination in economic policy questions. The final element holding the ZAG together was the generally recognized desirability of having some formal structure in which the "social partners" could discuss common policy, and, wherever possible, collaborate in a reasonable manner to their mutual benefit and for the good of the country as a whole. This more modest goal of mutual information, understanding, and conflict reduction was recognized and maintained even after the dissolution of the ZAG and played a large role in arguments for its revival by some industrialists and some unionists after 1924.

Having briefly and hastily outlined where the ZAG failed and where it succeeded, we may now raise the question of what its history reveals about the parameters of interest group action in Weimar society and what it suggests more generally about the role of interest groups in the processes of governance. To begin with, a close look at the ZAG suggests that one must be very careful in talking about what "interest groups" are doing or are capable of doing as entities. Business associations are, after all, composed of firms and concerns, the more powerful of which are in a position either to control the associations or to break ranks and act independently. On the employer side. the ZAG agreement was really negotiated by a powerful group of individuals, some of whom – Hugo Stinnes, Otto Henrich, Carl Friedrich von Siemens, Ernst von Borsig, Walther Rathenau, and Anton von Rieppel – were heading or directing large firms and concerns and who derived their status and authority from them, whereas others – Hans von Raumer and Jakob Reichert – were highly placed functionaries in major trade associations whose power derived from their close association with the prominent industrialists in their organizations. The actions of this group, which certainly showed remarkable initiative in the crisis, were resented by many of the bypassed leaders and functionaries of the peak associations and employer organizations. When the Reich Association of German Industry (RdI) was created in February 1919 at Jena, the perpetrators of the ZAG were attacked for making excessive concessions to the trade unions – possibly necessary in Berlin but not in the quieter provinces – and for compromising the autonomy of the business community by giving the worker representatives too great a voice in economic as distinct from social policy questions. One of the effects of the ZAG was to create a peculiar reversal of pre-war fronts on social questions where small and medium-sized business now took a harder line. They could not afford the concessions big business was prepared to make because it could pass on the costs to the taxpayers or its customers. Similarly, medium-sized and small business lacked the expertise and power to engage in complex negotiations and to play the inflationary game.

Although the creation of the ZAG required industry to organize its peak association and its various trade associations and employer organizations more fully than ever before, a situation certainly conducive to strengthening the role and power of industrial interest groups in the Weimar Republic, the old problem of heavy industrial and big business domination remained. Before the leadership of industrial interest groups could be mandated to undertake the kinds of arrangements involved in the ZAG, these organizations had to undergo a much higher degree of self-definition in terms of both organization and program. By the time this took place, however, important segments of big business had also turned against the ZAG, and it became clear that the peak associations could produce only the most general of programatic guidelines and negotiate only a relatively limited range of issues if they were not to face rebellion from the one or the other segment of their membership. The trade associations and employer associations were best equipped to deal with specific and discrete issues. In other words, the more industrial interest groups defined their specific roles and tried to develop coherent postures, the less appropriate their commitment to the ZAG became, insofar as the latter involved an assumption that they could regularly join with labor to influence a wide range of policy issues. Initially, some of the industrialist ZAG supporters were so obsessed with the need for an alliance with labor and so oblivious to the tensions within the business community itself that they actually proposed the appointment of the right-wing Social Democrat, August Müller, as business manager of the Reich Association of German Industry.[23] The reality was, however, that the peak associations' most serious task was not winning the confidence of labor but rather of their own constituencies. They found it extraordinarily difficult to formulate general policies that would bind their own members because, quite aside from internal institutional restraints, the dissimilarities and disparities within the "business community" were simply too great to permit consensus on more than a least common denominator of general policy or to sustain a general mobilization except in the most extreme cases. The attitude of businessmen toward their organizations was pragmatic and instrumental rather than ideological and sentimental. It was no accident that the most politically minded and aggressive industrialists sought to combine with powerful colleagues in ad hoc or informal arrangements to influence policy because the interest groups increasingly became either too specifically functional in their purposes or too inclusive to be manageable.

Similar problems existed for the trade unions, because if the trade union organizations were at once simpler and more highly developed at the time of the ZAG's founding, the actions of Legien and his colleagues were plagued by problems analogous to those of their industrialist partners. On the one hand, the trade union leaders were either not truly representing or not really controlling a large part of the constituency, whether in its older form or as it appeared in the form of the vast influx of new members who entered between 1918 and 1920. On the other hand, one of the chief reasons for the trade union leadership's willingness to accept the domination of people such as Stinnes in the ZAG was that, like many of the employers, they had few ideas and no real program of their own. Like the employers, the trade unions rapidly discovered that resistance from below made a retreat from the extreme commitment to the ZAG a necessity. The Metal Workers Union, the largest of the Free Trade Union groups, dropped out of the ZAG after October 1919 and Legien, after initial resistance, decided to support the Factory Councils Law of February 1920 despite strong employer opposition in the ZAG, because it was obviously more important that the trade union leaders recover their lost influence in the plants than that they heed the wishes of their alleged employer allies. Similarly, once the trade unionists began to rediscover their constituencies and their particular interests, they had a good deal more to discuss with the employers but a great deal less on which they could risk agreeing.

The fundamental dilemma for both employers and trade union leaders was that the commitment to industry–labor collaboration in the ZAG overstrained the organizational and ideological cohesion of their respective organizations. Opponents of the ZAG in both camps seldom contested the desirability of discussion and cooperation wherever they might prove possible and useful, but they did resist unrealistic pretensions to common interest that might impose limitations on the freedom of action of their respective organizations. Many of the employers who willingly accepted collective bargaining sharply criticized the initially proposed obligatory discussion of all economic issues with the trade union leaders so that "there was nothing left between heaven and earth that did not fall under the competency of the *Arbeitsgemeinschaft.*"[24] Similarly, although trade union opponents of the ZAG attacked it as a departure from the principle of class conflict, it would be a mistake to overemphasize the radical component of their position. The trade unionists in the Socialist Metal Workers Union who took their union out of the ZAG in 1919 supported collective bargaining with the employers and attacked the contention of the ZAG supporters that the ZAG was some kind of logical and necessary extension of the principle of collective bargaining.[25]

Indeed, where commitment to the *Arbeitsgemeinschaft* actually continued on both sides, as in the mining industry, consensus was no guarantee that agreement could be realized in action. Thus, in early 1920, the Ruhr mine union leaders refused to join with the owners in their industry's *Arbeitsgemeinschaft* and associate themselves with the ZAG proclamation of the industry–labor leaders in Berlin against the six-hour shift, because they feared being accused of betrayal of working-class interests by the miners – not because they disagreed with the proclamation. Just as the Ruhr trade unionists refused to take unnecessary risks with their constituencies for the *Arbeitsgemeinschaft*, so the Ruhr mine owners in 1923 yielded to the temptations of alleged necessity and tactical advantage by trying to extend the working day unilaterally at the end of passive resistance in the Ruhr. Their procedure was disapproved by many of their colleagues outside the industry and provided the immediate cause of the ZAG's final collapse. More generally, the example of the mining industry illustrates the fragility of the *Arbeitsgemeinschaft* concept. The internal politics of the interest groups, their ideological, sectoral, and regional differences, stood in the way of any continuing process of consensus and agreement.[26]

It was no accident, therefore, that the ZAG could not build its intended substructure and operate effectively as an organization. On the one hand, the interest groups involved were insufficiently homogeneous in character and inappropriately organized to achieve so complex an organizational structure as that envisioned by the ZAG's founders. On the other hand, the ZAG founders were compelled to rediscover and come to terms with their constituencies, a necessity that also forced them to define their functions and their programs in ways that were bound to cut the ZAG's purposes down to size.

At the same time, however well organized, important, and powerful, and however great the traditions of interest group politics in Germany, the interest groups really were in no position to bypass the state and traditional bureaucracy through the Demobilization Office. Koeth, as adept at "revolutionary economics" as he was at "war economics," would not wait for the ZAG to develop its projected structure, worked with what was at hand in his usual ad hoc manner, and, to the horror of the ZAG leaders, even gave way to radicals in the councils movement when this seemed useful. He thus disappointed many, if not all, of the expectations placed in him. Furthermore, once the initial emergency passed, the traditional bureaucratic agencies recovered the initiative, eliminated the Demobilization Office, and began to implement some of their own schemes for the organization of the economy. If the ZAG leaders had anticipated using the state as the agent of the will of the interest groups, they suddenly faced the danger they had intended to avert, namely, that the ZAG might be transformed into an instrument of a state-directed, planned economy as was desired by the undersecretary of the economics ministry and its idea man until July 1919, Wichard von Moellendorff. As in war, so in peace, Moellendorff hoped to use the emergency situation to achieve his ends and concocted remarkably complex schemes for a thoroughgoing organization of the economy along corporatist lines in which the ZAG with its intended substructure was to have a key place. Because of the fear of socialization and the councils movement, many of the industrialists and the ZAG temporized with Moellendorff, as did some of the trade union leaders who viewed such a "corporatively organized economy" as a useful middle ground between the socialization they did not want at the time and the unorganized private economy of the prewar era. Nevertheless, Moellendorff was opposed by various industrialist and labor leaders on two grounds. First, Moellendorff recognized that the German economy was composed of more than industry and labor and insisted that "self-governing bodies" for the various branches of the economy include consumer interests. Second, Moellendorff always considered economic self-government to mean self-government in the service of the national welfare. The industrialists were particularly hostile to the "consumer point of view," whereas the trade unionists were slow in rediscovering what it was until reminded by their constituencies as the inflation progressed. Both groups were hostile to the idea of submitting the ZAG to a bureaucratic state that vetoed and guided their actions. Basically, the ideology of the ZAG was that of voluntaristic collaboration and agreement arrived at autonomously on the basis of consultation and discussion and then accepted by the government and parliament because those directly involved had made up their minds.

This notion, however, was pitched at a level that made its implementation pure chimera for any society, let alone for one as strife-torn as that of Weimar Germany. This was amply demonstrated by the hapless and contradictory arguments and efforts made to legitimize the ZAG. Thus, the industrialist supporters of the ZAG in 1918–19 justified their alliance with labor not only on the grounds of political necessity but also with the claim that the trade unionists' participation in the *Arbeitsgemeinschaft* with the employers would help the former to understand and accept the employer point of view. In this way, the workers would be enlightened by their own leaders. The educative function of the ZAG was quite differently conceived by the trade union leaders, who told the rank and file that their collaboration with the employers would enable them to gain that practical command of industrial and economic problems that was necessary for the Socialist society of the future. Neither of these ideas was totally fanciful, because it is not difficult to find good evidence for employer co-optation of labor through collaboration, on the one hand, and for increased trade union understanding of the tricks of the managerial trade and capacity to deal with economic issues, on the other. At the same time, there was considerable incompatibility between the employers' hope to use the labor leaders as agents, and the trade unionists' conception of the ZAG as a preparatory school for socialism. In any case, the ZAG certainly had its legitimation problems on the ideological level, problems that could be ignored only as long as short-run considerations and inflationary trade-offs permitted them to be veiled. With the coming of stabilization and a change in the power relations of the two sides, these problems could no longer be avoided.

In defense of the ZAG leadership, it must be said that neither side had been totally oblivious to the implications of changes in their relative strength. They were conscious of the fact that a voluntaristic association of labor and industry would be tested by oscillations of the economic and political market. Their fundamental and very mistaken proposition, however, was that the rules within which their bargaining and negotiations would take place could be securely grounded in voluntary agreements. Thus, in 1918, Stinnes reported that

the trade unions say very correctly that that which is now introduced by the government under compulsion and which does not have any legal legitimation, does not have the same significance as a free agreement between the unions and the participating industry. The latter will remain, while the former is something that can be taken away again.[27]

Five years later, at the end of the inflation, when the employers were successfully eliminating the eight-hour day and reducing real wages below their prewar levels, the leaders of the industrial peak associations tried to persuade the unions to stay in the ZAG with precisely the suggestion that they too needed the ZAG because they could not count on the permanency of their successes. As Hermann Bücher of the Reich Association of the German Industry argued:

It would be wrong to disband it simply because the employers might win the upper hand in the near future, and he is of the opinion that the employers in such a case would, in the interest of the general good, be more moderate than the workers were after the Revolution. They would also realize that a reaction might otherwise come later.[28]

The top trade union leaders were by no means immune to such arguments, for they themselves had no real alternatives to the employer stabilization formulas of longer hours and lower wages. Consensus on such terms, however, was futile because it was unacceptable to the workers, and the union leaders could hardly find Bücher's assurances of moderation adequate grounds to give way to employer demands for complete freedom of action. Reluctantly, they accepted temporary government decrees setting aside the eight-hour day and a system of binding arbitration by the labor ministry as unpleasant but necessary forms of protection against that dictation by the marketplace that underlay the employer conception of the ZAG.

If the ZAG demonstrated anything, it was that the interest groups, insofar as they sought to deal with broad areas of executive action and general socioeconomic policy, needed the arm of the state and the sanction of law for both successful action and legitimation. This was implicit in the very call for a new demobilization office with "dictatorial powers" to implement the ZAG decisions. What the demobilization office and then the labor and economics ministries of the Weimar Republic clearly demonstrated, however, was that even governments as heavily influenced by interest groups as those of the Weimar Republic were compelled to be responsible to a variety of demands and would thus never prove sufficiently "dictatorial" in implementing interest group demands and never prove sufficiently tractable in dealing with the interest groups to live up to the kinds of expectations entertained by the ZAG founders.

The agreements made between industry and labor in the Stinnes–Legien Agreement, therefore, could not be purely private matters negotiated between the parties. Ultimately, it was the state that sanctioned the gains made by the workers through decrees of the revolutionary government, as in the eight-hour day question, just as it was the state that, in the emergency of 1923–4, sanctioned the abrogation of the eight-hour day. Indeed, most of the economic and social arrangements of the early years of the Weimar Republic were based on the exercise of the government's broad emergency powers, which were in turn an extension of the old wartime powers of the imperial regime. Because most of the demobilization decrees favored and protected labor as a consequence of the revolutionary situation, they were opposed by industry as restraints on economic development and the free decision making of businessmen as well as artificial barriers to the kind of voluntary agreements upon which the ZAG was based. Labor, too, was dissatisfied with having its rights guaranteed by decree, but it was not in the end willing to have its rights and gains based on voluntary agreements and good will either. At least as early as May 1919 many of the trade union leaders were taking the view that the ZAG was "lacking in interest to them because they will be able to push through most of their desires legislatively later on."[29] This did not prove as easy as then imagined, but the persistent efforts on the part of labor and, to a lesser extent, of industry subsequently to substitute law for decree and private agreement demonstrates that parliament had no more been eliminated as a vital element in the regulation of society and economy than had the state and the bureaucracy. Indeed, in the search for adequate legitimation for the social and economic system, parliamentary legitimation remained the only alternative to the private agreements that were unattainable and inadequate to that rule by decree that did so much to undermine democracy.

Underlying this necessity, however, were not merely the particular conditions of Weimar, in which industry's temptations to think more of a return to the old order and Socialist labor's tendency to retreat into old Marxist dogmas and formulas made consensus on the basic rules of the game difficult or impossible to achieve. Even under much happier and more stable conditions, such an extreme conception of corporatist collaboration and such a far-reaching effort to root the basic social arrangements of a modern industrial society in voluntary agreements between the parties concerned would face two sets of insurmountable difficulties. The first pertains to the incapacity of the interest groups themselves to sustain such a system because of their internal politics. The leadership of these groups must inevitably search for a balance between a policy of compromise that would mobilize the militants within their ranks against it and a policy of extreme militance that would deny the membership the benefits of useful compromise.[30] The second difficulty arises from this initial one, for it is precisely the limited capacity for consensus building between interest groups that makes a corporatist arrangement insufficient as a substitute for parliamentary government through parties. As Gerhard Lehmbruch has argued, corporatist and parliamentary "subsystems" may stand in symbiotic relationship to one another, the former permitting the latter to "absorb higher problem loads," the latter, because of its higher capacity for consensus building, relieving the interest groups of those fundamental and legitimizing decisions they cannot handle.[31] The effort to substitute corporatist for parliamentary systems, however, can only overload the first as it further burdens the second and ensure that societal corporatism will make way for an authoritarian corporatist solution.

As is well known, parliament and the parties of the Weimar Republic also failed for a host of other reasons of a political as well as of a structural and socioeconomic nature. The point here, however, is that interest group development in Germany during and after World War I indicates some of their limitations as institutions and demonstrates how "overloaded" they can become when seeking to supplant bureaucratic and parliamentary institutions and how essential it is to specify the optimally effective arrangements and rearrangements of this triangular relationship. In the long run, if Germany's development enabled the country to take a very big "two steps forward" in the interest group game, the Weimar experience demonstrated the necessity of a major "step backward" to the kind of relatively modest and intermittent "concerted action" that characterizes industry–labor relations today.

Acknowledgments

I wish especially to acknowledge the support of the Institute of International Studies of the University of California at Berkeley. Much of the empirical data on which this chapter is based is in either my previously published studies cited in the notes or my forthcoming "Die überforderte Arbeitsgemeinschaft. Studien und Dokumente zur Geschichte der Zentralarbeitsgemeinschaft 1918–1924" to be published in the *Schriftenreihe der Vierteljahreshefte für Zeitgeschichte*.

Notes

1 Thorstein Veblen, *Imperial Germany and the Industrial Revolution* (Ann Arbor: Univ. of Michigan Press, 1966) and Ralf Dahrendorf, *Society and Democracy in Germany* (New York: Doubleday, 1967).

2 Wolfram Fischer, "Staatsverwaltung und Interessenverbände im Deutschen Reich 1871–1914," in *Wirtschaft und Gesellschaft im Zeitalter der Industrialisierung. Aufsätze-Studien-Vorträge*, Wolfram Fischer, Kritische Studien zur Geschichtswissenschaft, Vol. 1 (Göttingen: Vandenhoeck & Ruprecht, 1972), pp. 194–213.

3 Rainer Lepsius, "Parteiensystem und Sozialstruktur: zum Problem der Demokratisierung der deutschen Gesellschaft," *Wirtschaft, Geschichte und Wirtschaftsgeschichte. Festschrift zum 65. Geburtstag von Friedrich Lütge*, eds. Wilhelm Abel et al. (Stuttgart: Fischer, 1966), pp. 371–93.

4 Dahrendorf, *Society and Democracy*, pp. 49–64.

5 For the classic attack on the historicist arguments, see Wolfgang Sauer, "Das Problem des deutschen Nationalstaates," in *Moderne deutsche Sozialgeschichte*, ed. Hans-Ulrich Wehler. Neue Wissenschaftliche Bibliothek, Vol. 10, Geschichte (Cologne and Berlin: Kiepenheuer & Witsch, 1966), pp. 407–36.

6 Marc Bloch, *Strange Defeat. A Statement of Evidence Written in 1940* (New York: Norton, 1968), p. 2.

7 Even if one does not share all the gloom so liberally dispensed in the present discussion of "governability," it is of great historical significance that the United States occupies so prominent a place in Michel J. Crozier, Samuel P. Huntington, and Joji Watanuki's *The Crisis of Democracy. Report on the Governability of Democracies to the Trilateral Commission* (New York: New York Univ. Press, 1975).

8 For discussions of "organized capitalism" in Germany, see the essays by Kocka, Wehler, and Feldman in *Organisierter Kapitalismus. Veraussetzungen und Anfänge*, ed. Heinrich August Winkler. Kritische Studien zur Geschichtswissenschaft, Vol. 9 (Göttingen: Vandenhoeck & Ruprecht, 1974). On societal and state corporatism, see P. C. Schmitter, "Still the Century of Corporatism?" *Review of Politics*, 36(1)(January 1974): 85–131, and for a very stimulating and penetrating application to Germany, see Ulrich

Nocken, "Corporatism and Pluralism in Modern German History," *Industrielle Gesell-schaft und politisches System. Beiträge zur politischen Sozialgeschichte. Festschrift für Fritz Fischer zum siebzigsten Geburtstag,* eds. Dirk Stegmann et al. Schriftenreihe des For-schungsinstituts der Friedrich-Ebert-Stiftung, Vol. 137 (Bonn: Verlag Neue Gesellschaft, 1978), pp. 37–56.

9 Jürgen Kocka, *Klassengesellschaft im Krieg. Deutsche Sozialgeschichte 1914–1918* Kritische Studien zur Geschichtswissenschaft, Vol. 8, 2nd. ed. (Göttingen: Van-denhoeck & Ruprecht, 1978), p. 205, n. 125.

10 Much of the discussion here and in subsequent pages is based on my published studies dealing with World War I: Gerald D. Feldman, *Army, Industry and Labor in Germany, 1914–1918* (Princeton, N.J.: Princeton University Press, 1966); "The Political and Social Foundations of Germany's Economic Mobilization, 1914–1916," *Armed Forces and Society,* 3(1)(November 1976):121–45; and "Der deutsche Organisierte Kapitalismus während der Kriegs- und Inflationsjahre 1914–1923," Winkler, *Organisierte Kapitalismus,* pp. 150–71. Important recent West German studies on the socioeconomic history of World War I are Kocka, *Klassengesellschaft im Krieg* and Friedrich Zunkel, *Industrie und Staatssozialismus. Der Kampf um die Wirtschaftsordnung in Deutschland 1914–1918.* Tübinger Schriften zur Sozial- und Zeitgeschichte, Vol. 3 (Düsseldorf: Droste Verlag, 1974). The major East German studies are those of A. Schröter, *Krieg-Staat-Monopol. 1914–1918. Die Zusammenhänge von imperialistischer Kriegswirtschaft, Militärisierung der Volkswirtschaft u. staatsmonopolistischem Kapitalismus in Deutschland während des Ersten Weltkrieges* (Berlin: Akademie-Verlag, 1965) and of Dieter Baudis and Helga Nussbaum, *Wirtschaft und Staat in Deutschland vom Ende des 19. Jahrhunderts bis 1918/19* (Berlin: Akademie-Verlag, 1978).

11 Cited in Feldman, *Army,* p. 281.

12 There is a particularly good discussion of Moellendorff's views in Zunkel, *Indus-trie und Staatssozialismus,* p. 56ff.

13 The legitimacy crisis is particularly well developed in Kocka, *Klassengesellschaft,* op. cit., pp. 131–7.

14 On the Reichstag and the political parties as well as on the general problems of parliamentarization in Germany during this period, see Udo Bermbach, *Vorformen parlamentarischer Kabinettsbildung in Deutschland. Der Interfraktionelle Ausschuss 1917/18 und die Parlamentarisierung der Reichsregierung* (Köln-Opladen: Westdeutscher Verlag, 1967) and Erich Matthias and Ruldolf Morsey, *Der Interfraktionelle Ausschuss 1917/18, Quellen zur Geschichte des Parlamentarismus und der politischen Parteien, 1. Reihe: Von der konstitutionellen Monarchie zur parlamentarischen Republik.* Hrsg. von W. Conze and E. Matthias (Düsseldorf: Droste Verlag, 1959). Arthur Rosenberg, *Birth of the German Republic, 1871–1918* (New York: Russell & Russell, 1962) is still very useful.

15 Feldman, *Army,* p. 197ff.

16 For the discussion that follows, see Gerald D. Feldman, *Iron and Steel in the German Inflation, 1916–1923* (Princeton, N.J.: Princeton University Press), pp. 71ff.; Gerald D. Feldman and Ulrich Nocken, "Trade Associations and Economic Power: Interest Group Development in the German Iron and Steel and Machine Building Industries, 1900–1933," *Business History Review* 49(4)(Winter 1975):121–45; Zunkel, *Indus-trie und Staatssozialismus,* Chaps 3–4; Kocka, *Klassengesellschaft,* op. cit., p. 57ff.

17 Emil Kloth, "Sind die Gewerkschaften Vertreter der Komsumenten oder der Produzenten?" *Sozialistische Monatshefte* 49(1917):1111–5. Kloth was a leader of the Prin-ters Union. On the trade unions during the war, see Heinz Josef Varain, *Freie Gewerkschaften, Sozialdemokratie und Staat. Beiträge zur Geschichte des Parlamentarismus und der politischen Parteien,* Vol. 9 (Düsseldorf: Droste-Verlag, 1956).

18 For the origins of the ZAG, the motives of its founders, and the details of its begin-

nings, see Gerald D. Feldman, "German Business Between War and Revolution: The Origins of the Stinnes–Legien Agreement," in *Entstehung und Wandel der modernen Gesellschaft. Festschrift für Hans Rosenberg zum 65. Geburtstag*, ed. Gerhard A. Ritter (Berlin: Walter de Gruyter, 1970), pp. 312–41; "The Origins of the Stinnes–Legien Agreement: A Documentation," *Internationale Wissenschaftliche Korrespondenz zur Geschichte der deutschen Arbeiterbewegung*, 19/20(December 1973):45–102; "Die Freien Gewerkschaften und die Zentralarbeitsgemeinschaft," *Vom Sozialistengesetz zur Mitbestimmung. Zum 100. Geburtstag von Hans Böckler* ed. Heinz Oskar Vetter (Cologne: Bund-Verlag, 1975), pp. 229–52.

19 Feldman in *Internationale Korrespondenz*, op. cit., p. 85.

20 On Whitleyism, see R. Charles, *The Development of Industrial Relations in Britain 1911–1939. Studies in the Evolution of Collective Bargaining at National and Industry Level* (London: Hutchinson, 1973) and Bernd-Jürgen Wendt, "Whitleyism – Versuch einer Institutionalisierung des Sozialkonfliktes in England am Ausgang des Ersten Weltkrieges," in Stegmann et al., *Industrielle Gesellschaft*, pp. 337–53.

21 On these tendencies, see the splendid discussion of Heinrich A. Winkler, *Pluralismus oder Protektionismus? Verfassungspolitische Probleme des Verbandswesens im Deutschen Kaiserreich*, Institut für Europäische Geschichte Mainz. Vorträge. No. 55 (Wiesbaden: Steiner, 1972).

22 A reliable older history of the ZAG is Heinrich Kaun, *Die Geschichte der Zentralarbeitsgemeinschaft der industriellen und gewerblichen Arbeitgeber und Arbeitnehmer Deutschlands* (Jena: Neuenhahn, 1938). Unless otherwise noted, the discussion that follows is based on Kaun and my own study of the ZAG papers in the Potsdam archives, a fuller account of which is to be found in my forthcoming "Die überforderte Arbeitsgemeinschaft."

23 See the June 1919 correspondence between Director Guggenheimer and General Director Rieppel, M.A.N. Werksarchiv Augsburg, K 75.

24 Remark by Dr. Curt Hoff, February 3, 1919, Sächsische Hauptstaatsarchiv Dresden, Gesandschaft Berlin, Nr. 776, Bl. 58.

25 See the debate in the *14. Ordentlichen Generalversammlung des Deutschen Metallarbeiterverbandes, abgehalten in Stuttgart vom 13. bis 23. Oktober 1919* (Stuttgart: Selbstverlag des Verbandes, 1919), p. 244ff.

26 On this, see Gerald D. Feldman, "Arbeitskonflikte im Ruhrbergbau 1919–1922. Zur Politik vom Zechenverband und gewerkschaften in der Überschiehtenfrage," *Viertel jahreshefte für Zeitgeschichte* 28(2)(April 1980):1–56.

27 Quoted in Feldman, *Internationale Korrespondenz*, op. cit. p. 88.

28 Meeting of the ZAG directors, November 27, 1923, Zentrales Staatsarchiv der DDR, Abt. I, Potsdam, ZAG, Nr. 7, Bd. 31/1, B1. 78.

29 Höltzendorff report, May 22, 1919, HAPAG Archiv.

30 The history of the ZAG gives strong empirical support for the arguments developed by Charles Sabel, Chapter 8 in this volume.

31 See Gerhard Lehmbruch, "Liberal Corporatism and Party Government," *Comparative Political Studies* 10(1)(April 1977):91–126.

7

Corporatism and official union hegemony: the case of French agricultural syndicalism

JOHN T. S. KEELER

The institutionalization of a corporatist interest system entails a fundamental alteration of the manner in which the favored interest groups relate to both the state and their members. Assuming the role of a "recognized" or official interest group involves, in the words of Claus Offe, "the exchange of some *gains* for some *losses.*" What an official group – for example, an official union – loses is a certain measure of its freedom to articulate the demands of its members; it becomes less able to appear as their ardent defender during periods of intense sectoral unrest, because the maintenance of its official union status is contingent on the acceptance of "certain constraints and restrictive obligations... for example, to behave responsibly and predictively, and to refrain from any non-negotiable demands or non-acceptable tactics."[1] The gains that an official union receives in exchange for fulfilling its obligations to the state are essentially of two types. The more obvious and more often discussed type is *biased influence:* structured access to the decision-making centers of the state and/or devolved authority for the administration of public policy. But a second type of gain, related to but analytically distinct from the first, is of more fundamental importance for an official union: *competitive advantage.* If an official union is to continue to respect its obligations to the state, which will at times mean disregarding the sentiments of many of its members, then it must receive organizational supports from the state sufficient to assure that its unpopular behavior will not imperil its sectoral hegemony through generating a massive departure of hostile members for rival union movements. The more an official union is compelled to "behave responsibly" in the face of its members' discontent with public policy, the more the state must provide its corporatist client with organizational supports.

Obviously there are limits to the state's ability to provide such

185

supports – that is, to act as the architect of syndical order[2] – in all democratic polities; however, these limits vary greatly not only from polity to polity but also from sector to sector. The state's ability to play an architectural role would appear to be least limited in a polity featuring a high degree of bureaucratic centralization and a virtual monopoly of governmental power by a single party or coalition and a sector featuring a high degree of state intervention. Given the political costs entailed in playing a major architectural role, the state must not only be able but also willing to do so; its willingness would seem to be maximized in a case in which there exists a profound need for the cooperation of an official union in the implementation of important public policies.

Assuming that a state in a democratic polity is both able and willing to act as the architect of syndical order, what are the means that it can employ to provide organizational supports for an official union? How precisely do these supports translate into competitive advantage? And to what degree can nonofficial unions exploit the limits to the state's architectural ability? In this chapter I will attempt to provide some answers to these questions through an examination of the dynamics of corporatism and official union hegemony in the agricultural sector of the Fifth French Republic.[3]

Since the early 1960s the governments of the center-right majority in France have been compelled, by their intense desire to accelerate agricultural modernization and their need for syndical cooperation in doing so, to develop a symbiotic corporatist relationship with the principal agricultural union, the FNSEA (Fédération Nationale des Syndicats d'Exploitants Agricoles). When the Gaullist government launched its agricultural reform policy with the Orientation Law of 1960 and the Complementary Law of 1962, state officials acknowledged that a comprehensive modernization program would "necessitate the active cooperation of the farmers." Given "the lack of education of the majority among them, their hostility to an evolution which condemns a certain number of them to leave," government leaders recognized that they would be obliged to "solicit the support of the professional organizations."[4] Despite initial misgivings and continued internal tension, the FNSEA has since the early 1960s agreed to engage in the *concertation* on which state reform policy has been predicated. Throughout a period in which state intervention in the agricultural sector has massively increased (between 1960 and 1976 the budget of the Ministry of Agriculture increased by 900 percent, whereas state spending on agriculture swelled from 5.4 to 13.5 percent of the total state budget), the FNSEA has provided the state with all of the essential services of a corporatist client: It has served as a fixed channel of communication, as a bargaining agent that aggregates and moderates agricultural demands and mobilizes sectoral support for policies that it participates in formulating, and as a supplemental bureaucracy that assists in policy implementation.[5]

The FNSEA's fulfillment of its corporatist obligations has been a source of sectoral discontent ever since it first became apparent, in the mid-1960s, that *concertation* would fail to produce the sort of new agricultural equilibrium which many farmers hoped for – and felt they were promised – at the time that the Orientation and Complementary laws were passed. Advocates of reform through concertation had envisioned the possibility of saving "the maximum" possible number of family farms (an estimate of 1962 was that only 15 to 20 percent of all farms would prove to be unviable), impeding the "capitalist concentration" of land, decreasing the regional disparities of income within the sector and – ultimately – achieving income parity with the industrial sector. Despite some signs of progress, none of these goals has been achieved. In fact, the exodus from the land has proceeded at a rate nearly twice as high as anticipated; the concentration of land has scarcely been slowed; and the regional disparities of income have actually increased since the early 1960s and remain greater than those found in any of the other nations of the European community. Also, although very few farmers can be said to have reached income "parity," the efforts of small farmers to achieve parity through modernization have resulted in an enormous increase in indebtedness and financial insecurity.[6]

As the FNSEA has continued on a *concertation* course, consistently behaving "responsibly" despite these disappointing policy results, the signs of faltering sectoral faith in the federation have multiplied. During a number of critical periods since 1967, many of the rank and file in economically depressed regions have ignored the leadership's pleas for "moderation" and engaged in disruptive – and sometimes violent – demonstrations. Unprecedented tensions at the *base* led to the convocation of a Congrès Extraordinaire in December of 1969; on this occasion the FNSEA president was forced to acknowledge that the organization was suffering from a "malaise," with the leadership "the object of permanent criticism" for maintaining "excessively intimate" relations with the state. By the mid-1970s at least four rival union movements had emerged to challenge the FNSEA, and one of these – the Communist-dominated MODEF (Mouvement de Défense des Exploitants Familiaux) – was able to attract roughly 20 percent of the national vote total in elections to the departmental Chambers of Agriculture. A public opinion poll administered in 1973 indicated that only 47 percent of the farmers queried were sufficiently confident in the FNSEA to state that it should be allowed to retain its privileged position as the sole agricultural union recognized by the state – and fully 55 percent of the farmers felt that the FNSEA and its youth organization (the CNJA, or Centre National des Jeunes Agriculteurs) "allow themselves to be influenced by the government."[7] In short, the "losses" incurred by the FNSEA have been substantial.

In exchange for these losses, however, the official union has received considerable "gains" from the state – not only in influence but also in competitive advantage. The cooperation of the FNSEA's leaders has been sustained, as the organizational supports provided by the state have so far been sufficient to assure the continued hegemony of the official union: In the mid-1970s the FNSEA remains the only farmers' union of truly national scope (with an affiliate, or FDSEA, in every department), claims the vast majority of unionized farmers, and generally wins about 90 percent of the seats to the popularly elected Chambers of Agriculture.[8] The hegemony of the FNSEA has been reinforced through five basic types of state action. The official union has benefited from: (1) *exclusive or privileged access* to the decision-making centers of the state at both the national and subnational levels; (2) *devolved authority* for the formulation and implementation of important aspects of agricultural policy; (3) *revision of regulations* governing elections to the Chambers of Agriculture; (4) *monetary subsidies* intended to further the modernization process; (5) *repression of rival unions*, either indirect or direct. As discussed subsequently, all these benefits have served to reinforce FNSEA hegemony by providing both union elites and rank and file with tangible and intangible incentives to remain active within – or at least stay on good terms with – the official union.

Exclusive or privileged access

Exclusive access

Perhaps the most widely recognized benefit granted the FNSEA by the state is the exclusive[9] right to participate in *formal* advisory councils, commissions. and committees. Such participation, as George Lavau has noted, provides groups with "invaluable means of accomplishing their objectives" and endows them with "considerable moral prestige." An indication of the utility and prestige value of the right to participate in advisory institutions is the fact that this right has been eagerly – and unsuccessfully – sought by rival unions, most notably by the MODEF and the FFA.[10]

Even before the age of systematic *concertation*, the FNSEA was "invited to send representatives to more than 200 committees, commissions and councils." Since the early 1960s, however, such institutions have increased dramatically in number and importance. At the *national level* the FNSEA now exerts considerable influence on the administrative councils charged with formulating policy pertaining to, for example, agricultural development (the ANDA), distribution of subsidies intended to further structural reform (the CNASEA), and state intervention in agricultural markets (the FORMA).[11] Moreover, the FNSEA is also the most influential sectoral representative at the highly visible and prestigious Conférence Annuelle. Instituted in 1971 at the FNSEA's request, the Annual Conference entails weeks of formal meetings of sectoral representatives with bureaucrats of the Ministry of Agriculture capped by a daylong conference between the chief leaders of the sector (most notably the FNSEA president) and the government (usually the prime minister and the minister of agriculture). As a rule, the major policy innovations of the year are announced at the conclusion of the conference – a procedure that effectively establishes a connection in the public mind between the articulation of demands by the FNSEA and their (at least partial) realization by the state. Although some measures may in truth be at least to a degree the response to pressure from nonofficial unions, they are made to appear to be the direct result of FNSEA influence – the fruit of *concertation*.

At the *department level* each FDSEA enjoys exclusive access to a parallel network of formal advisory institutions: councils or commissions that deal with everything from prices or tax policy to the administration of disaster relief. FDSEA leaders derive prestige and sometimes a great deal more from their seats on bodies such as the *commission des cumuls*, a commission established in 1962 to restrict the activities of so-called *cumulards* – nonagriculturalists who wish to buy land, evict the established tenant, and operate the farm with hired labor. An unfavorable judgment by such a commission can be of enormous consequence for a small farmer – and the possibility of such a judgment often serves as a powerful incentive to join or at least stay on good terms with the FDSEA. Organizers for rival unions often cite fear of the "malevolence" of these commissions as a major factor dissuading farmers from abandoning the FDSEA for a nonofficial union.

Privileged access

Privileged *informal* access to the government and the administration also furnishes the FNSEA with gains in both influence and competitive advantage. At the national level, the administration is readily accessible to the FNSEA and assists it virtually every day in the resolution of problems. More important, at the department level the privileged access granted to the FNSEA's affiliates serves – perhaps even more than formal access – as a powerful incentive for the attraction of members. Intermediation by FDSEA officials is almost a necessity for the many small farmers who cannot understand the workings of the state machine and are hesitant to deal directly with its faceless and fearsome bureaucrats. In most departments the FDSEA director can telephone the prefecture, speak with an assistant of the prefect, and – often immediately – resolve the particular problems of a farmer. Many FDSEA directors or presidents have earned the appellation of *préfet agricole* through manifesting, among other things, an astounding ability to cut through bureaucratic red tape. In contrast, the leaders of rival unions in most departments have difficulty even obtaining a hearing from the administration.[12]

Devolved authority

Since the early 1960s the FNSEA has not only been accorded the means to influence policy more than before through exclusive or privileged access but has also been granted the opportunity to formulate and implement policy at the subnational level. The authority for the administration of many important aspects of modernization policy has been devolved to a network of comanagement (*cogestion*) institutions staffed by representatives of "the profession" and, in most cases, dominated by the FNSEA. The most important comanagement institutions are the SAFER, the ADASEA, the SUAD, and the Chambers of Agriculture.

The SAFER[13]

Established by the Orientation Law of 1960, the SAFER are regional agencies designed to perform a crucial function in the structural reform process. Very briefly, the SAFER are intended to ameliorate farm structures by purchasing land as it comes on the market, implementing necessary improvements (e.g., by consolidating small parcels) and then selling this land selectively to render existing farms viable or to create new, viable farms. As of 1975, thirty-three SAFER were functioning in France with a combined budget of approximately 50,000,000F (an average of 1,500,000F per SAFER).[14] Comanagement of the SAFER thus provides "the profession" with the power to dispose of a significant sum of money and to make decisions affecting the most vital agricultural interests.

The comanagement of the SAFER operates in the following manner. By statute, each SAFER is defined as an association "con-

stituted . . . by the principal agricultural organizations of the departments concerned and controlled by the state." The participation of
the "principal" organizations consists of their delegation of representatives to a SAFER general assembly, which elects an administrative
council headed by a president elected from among its members. Although this president and his council are empowered to perform the
basic functions of SAFER, their activity is controlled by the state
through the *double tutelle* of the Ministry of Agriculture and Ministry
of Finance. Two state commissioners, one attached to each of these
ministries, must approve all operations of the Administrative Council
involving more than 60,000F or requiring the use of the *droit de
préemption* (a right of priority for the purchase of land placed on the
market).[15]

Although the comanagement of the SAFER is said to provide "the
profession" with devolved power to control its own affairs, the exercise of this power is restricted to the elites of the "recognized" organizations – especially those of the FNSEA. No statistics are available to
illustrate the degree of FNSEA influence within all thirty-three SAF-
ERs. However, in each of the regions that I have studied in depth, the
president of the SAFER was – as of 1975 – a major FNSEA official: In
the Nord-Picardie region the SAFER president was a vice-president
of the Aisne FDSEA; in the Aquitaine region, he was the president of
the Landes FDSEA; and in the Marche-Limousin region, he was the
president of the Creuse FDSEA. A passage in a report of one FDSEA
expresses quite well the FNSEA elite's vision of its relationship with
the SAFER: Although "not actually a direct branch of the FDSEA,"
the SAFER "has given an important activity to our organization."[16]

To what degree is the FNSEA's de facto control of the SAFER an
asset in its competition with rival unions? Judging from interviews
with both FDSEA and rival union elites, it would appear to be a
definite – although limited – competitive advantage. It is an advantage because, especially in departments in which the FDSEA is quite
strong, many farmers fear that an expression of opposition to the
FDSEA may provoke the "malevolence" of SAFER (as of the *commission des cumuls*), or at least make perhaps a crucial marginal difference in its decision.[17] However, this advantage is limited for several reasons. For one, the decisions of SAFER affect a relatively small
number of the farmers (much less than 1 percent) each year. For
another, even some rival union leaders express the opinion that the
tutelle of the state limits the degree to which the SAFER could "systematically discriminate" according to political criteria.[18] One informed, relatively objective observer summed up the significance of
the FNSEA–SAFER relationship in the following manner: "Many

farmers certainly fear abuse [of the SAFER power by the FDSEA], and there are some cases in which there seems to have been abuse, but in general the decisions are as fair as possible."[19]

The ADASEA[20]

The ADASEA was established in 1966 to "furnish the cooperation of the agricultural profession in the implementation" of the various programs of the FASASA: the IVD, the subsidies for occupational conversion, migration, and so on.[21] Each departmental ADASEA is controlled by a professional administrative council with a composition that virtually assures FDSEA predominance; in a typical council of sixteen, the FDSEA itself holds six seats; the CDJA, three seats; and the other recognized organizations (which are also generally close to the FDSEA), seven seats.[22] It is hardly extraordinary, then, that in each of the three departments I have examined closely, the president of the ADASEA has always been – like the SAFER president – an FDSEA official.

The benefits that the FDSEA derive from the ADASEA are far more tangible than those derived from the SAFER. The ADASEA personnel (a director and one or more counselors) are hired by the FDSEA elite, are subject to its directives, and are often housed in the same building as the FDSEA staff. Furthermore, in most departments the ADASEA-paid personnel work in close cooperation with "local correspondents" selected from among the elites of the FDSEA's cantonal unions and trained in ADASEA-financed "education and information" sessions. Because most farmers are unaware of the distinction between ADASEA personnel and FDSEA personnel (such confusion is encouraged by FNSEA/FDSEA proclamations that the ADASEA is a *réalisation du syndicalisme*), the former serve to enhance the image of the union even in discharging their proper functions – providing information on available subsidies, filling out necessary forms and transmitting them to the state, and so on. Moreover, ADASEA personnel are often used for a variety of syndical purposes, for example, the organization of union meetings, the transportation of union officials, the distribution of union literature – even the collection of union dues. In effect, then, the ADASEA personnel serve more or less as a state-financed adjunct of the staff of the FNSEA's departmental organizations.[23]

The SUAD and development

Most of the agricultural comanagement institutions were conceived and implemented during the first years of Edgard Pisani's term (1961–6) in the Ministry of Agriculture. The last two years of the Pisani era were largely devoted to the preparation[24] of another extremely important, complex package of *concertation* institutions: those concerning what had traditionally been termed *vulgarisation,* and what after 1966 would be termed "development." This change in nomenclature was intended to convey a profound conceptual change in this aspect of agricultural policy. Instead of merely serving to disseminate knowledge of technical advances in agriculture, the "development" program was also intended to accelerate structural reforms by "making farmers become conscious of the technical, economic and social problems" that would have to be solved to assure a prosperous future for their regions.[25]

Along with this change in conception, the new program instituted an important change in the manner through which the state would act to favor development. Until 1950, throughout what Pisani termed the "first age" of *vulgarisation,* the state had exercised a "quasi-monopoly" of the diffusion of technical knowledge; traditionally it had accorded such activity to the engineers of the administration's *services agricoles.* Because these public efforts were viewed as inadequate by many within the agricultural profession, further private efforts were made to advance the *vulgarisation* process, for example, through the establishment of the CETA (Centres d'Etudes Techniques Agricoles). The gradual recognition by the state of the utility of these private institutions engendered the "second age" of *vulgarisation* policy: In 1959 the government began to subsidize the CETA and similar groupings. With the passage of the 1966 development program, a "third age" was initiated: Henceforth the state would retain some power over the usage of development funds but would "grant to the agricultural profession itself the responsibility for the realization of *vulgarisation* and technical and economic progress at all levels."[26]

Since 1966 the "profession" has participated in the formulation of agricultural development policy at the national level and has been largely responsible for its implementation at the departmental level. At the national level, representatives of the FNSEA and the other recognized agricultural organizations are accorded ten of the twenty seats in the *paritaire*-style administrative council of the aforementioned ANDA. This council performs a number of important functions: It advises the agricultural minister on the general orientation of national and regional development programs, regulates the employment and training of development personnel, and manages a national development fund, which in 1974 amounted to 229,302,583F. Participation in the ANDA council thus provides a wide-ranging source of influence over agricultural policy to the elites of the recognized organizations – and especially the FNSEA. The president of the

ANDA council as of 1975 was Gérard de Caffarelli, the immediate past president of the FNSEA.[27]

At the department level, the "profession" exercises more complete control over development policy. The general orientations of the departmental development program are determined by a *paritaire*-style Conseil d'Etude presided over by the prefect. However, the day-to-day management of the program is entrusted entirely to the board of directors of the SUAD (Services d'Utilité Agricole de Développement), a board chaired by the president of the Chamber of Agriculture and composed of an equal number of chamber members and delegates from the other principal departmental agricultural organizations.[28]

Although this representational scheme does not accord the FNSEA de jure control of the SUAD, it translates into de facto FNSEA control. Virtually all FDSEAs are assured of a majority on the SUAD board through the combination of seats granted to the official union per se with seats obtained indirectly from FDSEA dominance within the Chamber of Agriculture (and, in most cases, dominance within the other recognized organizations as well). Thus, for example, in each of the three departments that I have examined closely, the SUAD council contains a vast majority of FDSEA members.

Control of the SUAD is an immense source of power for the FNSEA's departmental organizations: Not only does it enable them to exert great influence over the orientation of the development program but it also provides them with the opportunity to allocate directly – instead of merely solicit – public funds for the subsidization of their organizational activities. This opportunity arises because SUAD itself is essentially an institution for the coordination of development functions; nearly all its budget – normally about 2,000,000F in 1976 – is not spent by SUAD itself but rather disbursed to a variety of development organisms, many of which are related in varying degrees of intimacy to the FDSEA. For example, in virtually every department: (1) the FDSEA's "Woman's Section" commonly receives a subsidy (e.g., more than 34,000F in Corrèze and 20,000F in Aisne in 1976) that pays for a counselor or two specializing in farm management and accounting; (2) the CDJA receives a subsidy in every department – this is a stipulation of the national ANDA budget – for the employment of two counselors concerned with the technical education and information of the young farmers; this subsidy varies by department (e.g., from 50,000F to 90,000F) but is always significant and sometimes even greater than the entire CDJA budget; (3) the GVA (Groupements de Vulgarisation Agricole), which are "sections of the cantonal unions of the FDSEA," commonly receive subsidies of as much as several hundred thousand francs; (4) the EDE (Etablisse-ment Départmental de l'Elevage), which specializes in the develop-ment of livestock raising, and the CGER (Centre de Gestion et d'Economie Rurale), which assists farmers with management prob-lems such as the preparation of tax returns, both commonly receive subsidies of several hundred thousand francs; neither of these or-ganisms is directly controlled by the FDSEA, but both of them are supervised by administrative councils similar to that of SUAD and are thus generally subject to indirect FDSEA control. Although a number of organizations with no FNSEA connection also generally receive funding, few with overt ties to rival unions such as MODEF ever do.[29]

The Chambers of Agriculture

Established originally in 1924, abolished in 1940 and reestab-lished in 1949, the Chambers of Agriculture have developed into the most important of the "comanagement" institutions of agriculture at the departmental level. This development was unforeseen at the time of their creation under the Third Republic. The essential role of the chambers, as envisioned in this era, was to provide the state with a "consultative organism" representing the local interests of the ag-ricultural profession. To fulfill this role, the chambers were publicly financed (by a special tax) and their membership was determined by a state-controlled election, with suffrage granted to all farmers.

Since their creation, and especially since their reestablishment after World War II, the chambers have become increasingly important through their discharge of what was originally intended to be a sec-ondary role: the creation or subsidization, with public funds, of tech-nical and economic institutions or services in the "collective interest of agriculture." Until 1954, the ability of the chambers to perform this role was severely limited by their meager resources. In 1954, however, and again in 1959, the financial regulations of the chambers were altered in a manner as to expand greatly their ability to discharge an economic function. From 1954 to 1969, the combined budgets of the departmental chambers increased by a factor of 22, from just over seven million francs (roughly 80,000F/chamber) to 156,000,000F (roughly 1,800,000F/chamber). Since the advent of ANDA and the assignment of the SUAD to chamber control, the budgets of the chambers have been increased even further; as of 1976, ANDA pro-vided most chambers with a subsidy in the vicinity of 1,500,000F.[30]

This tremendous increase in the financial power of the chambers inspired one observer in the early 1960s to assert that each chamber president was becoming "a second DSA"[31] with an all-powerful di-rector commanding... several dozen neo-functionaries." Agricultural elites interviewed in the 1970s expressed similar sentiments, referring to particular chamber presidents or directors as the "*préfet vert*" or "*préfet agricole*" of the department. Such assessments are a bit exaggerated. The activities of the chamber elites are delimited and supervised by the state administration; their program proposals are subject to the approval of the prefect and their management of the chambers' funds is controlled by the Cour des Comptes (as discussed subsequently, this control by no means eliminates all "mismanagement.") Nevertheless, the elites of the Chambers of Agriculture do possess enormous power to affect agricultural policy through their representation on a multitude of institutions (as previously discussed) and their allocation of funds.[32]

A fact that has not often been acknowledged in the literature on French agriculture is that the elites of the Chambers of Agriculture also possess enormous power to affect the relative strength of the competing farmers' unions and that, with very few exceptions, this power has redounded to the benefit of the FNSEA. As noted in the introduction, the FNSEA regularly wins approximately 90 percent of the contested seats in elections to the chambers. The FNSEA's departmental affiliates control a majority of seats in all but a handful of departments.[33] As of 1975, 72 percent of the FDSEA presidents were members of their Chambers of Agriculture; 45 percent of the FDSEA presidents were members of their chamber's executive bureau. In 64 percent of the departments, the FDSEA and the chamber were housed in the same office building. In 10 percent of the departments, the FDSEA and the chamber employed the same administrative director – and in a great many more, the director of one of these organizations was the subdirector (and often functioned as the de facto director) of the other.[34]

The FNSEA's control of the chambers provides the federation with manifold organizational benefits. First, it affords the typical FDSEA even more influence – through the seats allotted to the chamber – over the comanagement institutions and advisory councils previously described. In fact, it provides the FDSEA with such a monopoly of power that, in the words of one dissident union activist, "one must work within the FDSEA if one wants to hold any important position and have any influence over policy; if one splits from the FDSEA, one can speak louder – but at the cost of not being heard."[35] Second, control of the chamber provides the typical FDSEA with indirect state subsidization of its infrastructure. While most rival unions are forced to operate with little in the way of infrastructure, the chamber-dominant FDSEA can make use – normally for a small payment if not for free – of the chamber's office building, its equipment (copying machines, telephones, etc.), library, and office supplies. Third, control of the chamber contributes – even more than control of the ADASEA – to the number of administrative personnel at the disposition of the FDSEA elites and thus provides the official union with an extremely important competitive advantage. Whether or not they are formally employed part-time by the FDSEA, virtually all the chamber personnel – from its director to cleaning women – perform important tasks for the union on occasion; moreover, in some departments the chamber (and SUAD) staff workers are virtually indistinguishable from those of the union. It is not uncommon for a chamber-paid librarian to be asked to compile a dossier on MODEF activities for use by FDSEA elites during a chamber election campaign, or for a technical counselor employed by SUAD to be asked to drive an FDSEA official to a union rally during such a campaign.[36] Not all chamber personnel are comfortable playing such a dual technical-syndical role, but even those who object tend to accept it with resignation. As one chamber employee who yearned to be truly "at the service of all of the farmers" lamented in an interview: "If I want to work for the Chamber, I must also work for the FDSEA ... the job is an *ensemble*."[37]

The de facto fusion of elites, infrastructure, and personnel almost inevitably leads in most departments to improper and even illegal activities. Official evidence of abuses of the chambers by FDSEA elites was presented in a report compiled in 1971 by theInspection Générale des Finances. This report, based on a study of the operation of seven chambers, uncovered many "abnormal" or "contestable" aspects of the relationship between the chambers and their respective FDSEA. Cited specifically in the report were cases in which the interlocking elites of the two organizations channeled "secret subsidies" from a chamber to an FDSEA, that is, financed with chamber funds most, if not all, of the cost of newspapers published jointly by the chamber and the FDSEA.[38]

The fate of this particular report is as noteworthy as its contents; it serves as yet another illustration of the preferential treatment generally accorded by the state to the official agricultural union. Despite the protests of rival unions, the report was never made public; its more essential contents became known only because they were leaked to the press. No effort was made by the state administration or the government to publicize and pursue evidence of the extensive mismanagement of public funds – evidence that could have been highly embarrassing to the official union.[39]

The revision of regulations

State action – or inaction – has also helped the FNSEA to maintain its dominance of the Chambers of Agriculture, the only comanagement institutions the official union gains control of through contested elections rather than through state appointments. On several occasions the state has altered the regulations for elections to the chambers in a manner seemingly designed to reinforce FNSEA strength. For example, by a decree of September 26, 1969, retired farmers – one of the major constituencies of MODEF – were removed from the college of *chefs d'exploitation* (which elects most chamber members – four per electoral district, twelve to twenty in a typical department) and placed in a separate college, electing only two chamber members per department. This "reform" reduced the voting power of retired farmers by approximately 71 percent nationwide: The retired farmers were accorded only one seat per 2,653 voters, whereas the active farmers were accorded one seat per 772 voters. An immediate result of this measure was the decline of MODEF seats in many of its departmental strongholds; in the case of Landes it produced the defeat of the only MODEF organization that had previously enjoyed a chamber majority. Although it is impossible to prove that the ministry created the retired farmers' college with the intent to combat the increasing influence of MODEF, the inference is certainly plausible (especially in light of some of the facts presented later). In Landes itself there was scarcely any doubt as to the intention of the 1969 decree. As a MODEF article commented after the 1970 election had put the FDSEA back in control of the chamber, the reform "has, as if by chance, favored certain candidates... An attempt is being made to find a formula in which the vote for MODEF will not count at all."[40]

Although the state enacted "reforms" like that of 1969, it has failed to adopt seemingly reasonable regulations that would weaken the FNSEA's hold on the chambers. For example, the agricultural ministry has consistently denied the demand of rival unions for state subsidization of costs incurred in chamber election campaigns – subsidization that has been granted to competitors in elections to the Chambers of Commerce and the Chambers of Industry. In the absence of such subsidization, rival unions are hard pressed to compete with the FDSEA, not only because of their larger budgets but because of their ability to exploit the resources of the chamber in their campaigns.[41]

Monetary subsidies

By far the least publicized benefit that the FNSEA derives from *concertation* is the receipt of financial grants from the state for the pursuit of a variety of union activities. Since the early 1960s the FNSEA has received millions of francs per year through various national subsidy programs. Rival unions have received no such subsidization. They have been systematically excluded from all subsidy programs administered by the "hierarchical-vertical" channel of the French governmental system. In some cases, rival unions have succeeded in gaining a share of the subsidies distributed by the "political-horizontal" channels, that is, the Conseils Généraux (see the next section).[42] Nevertheless, the amount of subsidization accorded to rival unions nationwide has been altogether insignificant compared to that received by the FNSEA. The federation's subsidies have been derived from two basic sources: the development program and the *promotion sociale collective* program.

Development subsidies

The goals, institutional structures (ANDA and SUAD), and department-level beneficiaries of the agricultural development program were examined in the second section. What remains to be discussed is the importance of development subsidies accorded to official unionism at the national level. Annual development subsidies have been granted for the past decade to the FNSEA itself, to the CNJA, and to various other organizations affiliated with the FNSEA.

In 1974, for example, the FNSEA per se received 893,800F from ANDA for the furtherance of development. The CNJA, charged with the implementation of development programs for young farmers, received an even greater sum: 2,968,100F. The organizational significance of the CNJA subsidy is enormous; in fact, Yves Tavernier has argued that the CNJA "only functions at the national and department levels thanks to the funds granted by the state." In some years, state subsidies have comprised as much as 92 percent of the total CNJA budget, with dues accounting for a mere 8 percent. Significant subsidies were also received in 1974 by a host of other organizations under more or less formal control of the FNSEA. Perhaps the best example of such an organization is the FNGVPA (Fédération Nationale des Groupements de Vulgarisation du Progrès Agricole),[43] an organization officially deemed to be a "section of the FNSEA" and headed – as of 1975 – by an adjunct secretary general of the FNSEA; the FNGVPA received 1,172,800F in 1974.[44]

Promotion sociale subsidies

The second major subsidy program from which the FNSEA has benefited is that for *promotion sociale collective*. This program, one not restricted to agriculture, was initiated by the government in 1959 with the espoused goal of aiding recognized interest groups in their efforts to educate activists who would eventually assume leadership roles and become interlocutors of the state.[45] As FNSEA officials have noted, the *promotion sociale* subsidy serves to further the process of concertation. Through enabling union leaders to become competent not only in "union techniques" but also in "economic, legal, fiscal, and social" matters, this program assures that "the union–administration dialogue can build on a base of common vocabulary."[46] Left unstated in FNSEA discussions of this program is that it also provides the official union with an immense competitive advantage over MODEF and other rival unions.

The funds for *promotion sociale* have been distributed in a preferential manner since their inception. Among industrial unions, for example, the CGT was accorded from one-eighth to one-fourth as much as the other major unions until 1969; and since 1969 it has received merely an equal amount, despite its demonstrated preponderance.[47] Among agricultural unions, none but the official FNSEA–CNJA has received any subsidization.

The *promotion sociale* subsidies granted to the FNSEA and CNJA increased steadily throughout the 1960s. In 1964 the FNSEA received 547,000F and the CNJA 450,000F – a total of 997,000F. By 1970 the total reached 2,200,000F, with the FNSEA and the CNJA receiving 1,100,000 apiece. The significance of this figure can be manifested by comparing it with the operating budget of the FNSEA's central organization in Paris; in 1970 this budget, comprised of the dues of all affiliated organizations, was slightly less than 3,000,000F.[48]

The *promotion sociale* subsidies have enabled the FNSEA to undertake an extensive nationwide program for the *perfectionnement des cadres*, that is, for the education and information of organizational elites and administrative personnel. From 1962 to 1973, 94,206 individuals participated in educational sessions; in 1973 alone, 11,389 individuals participated in sessions lasting an average of several days.[49] These sessions, financed at least 60 percent by state funds, have varied greatly in their subjects, participants, and locales. Sessions have focused on a multitude of subjects, for example, structural reform policy, tax policy, the common agricultural policy of the E.E.C., methods for improving productivity, and means of increasing participation in union activity. Some of these sessions – about 4 percent of the 1973 total – have been national or regional meetings of top-level elites (e.g., FDSEA presidents and administrative directors) initiated and organized by the FNSEA central office. Most sessions, however, have been departmental affairs involving the participation of one or more national FNSEA officials, all of the FDSEA officials, and many of the union's rank and file.[50]

These state-subsidized sessions serve not only to educate and inform the FNSEA's departmental *cadres* but also to increase the vitality and unity of the union's organization. They facilitate FDSEA efforts to elicit the participation of members by reimbursing them for travel expenses and by providing them with free meals, and they help the FNSEA elite maintain contact with the *base* by subsidizing travel from Paris to the localities. Moreover, they also assist in the *relance* efforts of weak FDSEA threatened by rival unions, as funds can be directed toward those departments featuring intense power struggles. In Landes during the 1960s, for example, extra sessions were held to revivify the FDSEA, and the FNSEA officials whose travel from Paris was covered by a state subsidy stayed after the "education" sessions to organize syndical meetings throughout the department.[51]

The repression of rival unions

The state has employed a variety of means to hinder rival union activity throughout France and especially in those departments featuring substantial organizational threats to the hegemony of the FNSEA. The efforts of the nonofficial unions have been indirectly hindered by the state's refusal to accord them subsidies, council seats, or access to state officials. Some rival unions, able to claim a large departmental following, have even been denied the right – routinely granted to the official union – to hold union meetings in public buildings. In Landes, for example, a 1975 request of the Cercle des Jeunes Agriculteurs – MODEF (by far the largest agricultural youth organization in the department) to use an amphitheater in the agricultural school in Dax for a union congress was rejected by the prefecture with the following brusque letter:

M. the Minister of Agriculture has specified in a very precise manner... the conditions governing the utilization of public educational establishments for meetings... only meetings requested by professional organizations which maintain official relations with the Ministry of Agriculture [are to be permitted].[52]

Faced with such a ruling, a nonofficial union has no recourse other than to register a (futile) protest or appeal to the ministry in Paris through the mediation of a sympathetic deputy.

Rival unions have been repressed more directly through every means, from the deployment of the riot police (the CRS) to interference with their attempts to exercise power in the Chamber of Agriculture. An intriguing example of such interference occurred in Landes in 1968. When asked by the prefect to propose a six-man board of directors for the newly established SUAD, the president of the chamber – the secretary-general of MODEF – did precisely what his counterparts in other departments had done: He proposed a board composed exclusively of members of his own union. Upon consultation with his superiors in Paris, the prefect learned that such a board would simply not be acceptable. Faced with a contradiction between his duty to implement governmental policy and his duty to maintain order in the department, the prefect found himself placed in a most difficult situation. "Everyone at the ministerial level," he noted months later, thought that the resolution of this dilemma would be an "impossibility." Eventually he did formulate a solution to the problem, admitting that it was imperfect but adding – rather wistfully – that it would not have been necessary "if I were in a department like the majority of rural departments in France where the problem is not posed in the same conditions."

The "compromise solution" was the following: Together with the six MODEF members designated by the chamber president, the SUAD board was to include six FDSEA members – appointed by the prefect – and four members of Conseil Général who would participate in a "consultative role" at all board meetings. Although the prefect noted that this solution was largely necessitated by opinion at the ministerial level, he justified his action essentially by arguing that "SUAD would not be able to function unless an accord were reached among all of the union *tendances* existing in the department." Only if he could "establish an equilibrium" among the competing unions, he asserted, would the programs of SUAD be effectively and properly implemented.

MODEF and its supporters in the Conseil Général objected to this "solution" but were forced to accept it when told that no SUAD funds would be forthcoming under other conditions. In noting his reservations, one general councillor expressed the hope that the prefect would also "follow the policy of equilibrium in choosing directors for the Maison de l'Elevage [the EDE]" and other comanagement institutions (such as the ADASEA), which were controlled exclusively by the FDSEA. This hope was never fulfilled, however. In fact, the "policy of equilibrium" was soon revealed to have been little more than a sham even in regard to the SUAD. After the FDSEA won control of the chamber in the 1970 elections (under the "reformed" regulations discussed in a preceding section), the new chamber–SUAD president was allowed to appoint a board composed entirely of FDSEA activists. With the SUAD board now safely in the hands of the official union, the prefect (after, one would assume, breathing a sigh of relief) discarded the "policy of equilibrium" and – despite vehement MODEF protests – refused to appoint a single member of the rival *tendance*. [53]

The limits to repression

Through the employment of a variety of repressive means, official union hegemony has thus been imposed rather effectively – if not easily, and if not without recurrent headaches for the prefect – even in departments where the FNSEA is extremely weak. Nevertheless, in recent years nonofficial unions have demonstrated some ability to challenge the official union system. Through mobilizing their members in the streets and exercising their influence in the Conseil Général, the rival unions of some departments have won at least some concessions from the state and have revealed the limits to repression.

Power in the streets

The case of Landes provides a vivid example of the state's inability to ignore completely nonofficial unions capable of manifesting power in the streets. For five years after the FDSEA displaced MODEF in the Chamber of Agriculture, the prefects of Landes attempted to adhere faithfully to the government's national policy of according a representative monopoly to the FNSEA. No seats were granted to MODEF leaders on formal councils; moreover, the prefecture pursued a policy of strictly denying even requests for informal meetings between MODEF leaders and state officials. The initial MODEF response to this "policy of discrimination" consisted merely of formal protests and a steady stream of threatening articles in the union newspaper. With the onset of the agricultural crisis of 1974, however, the MODEF leaders decided to back up their verbal protests with a series of mass demonstrations at the sous-prefectures and the prefecture. The culmination of these efforts occurred in February 1975 when, after receiving yet another refusal for consultations with the prefect, more than two hundred MODEF members stormed the prefecture and occupied it for two hours, thundering protests through a loudspeaker system; the demonstration ceased only after a violent clash with the riot police. "The Government has demonstrated once again in Landes," exclaimed the next issue of the MODEF paper, "how it conceives of dialogue with MODEF . . . by the intermediation of the CRS."

Soon after this disruption of the peace, the prefect was replaced by another more sensitive to the maxim cited by one of the subjects of

Howard Machin's study of French public administration: "To be a good Prefect you have to appreciate 'the art of the possible.'" Within a few months the new prefect acknowledged that the practice of this art in Landes would entail at least some steps toward the de facto recognition of MODEF. Since 1975 MODEF delegates have been accorded seats on most advisory councils as representatives of non-union organizations (e.g., cooperatives) and MODEF delegations have been grudgingly received at the prefecture. But the nonofficial union has continued to be rebuffed in its requests for de jure seats – and the FDSEA has thus retained control of all the formal decision-making bodies.[54]

Influence in the Conseil Général

Within the last few years, rival unions in a number of departments have – with varying degrees of success – begun to exploit their political influence within the Conseil Général in an effort to combat the official union system. In Corrèze, for example, councillors with ties to the department's two nonofficial unions – MODEF and the recently founded, Socialist-oriented MONATAR (Mouvement National des Travailleurs Agricoles et Ruraux) – refused to approve the 1976 budgetary allocation for the SUAD, charging that its employees were devoting much of their time to *animation syndicale* on behalf of the FDSEA and that its budget thus represented a "disguised subsidy" for the official union. Although they failed (by a margin of only one vote) to block the passage of the SUAD budget, they did succeed in conveying the message that they intended to monitor closely the use – and abuse – of public funds by the corporatist client of the government.[55]

In Landes, where the political influence of the FDSEA's opponents is greater and where two of the councillors (as of 1976) are MODEF officials, the Conseil Général has been utilized even more effectively. Here the MODEF sympathizers have loudly proclaimed their intent to work "against the injustice created by a government which recognizes only one category of unions, despite the fact that this is an anti-democratic position... a scandal!" Viewing as unfair the fact that only the youth organization of the FDSEA receives a subsidy from the national development fund, the majority of the Landes conseil has since 1972 adopted a *principe du rattrapage*, according a larger departmental subsidy each year to the MODEF Cercle des Jeunes than to the FDSEA's Centre des Jeunes: In 1975, for example, the MODEF group was granted 40,000F by the Conseil, whereas the FDSEA group received only 10,000F (to go along with the 50,000F allotted by ANDA in Paris).[56]

The powerful nonofficial union of Landes has thus experienced some success in exploiting the limits to the state's ability to shape the syndical order in France. Given the centralization of the political system, the nonofficial union has not been able to put more than a dent in the machinery that supports official union hegemony. But it has provided a vivid reminder of the extent to which the nationwide hegemony of the FNSEA rests on corporatist bases.

Conclusion

Some FNSEA opponents have charged that the official union's state-supported hegemony is reminiscent of the "totalitarianism of the *corporation paysanne* of Vichy."[57] This charge is somewhat misleading, as it fails to acknowledge the fundamental difference between the dynamics of Vichy corporatism and the dynamics of modern corporatism. In the Vichy corporatist system, the state simply declared that only one "union" had the right to exist. In the modern corporatist system, the state has declared that an unlimited number of unions have an equal right to exist – but that the official union is more equal than the others. Official union hegemony has been assured not through a decree, and not primarily through the direct repression of rivals, but rather through a more subtle process. The official union has been accorded exclusive access to formal councils, privileged informal access to state officials, devolved authority for the administration of important aspects of public policy, favorable reforms of regulations affecting the sector, and substantial monetary subsidies. These benefits have translated into nationwide hegemony by providing farmers with tangible and intangible incentives to support the official union regardless of its policies.

But if the dynamics of the old system and the new system differ substantially, their outcomes are quite similar. The modern corporatist system *is* reminiscent of the old corporatist system in that it manifests a successful effort by the state to act as the architect of syndical order. Future case studies will reveal to what degree and through what specific means the state has played such an architectural role in other sectors and in other democratic polities.

Notes

1 Claus Offe, "The Attribution of Public Status to Interest Groups: Observations on the West German Case." Chapter 5 in this volume.

2 This is a paraphrase of Charles W. Anderson's notion of "the state as architect of political order." See "Political Design and the Representation of Interests," *Comparative Political Studies* 10(1) (April 1977):130.

3 This paper is derived from my Ph.D. dissertation: "The Politics of Official

Unionism in French Agriculture 1958–1976: A Study of the Corporatist Bases of FNSEA Hegemony" (Harvard University, Department of Government, 1978). The dissertation will henceforth be referred to as "Official Unionism." The names of interviewees identified by number in the following notes are listed in Appendix I of the dissertation.

4 Yves Tavernier, "Le Syndicalisme paysan et la politique agricole du governement," *Revue française de science politique*, 12(3) (September 1962): 621–2.

5 *30 ans de combat syndical*, supplement to *L'Information agricole* (467) (March 1976):81; see also "Official Unionism," op. cit., Chaps. 2–3.

6 See "Official Unionism," op. cit., Chap. 3, pp. 164–7.

7 See "Official Unionism," op. cit., Chap. 3; the complete results of the 1973 opinion poll are given in Yves Tavernier, *Sociologie politique du monde rural et politique agricole*, fascicule III (Paris: Fondation Nationale des Sciences Politique, 1973), pp. 322–3, 358.

8 See "Official Unionism," op. cit., Chap. 3.

9 Exclusive of other farmers' unions, although not of other professional organizations; representatives of the Chambers of Agriculture and the cooperative associations are accorded seats along with the FNSEA–CNJA.

10 Georges Lavau, "Political Pressures by Interest Groups in France," in *Interest Groups on Four Continents* ed. Henry Ehrmann (Pittsburgh: University of Pittsburgh Press, 1958), p. 83. For a discussion of the efforts of the rival unions to obtain recognition, see "Official Unionism," op. cit., Chap. 4, p. 255, fn. 2.

11 ANDA – Association National pour le Développement Agricole; CNASEA – Centre National pour l'Aménagement des Structures des Exploitations Agricoles; FORMA – Fonds de Régularisation et d'Orientation des Marchés Agricoles.

12 "Official Unionism," op. cit., pp. 217–24; see also Tavernier's *Sociologie politique*, op. cit., pp. 216, 281; and Louis Prugnaud, *Les Etapes du syndicalisme agricole en France* (Paris: Editions de l'Epi, 1963), pp. 219–38.

13 SAFER is the Sociétés d'Aménagement Foncier et d'Etablissement Rural.

14 See "La SAFER Marche-Limousin au service de l'agriculture régionale," *Corrèze-Magazine* (163) (July–August 1975), and *L'Information agricole* (91) (December 1974): vi.

15 *SAFER: Organisation, fonctionnement* (Paris: FNSAFER, 1972), pp. 5–15.

16 Raoul Massetat, "Rapport moral," XXVIᵉ Congres FDSEA (Landes), p. 29.

17 "Official Unionism," op. cit., Appendix I, interviews 13, 52, 72, 89, 92, 94, 97, 99, 101, 56 and 65.

18 Ibid., interviews 89, 97, 99. As discussed in Official Unionism, op. cit., Chap. 7, such discrimination is virtually impossible in a department in which a rival union is extremely powerful and capable of applying external pressure on SAFER decisions.

19 "Official Unionism," Appendix I, interview 72.

20 Associations Départementales pour l'Aménagement des Structures des Exploitations Agricoles.

21 *L'ADASEA au service des agriculteurs* (Laon: ADASEA de l'Aisne, 1972), p. 8. The FASASA is a Social Action Fund for the Amelioration of Agricultural Structures established by the Complementary Law; the IVD (Indemnité Viagère de Départ), a subsidy for aged farmers who agree to an early retirement and render their land available for redistribution, has been the most important aspect of FASASA activity.

22 *L'ADASEA au service*, op. cit., p. 8.

23 Ibid., p. 23; *Le Sillon des Landes et des Pyrénées*, (219) (April 30, 1970):3 of the Landes section. ADASEA personnel perform FDSEA functions for a variety of reasons; some do so out of a commitment to the FDSEA's values and goals (many are former FDSEA members), some do so because they are friends (or even relatives) of FDSEA staff or members, others do so simply because they – or their bosses – consider it to be part of

their job. This assessment is based on my personal observations and many interviews, for example, "Official Unionism," Appendix I, interviews 14, 15, 52, 56, 61, 65, 72, 73, 74.

24 The "development" program was prepared under Pisani but was not enacted until after his departure in October 1966.

25 *Le Monde*, October 7, 1966.

26 *Le Monde*, October 7, 1966; see also Paul Houée's *Les Etapes du développement rural*, Vol. 2 (Paris: Les Editions Ouvrières, 1972), Chap. 6.

27 R. Thierry de Ville d'Avray, "Les Grandes étapes de la diffusion du progrès technique en France," *Paysans*, (111) (April–May 1975): 25; see also, in the same issue of *Paysans*, Gérard de Caffarelli, "Les Nouvelles orientations de l'ANDA pour un meilleur service des agriculteurs." pp. 38–43.

28 R. Thierry de Ville d'Avray, op. cit., p. 25.

29 Houée, op. cit., pp. 6, 124; "Le Développement agricole dans les Landes," Assemblée Générale, March 18, 1972 (St. Vincent-de-Tyrosse), especially p. 3; "Dotation aux Organismes Maitres d'Oeuvre: 1976," SUAD, Chambre d'Agriculture de la Corrèze; "Programme pluriannuel de développement agricole," SUAD, Chambre d'Agriculture des Landes, September 1974; "Programme pluriannuel de développement agricole: 1974–1976," SUAD, Chambre d'Agriculture de l'Aisne. For a discussion of the importance of the SUAD subsidy to the CNJA, see Tavernier, *Sociologie politique*, op. cit., p. 281.

30 P. Maurel, "Quel est le rôle des chambres d'agriculture?" *Paysans* (44) (October–November 1963):11–9; F. Maurel, "Syndicalisme et chambres d'agriculture," *Paysans* (42) (June–July 1963):5–14; *Le Monde*, February 1, 1964:18; Christiane Mora, "Les Chambres d'agriculture et l'unité paysanne," in *L'Univers politique des paysans dans la France contemporaine*, Yves Tavernier et al., eds. (Paris: Colin, 1972), pp. 507–31; "Le Budget des chambres d'agriculture: 1973," (Paris: APCA, 1973).

31 DSA (now DDA) – the chief departmental state functionary for agriculture.

32 See the two articles by Maurel listed in note 30. The president of the Chamber of Agriculture in Aisne was referred to as the "*préfet vert*" in interview 52; the director of the chamber in Corrèze was referred to as the "*préfet agricole*" in interview 99.

33 The most noteworthy exceptions to the rule of FNSEA dominance are Indre-et-Loire (where FFA controls the chamber) and Puy-de-Dôme (where anti-Débatisse forces control the chamber); MODEF controlled the Landes chamber from 1964 to 1970.

34 In Corrèze, for example, the FDSEA director performed the functions of the chamber director for almost two decades while maintaining the title of chamber sub-director; the activity of the *de jure* chamber director was limited to relatively mundane chores such as bookkeeping, bill paying and the supervision of personnel (interviews 75, 78, 79). Informed sources indicate that this is a rather common arrangement (interviews 13, 52, 79, 81).

35 "Official Unionism," op. cit., Appendix I, interview 56. This particular individual eventually did split from the FDSEA to organize MONATAR in Corrèze – and admitted to doubts as to whether he had made the proper decision, a decision that entailed abandoning his positions of influence within the powerful decision-making structures of the department. Had the FDSEA not been an "official union" with a monopoly on departmental power, he noted, he would have resigned from it long before he actually did.

36 "Official Unionism," op. cit., Chap. 6 and Appendix I, interviews 56, 78.

37 Ibid., Chap. 6 and Appendix I, interview 72.

38 *Le Monde*, August 19, 1971. For more details on FNSEA use and abuse of the chambers, see "Official Unionism," op. cit., Chaps. 5–7.

39 See, for example, *L'Exploitant familial: Organe national du MODEF*, (140) (September 1971); *Le Monde*, August 19, 1971.

40 See Yves Tavernier, "Le Mouvement de défense des exploitants familiaux ["Le MODEF"]," in *L'Univers politique des paysans*, op. cit., p. 479; see also the discussion of the Landes case in Chapter 7, especially pp. 470–476.

41 See *Les Informations agricoles* (MODEF-Mont-de-Marsan) (789) (June 6, 1975).

42 The "hierarchical-vertical" and "political-horizontal" terms are borrowed from Jean-Claude Thoenig, "State Bureaucracies and Local Government in France," a paper presented at the Harvard Center for European Studies, March 1975, p. 10. For examples of *conseils* that have granted subsidies to nonofficial unions, see "Official Unionism," op. cit., Chaps. 6–7.

43 The National Federation of the GVA, institutions that – as noted previously – are "sections" of the cantonal FNSEA unions.

44 "Quelques données chiffrées sur le développement agricole," *Paysans* (111) (April–May 1975):108–9; *L'Information agricole*, (381) (May 1968); Tavernier, *Sociologie politique*, op. cit., p. 281; "La Situation de l'agriculture et l'activité syndicale en 1974," 29ᵉ Congrès Fédéral-FNSEA, Versailles, March 18–20, 1975, p. 72.

45 See the series of articles by Joanine Roy on "L'Aide gouvernementale à la formation des syndicalistes," *Le Monde*, July 16, 17, 18, 1964.

46 *L'Information agricole* (431) (December 1972):43; (414) (May 1971):48.

47 See Michel Bazex, *L'Administration et les syndicats* (Paris: Editions Berger-Levrault, 1973), pp. 146–149.

48 *Le Monde*, July 18, 1964; *Les Informations agricoles* (MODEF-Mont-de-Marsan) (658) (November 10, 1972); "Rapport financier," 25e Congrès Fédéral-FNSEA, Nimes, February 24–26, 1971.

49 *L'Information agricole* (448) (June 1974):30.

50 *L'Information agricole* (414) (May 1971):49.

51 See "Official Unionism," op. cit., Chap. 7 especially pp. 447–9.

52 See "Official Unionism," op. cit., Chap. 7, p. 488.

53 See "Official Unionism," op. cit., pp. 488–91; the quotations are taken from "Procès-verbaux des délibérations du conseil général: Département des Landes," 2me Session Ordinaire de 1968, pp. 79–82.

54 "Official Unionism," op. cit., pp. 479–81; Howard Machin, *The Prefect in French Public Administration* (London: Crown Helm, 1977), p. 201.

55 "Official Unionism," op. cit., Chap. 6., pp. 390–2.

56 Ibid., Chap. 7, pp. 491–4.

57 "Rapport Moral: Les Agriculteurs face à la corporation anti-paysanne," 4ᵉ Congrès National, Fédération Française de l'Agriculture, Saint-Lo, October 23–24, 1974.

8

The internal politics of trade unions

CHARLES F. SABEL

It was frequently argued in the 1960s that economic growth and technological progress were making traditional ideologies obsolete in the advanced Western societies. The triumph of the pluralist state and with it the disappearance of ideological conflict was seen as part cause, part effect, of what promised to be a continual increase in material well-being. But the great European strike waves at the end of the decade, the slowing of economic growth, and the difficult struggle against inflation in the 1970s called into question the end-of-ideology argument and exposed the fragility of the existing forms of politics. To account for the political changes wrought by the growing determination of particular groups to hold society hostage to their demands, theories of the breakdown of the pluralist and the rise of a neo-, liberal-, or societal-corporatist state were developed.[1] Yet for reasons of their own, and with various degrees of hesitancy, these theories endorse a central conclusion of the older view: that debate about crucial social values, about the best way to organize modern society, will gradually be stilled. The argument in this chapter is that despite changed circumstances, such a conclusion is no more plausible now than it was in the 1960s. The reasons lie in the contest for power within corporate groups.

The older view of the end of ideology is too familiar and has been too often attacked to require extensive comment or criticism.[2] At the core of the argument is the notion of technological determinism. One central claim is that for every problem there is one and only one technological solution that makes the most efficient use of resources, given existing wants. A second claim is that any society that adopts a given technology obliges itself to adopt the uniquely corresponding forms of social organization as well. The first claim implies that debates between technical experts over questions of efficiency will re-

209

place debates between politicians over visions of a just social order – ideologies; and the second claim suggests that once the technical debates are at an end, the problem of social organization will solve itself.

Theorists of neo-corporatism reject the technological determinism of the older view. They do not think politics is reducible to choices of technology. Moreover, they observe that the party system and parliament no longer function as effective instruments for the execution of democratic procedure, but rather that the recourse to politics is itself disruptive, overburdening the state with unfulfillable demands. How, then, are the advanced capitalist societies trying to make essential decisions without precipitating a universally destructive war of all against all? Their answer is, in essence, by attempting to choke off political discussion within corporate interest groups.

One line of argument emphasizes the devolution of power from the state to private interest groups. Conflicts between groups become so intense that the state offers the leaders of these groups power over their members in return for a pledge to arrive at "reasonable" bargaining results. The state, for example, might legalize certain forms of dues collection that make union revenues independent of short-term changes in the members' opinion of the organization. The price for such legislation would be the leaders' agreement to an unpopular incomes policy. The more the state requires the leaders to disregard the spontaneous sentiments of the rank and file, the more securely it allows them to protect themselves against those sentiments.

Politics can be defined as struggle over the rules that limit who may demand what and the means that may be applied to satisfying demand. In this sense, politics is closely related to the notion of ideology as a vision of a just social order. Insofar as visions of a just social order are embodied in procedural rules broadly defined, politics is a struggle over which ideology will prevail. I will call the opposite of politics so conceived simply the struggle for power. In the struggle for power the rules of the contest itself are always explicitly assumed or simply ignored; they are never in question. The struggle for power is the game of the *éminence grise* (Bourdieu, 1977).

It follows that the more wide ranging and the better enforced the bargains of this neo-corporatist sort, the more likely that two forms of political activity within the bargaining groups will be stifled. First, the rules governing the relations between groups will be frozen as all pledge to defer to a common standard of "reasonableness." The effort by state authorities to convince business and the trade unions to limit wage increases to productivity increases plus a cost of living allowance is a classic example. Second, the rules controlling relations between leaders and rank and file in any one group will be withdrawn from discussion: Leaders will have the power simply to coerce the members to accept settlements.

A variant of the neo-corporatist thesis put forward by Pizzorno introduces the notion of progress in the division of labor, but only to arrive at similar conclusions by a different route (Pizzorno, 1978). As in the first case, leaders are said to refrain from exploiting the full market power of the groups they represent. They want to do this because their personal interests are tied to the long-term development of, not the short-run returns to, the group; they are able to do this because of their monopoly over the information that reaches the group members: Not knowing what their possibilities are, the latter must content themselves with accepting the course of action defined by the leaders as the only possible one.

This arrangement would be stable were it not that progress in the organization of work throws up new groups-in-formation, whose interests are not represented by the existing bargaining parties. As these protogroups struggle for recognition, they reinvent politics for two reasons. First, the protogroups need to shape the interests of their potential members so that they will undertake the effort of forming the group in the first place. The idea is that the members-to-be of the group must abandon their old self-definitions and realize that they can only esteem themselves insofar as they help create a world in which, according to the emergent ideology of the group, they are to have an honored place. No sacrifice, material or otherwise, for the creation of the new society (and group) will then be too great, because sacrifices and rewards can always be balanced by the immeasurably large benefits to be had in the future. The formation of a new group thus depends on the prospective members' willingness to place new demands on society and pursue them with unorthodox (because disallowed in the existing system of bargaining) means.

Second, a project of this magnitude requires allies. Therefore the ideology must be in some degree universal; that is, it must promise disparate groups a place in the new order. Otherwise they will refuse their support to the group being formed. In this way the birth of a new group reopens discussion about the existing order in the old ones.

Once the new group enters the system of bargaining, however, its political *élan* dissipates. Its leaders become concerned with their future in the institution; they begin to exploit their superior knowledge of the situation for the group's, or even their own, narrow purposes. Calculation of self-interest replaces the group-in-formation's appeal to universal ideology; and its selfishness disabuses the older groups of their newfound disinterestedness. As before, the pursuit by leaders, followers, and the group as a whole of well-defined advantage within well-defined limits comes to replace politics. So although this version of the theory is different from the first in insisting on a *ricorso* of politics, the two versions are similar in suggesting that ideological debate is not a continuous feature of the life of established groups. Despite many refinements, in neither case are we very far from Michels' theory of the Iron Law of Oligarchy.[3]

I want to make two kinds of arguments against the recent Michelsian versions of the end-of-ideology theory. The first set involves the regeneration of politics between corporate groups. The aim here is to show that there are tendencies inherent in those relations that undermine all efforts to construct a stable and enduring series of compromises. The claim is that the interest of the leaders of corporate groups in aggrandizing their own power sets important limits on their willingness to collaborate with one another in freezing the rules of the bargaining game. The second set of arguments, which forms the center of gravity of this chapter, concerns politics inside corporate groups. I posit that in their efforts to gain control of the group, and in the very act of establishing the institutional rules that would guarantee their power, leaders create organizational structures that can serve to reintroduce explicit political debate where none had seemed possible.

Reduced to a schematic, the link between the two levels of argument is that intergroup relations are fragile because both accommodation and continued conflict carry the same risks: paralyzing chaos and unpredictable radicalization. This fragility produces and is reflected in disputes over the rules of intergroup competition within the leadership of any one group; the ambiguities of the institutional structures by which power is exercised within the group make it possible for a faction within the leadership to try to strengthen its hand by winning the low-level officials away from its competitors; finally, because the struggle for factional control necessarily involves a discussion of the relations between leaders and followers, the self-interested pursuit of power by leaders embroils the whole group time and time again in disputes over politics in the sense of debate over the distribution of power within the group as well.

At the outset, three clarifications should be put in the way of as many possible misinterpretations of the argument I am advancing. First, I am not criticizing the neo-corporatist models for systematically underestimating the precariousness of inter- and intragroup relations in order to vindicate older pluralist views. Rather, my criticism is directed to an assumption shared by both pluralist and neo-corporatist conceptions, namely, the idea of a homeostatic or self-equilibrating institutional system. The structuring principle of the pluralist conception, as of the neoclassical models of the market from which they were often derived, is the idea of a self-regenerating set of institutional relations. The calculating pursuit of self-interest is supposed to force the actors to recreate, continuously and unwittingly, a set of formal relations among themselves. In the case of pluralism, the tug of war between organized groups reinforces their common subjugation to the rules and institutions of the liberal state; in the case of neoclassical economics, market transactors force one another to perpetuate a regime of free competition in which factors of production are paid their marginal product, and prices equal marginal costs. In both instances, then, the formal relations between the protagonists persist unchanged regardless of the substantive outcomes of their successive dealings. Moreover, in both cases the ideology of the protagonists is supposed to become in time a reflection of the social theorist's description of the bargaining regime. Thus market participants and pluralist politicians are presumed to realize that despite occasional though powerful temptations to the contrary, laissez-faire and the liberal state best serve their respective interests; and given that they are self-interested, what possible motive will they have for elaborating alternatives to them?

Approached in this way, a textbook neo-corporatist society would appear to be a species of a textbook pluralist society. As measured by official recognition of interest groups' rights and responsibilities, the connection between civil society and the state would be closer in the former than the latter. (Outside of textbooks, by the way, there have been many covert links between states and interest groups in societies described as pluralist – a point often downplayed by those who argue the novelty of neo-corporatist arrangements.)[4] But as far as I can see, the chief effect of this politicization of interest groups is in theory to shift what might be called the locus of rationality from the members of the group to its leaders. As under pluralism, a self-perpetuating system of bargaining is created. But this time the system serves the interests of the leaders, who by controlling the structure of incentives and above all the flow of information within their organizations make the system appear to be in the self-interest of their followers as well. Finally, self-interest is supposed to narrow the vision of neo-corporatist leaders as much as it does participants in the economy and polity under pluralism.

The view of political development I am advancing here differs then from pluralist and neo-corporatist conceptions in two fundamental ways. First, I claim that in industrial, capitalist society, self-interest is constantly tempting the leaders of groups to change the rules of the bargaining game to their own advantage. Second, I argue that the interest group leaders' reciprocal recognition of this temptation is itself a central cause of their inability to create a self-perpetuating system of bargaining. According to pluralist and neo-corporatist conceptions, systematic pursuit of self-interest will make alternatives to the established bargaining regime unthinkable. It seems more correct to say that systematic pursuit of self-interest will provoke thoughts about alternative courses of action that make it extremely difficult to establish a self-perpetuating bargaining regime.

The second clarification concerns the notion of the self-interested leader. For the purposes of this argument, I am assuming that leaders are interested only in increasing their own influence in national affairs. Leaders would not on this view gratuitously neglect the interests of those they represent but would do so whenever they could do it with profit to themselves. Of course most leaders think they are serving the interests of their followers; and many of those who think this do on important occasions take actions dictated not by their conception of self-interest but by their loyalty to the demands of those they represent. By abstracting from the numerous cases where leaders would find the neo-corporatist notion of systematic underrepresentation repugnant on its face, I intend to show that, even by stipulating an exaggerated but nonetheless central thesis of the neo-corporatist claim, the argument cannot stand. Taking interest groups not as I find them but as the neo-corporatist argument says they are, I try to show that they could not remain that way for long. The arguments set forth would then apply *a fortiori* to cases where leaders refuse to connive in corporatist schemes because of their convictions.

The third clarification has to do with the scope of the essay. To illustrate the tensions in intergroup relations I draw on the history of relations between capital and labor. The continuing debate on inflation and wage–price controls documents the centrality of bargaining between unions and employers in the economic and political life of the advanced industrial countries. As for the analysis of group factionalism, examples are drawn exclusively from the study of trade unions. One objection might be that members of trade unions are many. In isolation each is weak. The members of employers' associations are few, and individually they are strong. Because of these differences, might it not be misleading to suggest conclusions about the existence of factional struggles in employers' groups by reference to divisions in unions? Offe, in particular, argues that employee groups are distinguished from employer groups precisely by the fact that, in the former, the organization *forms* the interests of the individually powerless workers, whereas in the latter it merely publicizes the intentions of largely autonomous corporations (Offe, 1981). On this view, factionalism conceived of as struggle over strategy cannot by definition arise in employers' associations: Because leagues of capitalists express strategy but do not determine it, there is simply nothing to struggle about.

No doubt the problems of establishing and executing strategy in employer associations bear the marks of the relatively small number and relatively great autonomy of the members.[5] But for all that it seems equally true, although I will not explore this case here, that these problems exist in a general way as much for employer as for employee groups. To take only one example, firms, sometimes including the very largest, are often faced with a choice between a high-cost, autarkic strategy based on protectionism and a low-cost strategy of competition on world markets. Which course they choose will depend on whether the state can be brought to impose tariffs or to subsidize cost-cutting investments through tax credits. But the state's choice will in turn depend largely on the alliance that firms in this situation can form with other industrial and agricultural groups facing similar choices. In these crucial cases, each capitalist can fix his or her strategy only in consultation with other capitalists; and the struggle to build coalitions for one position or the other will be analogous in many ways to the battle to determine trade-union policy (Gourevitch, 1977). Once employers have decided on a strategy, their wealth and small number will give them important advantages over trade unions in executing it. But this is quite different from saying that their advantage over labor lies precisely in having an unambiguous strategy from the start.

The body of this chapter is in three sections. The first deals with the dilemma of establishing stable relations among corporate groups. The second aims to show the consequences of this dilemma for the internal organization of trade unions; and the third brings this two-part argument to bear on the analysis of the Confederazione Generale Italiana del Lavoro (CGIL) and the federations of the Deutscher Gewerkschaftsbund (DGB).

Why there is no enduring peace between corporate groups

There can be no lasting peace between unions and management because the risks of peace are for both sides in many ways the same as the risks of continued conflict. The failure to arrive at some agreement is associated with the closely related risks of paralyzing chaos and the unpredictable radicalization of group life. Leaders of one or both groups may have the motives and power to refuse to bargain with the other. But as long as one side is not completely powerless, failure to strike a bargain will produce one of two results. Changes will be imposed by the stronger party and the weaker one will bide its time, tallying a longer and longer list of grievances. In that case, at the moment economic conditions shift slightly in favor of the underdog there will be an explosion of protest against the application of *force majeure*. The Italian *autunno caldo* of 1969 discussed later is an object lesson to management and the unions alike of the possibilities for radical social transformation implicit in such situations. Or, out of fear of provoking a crisis, no changes will be made. But in that case, necessary innovations are postponed. International competitors steal a march on home industry. Neglect brings forth the demand for a relaunching of industry; but in the absence of a bargaining framework, industry can only be relaunched at the risk of creating just the crisis that was to be avoided. Aside from actually setting up some bargaining machinery, the only way out of this dilemma is to follow the example set by French industry after the defeat of the *programme commun* in 1978: Wait until your opponent is at his weakest, rationalize industry, then hope desperately (and if experience is a guide, vainly) that the rewards of economic reform will overcome the workers' indignity at its imposition.

But for both capital and labor the prospect of a comprehensive truce agreement is also associated with the twin dangers of paralysis and radical social transformation. Two cases can be distinguished under this rubric. In the first, negotiated stalemate produces demands for radical transformation; in the second, progress toward negotiated transformation produces radicalism and disintegration. Take first the problem of negotiated paralysis. Formal agreements between unequal partners give even the disadvantaged party certain rights. One of the attractions of such agreements – and of rules in general – for the weak is precisely that they set limits to the *de facto* powers of the strong. The more often trade unions and management compromise their differences and make an explicit principle of their practice, the greater the chance that each side will lose some essential part of its freedom of action – the greater the likelihood, in other words, that each side will eventually have enough rights to check some plan crucial to the other. As before, all necessary changes – rationalization of production is the obvious example – cannot be made. Eventually capital again faces the impossible choice between squeezed profits or reduced market shares, and something must be done.

One response of employers caught in this situation is to engage in a legal war of position. Rather than provoking a crisis by frontally attacking the existing system of rules, they interpret it restrictively in practice and press their interpretations in the courts. Their hope is to regain their freedom of maneuver with a minimal disruption of their relations with labor. This appears to have been the strategy of British industrialists around the turn of the century. Impressed by their American counterparts' successfully high-handed treatment of labor, they tried to bring their own trade unions to heel by holding them liable for civil damages in breach of contract suits arising out of strikes (Moore, 1978). Today, pressed in their turn by foreign competition, American industrialists are arguably pursuing an analogous strategy by attacking in various but related ways unions' rights to protect their members' jobs and – in a more fundamental challenge to the New Deal compromise – the rights of union organizers (Ferguson and Rogers, 1979).

Naturally, the more this strategy of the subversion of rights threatens to succeed, the more likely the unions will renounce the existing set of institutional arrangements as having been vitiated by the other side. One major reason the British unions abandoned the Liberals to form the Labour party (committing themselves to parliamentary socialism along the way) was their conviction that their old allies were unwilling to protect them against the legal offensive that culminated in the Taff Vale decision of 1901. In the United States, present legal setbacks are also moving the labor movement to consider new alliances and more militant strategies. Repeated failure to obtain redress in Congress against the courts has moved important union leaders, such as Douglas Fraser, head of the American Auto Workers Union, to the most critical discussion heard in a generation of labor's ties to the Democratic party (Fraser, 1979).

Capital can also try to break the negotiated deadlock by declaring a legal war of maneuver. The power of unions is pronounced too great, and the party of industry aims to limit it legislatively. The Taft-Hartley Act in the United States shows that this strategy can occasionally succeed. But as a rule such a frontal attack is, if anything, more likely to provoke an unpredictable radicalization of labor than more cautious methods. British experience is instructive on this score too. The Tory Industrial Relations Act of 1971 was designed to control labor unrest by forcing trade union organizations to bear responsibility for the acts of their militant, shop floor representatives. The act went into effect in February 1972 and was a dead letter by that summer. The civil penalties prescribed by the law were applied to the leaders of the Transport and General Workers Union for implicitly sanctioning an unofficial dockers strike; criminal penalties set out in the act were applied against five shop stewards for actually leading it.

The result was to bring Britain to the brink of a general strike; to discredit the courts and the government, which openly connived to reverse the legal decisions; and to set the stage first for the Tories' disastrous confrontation with the miners and then for the repeal of substantial portions of the act by the succeeding Labour government (Moran, 1977).

Agreement can lead to paralysis. But the reconciliation between corporate groups can also change the balance of power between them, and in ways that are perhaps more directly threatening to the power of the leaders of the disadvantaged group than a degenerating stalemate. Often the loss of one group's freedom of action augments the power of its opponent; and this augmented power feeds on itself to the point where the weaker group is in danger of being crushed by the superior force of its adversary.

Business leaders are, I think, genuinely horrified at the following prospect: Legislation is passed making it difficult to prevent the formation of the unions. Further legislation gives the union the right to have its dues deducted from the members' paychecks; welfare payments and unemployment benefits make it cheaper for the union to strike. Then a Social Democrat government allied to the unions comes to power. Its full-employment policies strengthen the workers' hand in a permanently tight labor market.

What can happen next is well illustrated by the evolution of the macroeconomic program of the trade-union confederation with the longest continuous and explicit history of neo-corporatist bargaining with business, the Swedish Landorganisationen in Sverige (LO).[6] During the Great Depression the LO advocated, and imposed on the Swedish Social Democratic party, a successful policy of deficit spending that amounted to a Keynesian program of demand stimulation *avant la lettre*. But by the early 1950s experience with this native Keynesianism had taught the LO two disturbing lessons. The first was that demand stimulation produced full employment only at the price of unacceptably high rates of inflation. The second was that inflation could be slowed by a strict incomes policy, but that an incomes policy strained the internal cohesion of the trade union movement (by disrupting accepted wage differentials between different groups in the work force, thus often provoking rivalries between the unions representing them) and tended to freeze, if not render still more inegalitarian, the distribution of wealth (because nonwage income proved to be difficult to control with an incomes policy).

To reconcile the maintenance of full employment with control over inflation and preservation of its organizational integrity, the LO adopted in 1951 and began to pursue in earnest a decade later the

Rehn model, named for the economist who formulated it. Rehn's idea was to exploit the existing segmentation of Swedish industry into sectors of high and low productivity and profitability, each with its corresponding, relatively closed, labor market, in the interests of the LO's triple end. Fiscal policy was to be used to maintain demand at a level that discouraged inflation, although guaranteeing the prosperity only of the productive, low-cost firms. Wage differentials between comparable jobs, but also between different industries, were to be gradually eliminated, the level of wages being pitched to the capacity of profitable employers to pay. The slackening of demand and the increase in wage pressure were calculated to squeeze the profits of high-cost producers, who either became more efficient or went under. In the latter case, workers who lost their jobs were to be supported financially by the state, which would also bear the costs of retraining and relocating them as their new jobs required. These were to be created in the growing high-productivity sector, part of whose expansion was to be financed out of what the state accumulated through its moderately restrictive fiscal policy. The Rehn model was thus to oblige employers to adopt the high-wage, high-productivity strategy made famous by Henry Ford and his five-dollar day while protecting workers from the costs of the forced-draft modernization.

By the end of the 1960s, however, two major defects in the strategy had become apparent. The state proved unable to compensate workers for the costs of industrial reorganization. Traditional communities were undermined, in one town as old factories closed and workers left in search of jobs, in another as new factories suddenly opened, bringing in outsiders. Even where established plants continued to operate, technological innovation destroyed old jobs, leaving the workers unsure of their rights and futures. Furthermore, just as the state had insufficient influence on where jobs were created, so it could not precisely control how many new jobs were offered. The result was that when growth in the high-productivity private-sector jobs did not fully offset the destruction of low-productivity jobs, to maintain full employment the difference had to be made up by creating work in the public sector, thereby straining the state budget.

The Social Democratic party and the LO were alerted to the growing discontent with the Rehn model by setbacks in the municipal elections of 1966 and growing rank-and-file discontent in the unions. As in the early 1950s, they responded to the discomfiture of their plans by attempting to extend their control over the economy by reshaping it still further. One series of reforms aimed at protecting workers from the consequences of economic change by increasing their job security and capacity to contest changes in workplace organization. Thus in 1973 a law was passed that essentially prohibits firing employees for anything but serious crimes. And the Codetermination Act of 1976 empowers trade unions to bargain with management on all "important" company actions; entitles them to information previously regarded as propriety by management; authorizes collective bargaining on *any* issue, including those decisions declared to be the exclusive prerogative of management in existing labor contracts; and expressly legalizes local strikes not approved by the central union leadership.

A second series of proposed reforms aims to resolve the problem of the location and number of new jobs by taking control over investment out of private hands. The basic idea, set out in the Meidner plan, is to require all firms above a certain size to capitalize some fixed proportion, say 20 percent, of their annual profits. Voting rights over the new shares would rest with workers' representatives designated by the trade unions. As new shares continue to be issued, control over the firm would gradually pass to the workers; meanwhile, the dividends from the new stock would be used to finance worker education programs and studies of how best to invest the accrued capital. After some hesitation the Social Democrats have pledged themselves to implement the Meidner plan if they return to power. Their electoral fate will depend in turn partly on their capacity to convince white-collar workers and their political representatives in the small Liberal party to accept the plan as well. But even though this is a story still without an end, its moral is clear enough: Disappointment with successive compromises has led the LO to demand ever greater control over the economy, whereas the very successes of those compromises – above all, a permanently tight labor market – have provided the foundation for the political power it needs to have its way.

In West Germany the postwar history of anything resembling neo-corporatist bargaining begins only in the mid-1960s. But here too, for organizational reasons to be elaborated later, the unions have pressed in recent years for a radical extension of their prerogatives. That they have been less successful than in Sweden is due to the peculiarities of the electoral alliance between the SPD and the liberal Free Democrats (whose passion for labor reform is held in check by their dependence on the financial support of certain industrial sectors and the electoral support of upper-level managers, the *leitende Angestellte.* What the DGB wanted above all was a revision of the 1952 Works Constitution Act, which would have raised its share of seats on the Aufsichtsräte or supervisory boards of large companies outside the coal and steel industries (where an earlier, more evenhanded law is in force) to one half, giving them full parity with capital. What it got was the Parity

Codetermination Act of 1976, which does indeed provide that seats on the Aufsichtsrat be equally divided between capital and labor, but requires the latter's representatives to include one *leitender Angestellte* and one white-collar worker. Still worse from the point of view of the unions, the 1976 act determines that tie votes in the Aufsichtsrat are to be broken by the board chairman, who is appointed by the shareholders. Thwarted in their original intentions by these provisions, the unions have declared their determination to secure revision of the law.

On this evidence, the capitalists are not always wrong when they complain that the unions' appetite for power grows with every taste of it. One line of defense against overbearing labor organizations is obviously to attack their leaders' ability to control the membership and to influence politics. By enforcing an organizational reform of the unions, which makes it easier for an internal opposition to establish itself and/or more difficult for the union organization to place war chests at the disposal of favored politicians, business can cut organized labor down to size. The Landrum–Griffin Act in the United States was, and the proposed Verbändegesetz now under discussion in West Germany would be, a step in this direction. But success here comes of course at a high price because it diminishes the chances that any leader will ever become formidable enough within his or her own organization to ride herd on the rank and file according to the neocorporatist formula (Scharpf, 1978).

The response of German industry to the Parity Codetermination Act of 1976 points to a second and more subtle defense against labor's encroachment on capital's authority. The industrialists challenged its constitutionality in court. Their official claim was that even in its present form it does not respect the rights of property anchored in the West German constitution. Commentators agree, however, that the intent of the challenge was not to overturn the law. Rather, the industrialists wanted to secure a restrictive interpretation of it that would set clear, unbreachable limits to the extension of participatory rights. In this way, they could have their definition of the social status quo written into the constitution, which could then be cited to defeat labor's future pretensions to greater power. But if this strategy is more sophisticated because it is less direct than official regulation of the unions' organizational statutes, it seems no more likely to succeed. The unions' immediate reaction to the challenge was to withdraw their representatives from the Konzertierte Aktion, a high-level wages and prices council. Under such pressure from the unions and pressed as well by Social Democratic politicians, the generally conservative Bundesverfassungsgericht or Constitutional Court upheld the constitutionality of the law on grounds that arguably concede the legality of further extensions of codetermination rights. But even had the court decision been less favorable to the unions, it is hard to imagine that they would not have been able to find, on the shop floor or elsewhere, a way to force industry to admit the possibility of further reforms.

From the union point of view, too, all collaboration with the powers that be is correctly viewed as a step that can lead to subjugation. Suppose, for example, that in return for state protection against employer interference with organization drives, a union agrees to rules restricting its right to strike and perhaps making it financially liable for certain violations of labor law. In times of economic disruption it is likely that the government will try to demand recompense for its services to the union by insisting that the latter restrain its wage demands, allowing profits to accumulate at a rate that stimulates investment and economic growth. Thus just in those moments when the union most needs to demonstrate its efficacy to its members, it is least able to do so: The union cannot press wage demands, nor can it actively support the spontaneous strikes that result when its members do so. To keep control over its members in such a crisis the union is then tempted to rely on precisely those forces – the employers and the state – whose embrace has been so confining in the first place. Deals with management to neutralize the troublemakers in this or that plant and deals with the government to constrain workers to continue their membership in unions solve the problem by further undermining the unions' capacity of autonomous action, thus increasing the propensity to compromise themselves still more in the next crisis.

One possible result of this line of development is that the unions are simply swept aside as rival and more radical organizations are founded to give voice to the workers' discontent. During World War I, for example, union leaders in Italy, France, Great Britain, Germany, and the United States collaborated closely with authorities in administering the war economies. Their principal motive was to assure official recognition of their organizations as entitled to organize and represent the working masses. But incapable of protecting those they claimed to represent from the effects of inflation and the rationalization of work, the union leaders were soon isolated from their followers. Mass strikes, sometimes factory occupations as well, repudiated agreements they had negotiated; workers withdrew their allegiance from national leaders and vested it in plant-level shop stewards' committees. Although the established leaders were often successful in reasserting their authority in the 1920s, in Germany the metalworkers' union came under the control of the militant Obleute or shop stewards; and in France many dissatisfied workers left the old unions to join rival organizations associated with the new French Communist party.

At the opposed extreme, compromised labor leaders can connive with the state to outlaw rival organizations and to join management in exercising an officially sanctioned condominium over the work force. Depending on the kind of state with which they connive and, relatedly, the sorts of coercion on which they depend, their situation will come to resemble that of trade unionists in Mussolini's Italy or Franco's Spain, on the one hand, or of the leaders of the official trade unions in Eastern Europe and the Soviet Union on the other. It seems presently quite unlikely that any liberal Western society would tolerate the denial of the basic democratic rights of free association that such collaboration requires. But even given the requisite political conditions, the historical evidence suggests that the state's power to terrorize and bribe is still insufficient to pacify the work force and to guarantee the tranquility of union leaders: Think of the periodic riots over changes in wages or prices in Eastern Europe, the decline of authority of the falangist Organización Sindacal Española ten years before Franco's death, or the rapid decline in the late 1950s of the power of the Brazilian *pelegos* – the labor leaders beholden to the corporative state who, like the sheepskin saddle blanket for which they were named, merely cushioned those who do the work from the weight of their masters.[7]

A third and intermediate possibility is that compromised trade unions adopt a more radical program, hoping to regain the support of the rank and file and thus free themselves from dependency on management and the state. As examples of this possibility I call attention to recent developments in the LO. If it is true that the LO put forward the Codetermination Act of 1976 and the Meidner plan in part hoping to aggrandize existing powers, it is no less true that the LO's second motive for suggesting them was fear of losing existing powers. As we saw, by the early 1970s, collaboration in economic policies that put labor at the mercy of capital in crucial areas (work conditions, creation of new jobs, rationalization) had estranged the leadership in various degrees from the rank and file. By further extending their control over the economy, the Swedish unions hoped to better protect their members' interests and to make surer claims on their confidence. In different ways developments in the Italian and West German unions, discussed later, illustrate this possibility as well.

Even when they did not lead to a recasting of the union's goals, however, the rank-and-file protests and waves of wildcat strikes that accompanied many of the experiments in neo-corporatist bargaining – the Renault strike of 1947 against a wage freeze agreed to by the French Communist party and the Confédération générale du travail, the strikes in West Germany in 1969 and 1973 against wage settlements judged to be inadequate, the dockers strike in Britain in 1972, and the repeated strikes by British Leyland workers against various incomes policies would be prominent examples – point up a fundamental contradiction in the logic of the neo-corporatist argument. The contradiction concerns the nature of the rank and file's relation to the union. It emerges most clearly in accounts of the genesis of corporatism, such as Streeck's, which attempt to explain why leaders of interest groups make deals that obviously restrict their freedom of action (Streeck, 1977).

Streeck divides the history of trade unions into two periods. The first (which is similar in many ways to what Pizzorno calls the phase of formation of a "new collective identity") apparently extends from about the middle of the nineteenth century to the middle of the twentieth (Pizzorno, 1978). During this early period of capitalism, the division of labor was such that work relations bound workers together on the job and fused their relations at work with their lives at home. Work thus gave rise to an all-embracing community. Implicit in the idea of community is the idea of solidarity; and the institutional face of solidarity in a working community was the trade union. In this period, membership in trade unions was thus more a sign of a particular social identity than the result of a calculation of expected economic benefits. The leaders of these organizations were not plagued by the free-rider problem, because paying dues was a moral obligation, not an investment.

But in the second and subsequent period (which corresponds to the phase of self-interested organizational behavior in Pizzorno's scheme), economic progress subverted the workers' sentimental attachment to the unions. Changes in the division of labor undermined workplace solidarity and the interpretation of life and work. As community succumbs to progress, workers withdraw to the nuclear family. Solidarity counts less and less. Workers' relationships become instrumental in the sense that they deal with others only because of the benefits expected. The same is true of the workers' relation to organizations. In particular, the workers exploit the union as free riders, raking in their share of the benefits it provides through collective bargaining without being willing to pay their share of the costs of obtaining them. Membership drops. Union leaders are forced to pledge to restrain wage claims in return for the state's help in encouraging or coercing workers to join up.

But – here is the contradiction – if the causes of the problem are as they are said to be, then the proposed solution is no solution at all. The state will legislate in favor of the unions only if the latter agree to underrepresent the members. The unions, however, need the legislation precisely because the rank and file have become so exacting in their calculations of cost and benefit. If workers disregard their leaders' pleas and pinch dues pennies, why should they tolerate being shortchanged in their wage claims? Rather, as Goldthorpe has argued, workers will want to "punch their weight" on the market; and if they do, the corporatist schemes will suffer for it (Goldthorpe, 1978). Whether or not workers have in fact become selfish in the characteristically middle-class way Streeck describes, the waves of wildcat strikes cited earlier are *prima facie* proof that they can assess their interests well enough to know when it is to their advantage to be a free rider and when they are simply being taken for a ride.

The upshot is that within the framework of a market economy in which the interests of workers and capitalists clash on a number of central points, there is no solution without substantial risks for the leaders who negotiate it. Of course everything is not up for grabs at every moment. Certainly there will be long periods in the development of a given country when stalemate, whether bargained for or not, is acceptable or when the predominance of capital or labor in one or another sector of the economy produces generally tolerable results. But the evidence is that in a changing world these arrangements do not endure; and, further, that the longer they do persist, the more dramatic and difficult the revision of strategy is likely to be in the period of renovation that succeeds them.

Let us assume that experience and tradition force the leaders of corporate groups to similar conclusions. And this will be so regardless of whether the leaders of the rival groups aim in principle at crushing one another or whether they are intent on mutual accommodation. If they are too forthcoming in negotiations, they know they risk either a revolt of the members or being swallowed by their opponents; if too adamant in their claims, they risk producing a chaotic situation in which the same results are possible. Corporate leaders, in other words, cannot put all their faith in a single strategic conception or even in a fixed idea of the range of permissible strategies, let alone a particular, single-minded strategy of cooperation. Even when they treat their opposite number as a partner, they must treat that person as an opponent as well, who is capable of turning the tables on them in a moment. If this image of the relation between leaders is accepted, two consequences directly follow.

The first is that there will be constant disagreement among the leaders of any one corporate group over the correct course of action: No matter how much more information they have than the members, they can never have enough to completely eliminate controversy among themselves. At issue will be the proper characterization of the facts of the organization's situation – what is the opponent likely to do if we act in such and such a way? – as well as the proper definition of the organization's ultimate purposes. Discussion of particular facts and organizational values will become intertwined, because given any set of facts, the organization's estimate of what constitutes a tolerable risk depends on the goals it is pursuing. Moreover, estimates of how one's opponents are likely to act are generally colored by the set of ideas that define the organization's purpose. Although they will no doubt agree on many issues, revolutionary Leftists and traditional Catholics will differ in their estimates of the ultimate reliability of capitalists as trustworthy partners and make correspondingly different judgments about the dangers of the same situation. If the definition of ideology is now extended to include a corpus of ideas used both to evaluate and describe the world, then the indeterminacy of corporate strategy means that there will be ideological debate among the corporate leaders: debate, to refer back to the earlier definition of politics, not just about which strategy to pick but about the criteria for picking strategies.

Because of the connection between comprehensive views of the world and judgments about particular situations, we should expect, and typically find, that persons who share the same ideological presuppositions repeatedly find themselves on the same side of division after division: In sum, we find that the necessity to search constantly for a middle term between too much opposition and too much collaboration produces factions within the leadership.

The second conclusion applies to the question of what unifies, rather than what divides, corporate leaders. Whatever its peculiarities, every leader's ideology tends to identify an irreducible antagonism between his or her corporate group and its rivals for power and wealth. In the case of relations between capital and labor this antagonism takes the form of a more or less clearly articulated idea of class animosity; agricultural groups will perceive a fundamental breach between town and country, and so on. (Indeed, even Fascist trade union leaders tried to keep alive a certain notion of their independence from and opposition to management, their affirmations about a harmonious corporatist order notwithstanding [Sapelli, 1975].)

The power of attraction of an idea like, say, class antagonism is directly related to the indeterminacy of corporate strategy. Clearly, unions and business groups will want to be able to press forward when their enemies are weak and defend themselves when they are strong. If one side is in the ascendant, then the belief in the implacable opposition of the opponent and in the ultimate irreconcilability of group interests justifies to the group's members and the public at large the demand for still more power. Conversely, if the group is losing ground, then the doctrine of antagonism serves as a cry to rally the members to self-defense and a warning that the group's leaders do not intend to be swallowed whole.

The logic of the situation requires each group to prepare for all contingencies by imputing aggressive motives to its opponent. To limit the unions' possibilities of transforming the social order through politics, business must suggest that despite their overt policy of collaboration, union leaders have revolution on the brain. Similarly, to protect themselves against being engulfed by business, union leaders must argue to their members and the public that their sincere dedication to partnership with capital is constantly being undermined by the latter's ambitions of complete domination. Hence each group's strategy of self-defense works against ossification of the rules of bargaining and limits the growth of mutual trust, the precondition of any enduring accommodation: Their reciprocal accusations fuel ideological debate and factionalism within each corporate group.

So far, the discussion has focused on the relations among leaders of rival groups. Now the focus shifts to the relation between the leaders of any one group, on the one hand, and the subordinate officials and members of that group, on the other. For if the possibility of an enduring rapprochement between rival leaders was a precondition for eliminating politics within corporate groups, then it is legitimate to ask how the impossibility of such a rapprochement might create internal political dangers for corporate leaders.

One crucial source of danger has already been identified in the Michelsian theories of the end of ideology (Pizzorno, 1978; Streeck, 1977). According to these theories, leaders seek to end discussion of ideology within their groups in order to safeguard their own freedom of action in negotiating with competitors. The less precisely the members can characterize their situation and the more they can be intimidated into remaining ignorant, the easier it becomes for the leader to represent any negotiated solution as the best obtainable under the circumstances. Conversely, the more explicit the debate about implications of the idea of fundamental conflict between groups, the more likely that members and lower officials will determine the best course of action on the basis of their understanding of the doctrine; and so the greater the danger that the leaders lose their freedom of action just as surely as if they had been trapped by their opponents at the bargaining table.

Hence a central dilemma of the corporate powers that be is that they both need a doctrine of group antagonism and are threatened by it. If they eliminate the ideological notion of group antagonism from the organization, they fall victim to their declared enemies; if they reintroduce it, they may run afoul of their friends. Alternating between de- and repoliticizing the organization, the corporate powers are constantly forced to undo with one hand what they do with the other. How they attempt to find an institutional solution to this problem and why the existence of factions among the leaders limits severely their chances for success are the themes of the next section.

Factionalism and the internal structure of corporate groups

In dealing with this problem, corporate leaders in general and union leaders in particular are faced with a classic dilemma of statecraft: how to use one's subordinates without ceding substantial power to them. Ideally, union leaders would like to construct an organization that would, first, efficiently collect and pass upward accurate information about the members' desires. In this way the leadership would never be in the dark as to the members' definition of the minimally acceptable settlement: A precise calibration of discontent would help put an end to surprising and unpredictable rank-and-file revolts.

Second, the organization would work on two levels at shaping the members' expectations of the union. More abstractly, the union will teach the related lessons of class antagonism and the need for a permanent, organized defense. The aim of this effort – really a continuation of the educational campaign out of which the union was born – is to convince members to define their self-interest in ways that permit sacrifices in time of struggle for the organization not justified by narrow calculations of immediate rewards. On the more concrete, day-to-day level, the organization would aim at convincing the members that the leadership is pursuing the correct strategy given their broadly defined self-interest. In other words, the first level of activity is directed toward making the workers accept certain general doctrines that make the organization powerful against its enemies; the second level is directed toward having them accept particular interpretations of the general ideas, which guarantee that the leaders can put this power to use.

But there are dangers inherent in this effort. If subaltern representatives of the organization are empowered to collect information, they may do so for their own purposes, not for management's purposes.

One way they could advance their position is by refusing to pass along all that they know unless given more power within the organization. Another possibility, related to the first, is that they simply begin to deal directly with the members themselves. Using firsthand knowledge of the situation, they arrange bargains between workers and management, thereby making the members their own – not the union's – clients.

The subaltern figures of the organization are also threatening in their capacity as exponents of official doctrine. To be effective in this regard, the underlings must be able to both teach dogma in its canonical form and apply it casuistically. But the better they are at these tasks, the better they are able to develop independent interpretations of the organization's ideas and defend them against the leadership's own constructions. The danger is increased by the underlings' superior grasp of the details of day-to-day industrial relations. More quickly aware of new developments and far less constrained by the need to harmonize the conflicting demand of disparate groups of members, subaltern figures are more likely than leaders to articulate doctrines that express the members' immediate experience of social life; hence they stand a good chance of winning the members to their notion of the organization's purposes.

This part of the argument now can be connected with the earlier discussion of factionalism. An obvious link between the two is that the probability of heterodox interpretations is further increased by factional struggles among the leaders. Other things being equal, it is easier to prevent deviations from official doctrine when all authoritative commentators agree in their definitions of orthodoxy than when they do not.

But factionalism does not only endanger the leaders by revealing the possibility of independent thinking. Far more threatening to their security is the permanent possibility that the underdog faction will try to muster support for its position among the subaltern functionaries and, through them, the members. How successful the dissidents will be depends among other things on the electoral procedures of the union, the possibilities for forming alliances with parliamentary or extraparliamentary groups, and the economic and political condition of the society at large. But whether or not the underdogs are successful is immaterial: What counts is simply the fact that orthodoxy and political control are contested. If the attempt is successful, the new masters of the organization owe a political debt to their underlings and rank-and-file supporters; if unsuccessful, then it is the old masters who are indebted to their agents and followers. Either way the autonomy of the leaders is diminished. Likewise, independent of its issue, the attempt will intensify ideological debate at the lower levels of the organization: Forced to choose between competing interpretations of doctrine, the low-level officials and the rank and file will have to learn how to defend their choices.

This much said we can begin to grasp the full measure of the leaders' predicament. Factionalism derives directly from the indeterminacy of trade union strategy as does the need for promulgating and monopolizing the interpretation of a doctrine of class antagonism. To say that factionalism undermines the leaders' monopoly of interpretation and helps embroil low-level bureaucrats and the rank and file in organization politics is to say that the logic of the situation undermines a strategy that it also requires. If leaders want to hold on to their offices and influence they will be forced constantly to make deals and enter debates with one another, their subordinates, and their followers. The best they can hope for is to discover maxims of prudence that, without eliminating the conflicts characteristic of the situation, reduce them to manageable proportions. The preceding discussion suggests two such maxims of prudence but also explains why they too can have only transitory success.

The first maxim is to teach subordinates only as much as they absolutely need to know about the organization's doctrine; tell them nothing at all, or at least as little as possible, about factional rivalries. The goal is to prevent subordinates from being seduced into factional struggles; or, when they are, to make them into less formidable opponents.

The second maxim is to tie subordinates to the organization – teach respect for loyalty and discipline. The goal is to make subordinates draw back from independently exercising their own judgment for fear of being disloyal to an organization they honor or fear.

The first of these maxims argues for emarginating subordinates (and, *pro tanto*, the members) within the organization. The second is a call to enfold them completely. Insofar as leaders successfully apply them, their subordinates are both included and excluded from the organization. Taken together, the maxims are thus a first step toward translating into the realm of daily politics the leader's general dilemma: how to make subordinates part of the organization without sharing power with them. Such rules of prudence need to be interpreted in the light of the union's general ideological self-definition. How they are applied will depend on the organization's preference for cooperation over antagonism or vice versa. To stake out the range of possibilities and for the purposes of the empirical discussion, we should distinguish two fundamental and opposed ways of applying these prudential rules, corresponding to two contrary ways of conceiving of the conflict between capital and labor.

One mode of application is associated with what are frequently called cooperative unions (Bergmann et al., 1975). Cooperative unions are those that openly declare their willingness to reach an accommodation with management within the framework of capitalism. This concessiveness follows from the view that the workers cannot secure (or would not benefit from) a fundamental change in the distribution of property and power in society. A corollary of this view is that such unions profess to see no underlying system in their demands: Union leaders ask only for Gomper's "more, more, more" – more money in wages, more job security; whereas lower-level officials treat members' problems as cases of personal hardship, requiring and only amenable to ad hoc solutions. By affirming the utility of the organization while disassociating its practical activity from any explicitly political principle, the leaders can limit the threat of heterodoxy: If the organization has no doctrine, then no one can challenge their right to interpret it.

With regard to the problem of loyalty, the leaders proceed in analogous fashion. Power relations between leaders and subordinates are personalized, as are the ties between subordinates and members. Patron–client relations, in other words, are the structuring principle of the organization's internal affairs as well as its connection to the outside world. Subordinates get ahead by including themselves in the retinue of a powerful leader; and it is the leader's power to reward and punish that offsets the perpetual temptation to establish independent enclaves of power within his or her territory.

Seen in this way, the lower levels of a cooperative union resemble a modern social welfare agency whose employees dole out help on a case-by-case basis and with as much attention to furthering their own careers as to reducing the suffering of their clients. Meanwhile at the top of the organization, the leaders, having encouraged the ignorance of the followers with bribes and threats, debate the necessary strategic choices among themselves.

The opposed type of organization might be called a revolutionary union, although it is of course no more likely to be consistently revolutionary in its acts than a cooperative union is cooperative. The defining feature of a revolutionary union is that all its actions are considered in light of the end of transforming society. With respect to both the articulation of doctrine and the institutionalization of loyalty, its cardinal principle is centralization. Every action is thought of as executing some part of a master plan for transformation. Those at the very pinnacle of the organization are thought to have a vantage point from which to formulate and interpret this plan; the work of subordinates is limited to applying, within the limits of their capacities and at the instruction of their superiors, first principles to particular cases.

The authority of leaders thus depends on their capacity to convince subordinates that great issues are always at stake, but that they, the subordinates, cannot discern for themselves precisely what these issues are. This relation colors in turn dealings between subordinates and members: Low-level officials instruct members in the necessity of certain notions as much as they help them in solving particular problems. Democratic centralism is the name generally given to this technique of eliminating political debate by reference to the omnipresence of politics.

With this the argument comes full circle. I began by showing that it was in the leaders' interest to avoid freezing the rules of bargaining with rival organizations. The next step was to suggest how pursuit of this end endangered their control over their subordinates, then, how they might reassert this control by applying certain maxims of prudence. But the more doggedly the maxims of prudence in either of the variations discussed are applied, the more they restrict the leaders' freedom to maneuver against their corporate enemies. The more the leaders as a group protect themselves against the members by personalizing power within the organization, the greater the tendency for the organization to dissolve into a series of independent baronies, dealing more or less independently with local representatives of capital. Ignored by their subordinates and unable to intimidate management with a coordinated show of strength, the leaders remain unchallenged only because no one values their position. Yet the more the leaders protect themselves by insisting on their version of doctrine, the more they cut the organization off from the day-to-day concerns of the members. Subordinates may continue to pass along leadership's orders, but the members will be looking for another organization to which to bring their cares.

Faced with either danger, some leaders break faith with the others and campaign for a change in the organization's self-concept and institutional structure. Factionalism, before confined to questions of the group's relations to its competitors, breaks out over dilemmas of the internal distribution of power. Politics is again the order of the day.

Two cases in point

Two brief case studies of trade union strategy will make these chains of argument more palpable. They are illustrative, not exhaustive. Their aim is merely to give a first impression of the fundamental similarity of the strategic choices that diverse institutional settings impose on leaders trying to make headway against their opponents.

Modern West German unions approximate in many ways my schematic description of a cooperative labor organization threatened by clientelistic disintegration (Bergmann et al., 1975; Müller et al., 1978). In the DGB unions the leaders are the hostages of their de facto representative in the plants, the factory counselors or Betriebsräte. It is the latter who ultimately set limits of union policy and are responsible for its execution. The proximate cause of disproportionate power of the Betriebsräte was the passage, against the union's bitter but ineffectual opposition, of the 1952 law on codetermination mentioned earlier. One set of provisions of this Betriebsverfassungsgesetz allowed the Betriebsräte to escape the tutelege of the national unions; a second encouraged their propensity to enter into clientelistic relations with management and the rank and file.

The law severely restricted the unions' opportunities for influencing company policy through participation in supervisory boards. As noted earlier, only one-third of the members of the Aufsichtsrat represented labor. Thus the unions had no means by which to control, bargain equally with, or simply bribe the Betriebsräte: They had neither managerial authority nor access to crucial information (because of their inability to control the composition of crucial subcommittees of the Aufsichtsrat) nor the right to dispose of well-renumerated posts.

At the same time that the union lost some of its means for influencing the Betriebsrat, legal restrictions were placed on the latter's capacity to cooperate with the union voluntarily. First the Betriebsräte were to be elected by all employees: They were not responsible just to union members. Second, as a consequence of the dominant conception of the firm as a community, the law imposed on the Betriebsrat a *Friedenspflicht*, an absolute duty to maintain peace in the plant. The Betriebsrat was thereby forbidden to organize strikes on its own or in the union's name, to encourage participation in strikes – whether or not they were legal – or even to aid in the preparation of disruption.

These provisions encourage a sort of clientelism at the plant level. To be reelected, the Betriebsräte must demonstrate success in bargaining with management. They can be successful in negotiations only if management has something to concede at plant level after agreement has been reached in national or regional negotiations. The Betriebsräte thus have an interest in seeing the union arrive at settlements that do not exhaust local management's ability to pay. And given their expert knowledge of company finances and the mood on the shop floor, they can often ensure that the unions' regional wage demands are in accord with their parochial interest.

More generally, the Betriebsrat has an interest in resolving all disputes ad hoc. The Betriebsrat is legally prohibited from participating in strikes; yet it can hardly expect to remain popular with the work force if its passivity puts it openly in management's camp at crucial moments. Its best hope is to avoid collective conflict requiring statements of allegiance. Hence, instead of emphasizing the common denominator of the workers' difficulties, the Betriebsräte treat them as a series of distinct personal difficulties with legal implications. In this way relations between subaltern union officials and the rank and file take on aspects of the relation between patron and client, with the Betriebsrat doing its best for the worker in return for the latter's loyalty.

But, as the preceding discussion of the limits of cooperation suggest, the factory counselors can pursue this strategy only so far. The Betriebsrat is prevented by the *Friedenspflicht* from organizing strikes. This prohibition extends to strikes meant to press demands by the Betriebsrat as well. The Betriebsrat's only weapon against management, therefore, is the more or less plausible threat that the union will organize and encourage discontent if need be, or that the workers will revolt spontaneously. This being so the Betriebsrat's interest in a weak union and a disorganized work force is offset or limited to some degree by its contradictory interest in a powerful organization of militants.

The union's view of its relation to the Betriebsrat is similarly ambiguous. A Betriebsrat that dominates the entire work force by distributing and withholding favors in the manner of a big-city political machine obviously threatens the power of the union. Yet a Betriebsrat that is unaware of the workers' discontents is also dangerous to the union. Virtually excluded from the plant by the Betriebsverfassungsgesetz, the union must count on the informal cooperation of sympathetic Betriebsräte in collecting the information it needs to formulate its demands. Nor is the union less dependent on a functioning Betriebsrat's judicious – which is to say, not actionable – violation of the *Friedenspflicht* in the execution, say, of its strike plans.

Thus the more closely the dealings between the union and Betriebsräte are examined, the clearer it becomes that a stalemate is likely. Each side fears the other but needs the other to escape domination by capital; each is repeatedly tempted to improve its situation by radically redefining the rules of collective bargaining. Broadly speaking, the Betriebsräte have an interest in cooperation with capital, the national leaders in opposition to it. But within these groupings there are factions whose very existence reflects the ambiguity of the situation.

Some Betriebsräte hold that they can only survive in the long run if the national union is strengthened; they will collaborate with the national organization whenever possible. Others, tempted by the idea of a company union, aim to cooperate still more with management in return for the concessions necessary to hold the allegiance of their clients. On the union side there is even greater division over the correct course to take. One strategy consists of pressing the state for more favorable social legislation. In this way the national leadership could bypass the Betriebsräte, recommending itself directly to all the workers as their immediate agent in government (and justifying at the same time its collaboration in incomes policies). A second, related, and typically neo-corporatist strategy – pursued most directly in the construction union – is to discriminate so much in favor of union members in industrywide collective bargaining that it becomes economically nonsensical for workers to avoid joining the union or to withhold dues once they belong. This strategy has the advantage of safeguarding the dues income of the national union without, however, necessarily antagonizing the Betriebsräte. In 1962, for example, employers in the construction industry agreed to contribute to the upkeep of several vacation resorts to be administered by the unions. It was tacitly agreed that workers could participate in the vacation program only on the recommendation of local union officials, thus guaranteeing that only union members would benefit from the resorts and that the officials would still have favors to bestow.[8]

Reform of the codetermination laws, discussed earlier, is a third possibility. If the unions can succeed in redrawing the rules governing their participation on corporate boards, they will realize their old ambitions of extending their control over the Betriebsräte from above at the same time they extend their influence in the economy as a whole. Alternatively, or additionally, the unions may try to increase their influence over the firms indirectly, by increasing their influence over macroeconomic planning: for example, through creation of a "social parliament," a joint labor–capital council that would give the unions the right to present legislative proposals regarding economic or social matters directly to parliament.

The fourth strategy is directed toward controlling the Betriebsräte from below. The chemical and metalworkers' unions have representatives in the plant – *Vertrauensleute* – responsible directly to the union. These *Vertrauensleute* are not bound by the same *Friedenspflicht* that ties the hand of the Betriebsräte (especially on those occasions when the latter want to appear bound). They have no motive to limit systematically the union's success. If need be, they can act as champions of class struggle, inciting the work force to protest the reformist policies of the Betriebsräte. Hence the *Vertrauensleute* can be used as an instrument for disciplining the factory counselors, who, anticipating the danger, have often brought the *Vertrauensleute* to heel with the promise of posts in the Betriebsrat, or the like.

Besides withdrawing from the Konzertierte Aktion and attempting to reform the Mitbestimmung laws, the DGB has recently toyed with the idea of reintroducing a call for the socialization of industry into its program. There have been bitter strikes by dockworkers, steelworkers, and printers. These militant outbursts might be explained as the vestiges of a traditional and fading class consciousness. But if the foregoing analysis is correct, it would be more correct to see these developments as but some – and hardly the most radical – of the possible consequences of a debate about union strategy that will continue as long as the DGB unions survive.

If the West German example reveals the limits of a cooperative policy, the example of the development of the Italian CGIL directs attention to the limits of the revolutionary union strategy. For the national leaders of West German unions, doctrines of class struggle have been one means to check the false pragmatism of their plant-level representatives; for the Italian leaders the problem has been to find an interpretation of the idea of class conflict practical enough to permit the unions to establish themselves as the workers' representatives at the plant level in the first place.

In Italy as in West Germany, the trade unions' dilemma had its immediate origin in the set of institutions that emerged from class conflict after World War II. The hold of the Betriebsräte over the national unions derived from the failure to obtain a parity codetermination law; the CGIL's isolation from the rank and file owed much to its early willingness to subordinate itself to the Italian Communist party (PCI). The thoroughgoing politicization of the unions was the outcome of the battle against fascism during the last years of the war. The struggle for national liberation fused with and eventually overshadowed the effort to reconstruct the trade unions. As a result, the latter came into being as appendages of the political parties, particularly of the PCI. The middle- and upper-level officials in the unions were drawn from and loyal to the PCI; and for its part the rank and file understood union membership not as a means of defending particular economic interests but as a political act. As Salvati puts it, the trade unions in this period gave the PCI "an almost unconditional power of attorney as to how and to what degree the new order should substitute the old" (B. Salvati, 1972).

The previous discussion of revolutionary unions suggests that this kind of politicization has both an opportunity and a danger. Politicization gives union leaders the opportunity to streamline the organization's structure and to coordinate the activities of its members. Where advantage is to be had by concerted action, it can be had in full. And of course this centralization of authority also increases the leaders' security in office.

The danger is that the more completely each part of the union is subordinated to the central political conception, the more helpless the organization as a whole becomes in the face of significant and unexpected changes in the political environment. What is the rank and file to do if the assumptions on which the central plan rests are overturned? Habituated to obedience, schooled to mistrust its own perceptions of local circumstance, it must choose between losing faith completely in the leaders or clinging to the hope that the future will vindicate them. So for fear of putting their authority to a test, the leaders will be reluctant to admit small mistakes, thus increasing the likelihood of large ones; and the larger the mistakes, the more corrosive the disillusionment of the disillusioned, the blinder the dedication of those who remain loyal. In the extreme case, the leaders are trapped by the fanaticism of followers who abide no deviations from orthodoxy and are deeply mistrusted by everyone else. Thus the very successes of a revolutionary union increase its vulnerability to disaster. The record of the CGIL in the early postwar period bears this out.

At first the Communists were successful in exchanging a guarantee of labor peace for the right to enter the government and participate in shaping the institutional armature of the emergent republic. But in May 1947 the PCI was expelled from the government. By the end of the year Einaudi's policy of deflation began to take hold. Mass unemployment and a collapse of the labor market became a possibility. In 1948 the electoral victory of the Christian Democrats condemned the PCI as a party of opposition and knocked down the props supporting its strategy of parliamentary participation. The PCI's indecisive reaction to the attempt on Togliatti's life a few months later revealed that it had no serious alternative strategy of revolutionary change. Finally, the Catholic wing of the labor movement declared its independence. The CGIL then discovered that it could no longer mount a defense of even the status quo in the name of all workers. The unions were reduced to calling for public investment to reduce unemployment. The reasoning was that tight labor markets would renew the CGIL's bargaining power. Until that happened, ideological appeals were to sustain the workers' loyalty. But for many union members, the leadership was as compromised ideologically as it was impotent in negotiations with capital.

After 1948 the workers began to leave the CGIL. By 1954 the metalworkers' federation was even losing elections to the *commissione interna* or factory council at FIAT. The workers began to look to the

Catholic CISL (Confederazione Italiana dei Sindacati Lavoratori) or to company unions to get satisfaction for their grievances. Capital's strategy of excluding the unions from the plants was clearly succeeding. By 1960 the CGIL admitted defeat and resolved that it was imperative to reconquer the factories by reconnecting the union's political aims with the immediate interests of workers on the shop floor.

During the 1960s the unions did in fact regain the workers' trust and reestablish themselves in the factories. Ultimately their success depended on the leaders' willingness to reconsider the organizational implications of revolutionary unions and to share power with the immediate representatives of the rank and file. But the preconditions for this sharing of power were structural and conjunctural changes in the Italian economy (Pizzorno et. al., 1978; M. Salvati, 1976). Structurally the key changes occurred during the last half of the 1950s and early 1960s. A capital-intensive, export-oriented sector of Italian industry was created. The work force in this sector came to enjoy certain limited but important employment guarantees. In time, the bargaining power of the workers in the export sector became independent from and superior to that of workers in the traditional part of the economy. Thus the labor market no longer automatically disciplined the whole work force as it had during much of the 1950s. Conjunctural developments then made this change in the balance of power in the export sector manifest by creating the conditions for spontaneous worker protest – which met with surprising success precisely because of the division of the labor market. Two episodes of this kind were crucial.

The first began with an expansion of demand in 1960, then of employment in 1961. The next year the level of conflict rose; the year after, the level of wages. But this period of struggle was a missed opportunity. The union's own indecisiveness tipped the balance against it in the early 1960s. The CGIL strategy in this period was to create *sezioni sindacali di azienda*, factory sections, elected by union members, as the means of reestablishing contact with the rank and file. But by creating *sezioni*, the union ran the risk of offending its loyal followers in the *commissioni interne*. Ineffectual as these factory councils were, they had survived the Cold War as a locus of union activity; and in the export sector, at least, the bureaucratization of industrial work was arguably transforming them into plant-level bargaining agents. Faced with the concrete choice between holding tight to what it had or taking risks to make organizational gains, the CGIL vacillated. Before it could make up its mind, the conjuncture turned, militance declined, and a new recession began.

At the start, the second cycle of militancy, which began in 1968 and ran through the first half of 1969, seemed as though it would be a repetition of the first. But disappointment at the failure of the parliamentary opening to the Left of the mid-1960s, the work speedups that had been capital's answer to the wage increases granted in 1962, and the radicalization of university students all worked to intensify debate. Two opposed conceptions of reform emerged. The first was based on the *commissioni interne*. The aim was familiar: to extend the contract powers of the *commissioni* to questions of work pace, promotions, and so on, and to link them to the rank and file and the union by the creation of *sezioni sindacali di azienda*. The contrary conception had complex roots in the history of the Italian left and Marxist thought generally. It was based on the figure of the *delegato di reparto*, the shop steward elected directly by a small, homogeneous work group and responsible primarily – in some versions exclusively – to it. In a union built on the *delegati*, the leaders would execute the will of the whole work force, not formulate and impose a general program on union members. The choice between these strategies recapitulated the leaders' dilemma after 1948: If they accepted the *delegati* as the organization's plant-level representatives, they put themselves at the mercy of unpredictable, perhaps antagonistic strangers; but if they rejected the *delegati*, they risked alienating the many prospective union members who rejected leaders distrustful of their own followers.

Both tendencies were represented in most large factories. Which one predominated depended on the local distribution of power. Where the *commissioni* were strong and worked harmoniously with the local representatives of the union (at Ignis or Ercole Marelli, for example), the traditional solution was favored. At FIAT, on the other hand, the *commissione* was weak, the level of unionization low, the competition from a company union menacing, and the idea of the *delegati* more appealing. Adopting the demand for decentralization of power only where they had none, local union leaders could have no consistent policy toward the *delegati*; for every case where radical democratization was a threat to the organization, there was another in which it was expedient. There was much talk of "empirical solutions."

It was the massive and unexpected participation of un- and semi-skilled workers in the industrial conflicts leading to the *autunno caldo* of 1969 that moved the leaders to adopt the *delegati* solution. Many of these workers were immigrants from southern Italy. They had come north hoping to earn enough to return home and establish their economic independence as small landholders or shopkeepers. When they began to realize in the 1960s that they were trapped in the northern factories for good, they reacted with the frustration and rage typical of peasants forced to submit to an alien work discipline. Convinced of the applicability of the unions' general doctrines of class struggle to their own situation, but disappointed in the unions' ability to protect them from work speedups, and encouraged in both sentiments by various radical groups, the southerners were natural partisans of the *delegati* movement.

In the summer and fall of 1969 the unions offered a compromise formula. The plan was to create new *comitati sindacali unitari* or unified union committees. Each work group in the plant would elect a delegate to serve on this committee, and *together* with the *commissioni interne* the *comitati sindacali unitari* would then direct the campaign for a new contract.

The appeal of this scheme to the leadership lay precisely in its ambiguity: On the one hand, it could be represented to the rank and file as a concession to the popular will; but it was equally plausible, on the other hand, to argue that the comitati were simply another avatar of the *comitati di agitazione*, that is, of the committees traditionally established in factories in times of conflict to win support for the unions' plans.

But the ambiguous formula proved to be not ambiguous enough. Attempts by the leaders to declare the period of mobilization at an end and to dissolve the *comitati* failed. Exercising their own powers of doctrinal interpretation, the workers regarded them as a permanent feature of factory life and made their participation in the union conditional on the institutionalization of the *delegati*. Grudgingly, drawn on by the prospect of greatly expanding their organizations, the leaders finally decided to take the risk. In December 1970 the CGIL declared that the *delegati*, elected by all members of each factory department independent of their union affiliation, would be its official representatives at plant level.

Simultaneously, however, the leaders were also searching for ways to reinforce their positions within the organizations. Thus they discussed broad questions of social reform with the government so as to demonstrate that they were uniquely adept at certain kinds of dealings. The paradox is obvious: If the leaders of the CGIL resisted internal democratization in part out of fear that it would undermine the union's subordination to the PCI, now it was the leaders themselves who were bypassing the party and thrusting the confederation directly into politics. Again, the struggle for power creates the possibility for the emergence of new social arrangements.

The leaders' attempts to regain control of the new structures continues today. Hierarchies and technical committees are formed in the *consigli* as a means of excluding some *delegati* from power; election districts in the plants are sometimes redrawn to favor the leadership's candidates; and so on. But for all that, the *delegati* – and through them the rank and file – retain substantial autonomy.

The irony is that the CGIL has become more powerful than it was. It deals more with government and business than it did and might therefore be said to be closer to neo-corporatist integration into Italian society than in the past. Yet the CGIL is also more political than before, if politics is understood not in the context of the ideal type of the revolutionary union but rather as struggle over who may demand what. Within the organization there is more questioning of the relation between leaders and followers than there had been. And, precisely because of its success, the organization as a whole is forced to explore the possibilities of reshaping its relations to the rest of society as a way of transforming society itself. In the 1970s, for example, the unions made it virtually impossible to fire workers. Firms responded by refusing to hire workers to replace those who quit or retired; when output had to be increased, they hired labor indirectly, farming out production to small job shops where the unions are powerless or by increasing productivity through the introduction of new machinery. To defend the strongholds of support in the large factories that they conquered in the 1960s, the unions are now trying to find ways to police decentralization of industry, control the disorienting and potentially divisive effects of rationalization, and regulate labor mobility so that the efficient use of labor is not established – as in Sweden – at the cost of disruption of working-class communities. In formulating this self-defense, they are of course calling into question the accepted distribution of power between labor and capital (Bulgarelli, 1978).

In sum, self-interested leaders are trapped. The attempt to create the preconditions for what might be called the ideal foreign policy subverts their domestic position, the pursuit of the ideal domestic strategy thwarts their foreign ambitions. Weakness in foreign dealings is soon their ruin at home. Thus whatever single course they choose, they choose wrong. They reveal their skill not by their ability to avoid mistakes, but to catch them in time. And catching them the best they can, leaders still cannot stop, and often contribute to, the redefinition of politics within their organizations and the society at large. Leaders who have learned all this, and the successful do, know as well that it is not possible to abolish political struggle in modern society, but only to transform it.

Notes

1 Lehmbruch (1977), Offe (this volume), Panitch (1977), Schmitter (1977), Streeck (1977), Winkler (1976). Of these, some are fascinated by the potential stability of a

neo-corporatist system because of alleged economic efficiency (Winkler) or as an elegant solution to the organizational problems of interest groups (Streeck). Whereas others (Lehmbruch, Offe, Panitch, Schmitter) are more attentive to the sources of instability in the neo-corporatist system as well as its potentially authoritarian cast, my own aim is to present a rigorous argument in support of the claim that a neo-corporatist solution to the problem of group conflict is inherently contradictory. Many of my ideas have been anticipated by other writers, at the latest by A. J. Muste in 1928; but I will not indicate all the ways my thinking converges with or diverges from the work of those who hold a similar position.

2 Kerr et al. (1960); a succinct critique of the related literature is Scase (1977).

3 For Michels' statement of the Iron Law, see Michels (1966). The point of convergence between his notion of oligarchy and contemporary writings on neo-corporatism is the twin idea that power naturally comes to rest with the leaders of large organizations and that the powerful are sufficiently united by common cultural and material interests so as to harmonize their actions. Because modern trade unions are so frequently taken to task for their more or less undemocratic internal procedures, students of labor have been particularly interested in testing the validity of the Iron Law. For a critical review of the political science and sociological literature, see Eldridge (1977) and Ramaswamy (1977). Typically such empirical studies of union democracy produce contradictory results. The law is held to be generally confirmed insofar as the long tenure in office of many union leaders can be explained in part by their efficient (i.e., useful to the members) monopolization of various kinds of information. But at the same time, it is also noted that the leaders' tenure owes a great deal to a series of quite particular electoral and recruitment procedures whose origin and survival cannot be explained at all from the viewpoint of organizational efficiency. Two recent examples of this sort of research, both of which leave typically unresolved the question of whether efficiency or skulduggery count most in explaining oligarchy in organizations, are Gamm (1979) and Hartmann (1979). In any case, their often-confirmed finding that the maintenance of power in organizations requires constant interpretation, defense, and manipulation of the rules is consistent with the line of argument advanced here.

4 On the complex relations between the state and industry in what is reputedly the most pluralist of societies, the United States, see Horwitz (1977) and Noble (1977).

5 Employers' associations are but one, and often not the most important, means by which capitalists coordinate their strategic choices. Others are trusts, cartels, and mergers. Furthermore, control over whole industrial sectors may be in the hands of powerful bank syndicates, as is frequently the case in West Germany; or, as in the United States, industrialists may use nominally public regulatory boards that they dominate as a means of enforcing joint strategies. Even employers' associations often have the means to discipline members, for example, in Austria, where they pressure the government to force individual firms to obey wage–price guidelines. On cartels and mergers see Chandler (1977); on the influence of banks, Shonfield (1969); on the private use of public regulatory bodies, Kolko (1963); on the sanctions available to employer associations, Pütz (1966).

6 This account follows closely the periodization set out in Martin (1979).

7 Conversely, the workers' loyalty to the docile Argentinian trade unions in the 1950s has been explained as the result of the confidence and hope those same unions inspired by their aggressive pursuit of popular goals in the late 1940s. See Doyon (1975).

8 Agreement to the union's rights of selection had to be tacit because of legal considerations relevant to the present argument. West German law guarantees and small employers vigorously defend the citizen's right to negative *Koalitionsfreiheit*, roughly, the right not to be coerced into joining an organization. This right, which has been

repeatedly affirmed by the courts, limits the degree to which employers and union officials acting in concert can compel membership in the unions, as in the previous example, and nicely illustrates the way in which the liberal state may trip over its own feet walking down the neo-corporatist path.

Bibliography

Bergmann, Joachim, Jacobi, Otto, and Müller-Jentsch, Walter. *Gewerkschaften in den Bundesrepublik: Gewerkschaftliche Lohnpolitik zwischen Mitgliederinteressen und ökonomischen Systemzwängen.* 2 vols. Frankfurt am Main: Europäische Verlagsanstalt, 1975, p. 1.

Bourdieu, Pierre. *Outline of a Theory of Praxis.* Trans. Richard Nice. Cambridge Eng: Cambridge University Press, 1977.

Bulgarelli, Aviana. *Crisi e mobilità operaia.* Milano: Mazzotta editore, 1978.

Chandler, Alfred D., Jr. *The Visible Hand: The Managerial Revolution in American Business.* Cambridge, Mass.: Harvard University Press, 1977.

Doyon, Louise M. "Conflitos operários durante o regime peronista." *Estudos CEBRAP* 13(July–September 1975):81–122.

Elderidge, J. E. T. "Trade Unions and Bureaucratic Control." In *Trade Unions under Capitalism,* eds. Tom Clarke and Laurie Clements. London: Fontana/Collins, 1977. pp. 175–83.

Ferguson, Thomas, and Rogers, Joel. "Labor Law Reform and its Enemies." *The Nation* 228(Jan. 6–13 1979):17–20.

Fraser, Douglas. "Beyond Collective Bargaining." Interview. *Challenge* 22(March–April 1979):33–9.

Gamm, Sarah. "The Electoral Base of National Union Executive Boards." *Industrial and Labor Relations Review* 32(April 1979):295–311.

Goldthorpe, John H., "The Current Inflation: Towards a Sociological Account." In *The Political Economy of Inflation,* eds. Fred Hirsch and John H. Goldthorpe. London: Martin Robertson, 1978, pp. 187–214.

Gourevitch, Peter. "International Trade, Domestic Coalitions, and Liberty: Comparative Response to the Crisis of 1873–1896." *Journal of Interdisciplinary History* 8(Autumn 1977):281–313.

Hartmann, Heinz. "Works Councils and the Iron Law of Oligarchy." *British Journal of Industrial Relations* 17(March 1979):70–82.

Horwitz, Morton J. *The Transformation of American Law 1780–1860.* Cambridge, Mass.: Harvard University Press, 1977.

Kerr, Clark, Dunlop, John T., Harbison, Frederick H, and Myers, Charles A. *Industrialism and Industrial Man.* Cambridge, Mass.: Harvard University Press, 1960.

Kolko, Gabriel. *The Triumph of Conservatism.* Chicago: Quadrangle Books, 1963.

Lehmbruch, Gerhard. "Liberal Corporatism and Party Government." *Comparative Political Studies* 10(April 1977):91–126.

Martin, Andrew. "The Dynamics of Change in a Keynesian Economy: The Swedish Case and its Implications." in *State and Economy in Contemporary Capitalism,* ed. Colin Crouch. London: Croom Helm Ltd., 1979. pp. 88–121.

Michels, Robert. *Political Parties,* trans. Eden and Cedar Paul. New York: The Free Press, 1966.

Moore, Roger. *The Emergence of the Labour Party 1880–1924.* London: Hodder and Stoughton, 1978.

Moran, Michael. *The Politics of Industrial Relations: The Origins, Life and Death of the 1971 Industrial Relations Act.* London: Unwin Brothers Ltd., 1977.

Müller, Gernot, Rodell, Ulrich, Sabel, Charles, Stille, Frank, and Vogt, Winfried. *Ökonomische Krisentendenzen im gegenwartigen Kapitalismus*. Frankfurt am Main: Campus Verlag, 1978.

Muste, A. J. "Factional Fights in Trade Unions: A View of Human Relations in the Labor Movement." In *American Labor Dynamics*, ed. J. B. S. Hardman. New York: Harcourt, Brace and Company, 1928. pp. 332–48.

Noble, David. *America By Design: Science, Technology and the Rise of Corporate Capitalism*. New York: Alfred A. Knopf, 1977.

Offe, Claus. "The Attribution of Public Status to Interest Groups." This volume.

Panitch, Leo. "The Development of Corporatism in Liberal Democracies." *Comparative Political Studies* 10(April 1977):61–90.

Pizzorno, Alessandro. "Le due logiche dell'azione di classe." In Pizzorno, Alessandro, Reyneri, Emilio, Regini, Marino, and Regalia, Ida, *Lotte operaie e sindacato: il ciclo 1968–1972 in Italia*. Bologna: Il Mulino, 1978. pp. 7–45.

Pizzorno, A., Reyneri, Emilio, Regini, Marino, and Regalia, Ida, *Lotte operaie et sindacato: il ciclo 1968–1972 in Italia*. Bologna: Il Mulino, 1978.

Pütz, Theodor, ed. *Verbande und Wirtschaftspolitik in Osterreich*. Berlin: Duncker and Humblot. 1966.

Ramaswamy, E. A. "The Participatory Dimension of Trade Union Democracy: A Comparative Sociological View." *The Journal of the British Sociological Association* 11(September 1977):465–79.

Salvati, Bianca. "Rebirth of Italian Unionism, 1943-54." In *The Rebirth of Italy, 1943–1950*, ed. S. J. Woolf. London: Longman, 1972, pp. 181-211.

Salvati, Michele. *Sviluppo economico, domanda di lavoro e struttura dell'occupazione*. Bologna: Il Mulino, 1976.

Sapelli, Giulio. *Fascismo, grande industria, e sindacato: il caso di Torino 1929/1935*. Milano: Feltrinelli Editore, 1975.

Scase, Richard. *Social Democracy in Capitalist Society: Working Class Politics in Britain and Sweden*. London: Croom Helm Ltd.. 1977.

Scharpf, F. W. "Die Funktionsfähigkeit der Gewerkschaften als Probleme einer Verbändegesetzgebung." Berlin. International Institute of Management, discussion paper 21, 1978.

Schmitter, Philippe C. "Modes of Interest Intermediation and Models of Societal Change in Western Europe." *Comparative Political Studies* 10(April 1977):7–38.

Shonfield, Andrew. *Modern Capitalism: The Changing Balance of Public and Private Power*. London: Oxford University Press, 1969.

Streeck, Wolfgang. "Gewerkschaften und Mitglieder. Zur Soziologie gewerkschaftlicher Mitgliederrikrutierung." Berlin: International Institute of Management, discussion paper 65, 1977.

Winkler, J. T. "Corporatism." *European Journal of Sociology* 17(1976):100–36.

Part III

State, society, and representation: the changing relationship

9

Interests and parties in pluralism

ALESSANDRO PIZZORNO

In the introduction to *Law and Public Opinion in England*, the 1913 edition, Dicey analyzed the principal acts passed by the English legislature during the first thirteen years of the century. He showed, from the 1908 Old Pensions Act to the 1911 National Insurance Act, and from the 1906 Trade Disputes Act to the 1910 Finance Act and the 1913 Trade Union Act and others, the rapid advance of the collectivist movement that had emerged during the last decades of the Victorian era. For Dicey, a student of the relationships between legislation and society, it was clear that a new era had begun, supplanting the liberal age with its emphasis on the individual and laissez-faire. He named this period the collectivist era.[1] Since Dicey's times the debate continues over the existence of a liberal age. And since Brenner's 1948 revisionist articles on laissez-faire and state intervention in Great Britain, the argument that the age of laissez-faire never existed has gained considerable ground.[2]

For the most part, however, the debate has sought to ascertain whether the state was still present in the economy, whether public administration grew continuously (it did), and whether there was a fall in the trend of growth of public expenditure (there was, between 1830 and the beginning of the twentieth century). It has *not* been a debate over changes in the system of representation.

Yet, certain characteristics quite clearly differentiate the formal aspects of the political system and the system of representation, in particular, in capitalist societies just before and immediately after World War I from those of fifty or more years previously. These new characteristics were: the virtual completion of universal suffrage, and the presence of organized mass parties, of permanent organizations representing special interests and playing a new institutional role, and of new forms of legislation that reflect the gradual shift away from the universalistic laws of the age of classical liberalism toward both more specificity in the content of laws and delegation of power to administrative agencies.[3]

Was this evolution already implicit in the principles of classical liberalism? Had not Locke already recognized the legitimacy of the political action of various interests – land, commercial, and financial? Indeed, had not Madison named, at the origins of the American republic, those very same interests and added to them that of manufacture? But neither Locke nor Madison could have imagined such interests formally organized and durable over time or the presence of the interests not linked with private property. Moreover, they never dreamed of stable organizations, permanent agents on the political scene, which would be inspired by an ideology distinct from the dominant one of the political system. Only religious groups were thought to have such characteristics.

Even if the two principles – all members of a political community have the right to be fully represented and any group of persons with specific shared interests has the right to form a stable organization to promote these interests – were originally generated by the liberal mind, once effectively put into practice, they brought about a radical change. Another principle which was perhaps less visible but had far more significant consequences, was added to these two. That is, although each citizen is the best judge of his or her own interests, this is true only for his or her immediate, visible interests; for long-term interests, however, these can be perceived more clearly by another person, someone whose profession it is to deal specifically with such matters. This was the principle of *political professionalism*.

An awareness of the changes that the liberal state was undergoing can lucidly be found in the political thought of the time. Gierke, with his reappraisal of the importance and continuity since German medieval times of the *Genossenschaft*; Maitland, with his reappraisal of the relationship of trust; the Catholic corporativists; Laski and Cole and the English guildists; Durkheim in the preface to the second edition of *The Division of Labor* and his followers among the French "institutionalist" jurists; the American institutionalists; Bentley, with his methodology of political groups; Santi Romano and his juridical school and many others[4] saw the pluralist and corporative seeds of the new system.

One common theme in these otherwise diverse currents of thought was recognition that the idea of a direct relationship between the state and individual was unrealistic; that conceptual models and institutional projects should be worked out to cope with the reality of more or less independent intermediate bodies, of organized interests and, in general, of groups capable of autonomous collective action. However, it was not only from such theorists that proposals came for a new conceptualization of the changing reality of the contemporary state but also from those who directed their attention toward a slightly different type of phenomena: the modes of mediation between social reality and the state, the various forms of displacement and distortion of interests, and the indirect connection between the demands of civil society and the reply offered by the state. Mosca's view of the political class as an autonomous subject; Kautsky, Lenin, and Gramsci elaborations on professional revolutionaries and intellectuals; Michel's description of party and union functionaries; and Weber's analysis of professional or charismatic politicians were all tentative theories meant to explain why there is no one-to-one correspondence between civil society and the state, between class and party, and between the represented and the representatives.

In other words, the political thinkers witnessing the transformation of the liberal state were not blind to the importance of autonomous collective identities (whether political or social) being constituted within the state, as well as to the consequences of the process of mediation between socioeconomic interests.

In the following pages I will analyze the historical "object" that began to emerge at the end of the past century, as if it were a system. I will examine how its main components interrelate, and how its main processes produced unintended and contradictory consequences. This can be done by examining how, in this system, interests are being identified and defined, how they are selected and excluded from representation, and how the autonomy of the national state in these processes has changed. In the second part I will deal with some recent developments.

The identification of interests

The simplified image of a system of representation postulates the existence of a set of "interests" that "civil society" (the market, the social structure, the system of the division of labor) presents to the political system, and to which this latter, with its various mechanisms (organizations and institutions), provides responses. In this formulation, "interests" mean "demands," that is, explicit requests for political measures. But who is authorized to or is able to voice requests, given the fact that these demands are potentially unlimited in number? Certain criteria are needed to define the agents entitled to act as bearers of interest and to define the resources they may offer in exchange for satisfaction of their demands.[5]

In the estate system (*Ständestaat*), there was no problem of this sort.

The collective subjects entitled to representation were defined by the social structure itself. That is, the recognized components of the social structure coincided with the subjects entitled to be represented. As the estates gradually lost power to the absolute monarchy and were finally abolished by the liberal regime, the criteria used for defining the units of representation underwent a substantial change and geography became the criterion of electoral constituencies. At the outset, this definition may indeed have corresponded to some real division of interests, because the formation of the national states implied a conflict of interests of a territorial nature (center versus periphery, differentiation between provinces, etc.).[6] But the phenomena just described – the tendency on the part of the ruling class to differentiate itself in a lasting, organized fashion, the widening of suffrage, and new territorial communications – tended to make the principle of the territorial identification of interest quite inadequate. The appearance of organized mass parties and stably organized interest groups would introduce new principles of identification.

The organized mass party

In its pure form, the organized mass party proposes an ideology as a principle of identification. It presents demands that are elaborated with a view to a future state of affairs to be achieved through political action (often working out projects to this end on the basis of an overall interpretation of society). As a consequence, the goals of the representational unit (the party) lack in specificity and become more rigid, and the representational structure acquires an autonomy of its own.

The goals lack in specificity because they must be "formulated" having in view the interests of society as a whole. They cannot appear to be the goals of a particular section of society, unless the interests of this section are seen as coinciding with the interests of the whole society. (This is the case, for example, of the Marxian view of the coincidence, in the long run, between the interests of the working class and the interests of society.)

Because representation is not predicated on the specific interests of a section of society, the goals of collective action tend to be rigid and nonnegotiable. In fact, when the interests of a specific group or section of society constitute the basis of representation, collective identity can persist through the renewal of goals and is not lost with the loss of a certain objective. Whereas when the collective identity is predicated on the ideology, and a goal becomes unattainable, the collective identity itself is threatened. By postulating goals as nonnegotiable this threat is eluded.

Or, ideological organizations may develop a special function (that is, a special layer of functionaries) devoted to the continuous reinterpretation for internal, esoteric use of goals that are defined as nonnegotiable for the external audience. Something very similar to the phenomena described in the theory of cognitive dissonance happens here, which becomes essential to the survival of the organization. Organizational (bureaucratic) power and intellectual capacity to reinterpret ideology reinforce each other. The outcome is the permanence of the apparatus as a collective body generating interests of its own.

Party subcultures, such as Catholic, Socialist, and Communist, can be analyzed from the standpoint offered here. They embody the very opposite of the phenomenon found in the system of representation by estates. Whereas in the estate system the social structure defined groups that participated as such in the political process, which in no way attempted to redefine them, in the new conditions political subcultures represent social entities that emerge through the workings of the political system itself, and especially over struggles for entry into it. (Such subcultures are particularly strong in regions where certain parties have been in opposition for a long time, although they arise in other conditions as well.) A split similar to that between social basis and political organization, between class and party, can then be found between "the interpreters of the ideology" and the followers (militants and active members). This split reintroduces the possibility of selection among goals via a reinterpretation of the ideology. Because it is up to "the interpreters of the ideology" to decide on the type and degree of coherence between short- and long-term goals, the rigidity of the political relationships generated by the introduction of the ideology can be attenuated by a certain latitude in its interpretation. This latitude is beyond the control of the represented.

Thus three levels can finally be distinguished; each one has its own criterion of rationality in political action. The first is that of the *social basis of interests* (corresponding to what Socialists called the level of the class). Here we find individuals with objective interests in common but who evaluate in individual terms what they will do. The criterion of rationality for political action is based on the maximization of individual utilities, which means that political action is performed strictly in exchange for the utility it procures. But because this type of action is normally performed collectively, the Olson argument is applicable. That is, the cost of participating in collective action is always greater (except in small groups) than the utility it procures. As a consequence, if those who operate at this level (normal citizens) are to receive utility from political action, a second level must be assumed where active participation and militancy are consistent with a different criterion of rationality.

This second level is that of the active party or the social movement members. Here the criterion of rationality is based on the reinforcement of collective solidarity. Collective political action is not a way of maximizing individual utilities according to preexisting interests but, rather, is an end in itself; in other words, it tends to maximize the values of membership and solidarity. Here extremism is more likely to flourish than moderation, because in pitting the group against its adversaries, group solidarity is created, which becomes a prime objective. For the same reason, this criterion of rationality will be found more often in opposition parties than in governmental ones.

The third level is that of the leaders, the political professionals. Here again, the criterion of rationality in political action is the maximization of individual utilities, but in terms of acquiring power. To be in politics means to perform a special role in the social division of labor; politics becomes a profession, a career specifically remunerated in terms of power. And because power can be enjoyed only if others recognize it, involvement in politics on this level means reciprocal recognition, negotiation, and compromises.

These three criteria of rationality in political action constitute an analytical classification. Real cases are obviously less cut and dried and cannot always be so precisely classified. Particular individuals may aim to increase their own personal advantage even when they are "participating" just as they may use their militancy to further their own careers. Nevertheless, in the logic of their visible action, one of these criteria of rationality can always be discovered.

So far our description has been based mainly on the concrete case of the parties arising from the workers' movement, because these are the closest to the pure type of organized mass parties. The Catholic parties approximate less closely to this model and Liberal and Democratic-Liberal parties are still further removed. The variations that occur in these party types, with respect to these characteristics, are usually a function of two factors, which often tend to work in the same direction: the social categories a party represents and its chances of coming into power. Hence the workers' party in opposition is the closest approximation to the pure type described, whereas the bourgeois party in power is the most removed.

The reasons for this are fairly obvious; nevertheless, a closer look at them may be useful. The less a social group possesses resources of an economic nature, the more it will have to depend on numbers for political action; hence it will rely on participation. In turn, organization may be considered as the capitalization of the resources of individual participation. Instead of letting the participation of the various individuals be consumed wherever it takes place, organization is a tool for channeling, regularizing, and concentrating participation (through enrollment, meetings, etc.), so that it can be used strategically at chosen moments. The effectiveness of participation is further increased by the application of various techniques (techniques of participation, rituals, expert advice, training, information, etc.). Ideology itself can be seen as a technique for reinforcing organization.

In fact, ideology reinforces the solidarity of those who belong to the organization by generating the feeling that all of them share certain goals toward which *durable* collective action can be oriented. Furthermore, it can coordinate the specific action of various centers of decision, because from the general principles contained in the ideology it is possible to deduce rules for action to be applied in particular occasions, thus avoiding the burden of detailed prescriptions from the center. Finally, ideology offers a criterion by which to check the performance of the leaders, even when their action *does not produce immediate satisfaction of interests.* [7]

This last point suggests why ideological mass organization is more functional for opposition parties than for parties in power. In fact, the links among parties in power, their followers, and their constituency are founded on the satisfaction of interests brought about by governmental action. In principle, there should be no need for organization or ideology to unite the followers of a governmental party. The choice is a simple matter of individual utility: Those whose interests are satisfied by governmental measures will vote for the party, and the others will vote against it. For the opposition party, however, there is no performance on the basis of which it can be judged. There are only promises and – if the party is likely to remain in the opposition a long time – promises for the distant future. Here trust is needed, which must be based on ideological arguments and a feeling of common belonging. Of course, the party in government also is judged on its promises, to the extent that what is done is done and does not necessarily constitute a guarantee for the future. Those favored by the previous legislature may think they will be less well served by the next one (although this is a different kind of judgment whose plausibility rests on extrapolation from experience). Here too, some sort of trust of the electors in their representatives must come into play, at least the belief in links of common membership and some common goals.

This observation suggests that although a party may get quite close to the "individual representation" type, (nonideological, without party discipline, with multiple, short-lived identities), the party can never really reach it. Even in bourgeois parties with long experience in government, the need for maintaining a distinct identity, along with the need for maintaining the support of all those who do not receive any advantages from its term in office, is bound to produce some form of ideological symbolism and ritual, operating as incentives for activism and thus permitting the saving of other organizational resources.

The pure type of ideological party is never reached either, and the closer it is approached, the more unstable the organization becomes. In fact, because its goals are projected far into the future and it is unable, as a pure type, to pay its militants back immediately (to distribute "selective incentives" to use Mancur Olson's terms), the purely ideological party would not be able to set up an efficient, lasting organization. It does, of course, offer the satisfaction of belonging, but this will be short-lived, because it leads to the following paradox: The grounds for belonging disappear once the collective goals are reached, for then collective action is no longer needed. They also disappear if the goals turn out to be unattainable, because this, too, would mean that collective action was in vain.

In sum, in durable ideological mass parties three different sorts of motivations are present. For the functionaries, leaders, and the professional party workers, the motivation is individualistic, that is, tending toward individual advantages measurable in terms of power, prestige, income, career, and their possible advancement. For simple participants, on the other hand, the motivation is the gratification of belonging, sociability, mutual support, and the sense of identity that is derived from these. For voters the motivation is again individualistic, aimed at the maximization of individual utilities through the process of representation.

This analysis not only brings us close to the Schumpeter–Downs model of professional politicians as entrepreneurs aiming at winning over political clients but also shows how inadequate this model is. It is true both that there is a supply of representative services that is motivated by the prospect of political "profits" (power, prestige, etc.) and that this supply is found in ideological mass parties as well as in other parties. But it never consists solely in the supply of political goods (government decisions, and the like) to be evaluated in terms of individual utilities.

How else could one explain the durability and persistence over time of political identities? We should be forced to assume a continual *tâtonnement* by voters in search of the most attractive promises. Nor would there be an explanation for political commitments or participation in general, whose costs inevitably outweigh individual gains. In other words, in such circumstances Olson's "free-rider" objection could not be overcome.

To go beyond these theoretical difficulties, we have hypothesized that some kind of collective identification – structures of trust and solidarity, ideologically determined common goals, or a common cultural, religious, ethnic, and so on, background – must precede the political choice made to maximize individual utilities. In a regime of representation by estates, these collective identities were constituted by the estates themselves, that is, by social groups and categories formed by the division of labor and geography and recognized by the political authorities. Political parties represent the solution to the problem of political identity wherever such ascribed identities have completely disappeared and where mobility and freedom of choice are maximal, that is, in a situation in which numbers can best be used as a political resource. Parties, then, as more or less long-lived social bodies, become the focus of identification and expression of politically representable interests. Inasmuch as they are forms of collective identification, however, parties also tend to respond to needs that arise from the decline of traditional identities and from individual situations of mobility, freedom of choice, and uprooting. Thus it is probable that the more those needs become secondary or can be met by other structures, the further away political parties will move from their pure form.

Summing up, we describe the effects that the rise of organized mass parties had on the system of representation as follows.

1. A strong tendency arises to see interests in aggregate form, hence furthering highly general demands. Consequently, to deal with specific interests appears as logrolling or dirty politics and is seen as negative.

2. A high degree of aggregation likely goes together with some ideology. Thus not only are different interests grouped under a general idea, but also their satisfaction is conceived in total terms and projected into the future in such a manner so as not to be the object of political negotiation. The representation of immediate interests, as well as of special interests, appears then excluded. Action is ostensibly undertaken in view of long-term general interests.

3. The capacity for defining interests is unequally distributed across the party hierarchy. Ordinary voters must, at least in part, accept the political definition of their interests suggested to them by the members of organizations, although these latter must, at least in part, accept the definitions of political goals handed down by activists and leaders.

4. The job of mediating between interests and the centers of decision making becomes a professional task. To this end, there emerges a specialized category of mediators – the professional politicians – who although they compete among themselves, develop stable com-

mon interests in exercising a sort of monopoly over political language, techniques, and resources.

These consequences do not extend to the whole field of political action. In fact, when any strong interests or needs emerge in society, different forms of political action correspondingly arise. Certain aspects of local politics, for example, clientelism or self-government, constitute possible alternatives to rigid aggregation and to professionalism and ideological politics. Social movements are another alternative. But the most important alternative is the one that relates to the durable representation of special interests. This form, even more than organized mass parties, characterizes the pluralist system of representation.

Organized interest groups

In the system of representation by estates, all the interests represented were by definition "special" interests. The only bearer of general interests was the sovereign, himself a former bearer of a special interest that had become "general" by defeating other special interests in a given territorial area. The religious foundation of monarchical legitimacy excluded the conception of a state that was legitimized solely by its capacity to represent all interests. Indeed, it would have been dangerous during the formative period of the national state to give legitimacy to peripheral and particularistic interests.

The final abolition of special (corporate) representation took place in the liberal regimes. In reality the narrowness of suffrage and hence the actual power of the few individuals who had the right to be represented allowed a direct transmission of special interests, even when these were not organized on a permanent basis. With the widening of suffrage and the emergence of organized parties, each party, as mentioned earlier, although representing only a fraction of the population, will present itself as defending general interests. Thus the need for structures that defend special interests is again bound to arise.

Soon after the decline of the estates (*Dekorporierung*), carried out in various ways and in different degrees by the liberal regimes, and once beyond the first short phase in which association rights were denied, voluntary associations flourished.[8] These were groups created through the free choice of their members, who could leave whenever they desired, and which pursued specific, declared goals by means of collective action.

These associations still could not really be considered organized interest groups, although in some cases they gave rise to them later.

They aimed mainly at mutual support and security, promoted forms of sociability, or, more often, economic, cultural, artistic, professional, religious, moral and charitable activity. Goals were fairly specific and their membership was more often local than national. Legally they were subject only to negative norms in that they were considered as private, contractual relationships.

In time, these voluntary associations gave rise to real interest organizations. The changeover was a gradual process, the first sign of which was an increase in size as a result of the widening (functional and territorial) of the range of activities. Consequently, there was a shift from associations oriented to a particular goal to associations pursuing a range of aims, that is, representing interests to be defined in an open-ended way. These organizations have national dimensions; they set up their own bureaucracies and their own experts; and their leaders no longer act by the members' mandate, or do so only partially, because the "possibilities of interpretation" leave ample space for autonomous action.

Processes of this nature take place gradually and at various points in time in the different industrial countries. Roughly speaking, however, they were most clearly observable during the last decade of the nineteenth century and the first one of this century.

The final stage of this process (the historical moment that varies from country to country and from field to field of representation) is the politicization of the interest organizations, when their status is legally recognized and various public functions are officially handed over to them.[9]

As in the case of the political parties, we have chosen to describe here the formative process of one pure type: the type that leads from voluntary associations pursuing specific goals to organized interest groups pursuing various, wide-ranging goals, having their own bureaucracies and national headquarters and enjoying a monopoly of representation and a public or semipublic status. Again, the degree of approximation to this pure type varies from country to country and from one type to another of organization. The larger unions, employers' associations, and professional bodies all have, to a greater or lesser extent, the characteristics we have just described: the pursuit of differentiated goals, a national bureaucratic setup, a tendency toward representative monopoly, and the assumption of public functions by delegation. The variations within these characteristics are, however, fairly substantial. Furthermore, in a pluralist system of interest representation, classical types of voluntary association remain important, with their specific goals – nonexistent or relatively small bureaucracies – and substantial autonomy.

Summing up, we can say that the degree of *multiplicity and diffusion of the association goals* and the degree of *coordination to which the association is submitted* are the two main variables we should use in analyzing a system of associational interest representation.

1. The degree of diffusion and multiplicity of the association's goals is important in explaining relationships among associations. In fact, the more widespread and multiple the goals of the association, the greater its possibilities of gaining a monopoly position in representing a given category of interests. The inverse relationship is even more probable: The greater the monopoly of representation, the wider the range of goals pursued. The same variable is important for determining the types of relations between the organization and the single individual who belongs to it or who is legitimately represented by it. Actually, if the goals of a voluntary association are specific, an individual's decision to join amounts to a declaration of consent to that association's action in pursuing those goals. Disagreement is expressed, however, by withdrawal from the association, that is, by "exit," to use Albert Hirschman's terms, and there is little or no need for "voice." If there are many cases of "exits," the association will modify its policies or disappear altogether, making way for other associations. The "theorem of identity" of democratic theory is valid in this case. In Teubner's words: *"Zweckmotivation gewährleistet, dass sich die Organisationspolitik mit den Interessen der Mitglieder weitgehend deckt. Divergenzen werden durch Austritt Entscheidungen bzw. Zweckänderungen eingeebnet."* [10] If the goals are multiple, on the other hand, the decision to participate and the expression of consent do not necessarily coincide. They coincide even less when the organization enjoys something close to representational monopoly. In this case, in order to have a democratic organization, or even to obtain enough information for efficiency, "voice" – the vote, protest, or other ways of expressing opinions on the part of the members – must be guaranteed.

2. The degree of coordination to which the association is submitted, the second variable, calls for an evaluation of the degree of autonomy or heteronomy of individual organizations with respect to the state (for the various forms of heteronomy, cf. Offe, Chapter 5 in this volume), and hence of the process through which the coordinated decisions are carried out. This process may vary from open negotiation to pure institutional incorporation. The first of these is generally referred to as a *pluralist* situation. The second, which tends to be accompanied by a representative monopoly, bureaucratization, and delegation of public functions, is referred to as a *corporative* system. [11]

The literature on interest groups obviously offers other criteria of classification, in addition to the dimensions of goal specification and coordination. The classificatory scheme we propose has the advantage of focusing on both the relationships that individuals, categories, and classes have with the groups and organizations that represent them (multiplicity and diffusion of goals) and the relationships that these groups have with the system of representation as a whole (coordination).

We shall deal with another crucial aspect of the question – the access of new groups to the system – later, in the section on the modes of exclusion. Before discussing this and the problem of the system's autonomy, we need to make some general observations about the efficiency of the system of representation we described so far.

Does the pluralistic identification of interests assure efficiency?

The output of a system of representation may be evaluated either in terms of efficiency in the satisfaction of demands or legitimation. With regard to efficiency, the usual argument is that although a pluralist system is efficient because it is capable of sounding out the main demands of the (organized) population, and hence has the best possible information on what real needs are, it suffers from the fact that because everybody is entitled to ask and to press for his or her demands, the responses of the system are inadequate and contradictory. But three more specific arguments may be advanced for the efficiency of pluralism: arguments of balanced realism, of flexibility, of self-screening (or decentralized control).

1. Pluralism operates with *balanced realism* because it satisfies interests according to a weighted calculation of their strength. It takes into consideration both the economic resources and the participational (numerical) resources (capacity of activism, militancy, and the like) of a subject. The outcome of the pressures for political decision does not reflect market forces exactly; neither does it exactly reflect participational (electoral, order-threatening, etc.) resources. It reflects a mixture of the two, sanctioning the "real," that is, prepolitical equilibrium of power existing among the social bearers of interest.

2. Pluralism operates *flexibly* because it allows and favors negotiation all the time and everywhere. The norm for flexibility is that every decision can be bargained over. Negotiation is not efficient because it satisfies expectations, but because it *redefines* expectations in the process of reaching a decision, adjusting them to the achievable outcome. Moreover, negotiation continuously produces useful information. It replaces prices as a means of collecting the necessary information for decisions.

3. Pluralism allows for the screening, or *selection*, of a multiplicity of demands in the process of "representing" them. Interests have to be represented in order to gain access to the centers of decision, and an interest is stronger when it is organized. But organization implies, to some extent at least, selection and the sacrifice of immediate demands. As a consequence, the very process of representation of interests operates so as to moderate them, thus allowing room for the respect of "general," "common" interests.

But there are also powerful arguments speaking for the inefficiency and inner contradiction of the system. Negotiation brings expectations nearer to realistic outcomes *for those who take part in it*, and it may also widen the gap for the nonparticipating expectants. Indeed, it increases their frustration, because they do not see why their representatives have abandoned the original aims, and hence feel betrayed by them. The practice of negotiation, therefore, may have either moderating or alienating consequences, according to the extent of participation. But large participation in negotiations is costly or produces dispersion and dissipation of results, so that the only case in which negotiation is efficient without being alienating is when there is high trust in the negotiators. However, the conditions of high trust are not a product of the pluralistic mechanisms. They have to be presupposed and depend on collective identities that preexist, or that have been formed for reasons different from the representation of interests.

The pluralistic virtues of flexibility in negotiation and of professional skill in screening demands, moreover, have a high cost in economic terms because of the vast apparatus of mediation that they make necessary. This apparatus expands continuously, often provoking conflicts that are "artificial" because they do not arise from the cleavages generated by the organization of production but, rather, from the apparatus of political mediation. The growth of a professional political class, coterminous with the growth of the pluralist system, becomes costly not only because it is paid out of taxes, but also because it generates a vested interest in political competition. Thus we have the paradox that when the political class is unified and tendentially monopolistic, it is capable of extracting more surplus value from the population (hence, in a way, exploiting it); when divided, however, it tends to provoke wasteful conflicts.

The assumption that a pluralistic system is a system in equilibrium, also stems from an unwarranted analogy – that collective competition is analogous to atomistic competition in that it will operate to bring the cost of production down to its lowest level. Through atomistic competition the actors in a market are forced to produce more, or to consume less, thus contributing more to social wealth, if they want benefits. However, the same cannot be assumed in collective competition dealing with redistribution. Here, in order to gain advantages, the collective subject will *not* work more or consume less but, rather, will threaten to withdraw the resources that it normally puts into the production process (either capital or labor power or information or conformity to the productive and public order). Thus, the very modes of the competition for redistribution tend to curtail the amount of benefits available, making the system inefficient. Lacking a self-equilibrating dynamic, the system therefore needs a special mechanism that evaluates to what extent and in what direction the contribution of the system as a whole (taxes, services, commitments of some sort) will be redistributed. This mechanism is the state. The more benefits are redistributed as an outcome of collective competition, the larger is the intervention of this mechanism, and the higher is the burden put on the efficiency of the system.[12]

With respect to legitimation, the main argument in favor of pluralist systems parallels the case for efficiency: Because everybody can be heard, all decisions will be supported by everybody. There is no need to obtain consensus on the *content* of a decision. Consensus is given to the procedures that allow the "voice of the sovereign people" to be heard. Conflict is part of the procedure, not an expression of dissent. Legitimacy is an attribute of the state as an "order" – that is, as a system – not as an agent or subject of decisions.

Two arguments, however, are not taken into consideration in this defense. One refers to the *delegitimation of the representatives* and is linked with the second and third arguments previously discussed, on the inefficiency of pluralism. We have seen that the practice of bargaining and the constraints of mediation lead to at least a partial divergence between the utility functions of the representative and of the represented.[13] As a consequence, the representatives may be threatened by a process of delegitimation. They lose consensus, hence they lose the power and the right to exercise their roles. It is not necessary that the "system" as such (the regime, the state, or other) be delegitimated – it is not even clear what that would mean, because the pluralist system foresees and acknowledges the occurrence of conflicts. But the loss of legitimation of the structure of representation – the interruption of the channels of institutional expression of demands – is risky for the system as a whole. When this happens, factions and splinter groups within an organization will propose new goals, new definitions of the collective identity to which they belonged; on the other side, new collective identities will try to force their way into the system of representation. In both cases, conflicts will be provoked depending on a recognition of identity, which is a nonnegotiable issue. They can become more or less serious, but they are potentially critical.

The second argument concerns the *decomposition of the state*. The practice of negotiating every decision tends to decompose the core of the political system, the state as the ultimate public authority and unitary coherent subject. In order to be able to negotiate with private individuals, an agency of the state needs a certain degree of autonomy. This increasing autonomy in negotiations gradually transforms parcels of the state into semiautonomous agents similar to their private counterparts, that is, "widespread, not integrated, centrifugal."[14] It may even lead them to act on behalf of "private" interests in dealings with other state agencies. Various studies carried out in different countries show that ministers of agriculture tend to act with respect to the government as though they were representatives of the organized interests of the farmers; ministers of industry do the same for the industrialists; and so forth.[15] The meetings of the cabinet have been described as negotiations between representatives of the interests of departments.[16] It is no less difficult to coordinate the action of parts of the state that have thus become autonomous in a joint program than it is to coordinate the vast network of private interests "outside" the state. Private interests outside what is traditionally called the "state," and "private" interests (be they political or bureaucratic) of more or less autonomous subjects within the state, may thus be thought of as lying along a continuum. To borrow a picturesque phrase from C. Wright Mills, when private and public bureaucracies negotiate on two sides of the table, "their myriad feet interlock in wonderfully complex ways."[17]

It becomes difficult, therefore, to define such a process of "representation," because the body that should receive the representation is no longer an entity, but a "market," or better still, a potential battleground for armies, divisions, companies, and sharpshooters, that is, for those "groups" (parties and their factions, associations, clienteles, firms – when they represent themselves – departments and offices of public and semipublic administration) that open fire or negotiate, ally, and separate again. Each waves its own banner, from electoral mobilization to the withdrawal of capital or labor, from information about an economic sector to the control of a public project or the handling of a case, and so on.

Our argument can be summarized by saying that within a pluralist system we cannot conceive of a unitary entity whose action may be evaluated as legitimate or illegitimate. Legitimacy or consensus – illegitimacy or dissent – are attributes of the process of representation, of the links that make up the collective identity that "legitimizes" representatives. The separation between autonomous functional spheres (postulated in the work of functionalists such as Luhmann and Poulantzas)[18] corresponding to specific structures (administration, parties, interest groups) not only fails to explain the mix of structures and functions, but also fails to acknowledge the "private" (i.e., uncoordinated, but for exchange) nature of all those collective agents, striving with similar resources toward competing goals. Neither the traditional pluralist nor the "functional-statist" view, moreover, can account for the restabilizing mechanisms that we have shown to lie in the nature of competition among collective identities. To understand the working of the system, we need to trace the way stability is regained. This essentially happens by placing some (potential) bearers of interest in a position to generate less dissent than they might, excluding them from access to the redistribution process, limiting their entitlement to forward demands, or screening the demands they can forward. This process will be analyzed next.

The modes of selection and exclusion

Let us return to the idea of a system that "generates" demands, because its benefits are distributed unequally so that all the recipients have an "interest" in improving their position with respect to that of others and in defending that position from others' attempts to degrade it. As we see it, this is a zero-sum system. Quite possibly, all the positions in the system may "improve" with respect to the past without altering relative positions. Thus it is likely that all the members of a system may have an "interest" in improving their future positions, with respect to their past ones, "together." But this is simply an *additional* interest to the continuous one that everyone has in improving his or her own position in relation to that of others. In other words, the intertemporal comparison is an addition to and not a substitution for the interindividual comparison. The relative improvement may be achieved through the action of every individual within the same system (say, "M") or through the action of chosen representatives within another system (say, "R").

If all the subjects active in "M" have access to "R" with the same force that allowed them to attain their position in "M" – if, that is, the resources available to them are the same in the two systems – the existence of "R" brings about no change and hence ceases to be important. But this is not the case, for access to "R" also depends on resources of another sort, linked with political participation and its organization. This is not the only difference, however. The subjects with access to "R" are rarely the same as those to be found in "M." What takes place is a process of decomposition and recomposition, which comes about in three different ways. One is by *aggregation*. The subjects that operate on their own in "M" (individuals, firms, etc.) join together in order to act in "R," forming associations, unions, and various other organizations. In this case, the interest represented is an average one, or the outcome of the recomposition of more or less disparate interests. In any case, individual interests will manage to get only some of their demands represented and will have had to give up others.

Another way is *institutional specialization*. An interest, individual, or aggregate, can never be presented as such, that is, with the demand for improving its relative position but, rather, must put forward particular requests, raise definite issues, and single out particular goals. This specialization is dictated by the division of labor within the administration and by the institutional setting in general. In other words, the subdivision of goals that a particular subject may have depends on the definition of the issues by institutional structures. As D. Marsden says, "Such a division (of one subject from another) can be brought about by the definition of issues in a particular way and by their channelling through different institutional bodies." Marsden's example of typical institutional specialization is the system of industrial relations in Germany. The general interest in improving the conditions of the working class can be broken down into various goals: the increase of the minimum contractual salary, the improvement of work conditions, of health conditions, and so forth. For each of these goals there is a different institutional subject and correspondingly a different agent of representation (the union, the *Betriebsräte*, parity commissions, etc.) which act autonomously, possibly even disagree with one another. Thus there is a possibility of selecting and excluding goals according to how institutions are structured.[19]

A third way of breaking down interest is between *short and long terms*. Wanting the satisfaction of certain interests immediately and wanting it in the future are two different things – indeed, the achievement of interests in the short term may have negative effects on the achievement of future interests. There may be two sorts of factors that influence the preference for short- or long-term satisfaction. First of all, there is the *degree of power of a given organization*: A strong organization (representing powerful interests in the system) may allow itself a strategy envisaging sacrifices, because it has relatively good chances of recuperating in the future what it has given up. In fact, a strong organization assumes that it will influence the way the system works; that is, the system may be seen as an oligopolistic market. An organization of weak interests with no hope of influencing the system will, on the other hand, be well advised to obtain everything it can right away.[20]

Another factor that determines preferences for short- or long-term gains is the *degree of autonomy of the representatives within the organization*. If the representatives are frequently called on by those they represent to account for their actions, they are likely to favor immediate goals. If, on the other hand, there is no risk of being shown up and brought to task, they may as well oblige those they represent to make short-term sacrifices in favor of long-term goals.

Aggregation, institutional specialization, and orientation toward long-term goals are modes of selection and exclusion of interests. They become important when *explicit exclusion*, that is, the exclusion from franchise, characteristic of the liberal system, ends.

Moreover, the development of functional representation impairs the mechanism of exclusion through the division of majority and minority. When the transmission of political demands is accomplished by interest organization, no interest is predictably excluded, because choices are the outcome of pressures, and the weight of pressures cannot be systematically calculated in advance because it is the product neither of competition in the market nor of the numerical majority of the interest bearers.

Exclusionary mechanisms, however, come to operate again, because of the way representation is organized, and in particular because of the new type of organizational stratification that arises, which was described earlier. Because leaders of the organizations have an interest in maximizing power, they will represent the interests of those who elected them only to the extent this helps to increase their own power. The power they seek to maximize is not personal but, rather, is contingent on them as leaders of social organisms destined to last in time. "Power" can be defined here in Hobbesian terms as *the capacity to procure future benefits*. Increasing the power of the organization thus implies a preference for those actions that ensure *future* benefits for its members (and those who are represented by it), rather than for actions that satisfy *immediate* interests. In this sense the pursuit of power, because it implies a lasting collective identity that is recognized by the other bearers of collective identities in the system, must take place within the rules of the system and within the "general interests" of the system. For this reason there is a functional interest on the part of the representatives, linked as they are to a permanent identity in a system of recognition, in not *fully* pursuing the satisfaction of the immediate interests of those they represent if and when such satisfaction clashes with the other interests of which the system is composed.

Ideology sanctions and facilitates the acceptance of delayed satisfaction by the represented and thus reinforces the mechanism previously described. Paradoxically, an ideology that commands the consent of a group of interest bearers, even though it may appear to present nonnegotiable aims inasmuch as it produces disciplined behavior, in fact, works to select and postpone the satisfaction of interests and thus facilitates the functioning of the system.

Political professionalism, that is political practice considered as the domain of expertise, with a specialized language and technical information, operates in the same direction. The interpretation of the policies necessary for defending certain interests cannot be controlled (particularly if it is a question of medium- or long-term interests), which leaves room for discretion about what should be negotiated and what should be excluded. The unequal distribution of political resources such as political competence, education, access to information, and opportunities for communication works in the same direction.

The most important exclusionary mechanism is, however, what, by analogy with the model of monopolistic competition, we might call "entry control." The subjects already represented in the system have an interest in limiting their number and try to preclude other subjects from having access to representation. A typical example of techniques used to this end is *raising the organizational threshold*. When new bearers of interest appear on the representational scene, the subjects already occupying the scene propose actions (e.g., popular demonstrations, and so forth) or levels of negotiation (centralized rather than local) or other requirements that cannot be achieved by the new subjects, which will result in their exclusion.[21] Another technique is the exclusion of "issues" by limiting the topics with which the system will deal ("control of the agenda").[22]

So far we have been dealing with forms of exclusion that work within the system of representation. Recent political history shows, however, a more open form of reaction to the widening of representation: the reinforcement of the executive, which is related to the changing degree of autonomy of the system.

Growth and decline of the autonomy of the system of political representation

A representative system includes certain individuals (the citizens) and not others: It has boundaries. Within these boundaries there are one or more decision-making organs that respond to demands, selecting them according to certain criteria and ensuring that their redistributive effects are acceptable. At the risk of being obvious, mention of these circumstances allows us to identify the two main processes in the formation of the modern state: on the one hand, the formation of the identity and territorial distinctiveness first with regard to the empire and then to the other national states; on the other hand, the affirmation of central monarchical power with respect to local, feudal, and corporate power.

A third element in the process of historical development of the modern state that is worth mentioning because it corresponds to a third analytical dimension of the problem of the autonomy of the system is the emancipation of the state from religion and the resulting legitimation of the state as caretaker for the long-term interests of society. On this basis, nations were able to develop as more than mere territorial units, and constitute cultural and even, in some cases, ideological identities. The assumption of a national ideological identity, in fact, plays an important part in the formation of systems of representation from the outset. The idea that in the long term a nation's interests subsume all individual interests made it possible to portray the member of a national parliament in the liberal constitutional doctrine as "representative of the whole nation" and not merely of the particular interests of the constituency that elected him. This is what allows political representation to take place in *plena potestate* and not by mandate.

How these three aspects of the problem of autonomy – the relationships between the system and what surrounds it, the capacity on the part of a central organ in the system to act with respect to the particular interests within it, and the capacity to pursue long-term interests – relate to each other can be seen in the events that lie at the origins of the post-liberal system. The emergence of big organized interests with their capacity to control the market led the state to expand in order to meet the new demands for services and support of the economy. It also led to, or strengthened, a policy of protection against the outside world and, in general, of defense of national interests. This first phase of oligopolistic capitalism – and it was "state" capitalism in the sense that it required state protection – involved a power policy at the international level. Thus nationalistic ideologies were developed along with myths about "manifest destinies" to support the state's expansionistic policies, on the one hand, and to uphold the policy of coordinating the main organized interests and of integrating, where possible, the working classes, on the other.

The period of marked expansion in international trade that followed World War II throws this relationship among central power, international constraints, and big private interests into question. International constraints grow more rigid as each country is increasingly exposed to international trade. The big private interests, in view of the increased rigidity of the international constraints, can raise the price of their cooperation. In addition, private interests of a multinational nature grow stronger and constitute further constraints to the actions of the central national authority. Thus with respect to the first phase of organized capitalism, national economic systems tend to lose their autonomy. Hence, although part of the production of goods and services covered by the so-called public administration expands continually, the capacity of the central organs to choose between alternative policies declines.[23]

The new conditions of pluralism

During the sixties and seventies the pluralist system of representation seems to have undergone a crisis. The signs of the crisis are found in the operation of new and unforeseen collective movements or groups, threatening to wage unconventional social wars; in the decline of the political parties, too weak to be able to integrate their followers in a unitary will, to screen demands, and to propose realistic alternatives for the conduct of the modern polity; and in the consequent excess of tasks that overburden governments, paralyzed by the diffusion of veto powers and the extenuating process of incessant negotiations.

These signs become more ominous when they are seen in the context of an economic crisis, or "depression," which is probably, after the 1873–96 great depression and the crisis of the thirties, the third great crisis of the capitalist economy. Given its international dimensions, the economic crisis contributes to the impotence of the central organs of the national political systems, because economic constraints become more rigid; whereas changes in the socioeconomic structure brought about by changes in the international division of labor provoke tensions that the traditional forms of representation are unable to express. Moreover, the expansion of national income is much slowed down, which frustrates demands that previous growth had spurred.

But these conjunctural economic factors cannot be held responsible for the signs of cracking in the pluralist system. These were there before, even if less visible. The impasse of the gradual blurring of party programs, the decline of party functions, the difficulties of political reproduction, and the strains provoked by the emergence of new collective identities could have been predicted from the first appearance of the pluralist system. We shall now try to show how their explanation can be integrated in a theory of pluralism.

The convergence of programs

It has been frequently observed that despite the wide range of parties in the parliaments of the representative democracies they tend increasingly to say the same things to their electorate. Tingsten in 1955 backed up this observation with systematic data, and recently J. C. Thomas,[24] in a thorough inquiry into party programs presented in the parliaments of eleven countries,[25] has shown that over the past forty to sixty years the average differences among party positions on ten principal programmatic themes have constantly decreased. Likewise diminished is the intensity with which reforms are advocated in these programs: "There has been a dramatic narrowing of the scope of domestic political conflict between parties in western nations. The limit of this narrowing is just short of zero, like in American parties."[26] Observations on the marketing style of latter-day electoral campaigns, on the way the various parties compete to represent the same social groups and hence the development of what Kirchheimer called the "catch-all" parties, constitute less systematic but nevertheless telling proofs of the same phenomenon.

Is this phenomenon restricted to program "enunciations," or does it reflect a deeper lack of political alternatives, some impracticability of real options in pluralist regimes? Is the trend it delineates a secular one, or does it show a cyclical pattern? And does it represent a decisive alteration of the pluralist machinery? I shall try to discuss these three questions, being aware of the fact that a definitive answer is not possible at the current state of our knowledge.

1. Are political alternatives only illusory in pluralistic regimes? It is possible that although party programs tend to converge, real party policies, when parties are in government, do not. Certain research and commonsense observation would tell us, for example, that Social Democratic parties pursue policies favoring full employment, whereas liberal and conservative parties pursue policies aiming at reducing inflation at the expense of unemployment. Neither commonsense observation nor the current state of the research is convincing on this point.[27] In fact, the relevant data should be analyzed on three levels: What the parties say, what the parties try to do, what the effective outcome of their policies is. On the third level, obviously so many other factors and constraints (foreign and internal) are operating, that we may not reach any well-tested conclusion. On the second level, what the parties try to do when in government, depends at least as much on the pressures they receive and the evaluation of the needs for coalitions, compromises, and so on with other social and political forces, as from the need to identify with the program submit-

ted to the electors. For the first level, the declarations about their own intentions obviously depend on the evaluation of their effects on the electors, given the constraints of maintaining some distinction from the other parties. But distinctions can also be secured through either general ideological construction, not requiring detailed program specification, or techniques of image building, leading the electors to identify with personal or group characteristics more than with policy orientation.

The distinction between the first (what the parties say) and the second level (how they operate) suggests a corresponding distinction in political languages. To the first level correspond the open, exoteric, generally programmatic language, formulated with electoral goals in mind. Here different speakers are hardly distinguishable. To the second level corresponds an esoteric, subtle, allusive, language, directed at the public of those who represent interests and understand the allusions that escape others. At this second level the messages aim at negotiating alliances, working out exchanges, and prospecting demands and supports. Here the specialized public can easily tell one speaker from the other.[28] Alternatives are real for specialists, they are illusory, or fragmented in thousands of contradictory measures, for the general public.

2. Are we witnessing a secular trend toward programmatic convergence as Thomas's findings tend to suggest? Several observations invite us rather to consider a possible cyclical hypothesis. Until about World War I, with variations from country to country, the trend was toward differentiation. The cause of this was clearly to be ascribed to the "new entries" (Socialist and Catholic parties) into parliament. (In fact, the United States did not experience any differentiation.) Elsewhere, new "external" parties (in Duverger's sense) representing interests that had formerly been excluded, forced their entry into Parliament. Their first need was to affirm their separate identities, hence to emphasize the differences between themselves and the older parties constituting the "system." As a consequence, their programs were "radical" and their goals nonnegotiable. Once taken inside and recognized and accepted by the others, they felt a lesser need to affirm their identities. The continual interaction with the other actors within the system, the awareness in general of the constraints that limit the achievement of any political goal, the need to appeal to the marginal voter, discourage excessive differentiation – hence the phenomenon of convergence. We can confidently conclude, therefore, that, *ceteris paribus*, new entries result in more program differentiation, whereas a lack of new entries, that is, a long permanence of the same subjects in a system, produces convergence.

This also helps to throw light on the famous dispute over the "end of ideology." If ideology means differentiated proposals for long-term goals, there is no doubt that the political forces are more inclined to abandon this kind of message the longer they stay in parliament. But this message is not likewise abandoned by the "social forces," the collective subjects outside parliament. On the contrary, it is probable that, in certain periods at least, the less ideological are the messages (i.e., proposals of long-term goals) issued by the parties pursuing governmental power, the greater will be the number of producers of ideology outside the parliamentary system. These are not bound by the rules of the political game in the same ways as those inside and hence can propose programs, the realism of which need not be immediately verified.

If the process of program convergence approaches the point where all distinctions are canceled, the electors become unable to choose for want of separate identities, and participation in political life approaches meaninglessness, except when professionally motivated. The old parties will then be either exposed to schisms or threatened by new entries. A more or less durable revamping of the ideological stance, hence of the identity, of a party may then be the most convenient response. The Thatcher case in the United Kingdom, followed by the organizational reform in the Labour party, which has increased the power of the "ideological core" of its supporters, can be considered an example of how separate identities need to be restated when policy constraints have blurred all distinctions. There is another suggestion here that the convergence/divergence path of parties' programs may follow a cyclical pattern.

A different way out from this impasse may be to shift to personalities for the task of representing alternatives. Choice among parties, ideologies, and programs – or among subcultural memberships – is then replaced by choice among images of personalities in which the electors are asked to put their trust. (U.S. politics come closer to this ideal type). Here the choice is dissimilar from the choice between programs – and more similar to the choice between ideologies – in that it is not binding on the specific policy of the elected, and therefore allows the governing groups to adopt very similar policies even if their images are distinct enough to make a choice possible. The deep factors generating program convergence are hence not interfered with.

3. The third question is the most relevant to our general theme. Does this decline in distinction among party programs signify a relevant alteration of the pluralist system?

To answer this question, we first consider another aspect of the evolution of the political parties: the weakening of their function of "social integration." Parties no longer represent or do not represent to the same extent (Austrian parties and the Communist party in Italy being the main partly deviant cases) a source of social integration for their followers. Neither are electoral cleavages as stable as they had been for the more than sixty years since they were formed as a reflection of class and religious differences at the end of the last century.[29] The European electorate – as well as the American – has become more fluid, and shifts in preference from one election to the next have become increasingly frequent.[30] It is not easy to judge the depth of such a change and its causes today, but we may at least say that it is linked with the long-term decline in the programmatic function and the integrational function of the parties. A general explanatory hypothesis can be offered that "integration" parties, stable electoral cleavages, and clear alternatives in party program are more likely to be found in periods of intense social (mainly occupational and geographic) change and of consequent strong pressures by new categories of interests to enter into the political system.

If this hypothesis is true, strong parties, with clearly delineated programs and integrated membership, are a temporary phenomenon. They emerge both to strengthen and to control the access of the new masses into the political system and become redundant once both entry and control are achieved. If they are typical of pluralism, then, they are typical only of its first "generative" phase, when the big collective actors are admitted to share power into a system of representation; they still tend to control their followers as whole persons, not just to represent them in specific roles. Typically, there is no pluralist "political market" in this phase, no crosscutting of memberships. Although this "integrated" form of representation seems characteristic of the working-class parties, that is, of the parties organizing a class that is excluded from the individualistic access to multiple public roles, after World War I, and in certain cases even before, in more than one country, bourgeois parties and movements organized themselves in the same "integrated," almost totalitarian, way.

This phase may last longer in certain countries (Italy, France, Austria) and be almost nonexistent in others (e.g., United States), but sooner or later it makes place for a situation in which no irreducible political identity is at stake and political demands all become negotiable. Interest groups asking for specific policies are the main actors on the political scene whereas the political parties, in their effort to represent multiple interests in order to conquer the marginal voter, as well as to have the support of as many interest groups as possible, tend to lose their programmatic and organizational identity.

The analysis that we have been conducting until now should give us the clue to explain how this phase of pluralism has come about. We can summarize the main factors responsible for the change as follows.

The acceptance of the rule of electoral choice tends to bring parties to resemble each other more and more, to rub this distinctiveness out. The growing economic interdependence, both national and international, strengthens the veto powers of international and private national actors, restricting the autonomy of the central authorities of the system, their capacity of pursuing long-term policies and of achieving a unitary will to modify society according to some overall program. This obviously makes the tools for the elaboration of coherent programs obsolete. Because political decisions are entirely the outcome of negotiations between separate interests, political parties have to adapt their structure to the needs of the real actors, the interest groups.

Not all political decisions, however, are the outcome of negotiations between private interests. Even in a pluralist polity, a level of decisions escapes the pluralist procedures of representation because it deals with problems of the system as a whole in its relationship with the other systems on the international scene. Here is the domain of *arcana imperii*: Decisions are secret, secluded, momentous. Neither interest organizations nor political parties are the fittest structures to intervene in forming the decision, but small groups of power holders, or of persons informally related to them are. (This does *not* mean that all decisions of foreign policy pertain to this level; a large part is the outcome of negotiations among all sorts of interests.)

A dualistic structure of power seems therefore to constitute the natural outcome of pluralistic regimes: a caesaristic, secluded level of decisions and an effectively pluralistic, polyarchical, negotiated one. On both levels a contradictory logic is at work. At the caesaristic level the contradiction is between the "absolute" unitary nature of the decisions to be taken and the dependence of the incumbent on the multiformity of public opinions. On the polyarchical level the tension is between the trend toward an institutional (corporative) definition of the interests to be represented and recognized and the continuous surge of new issues and the aggregations of interests around them. On neither level do the political parties seem the most appropriate instruments.

A third level of "nonpower" should be added to these two levels of power, where the "excluded" interests are located: those of the population that is going in and out of the labor market, enjoying no security, belonging to no union or party or other association, without real contact with any structure of political representation, voting or not out of mechanical allegiances. Political parties could probably be interested in this stratum of the population, but the cost of mobilizing it would be too high for them.

Five hypotheses to explain the survival of political parties

One question is now open: If they appear redundant, how is the persistence of political parties in representative regimes to be explained? Obviously, we could surmise that political parties are structures born in response to the initial needs of these regimes and now outdated. The particularistic interests that have in time built up around these structures would be sufficient to justify their survival, considering their reliance on the institutionally guaranteed monopoly over the selection of political personnel. But this would not explain those cases in which the party system was interrupted and later reestablished. Although not a prerequisite, the presence of at least one party does in fact seem to be closely associated with all types of government in advanced industrial societies. Four hypotheses can be put together from the existing literature to explain this fact:[31]

1. The hypothesis of *illusory choice.* Because the principle of popular sovereignty implies that the people must somehow choose, the parties are there to permit them to do so. The principle of popular sovereignty might be merely ideological were it not for the fact that it actually makes governing society easier, for the illusion of being able to choose their governors prevents the population from opposing the regime. Thus parties last because they help maintain consent, which they do by constituting conditions of choice. Although choice would exist even if there were only individual representation without organized parties, parties offer more or less stable collective identities as the basis of choice. Indeed, here we might use the concept of *illusorische Gemeinschaft,* which Marx used for the state. Just as the state takes the place of religion to offer the illusion of a community within which conflicts of particular interests are eliminated, so the parties offer the same illusion, once the state can no longer do so (its possibilities of doing so have been undermined by the very struggles of the ideological mass parties). The party appears as a collective body within which particularistic interests disappear. This fosters the illusion of being able to choose rulers and also to choose them according to general criteria shared by a solidary and stable collectivity rather than for individual utilities.

This hypothesis has two parts, one on the plurality of parties, hence the *illusion of choice,* and the other on the parties as a collective body, hence the *illusion of community.* The force of the hypothesis may correspondingly be summed up in two formulas. (1) If the illusion of choice were to disappear, an important instrument of consent would be lost and thus it would be more difficult to govern society. (2) If the illusion of community were to disappear, the members of a population would be reduced to judging public affairs according to criteria of individual utility, and there would be no way that was not arbitrary of passing from individual criteria to criteria capable of defining collective utility. This would also make government more difficult, and hence the need for parties.

The objections to these hypotheses are the following. The illusion of choice cannot be considered an indispensable instrument of government because many advanced industrial societies have only one party (and even if the repression in these countries seems to be harsher, it does not necessarily cost more than it does in multiparty countries). The illusion of community, on the other hand, is very strong within ideological parties in opposition, where obviously it does not aid but rather hinders governmental action. The illusion of community is also strong in parties governing with opposition. But here it is bound to be confused with the illusion that the state itself is a community immune from fundamental conflicts of interests, and this illusion should be sufficient to induce the population to consent to state action. Hence where this is their only function, parties should disappear.

2. The hypothesis of *cohesiveness*. The upper-level bureaucrats and also the political personnel deriving from their ranks are bound to have a sectoral view of government. The goals they pursue are those of administrative efficiency rather than those derived from a certain view of society in general. Furthermore, they remain attached to the administrative environment from which they came. This makes it difficult for them to govern impartially. To overcome this, the political personnel in government would have to be made up of a cohesive group of individuals, who know each other, are able to communicate easily, and have some end in common so that they would consider administrative efficiency as a means rather than as an end. This would make them something close to a party, a social body that can guarantee internal homogeneity and easy communication. In a party, though, these are bound to have developed in the struggle against other parties.

The hypothesis makes public virtues (cohesiveness and coordination of purposes) derive from private vices (cliquishness or complicity between the members of a group who want to overpower another group).

The objections arise from the observations we have made earlier. If in fact the programmatic function in the party weakens, there will be little to distinguish the party's political personnel from the bureau-

crats in the various administrative sectors. The inferior specific competence of the former will no longer be compensated by a vision of
general goals built up in party action. And if the function of social
integration and cultural formation gets weaker in the parties and no
synthesis or mediation takes place among the various interests represented, the individuals that move from party to governmental positions will lack a common vision and will be no more able to communicate among themselves than any other group of individuals can. Thus
if parties' only function were the formation of a governing group that
is organic and has common goals, their presence would not be justified.

3. The hypothesis of *responsible polling*. The representatives are in a
position to carry out a survey of the electorate and thus to transmit
information useful for government. It is true that any good public
opinion research organization can do better surveys as far as reliability is concerned than can the representatives of the people; these
latter, however, carry them out with "responsibility"; that is, if their
information is not adequate, they may be punished by their electorate. But polls of this sort are bound to be vague and erratic. Even if
they were efficient, there would still be no need for parties but only
for individual representatives.

4. The *reduction-of-complexity* hypothesis. Political parties reduce
the excess of problems that the state would have to address if all the
demands of society reached it directly. That is, they reduce the
number of options that the executive organs have to consider. At the
same time, because the public recognizes itself in the parties, at least
partially, such a reduction of options appears acceptable. Consequently, the parties, on the one hand, facilitate the choice for the
electors inasmuch as they present them with large, general problems
on which to decide; on the other hand, they facilitate administrative
decisions in that they reduce the area of what is considered politically
possible.

But this "screening" function, as we have seen, can be performed
also by interest organization. Moreover, how does one explain the
long-term historical tendency toward programmatic convergence that
makes general choices illusory? And how does one explain that in
many of the most advanced industrial countries such as the United
States the parties are less well aggregated than in other, "simpler"
societies? In what sense can one say that the work of political parties
serves to sustain and to legitimize the decisions of the government?
Certain parties sustain them; others oppose them. A parliament of
individual representatives is sufficient to define a majority and a
minority; organized parties are not required.

5. Each of the four hypotheses that I have reconstructed to understand the reasons for the survival of the political parties in spite of the loss of their most obvious functions appears inadequate in itself, although they all contain insights. A fifth hypothesis may be put forward. We should first consider the specific role of party politicians in the decision-making process. They seem legitimated to take part in it so long as they enjoy the trust of others. Because the same is true also for representatives of special interests, one might infer that what is special about the party politicians' position is that they present themselves as potential representatives of general interests. But this is hardly plausible. We shall argue rather that the party politician acts to guarantee the currency that is exchanged on the political market.

In other words, if representatives of private interests want to obtain a particular measure, they can offer in exchange to the decision maker those resources they control (money, favors, votes, etc.). This kind of exchange is limited to two actors and to rather short-run effects. If long-term political transactions involving a large number of actors are to be made possible, a class of identifiable mediators becomes necessary; durable trust in them will act as a guarantee for the deferral of payments. The party, with its durable structure and public exposure, is a sort of guarantee of political mediation, a kind of "political credit" institution, made possible by a continual verification of the available credit, through the electoral process.

If creation and preservation of political trust is to be considered the ultimate function of political parties in a representative regime, we may conclude, as previously indicated, that political parties are thriving when other bases for trust (religious, ethnic, associational, local, etc.) are lacking or politically dormant, and citizens are in need of stable structures to which they can trustfully refer to orient themselves not only in their utilization of political machineries but also in their acquisition of new social identities. Parties decay when these conditions do not obtain.

The difficulties of political reproduction

In what way has the operation of pluralist systems of representation influenced the process of reproduction of political forms over the long run? Such phenomena as the weakening of large political identities, the disaffection with institutions and with patriotic sentiments and, most important, the revolt or alienation of youth, show that the mechanisms of political reproduction do not function without serious problems.

A certain permanence in the social determination of interests should be assured for a system of representation to regenerate without tearing itself apart in the process of reconstituting its identity. (Thus, paradoxically, one could say that a pluralistic system could be better balanced if it were the expression of an estate society.) But in an industrial society interests are mobile and continuously redefinable, and social aggregations that pursue them disintegrate and recombine. Furthermore, certain parts of the population, such as youth, remain outside of the largest categories of interest. In this sense the problem of including new generations in the system of representation is one of the crucial problems of pluralism. The later that young people enter into the professional system, and the longer that they are suspended from the organized representation of interests, the greater will be the instability of the system.

Historically, this problem has been resolved – or attenuated – through ideology. At times this has meant nationalist ideologies, of various colors, propagated through the state institutions (such as schools) and through the family. At other times it has been the presence of contrasting "ideological" families, each with its own "political church" and its own subcultural networks, generally based on class identity, all of which assures political socialization and helps stabilize the reproduction of political forms. At other times, finally, an analogous function has been carried out by prepolitical social identities – religious, ethnic, linguistic, and the like.

These observations suggest that political reproduction operates smoothly when it takes place within identities that do not represent *specific* interests and that are determined prior to politics – identities that operate throughout the life of the individual, are intergenerational, and are not limited to professional or "civil" life. Youth political orientation can be given meaning by an ideology or membership in a "cultural" (religious, ethnic) identity, not by an interest organization based on an occupational system of which youth is not, or barely, a part.

Thus the more a system is organized to represent the interests of large occupational categories and the less place, therefore, it leaves to ideology, the more difficulties it will encounter in assuring the reproduction of its forms of political representation.

The threat of the new collective identities

From the American civil rights movement to the student movements of various countries, to the ethnic and linguistic movements, to the feminist movements, to the "senior citizens," to the ecologists, to the multiplication of new interest groups, and to the reinforcement of traditional organizations that now present new kinds of demands, the last twenty years have seen new actors, or old ones acting in apparently new ways and raising new issues, burst onto the scene. Is this merely a sign of the smooth functioning of a system that should allow every new interest to come onto the scene in its time? That these movements have not been transformed into true and proper political organizations – except in a few cases in countries where pluralism has still some characteristics of its early phase (such as in Italy or Germany where splinter movements have been transformed into terrorist organizations) – would appear to confirm the notion that pluralism is capable of giving to each collective actor space for expression.

This interpretation is too optimistic, however. It does not explain the violent conflicts that have often accompanied these movements, nor their often rapid subsequent decline. More important, it does not explain the nonnegotiability of many of their demands, which in several cases has generated a kind of politicization *external* to the political system, with the consequent tendency not only to reject party channels but to fight them. Meanwhile, the political systems have generally showed themselves incapable of reacting positively to the impulses they received. Even where this great effervescence has had some effect in terms of reforms, it has been very small compared to the activism, the militance, and the conflicts certain issues had generated.[32] In some cases the effect has even been detrimental to reform, because institutions have rigidified, groups in power have become entrenched, and state action has become repressive. Perhaps this is a predictable effect of too many demands, but why are there *too many* demands? And why does a pluralistic system not have mechanisms to channel and reformulate them?

This can be answered if we recall how pluralistic mechanisms bring about an unlimited possibility for the redefinition of interest and for the access of collectively shared private needs to a "public forum" without being capable, by themselves, of defining a "common good," or, in general, goals that every section of society should accept as its own. The maintenance of the rules of the game, the "form" of political relations, seems to be the only "interest" that everyone must share if they want the system to survive. But this is not enough to induce moderation in the pursuit of particularistic interests when necessary.

Furthermore, as we have seen, because the proper functioning of a pluralist system progressively weakens the ideological and programmatic ambitions of the parties that have access to positions of government, reduces their socially integrative activities, and increases the distance between representatives and represented, a situation is generated that leaves room for new expressions of collective feeling, followed by struggles for the recognition of a new collective identity.

On the other hand, in a pluralist "representative" system, with universal franchise and freedom of association, everybody – every social category – *is* represented, at least according to a certain classification of interests. Where can new collective identities come from? Why should a worker already represented as a worker, prefer to be represented as a black – or as a woman, or as an Irishman? Why should an *already represented* citizen join collective action to obtain a law on abortion? If this is a *new* issue, why does it emerge from outside the existing channels of representation? An answer to these kinds of questions can only be given if the *process of identification* is considered to precede and encompass the process of definition of interest and also to constitute a goal in itself when either no collective identity exists or the old ones are weakening.

This can be shown in the wave of collective movements that appeared at the turn of the century. Because it represented the entry into the system of classes that until then were excluded, the movement crystallized in unions and political parties.

The goal (as it was redefined, even if it was not the original one) had been to acquire a *durable* position of power within the system – because the original social condition of the mobilized groups (as defined by the occupational system) was a durable one. Not so in the recent wave, when identities are defined according to either cultural–biological criteria (sex, ethnicity, generation) or issues (abortion, ecology, rights of an external identity: civil rights, Vietnam War, etc.) These two kinds of criteria, even if they seem to be very distant from each other, have, however, some aspects in common. They both refuse the occupational criterion as the source of the process of identification. And they both stress the principle of distinction and incompatibility: the cultural–biological movements because their bases are obviously exclusive; the "issue" movements because an issue being the only reason to act together, if it is bargained over, no other collective identification exists. What is implied in this latter type is the striving toward the formation of a community of value-sharing individuals. But this is not different from what is implied in the former type, where the new community is seen as finding its roots in a common heritage; the latter proposes a commonly built future. In both cases the goal is the constitution of a new community having certain desired characteristics – not the improvement of the position of a certain social category within a given system of value distribution.

The principle that inspires this kind of movement seems then to express a reaction against those mechanisms at work in contemporary society that tend to dissolve the bonds of collective identities. Therefore the content of their goals is changeable, even if a pattern can be

found in a double direction: toward either reestablishment of particularistic solidarities or claims of a higher universalism than the
current social order permits. And their social basis is *not* the product
of a particular process of change in the division of labor, although it
can be said that certain forms of collective mobilization are possible
because of the particular position of youth in the social structure and
because of the process of "liberation" from labor of part of the middle
classes.[33]

As for the impact on the pluralist system, we may well observe that
after this wave, as after others, the system is generating its own
remedies. Representatives of the traditional organizations incorporate
some new demands, reinterpreting them so that they can be negotiated with other actors in the system. The top representatives of
the new interests are co-opted and allocated more or less institutionalized functions. Sectional monopolies of representation get
reestablished or reinforced. The international constraints on which
the control of the economy depends (balance of payments, etc.) are
shown to be decisive. Thus the technical nature of fundamental political decisions is made clear: They are well out of the range of any
"political skill" possessed by the masses; this extinguishes any ambitions for participation and induces the population to abandon politics.
New decision-making centers (for the economy, public order, secret
information) are set up out of public reach and kept in the secluded
sphere of politics.

Only one traditional remedy seems not to have been tried this time:
the diffusion of nationalist mass ideologies. The de facto dependence
of national political bodies on the international system seems to render this technique of reaction inapplicable. In any case it would
bring obvious inconveniences, both internationally and internally, in
that it would provoke forms of mass mobilization. It is much safer to
encourage the depoliticizing effects that the other techniques assure.

All this does not indicate that the pluralist equilibrium works. On
the contrary, the emergence of new identities and the maneuvers to
exclude them express the intrinsic instability of a system that demands that interests be identified "categorically," but does not offer
stable criteria for such identities and instead favors their multiplication. The theory by which a pluralistic system is automatically legitimated insofar as it allows a voice to every interest that emerges from
civil society, assumes that the members of the system will agree not to
consider how well their interests are satisfied and will only consider
how well the procedures operate. This alone is a difficult assumption
to justify, but we have already seen that there is more. The functioning of the system itself generates unpredictability and wears down

activism and political commitment. It creates tensions and strains in the development of personal identities, which, having been generated during the formation of collective identities, are mortified when social movements dissolve or are bureaucratized. The waste and loss of social commitment seem thus to grow unbearable after each process of restabilization. Pluralism, the proud product of Western political invention, increasingly begets indifference or pessimism.

Notes

1 A. V. Dicey, *Law and Public Opinion in England* (London: Macmillan, 1962), p. 32 ff.

2 The debate is analyzed in A. Taylor, *Laissez-Faire and State Intervention in Nineteenth-Century Britain* (London: Macmillan, 1972). Brenner's article with the same title is in *Journal of Economic History* 8 (1948).

3 Cf. Th. Lowi, *The End of Liberalism* (New York: Norton, 1969), Chap. 5. For an overview of several interpretations on this theme, cf. M. Corsale, *Certezza del diritto e crisi di legittimità* (Milano: Giuffrè, 1979), Chap. 5.

4 An analysis of the political thought that was first aware of the inception of the pluralist system is in R. Eisner, *Pluralismus zwischen Liberalismus und Sozialismus* (Stuttgart: Kohlhammer, 1972), Chaps. 4, 5.

It should also be clear that what we mean here by pluralism is an historical phenomenon, *not* a political doctrine. Of course, the literature concerned with the political doctrine of pluralism expresses a certain view of how pluralist traits exist in reality, all of which has an influence on the formulation of the doctrine. (See a recent exhaustive analysis in Hans Kremendahl, *Pluralismustheorie in Deutschland* (Leverkusen: Heggen, 1977). But now we are interested in the analysis of how a certain system of representation works, independent of the preferences or criticisms that certain authors can manifest toward an ideal model of it.

This analysis, being historically specific, should also be differentiated from the "pluralist theory," or better, "group theory" (Bentley, Truman, etc.), which applies the notion of "group" to any type of political system.

5 I deal with this definition of interests in *Le Regole del Pluralismo*, (Bologna: Il Mulino, 1980), Chap. 2.

6 The *locus classicus* for the history of representation in the West is O. Hintze, "Weltgeschichtliche Bedingungen der Repräsentativverfassung," *Historische Zeitschrift* 143: 1–47, now in O. Hintze, *Staat und Verfassung*, 147–85. See also G. Poggi, *La vicenda dello Stato moderno* (Bologna: Il Mulino, 1978), Chap. 3.

7 This analysis of the relationships among social basis, ideology, and organizational cohesion in a political party is obviously very sketchy. A good analysis is E. Ozbudun, *Party Cohesion in Western Democracies*, Sage Professional Paper, no. 01–006, 1970.

8 Cf. G. Teubner, *Organisationsdemokratie und Verbandsverfassung* (Tubingen: Mohr, 1978), Chap. 2. Much of what I say in this section is based on this book.

9 Op. cit., p. 57 ff.

10 Op. cit., p. 39.

11 See note 5.

12 I elaborated this theme in "Political Exchange and Collective Identity," in *The Resurgence of Class Conflict in Western Europe Since 1968*, eds., C. Crouch and A. Pizzorno p. 278 f.

13 See D. A. Smith, "Labour Market, Institutions and Inflation," *British Journal of Industrial Relations* 14 (1): 35–42 and A. Pizzorno, *op. cit.*, p. 284.

14 H. Kariel, *The Decline of American Pluralism,* (Stanford: Stanford University Press, 1978). See also G. Ionescu, *Centripetal Politics* (London: East Davis, 1975).

15 Among others, J. Lapalombara, *Interest Groups in Italian Politics* (Princeton, N.J.: Princeton University Press, 1964).

16 R. Crossman, *The Diaries of a Cabinet Minister* (New York: Holt, Rinehart, and Winston, 1975).

17 C. W. Mills, quoted by H. Kariel, *op. cit.*, p. 102.

18 See N. Luhmann, *Politische Planung* (Opladen, 1971) and "Soziologie des Politischen Systems," in *Soziologische Anfklärung,* (Opladen, 1970), p. 154 ff. N. Poulantzas, *Pouvoir politique et classes sociales,* (Paris: Maspero, 1968).

19 D. Mardsen, *Industrial Democracy and Industrial Control in West Germany, France, and Great Britain,* Department of Employment, Research Paper n. 4, London, September 1978.

20 Cf. the analysis in A. Pizzorno, "Political Exchange and Collective Identity", *op. cit.*

21 Cf. A. Pizzorno, "Le due logiche dell'azione di classe," in *Lotte operaie e sindacato: il ciclo 1968–1972 in Italia,* Pizzorno, Reyneri, Regini, Regalia, (Bologna: Il Mulino, 1978), p. 32 ff.

22 Cf. Bachrach and Baratz, "Key Concepts: Decisions and Non-decision" in *Power and Poverty* (London: 1970) and C. Offe, "Klassenherrschaft und politische System. Die Selektivität Politischer Institutionen," in *Strukturprobleme des Kapitalistischen Staates* (Frankfurt: Suhrkamp, 1972).

23 Cf. A. Lindbeck, "The Changing Role of the National State" *Kyklos* 28 (1): 23–46.

24 J. C. Thomas: *The Decline of Ideology in Western Political Parties* (London: Sage Publications, 1975). It should be remembered that Thomas's data go only until the early sixties.

25 Australia, Austria, England, France, Germany, Italy, Japan, New Zealand, Sweden, USSR, U.S.A.

26 J. C. Thomas, *op. cit.*, p. 46.

27 In "Political Parties and Macroeconomic Policy," *American Political Science Review* (December 1977), D. Hibbs argues that "governments pursue macroeconomic policies broadly consistent with the objective economic interests and subjective preferences of their class-defined core political constituencies" (in his rejoinder to the criticism of J. Paine, (*American Political Science Review* 73 (1) (March 1979): 185) and precisely that leftist governments pursue economic policies reducing unemployment and increasing inflation; whereas the opposite is true of the conservative governments. The successive debate has shown that the evidence is still very uncertain on this point. And the experience of the seventies would add to the contradictory elements.

Interesting data are also contained in E. S. Kirschen et al., *Economic Policy in Our Time* (Amsterdam, 1964), p. 225 ff. If they show separation in the economic policies preferences among the political parties, they underscore the effect of the differences among interest groups' preferences. This brings us back to the distinction between the first and the second level of the analysis we propose.

28 This distinction between the first and the second level is similar to the one G. Sartori draws between *visible* and *invisible* politics in *Parties and Party Systems,* (Cambridge University Press, 1976, p. 143), even if it can hardly be maintained that the second level of action is "invisible," because it is still performed through public language, although specially codified. I would not agree, however, with the statement that "the lesser the ideological bent . . . the greater the (relative) proximity and conver-

284   ALESSANDRO PIZZORNO

tibility between rhetoric and feasibility, between image selling and deeds."
"Nonideological" image selling may be as distant from real action as the most abstract
ideology.

29 S. M. Lipset and S. Rokkan, "Cleavage Structures, Party Systems, and Voter
Alignments: An Introduction," in *Party Systems and Voter Alignments* (New York: Free
Press, 1967), pp. 1–64.

30 S. B. Wolinetz, "Stabilità e mutamento nei sistemi partitici dell'Europa Occiden-
tale" *Rivista Italiana di Scienza Politica* 1(1978):3–56.

31 These hypothesis are reconstructed here as four self-justifying arguments. All of
them can be found in a somewhat diffuse form in the literature, but none of them can
be attributed to one specific author or school. Only hypothesis (4) is typically to be
found in Luhmann's systemic approach.

32 S. Berger, "Politics and Antipolitics in Western Europe in the Seventies",
Daedalus (Winter 1979):27.

33 On this particular point we diverge from A. Touraine's analysis, which we think,
however, constitutes one of the best interpretative syntheses of the content of the new
wave of collective movements. Cf. A. Touraine, "Les nouveaux conflicts sociaux"
Sociologie du Travail 1 (1975):10–18.

10

Interest intermediation and regime governability in contemporary Western Europe and North America

PHILIPPE C. SCHMITTER

Virtually all efforts to understand the generic nature of contemporary political behavior and its policy products rely on the notion that the promotion and protection of self-regarding objectives "rightly and rationally understood" provide the motive force, and the capacity to prevail over the interest efforts of others provides the explanation for likely outcomes. The emergence and triumph of capitalism and industrialization have provided not only a differentiated set of categories for identifying and a suitable means for calculating those interest(s); they have also ensured through interdependence and competition that one must indeed consider self-regarding objectives or suffer dire consequences.

The purpose of this chapter is not to lament the replacement or effacement of more "noble" motives in political life. Nor is it to measure the extent to which selfish, vested behavior is, in fact, characteristic of the politics of advanced industrial/capitalist societies.[1] Rather, it assumes the predominance of such motivation and seeks to explore (and tentatively to test) the consequences that the emergence of different modes of formalized interest intermediation have had on the governability of contemporary Western European and North American polities.

Implicitly, if not explicitly, much of the existing literature on "(un)-governability" or on its predecessor "(in)stability" denies the relevance of the question posed in this manner. The traditional wisdom of politics identifies regime survival with the art of "high politics," with the statecraft and statesmanship of leaders responding, with more or less skill, to the exigencies of the international system, the demands of public opinion, the imperatives of moral conscience and/or the dictates of the "spirit of the age." Both the form and content of interest(s) are confined to the realm of "low politics" – annoy-ing and at times confining, but fundamentally incapable of threaten-ing the global viability of political order. Only failure of judgment, weakening of community, decline in legitimacy, or exogenous catas-trophe could lead to ungovernability.

The neotraditional science of politics may recognize and even exalt the pursuit of interests but concludes that the very logic of industri-alization will produce such a multiplicity of dynamic, ephemeral, overlapping and countervailing efforts to protect and promote self-regarding objectives that the resultant "pluralist" system will be both self-equilibrating and self-legitimating. All with interests will get a democratic chance to play in the game; none, however, will be capa-ble of controlling its course or rigging its outcome. From this perspec-tive, the danger of ungovernability and/or instability arises from outside the game of interest politics – from passionate, irrational subver-sives who refuse to play according to the established rules, who insist on turning the game toward more exalted goals, and who force the otherwise benevolent umpire to use coercion in order to ensure the continued governability of the system.

The currently fashionable perspective of the "policy sciences" suggests yet another explanation for (un)governability or (in)stability. Again, the pursuit of ignoble, vested interests is acknowledged as providing the predominant motive for political action, but in contrast to the optimism of pluralists, the "policy scientists" see a real danger in such unbridled selfishness. Too much of it by too wary and too well-organized actors leads to "overload," to an excess of demands on public authorities beyond their capacity for satisfying such claims. As the governing systems of advanced industrial/capitalist societies decline in efficiency, efficacy, and legitimacy under such an imbal-ance, more and more dissatisfied interests find they must make more and more noise and engage in more and more unconventional be-havior to gain effective access – and this leads only to more and more overload and ungovernability.

This chapter contends in particular with the latter, "overload school." In the process it will advance arguments (and marshal some data) to demonstrate that the pursuit of lowly self-regarding interests can have high-level consequences for the governability of advanced industrial/capitalist polities. Arguments are also proffered that pluralism is *not* the likely form that interest intermediation will take in these polities, and moreover that where it has been most prevalent it has had an effect on governability contrary to that presumed by its leading theorists and ideologues.

The "mode" of interest intermediation and the problem of governability

The principal orienting hypothesis of this chapter is simple: *The relative governability of contemporary, highly industrialized, advanced capitalist polities is less a function of aggregate overload, of "imbalance" between the sum total of societal demands and state capabilities, than of the discrete processes that identify, package, promote, and implement potential interest claims and commands.* In an aggregate sense, there has always been more of a demand for imperative coordination and authoritative allocation than the state was capable of supplying, and the "gap" was (and still is) filled by physical repression and symbolic manipulation. It is indeed questionable whether the sheer volume of demands, even politically "weighted" ones, has increased out of proportion to state capabilities. Certainly the monopoly of organized physical violence has never been more overwhelmingly concentrated in the hands of state authorities – even if occasionally vulnerable to blackmail and disruption by determined minorities. Although one could point to a marked decline in the capacity of legitimate state actors for symbolic manipulation in an age of desacralization of authority and disenchantment with rational efficiency, at no time in recent history has there been such a dearth of plausible ideological alternatives. No "counterarrangement" has yet to mount a coherent appeal or attract a significant and lasting mass following. The outbursts that have occurred – from *Poujadisme* to counciliar communism – have fizzled in short order, leaving "bloody but unbowed" the liberal-bourgeois-parliamentary-electorally competitive order as the ultimate focus of legitimation in the polities of Western Europe and North America.

What have changed extensively and irreversibly are the processes of political intermediation by which the potential volume of societal demands is captured and focused and through which the eventual pattern of public policies is evaluated and sifted. To an extent this has been recognized in the literature on ungovernability and overload, but the emphasis has always been placed on the party, legislative, and cabinet nexus. The narrowing margins of electoral victory, the shifts in partisan allegiance, the decline in party identification, the rise in the proportion of independent voters, the increased frequency of minority governments, the unstableness of "reigning but not ruling" coalitions, and the specter of Communist participation in national executive decision making have been taken as both *cause for* and *evidence of* declining governability. This tendency to attribute the ills and distempers of advanced industrial/capitalist societies to an overloading of their party-electoral-legislative-cabinet circuits is, I submit, in large part the product of an instinctive intellectual reaction similar to that of the drunken sailor who knows he has lost his key elsewhere but searches for it under the street light because it is more convenient to do so. Liberal social science has, indeed, illuminated that arena of political life quite extensively but has not taken much of a concerted, systematic look at the other processes of intermediation that link social cleavages, class relations, and organizational interests to political choice and state action, bypassing, if not subordinating, the classical liberal mechanisms of individually articulated preferences and territorially based representation.

My second hunch, therefore, is that although those who have emphasized the confusion and decline in party and parliament focus correctly on the distinctly *political* processes of intermediation, they have mistaken the symptoms for the disease. The key to understanding the various crises of governability lies in the dimly lit arena of functional interest intermediation through highly formalized and specialized organizations in direct relation with the bureaucratic apparatus of the modern state. The collapse of new social contracts; the burgeoning demand for guaranteed and privileged access; the clash of representative jurisdictions; the quest for authenticity and participation at all levels of authority, private as well as public; the mobilization and militancy of previously quiescent groups such as civil servants and public dependents; the clamor for and revolt against raising state expenditures and governmental regulation; the increasing sensitivity to relative deprivation and inequalities within as well as between social classes; the explosion of subnational ethnicity; the sudden emergence of single-issue movements, not to mention the principal defining characteristics of (un)governability (to be discussed *infra*): (1) the tendency to resort to unprecedented, extralegal means of political expression; (2) the dwindling of elite cohesion and hegemony; and (3) the diminished capacity of the state to secure resources and implement policies – most, if not all, of these find their expression in and irresolution through the structures of specialized intermediation for class, sectoral, professional, regional, ethnic, sexual, and generational interests. It is not parties and elections that bring most of these problems, dilemmas, or contradictions to the agenda of the state, although they may be indirectly affected by them. Individual partisan allegiance and the territorial clustering of notables, those two pillars of the liberal democratic, civic-cultured, bourgeois-dominant political order, have been gradually but firmly overtaken by the third, heretofore less prominent, aspect of that mode of domination: the implacable pursuit of self-interest, rightly and rationally understood, through specialized, functionally differentiated organizations. De Tocqueville warned long ago that *"la liberté d'association est la dernière qu'un peuple puisse supporter,"* and we may soon find out if he was correct.

This "organizational revolution" was rather slow in coming, and, until quite recently, it seems correct to say that the full potential capability of interest associations was not realized or exploited. This is for two basic reasons: the first politico-historical, the second politicological. Here I wish simply to repeat the argument I have developed elsewhere:

All Western European societies passed, unevenly and asynchronically, through some of the same structural transformations in their organized-mediated relation between civil society and the state. From a set of "ancient associations" – involuntary, exclusive, monopolistic, quasi-public, semireligious guilds – most moved (with varying degrees of partiality and brevity) toward a situation of "freedom of contract" or "freedom of labor" as a result of the abolition of guild privileges and monopolies, and the more gradual assertion of liberal notions of individual citizenship and territorial-parliamentary representation – those reforms in turn impelled by the spread of capitalist relations of production and distribution. In extreme instances, e.g., France under the loi Le Chapelier, all forms of effective intermediation between citizen and state were formally abolished. Elsewhere, legal codes and judicial practice were differentially destructive of class-based organizations, e.g., the Combination Acts in Great Britain. Finally, in a few Continental European cases, the intervening period of individualistic liberalism was quite short and incomplete as monarchic autocracies and conservative oligarchies attempted to make over from above medieval corporations into modern interest associations (e.g., Germany and, especially, Austria).

By the latter quarter of the nineteenth century, the "art of association" could no longer be formally denied – even to potentially subversive working-class majorities and ethnic minorities. With varying degrees of delay, reluctance, and reservation, European governments began to recognize "freedom of association and petition" as one of the fundamental rights of citizenship. In at least one case – Switzerland – the constitution also recognized one's "freedom not to be forced to associate," prohibiting all forms of *Zwangsverbände*. This change in legal norms and ideology, combined with a protracted economic depression, a wider agenda of policy choices (e.g., tariff debates and the institutionalization of social insurance), changes in the nature and structure of productive units, and the extension of capitalist relations to all sectors of the economy, seems to have produced an outburst of formal interest associability in the 1870s–1890s. During this period something like a modern system of representation based on extensive functional coverage and intensive interest specialization began to emerge at the national level, as well as in municipal and provincial subunits. At first, most of this associability took a pluralist form. The units of representation were spontaneous in formation; multiple, dispersed and overlapping in their claims to jurisdiction; competing for members; ideologically divergent in their goals; and praxeologically distinct in their techniques of intervention. Nevertheless, differences in modes of representation emerged quite early. The degree of hierarchy and vertical structure and, with it, the relative importance of peak associations varied considerably, as did political and organizational independence from the State and political parties, and influence in setting the agenda and determining the outcomes of public policy.

Some of this initial diversity in structure and behavior was reduced by the impact of World War I. Everywhere, even in non-belligerent powers, the tasks of wartime mobilization, rationing, planned resource allocations, price control and so forth, encouraged the consolidation of previously competitive associations, the formal delimitation of interest jurisdictions, the nationalization and centralization of organizational structures, the monopolization of representation, the acquisition of quasi-public functions, and the interpenetration of public and private realms of decision making, as well as enhanced the legitimacy and influence of interest associations in their direct interaction with the state bureaucracy. When, as Charles Maier has argued, bourgeois Europe was "recast" in the tense aftermath of the War, a reinforcement of neo-mercantilist policies and neo-corporatist organizations was part of the mold.[2] In the 1920s and 1930s, the primary issue in many European countries was whether these trends would develop autonomously and selectively within the sinews of civil society, occasionally culminating in privatistic "social peace treaties," or whether they would be forced to develop under the watchful eye and compulsory muscle of the State, eventuating in the impressive corporatist façades of Fascism and other forms of authoritarian rule.[3]

While these different historical starting points and developmental patterns were leaving Western Europe and North America with markedly different configurations of interest organizations, a second "politicological" factor was at work. As long as the basis of associability in the liberal democratic order was exclusively voluntaristic – with freedom both to join and to leave – the whole process of specialized interest intermediation was trapped in a serious dilemma. The incentive structure of rational individual choice was such that the potential interests that were most likely to make a difference in influencing both policy outcomes and member preferences were the least likely to find initial associational expression. New interest organizations might be founded by some unrealistic entrepreneur or ideological zealot, but given the sheer numbers involved, the probable dispersion of preferences, and the ease with which any initial success would attract competitors – not to mention selective incentives not to join or repression costs if one did – such organizations were unlikely to survive or prosper. Where the number of potentially interested actors was small or concentrated, an association might have been more likely to appear, because each participant would contribute measurably to its success, but its organizational demands would not deviate very much from existing member interests, nor would its policy influence vary much from what ad hoc or sporadic forms of class or sectoral collusion might achieve. Under such conditions, only moderate-sized, highly specialized associations – usually of propertied or professional interests – might be expected to avoid both *free booters* (individuals and firms with sufficient knowledge, market power, and/or political clout of their own to do without collective intermediation) and *free riders* (individuals and firms with insufficient incentives to join but an interest in vicariously reaping the benefits of collective intermediation) and therefore to realize the full potential of the organization weapon.[4] Those classes, sectors, professions, regions, *éthnies*, and so on with a large and dispersed clientele would offer weak incentives to form or join, but ironically, once established, associations representing such interests would be the most likely to enlighten or manipulate member preferences, to develop independent organizational resources and leadership, and thereby to introduce significant new forces into political life.

Although some mass-based associations managed to break out of this dilemma through ideological conviction, class consciousness, and subcultural solidarity (e.g., trade unions and some *Mittelstand* groups), or through peripheral *ressentiment*, moral outrage, and transnational sponsorship (e.g., temperance movements and lay Catholic organizations), the real change depended on a shift in the nature and extent of public policy. Only the coercive intervention of the modern bureaucratic state to subsidize organizational existence; to license respective jurisdictions; to grant monopolistic access; to delegate tasks; to ensure selective privileges; to render membership obligatory *de facto* or *de jure*; to define issues, and hence affected interests; to insist on the provision of associated information; to encourage the formation of functionally organized "partners" for the implementation of public policy; and so forth is likely to bring forth such an organized response from civil society. In a sense, the historical process sketched briefly here overwhelmed the politicologic of pluralistic spontaneity and liberal voluntarism. Once the social-insurance schemes, subsidies for capitalist accumulation, regulation of "unfair" competition, war- and peacetime rationing and price control, indicative planning, promotion of exports, negotiation of social peace treaties, extension of contracts, and so on had introduced elements of compulsion and collusion into the relationship between state agencies and privileged interest associations, the whole process of intermediation between civil society and the state began to change.

Not only did the distinction between private and public action weaken, but also the organized intermediaries themselves acquired new resources and tasks as private governments and semipublic spokesmen. Increasingly bureaucratic in nature, their survival became more independent of member preferences, their leadership more professionalized, their activities more diversified (and, in some cases, more commercial and financial), and their goals more determined by their collusion with power and capital. The *density* or associational membership grew rapidly given the new elements of compulsion and selective access to benefits. The *coverage* of organized interests expanded functionally and geographically to fill out national networks of effective intermediation as existing associations invested financial capital and human resources to spread the message and as competing or conflicting interests struggled to emulate threatening forerunners. *Concentration* in the channels of specific interest intermediation advanced rapidly, propelled by strategic calculation and by administrative convenience, until hierarchically centralized, monopolistic associations had forged symbiotic, "responsible" links with corresponding state agencies.

In those countries in which individualistic liberalism was weakest, premodern forms of associability most resilient, ownership and geographic locus of capital most concentrated, expansion of state policy earliest and most extensive, strength of reformist social democratic parties greatest and most protracted, a mode of interest intermediation emerged, which at its most extreme can be called "societal corporatism." It is corporatist in the sense that its constituent units are organized into a limited number of singular, compulsory, hierarchically ordered and functionally differentiated categories, recognized, licensed, or encouraged by the state and granted a representational monopoly within their respective categories in exchange for observing certain controls on their selection of leaders and articulation of demands and supports. It is societal in the sense that this arrangement came into existence largely, but not exclusively, as the result of interassociational demands and intraorganizational processes – from below, so to speak, rather than from a conscious effort by those in power to mold the type of interest intermediation system most congenial with their authoritarian mode of domination. Corporatism from above we would call *state* corporatism.[5]

Now we are in a position to make our second hunch more explicit. The key to differing degrees of governability lies less in the "objective" magnitudes of macroeconomic performance, social cleavages, and class relations than in the way differentiated interests are "intermediated" between civil society and the state. Our discussion has suggested the specific empirical dimensions relevant to the explanation of differences in outcome: representational coverage, membership density, and corporatist structure. *Polities in which interests are*

processed through formal associations that cover the widest variety of poten-
tial interests with national networks of representation, that have the highest
proportion of those potentially affected as members, and whose pattern of
interaction with the state is monopolistic, specialized, hierarchical, and
mutually collusive should be more orderly, stable, and effective, at least in
the short run, given the conditions of contemporary governance. Put
a different way, those countries previously "fortunate" enough to
have developed a pluralist mode of interest intermediation with its
multiple, overlapping, spontaneously formed, voluntaristically supported, easily abandoned, and politically autonomous associations,
are likely to find it a serious impediment to governability in the post-
liberal, advanced, capitalist state.

Unfortunately, we cannot explore even tentatively all three of these
dimensions of intermediation. The pattern and extent of associational
coverage have yet to be satisfactorily measured – much less reduced to
a single indicator or rank ordering. *Density* is less of a problem even if
the reliability of membership figures for trade unions is questionable
and little or no comparable or comparative data are available for employers', professional, civic, and religious associations. Presumably
where unionization is "dense," so will be membership in these other
types of associations. In any case, it is possible to rank the fifteen
polities of Western Europe and North America[6] according to the
proportion of wage and salary earners that are formally enrolled in
blue- and white-collar unions. This variable takes on an impressive
range – from 76.7 and 72.6 percent for Sweden and Finland, respectively, to 18.2 and 23.4 percent for the United States and Canada.

Devising an indicator of societal corporatism is more difficult given
the multivariate nature of the concept and the need for qualitative
information about a wide number of associations and their practices.
In Table 10.1, two core structural characteristics of the trade-union
movement – (1) the degree of organizational centralization and (2) the
extent to which a single national central enjoys a representational
monopoly – are combined into a single rank ordering. The organizational centralization measure was created by Bruce Headey and is
based on information on size of (con)federation bureaucracy, existence of strike funds, and degree of control over member associations.[7] The degree of associational monopoly was derived from recent
data on the number of distribution of union (con)federations, as well
as on information on whether blue- and white-collar workers were
grouped in the same peak association (e.g., Norway) or in separate
ones (e.g., Sweden). It is also a presumption of this indicator that
where workers' associations are highly centralized and monopolistic,
other interests will be correspondingly organized.

Table 10.1. *Indicators of societal corporatism: simple rank order and combined rank order*

	Simple rankings		Combined ranking
	Organizational[a] centralization	Associational[b] monopoly	Societal[c] corporatism
Austria (A)	1	3	1
Belgium (B)	3	(9)	7
Canada (CDN)	(13)	(9)	(11)
Denmark (DK)	8	(1.5)	(4)
Finland (FL)	(5)	(4.5)	(4)
France (F)	10	(14)	13
Germany (D)	9	6	8
Rep. of Ireland (IRL)	(13)	(9)	(11)
Italy (I)	(13)	(14)	15
Netherlands (NL)	2	(9)	6
Norway (N)	(5)	(1.5)	2
Sweden (S)	(5)	(4.5)	(4)
Switzerland (CH)	(7)	(14)	9
Great Britain (GB)	(13)	12	14
United States (USA)	(13)	(9)	(11)

rho = 0.52

[a] A composite score of indicators of (con)federal powers to engage in collective bargaining, to support strikes with own funds, to maintain a large staff, and to collect dues from members. Scores for Switzerland and Canada have been calculated by this author.

[b] A compound-additive score with three components: (1) presence of single national labor (con)federation equals 1; presence of two national (con)federations or one national plus important nonaffiliated unions equals 2; presence of three or more national (con)federations equals 3; (2) joint organization of manual and nonmanual workers equals 1; manual and nonmanual organized separately into national (con)federations equals 2; manual and nonmanual organized separately with no nonmanual national (con)federation of importance equals 3; and (3) no stable factions within national (con)federation(s) equals 1; stable faction within national (con)federation(s) equals 1.5.

[c] A combined rank ordering of organizational centralization and associational monopoly.

Sources: (a) Bruce W. Headey, "Trade Unions and National Wage Policies," *The Journal of Politics* 32(2) (May 1970): 407–31; (b) *The Europa Yearbook*, Vols. I and II (London: Europa Publications, 1976).

The use of the concept of "corporatism" by other authors in this volume and the even more varied uses to which it has been put elsewhere[8] makes it necessary to spell out the definition used here and its operational limitations. First and foremost, "societal corporatism" does not refer to any historically specific ideology, world view, political culture, or even any set of collective aspirations.[9] Notions of functional harmony, class collaboration, self-administration, and so forth are usually not far removed from this institutional arrangement, but they have been so disparate in their intellectual origins and social support, so deviant in the past in their *praxis* from their promised ends, and so divergent in the present from explicit ideologies and intentions, that little can be gained from defining or even associating the term with this fleeting "world of ideas and symbols." Societal corporatism as used here is located in the realm of institutional behavior, not that of individual values or collective aspirations.

Second, it refers to a mode of arranging the political process, indeed, structuring part of the political process. It is not a way of organizing all of society or running the economy. Societal corporatism is "compatible" with a wide range of social institutions and is not an "alternative" to capitalist exploitation but, at least in some countries, an integral part of it.

The part of the political process to which societal corporatism refers I have called "interest intermediation." It encompasses both the means through which interests are transferred from, aggregated over, and articulated for members to collective decision-making bodies, public or private (*representation*), and the ways in which interests are taught to, transmitted to, and imposed on members by associations (*social control*). The concept "intermediation" is also meant to convey the likelihood that interests may be generated from within formal associations themselves, independent of member preferences and authoritative commands.

Much of the burgeoning literature and several of the chapters in this volume use corporatism (with such prefixes as neo-, liberal, societal) to refer to a closely related but analytically distinct aspect of the political process: as a mode of policy formation, in which formally designated interest associations are incorporated within the process of authoritative decision making and implementation. As such, they are officially recognized by the state not merely as interest intermediaries but as co-responsible "partners" in governance and societal guidance.[10] Ostensibly private and autonomous associations are not just consulted and their pressures weighed. Rather, they are negotiated with on a regular, predictable basis.[11] Their consent becomes necessary for policies to be adopted; their collaboration becomes essential for policies to be implemented. In the most extreme or pure case, such corporatist policy making would involve "private" agreements between associations that eventually receive the *pro forma* approval of parliament or executive authority – rendering them enforceable as public law and thereby making them binding on noncontracting parties, up to and including the public as a whole. These agreements are subsequently implemented through the associations themselves – thereby lightening the load of public agencies, removing the issues from accountability to wider publics, and legitimating the outcome for the affected, "represented" parties.

Now corporatism as interest intermediation and corporatism as policy formation are neither theoretically nor empirically synonymous. One can exist without the other. For example, a regime may incorporate multiple, overlapping, competing, autonomous interest associations into policymaking and implementation. Inversely, a regime may tolerate and license singular, monopolistic, functionally differentiated, hierarchically ordered associations but deny them the access or capability to do more than "pressure" for their preferred outcomes from without and refuse to rely on them for implementation purposes.

There is, nevertheless, considerable evidence of an elective affinity, if not a strong element of historical causality, between the corporatization of interest intermediation and the emergence of "concerted" forms of policymaking.[12] It is no accident that virtually all the authors using different definitions of corporatism[13] agree on the countries and policy arenas they chose as exemplars for theory building or cases for hypothesis testing.

The rank orderings suggested in this chapter as measures for "societal corporatism" are compiled only from data on the institutional structure of interest intermediation. They contain no data and make no presumptions about the extent of policy concertation that may be simultaneously or concomitantly present in these countries. They do not include (for lack of information) the one "policy" dimension that was stressed in its formal definition, that is, the extent to which interest associations are recognized by the state and, in exchange, exercise certain restraints in their selection of leaders and articulation of demands.

The operational indicator also makes the assumption that the institutional configuration for workers' interests will be somehow "mirrored" in that of other classes, sectors, and professions. In short, it presumes a sort of organizational symmetry between organized interests – a presumption that is demonstrably false with regard to capital and labor in certain cases,[14] and generally not applicable to the organization of agriculture and the professions that seem to have quite distinctive patterns of associability.[15]

Before examining the correlation of these newly derived rank orders of membership density and societal corporatism with our correspondingly measured indicators of governability, let us consider briefly their relationship to each other. In a liberal political economy, one might expect the relationship to be negative. Singular, cen-

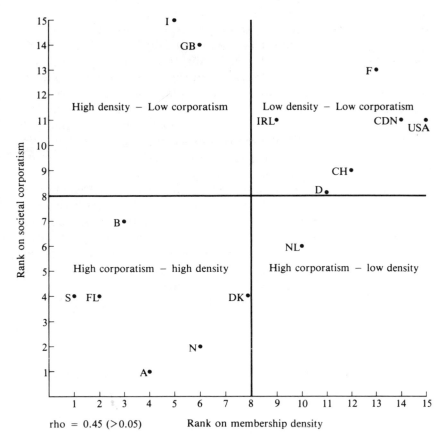

Figure 10.1. Relation between societal corporatism and membership density. Key: (A) Austria, (B) Belgium, (CDN) Canada, (DK) Denmark, (FL) Finland, (F) France, (D) W. Germany, (IRL) Rep. of Ireland, (I) Italy, (NL) Netherlands, (N) Norway, (S) Sweden, (CH) Switzerland, (GB) Great Britain, (USA) United States.

tralized, monopolistic associations should not have a competitive incentive to attract and hold new members; therefore, where societal corporatism is high, membership density should be low. If, however, we drop the assumption that associability functions according to the voluntaristic exchange principles of a market and emphasize the elements of compulsion, coercion, selective access, and organizational control that have increasingly crept into modern systems of interest intermediation, then our expectation is reversed. The more societally corporatist a system, the more members will have no choice but to participate in it – however begrudgingly.

Figure 10.1 shows that for Western Europe and North America

neither of the hypotheses is thoroughly compelling. The clear trend is toward a positive association of corporatism with high density and pluralism with low density. There are practically no highly corporatist cases with low proportional memberships (the Netherlands and West Germany are borderline instances), but there are two highly significant exceptions to the notion that multiple, overlapping, organizational decentralized worker peak associations must be less capable of attracting a high proportion of those potentially eligible to join: Italy and Great Britain. Even if some of this exceptionalism is due to inflated membership claims (especially in the case of Italy), nevertheless, the scatter in Figure 10.1 will allow us to test for an important difference in the role of modern interest intermediations. Are polities becoming more unruly, unstable, and ineffective simply because everyone is finally getting organized, and hence the sheer volume of information, the quicker timing of responses, the more specialized nature of demands, and the greatly augmented weight of organized claims threaten to overload the decisional and implementational channels of decision making? Or, is relative governability more related to the quality than to the quantity of associability – to the form that interest intermediation has taken rather than its coverage or density?

The nature of contemporary (un)governability and its alleged causes, concomitants and consequences

The joyous celebration of the end of ideology in advanced industrial societies had barely begun, when it turned into a gloomy wake mourning the end of governability in liberal democratic polities. At the very moment social scientists had predicted the definitive supercession of "archaic" cleavages and the triumphal emergence of a consensual "postproblematic" political order, Western Europe and North America seemed to plunge into a generalized regime crisis of alarming and certainly unexpected magnitude.

Much of the literature on the subject of ungovernability can with hindsight be dismissed as strictly *événementielle*, consisting of either overextrapolations of short-term trends or overreactions to immediate occurrences. Disturbances or revolts of very diverse origins – students, draftees, public employees, taxpayers, "rank and file," regionalists, ecologists, and so on – were seized on, enlarged, and projected forward until they appeared to cast an ominous shadow over the stability of political regimes and the very fabric of social order. Lacking historical perspective, such analysts failed to recognize that many such disturbing events lie within the normal range of political life in Western democracies. They only seem alarming when contrasted to the highly abnormal quiescence and conformity of the decades following World War II. The issues they raise and the challenges they pose are by no means unprecedented in nature nor unparalleled in magnitude. Most European polities (and, to a lesser extent, the United States) were not specifically designed to be governable, but evolved as compromises, second and even third best solutions to a continually changing panoply of cleavages and saliences. As such, their normal state has been unruly, unstable, illegitimate, and overloaded – at least in the eyes of and due to the efforts of significant discordant minorities. Widespread consensus on governance and, with it, citizen acquiescence, regime stability, and state effectiveness, have been more the exception than the rule over the long haul.

Another substantial proportion of the literature on governability can be dismissed not as the shortsighted and erratic product of academic fashion, but as the perpetual and predictable reaction of spokesmen for decadent political elites and the declining social classes. Faced with economic and social transformations that threaten their bases of property and privilege or with political crises that challenge their hegemonic domination, they have responded by declaring the polity ungovernable and sought to cover up their own displacement and incapacity by proclaiming a general collapse of civilization, reason, order, democracy, virtue, and so forth. Although intellectuals and even academics in the past often were found in the front ranks encouraging and celebrating the declining governability of decadent regimes and ruling principals, today most have retreated to the back ranks of passive mourners, leaving the actual pallbearing to politicians and economists.

If one eliminates the overreactors who read cataclysm into the slightest manifestation of obstreperous political behavior and the reactionaries who use threats to the existing order as a convenient excuse to roll back expectations, participation, and accountability, not much is left of the existing literature. Although they may be interesting and comprehensible in psychological or ideological terms, their views hardly provide an adequate basis for empirical inquiry or even further conceptualization – unless one is particularly subject to "future shock" or deeply respectful of existing class and elite arrangements. Indeed, after a cursory reading, the whole topic of ungovernability looks hopelessly speculative and/or ideological, subject to the most divergent and specific influences of time horizon, class prejudice, and national experience. Not until I discovered a special issue of a highly reputable journal in the country most frequently selected in polls as "the best governed in the world" devoted to the topic: *Wird die Schweiz unregierbar?* did I really sit up and take notice.[16] If no one regarded it as ridiculous to even ask the question, there must be something to the notion of a general crisis of governability in advanced industrial/capitalist societies. If its specter haunts even Switzerland, its presence may well be a real nightmare elsewhere.

But the fact that ungovernability is signaled everywhere calls attention to one of the concept's major difficulties, namely, that the condition it describes is likely to be very, very relativistic. However measured, its quantification/calibration would have to be measured on a scale with intervals that varied enormously from case to case. Consider, for example, Switzerland and Sweden, two countries of nearly identical economic product, level of affluence, size, international status, and dependence on foreign trade. Yet what are perceived as major challenges to the present governing order of the Swiss would be seen by the Swedes as minor institutional and policy reforms long since accomplished and assimilated without disruption. Threats to the current stability of the latter, however, involve degrees of interference with the market, levels of citizen involvement, types of public disclosure, magnitudes of fiscal resources, and capacities for state action far beyond the imagination (and certainly beyond the tolerance) of the former. Whatever its multiple dimensions may be, ungovernability is likely to be difficult to pin down to simple linear associations and equivalent magnitude effects. Furthermore, there may not be, as much of the literature assumes, a single crisis of governability in highly developed, advanced capitalist societies but, rather, several distinct, even unrelated crises linked together only by the common fears and uncertainties they generate or by timing. Although it is indeed striking that so many Western polities are being "spooked" simultaneously, it is by no means obvious that the same specter is to blame.

These suspicions of extreme relativism and multiple guises may account for the confusion in the literature about the empirical referents of ungovernability, but this seems more likely to be caused by inchoate, unit-specific assumptions and/or a preference for prudential terminological vagueness. Defining conditions that permit ordinal, much less cardinal judgments are rarely offered. One lacks not only a clear notion of what the baseline of normal governability from which to make assessments of trends might look like but even the most tentative grounds for stating that polity X is (or, better, has been) more ungovernable than polity Y. Thus discussions tend to be disjointed and country-specific, and that, in turn, renders comparative analysis powerless to provide even modest insight, much less compelling arguments about cause and consequence. Compounding

these ambiguities is the propensity of most analysts to bundle together indiscriminately the alleged causes, consequences, concomitants, and characteristics of ungovernability into a single package of
contemporary dysfunctions and misfortunes. Inflation, slackening
rates of growth, political indirection, policy impotence, loss of trust in
government, public *incivisme*, intellectual disillusionment, frustrated
expectations, leader incompetence, fiscal crisis – are presented as
basic *causes* for, mere *covariants* with, defining *conditions* about and/or
ineluctable *products* of ungovernability – when they are not simply
described as component parts of the same gestalt.

To the extent that even a rudimentary theory of the phenomenon
(or phenomena) exists, it tends to rely heavily on an ill-specified and
inappropriate metaphor of "balance." Inputs are said to outweigh
outputs; mobilization outruns assimilation; participation outpaces institutionalization; expectations overwhelm realizations; demands
overcome satisfactions; suspicion undercuts trust; class consciousness
undermines hegemonic dominance; and so forth. The political process, it is suggested, operates as if it were some gigantic and unique
balance-beam scale that lumped together, on the one side, citizen
demands, individual expectations, and collective loyalties and, on the
other, piled up authoritative allocations, political socializations, and
symbolic satisfactions.[17] In normal (i.e., governable) times, there is
(why?) a dynamically stable equilibrium between the two packages.
Ungoverning or undergoverning presumably occurs when the scale
tilts excessively and/or protractedly to the "input," or societal, side.
Overgoverning would occur metaphorically when the scale slants in
the opposite direction. The imagery is particularly attractive because
it suggests solutions: One could "lighten" the input load by shifting
expectations or reducing demands, or one could "weight" the output
performance by more efficient, authoritative, and repressive measures – or, better, do both simultaneously. In any case, the normal
metaphor for the polity is an even balance, lightly or heavily weighted
down.

Of all the images used to describe the modern state, this seems to
me to be one of the most misleading. First, there is the obvious problem of assuming homeostasis when the external parameters on political action are changing in such rapid, unpredictable, and interdependent ways. Sudden added weight in one country's output "pan" is
likely to be due to a diminished and unexpected change in the capacity of another's input "pan" – and vice versa. Second, it is difficult to
imagine how such a multilayered, overlapping, heavily intermediated
set of decisional bodies within a polity could possibly be coordinated
to produce a global equilibrated outcome. Efforts to do so – whether

by visible or invisible hands – would only seem likely to generate new and further imbalances. Finally, because one of the most notable characteristics of contemporary capitalist polities is the interpenetration of private and public allocations, self- and societally regarding interests, communitarian and national loyalties, it would seem impossible to separate neatly inputs from outputs, expectations from satisfactions, demand from supply – much less to maintain the two "sides" in some stable equilibrium. Most of those who write on the ungovernability of contemporary polities in Western Europe and North America emphasize irreversible structural changes in state–society relations but continue inconsistently to employ a metaphor of governance that is anachronistically liberal.

Governability, or better, its inverse, ungovernability, would seem, from the literature on Western Europe and North America, to be composed of three general properties:[18] (1) *unruliness* or citizen-initiated efforts to influence public choices in violent, illegal, or unprecedented ways; (2) *unstableness* or the failure of efforts by elite political actors to retain their positions of dominance or to reproduce preexisting coalitional arrangements; (3) *ineffectiveness* or the decline in the capacity of public executives or administrators to secure compliance with or to attain desired collective goals through the imperative coordinations or authoritative allocations of the state. The literature suggests that the three dimensions are covariant, that is, the postindustrial, advanced capitalist state is simultaneously becoming unruly, unstable, and ineffective. A closer inspection of nationally specific studies, however, reveals important differences in emphasis. Some countries are described as unruly in their patterns of citizen behavior but quite stable institutionally and still reasonably effective in administrative terms (e.g., France and the United States), whereas others are seen as peaceful and orderly in mass political and social behavior but unstable in their elite combinations (e.g., Finland and Denmark). Finally, there are those that seem ungovernable in all three dimensions (e.g., Italy and Great Britain) and therefore are regarded as prototypes for future disorder.

Setting aside the very troublesome problem of the concept's relativism – that objectively similar manifestations of unruliness, unstableness, and ineffectiveness may be experienced quite differentially, with a single wildcat strike sending tremors through Swiss politics but passing unnoticed in Italy – let us for exploratory comparative purposes look at some operational indicators of these dimensions of governability to estimate the distribution of variance and extent of their interrelation in Western Europe and North America since the mid-1960s. Unfortunately, we are initially stuck with the first two dimensions. No one has yet developed a valid indicator of the effectiveness of government that is sensitive to differing collective goals and policy efforts. If we could assume that all polities want equal amounts of economic growth, price stability, full employment, income equality, and fiscal balance, would expend equivalent public efforts to meet those goals, and therefore should enjoy some a priori similar chance of success from those efforts, then we might be able to use relative differences in macroeconomic performances as surrogate, unobtrusive indicators for effectiveness. These being manifestly unacceptable assumptions (despite the convergence in goals and programs of recent decades), we are forced to concentrate our attention initially on those more directly observable dimensions, *unruliness* and *unstableness*.

To emphasize the large error margins, varying time periods, and tentative validity of the operational indicators and to render them comparable to our measures of societal corporatism and member density, we have transformed all data into rank orderings.[19] Presumably, these cruder measures will be relatively insensitive to changes in selected indicators, more appropriate specification of time periods, and even the addition of more recent data. All have been ordered so that the highest degree of "ungovernable" performance will receive the top rank. Hence in Table 10.2 the United States had the greatest levels of both collective protest and internal war from 1958 to 1967 (more recent data are not available); the Netherlands and Norway tied for last place. In strike volume, changes in chief executive and major ministries and decrease in the governing margin, Italy is at the top, whereas Norway suffered the greatest increase in party fragmentation.

Each of the two dimensions has been collapsed separately into a single rank order – a summary indicator for relative citizen unruliness and another for governmental unstableness. Data for different time periods and on other potentially relevant indicators might have produced some change in relative values, but the combined rank orders appear both empirically reliable and temporally stable.[20] In addition, they do not violate commonsense evaluations present in the specialized literature and general press. France, the United States, Italy, Great Britain, Canada, and Belgium are ranked, in that order, as unruly places; Norway, the Netherlands, Switzerland, and Sweden seem to deserve their reputation for orderly citizen behavior. As for the unstableness of executive and electoral institutions, however, Norway and Denmark unpredictably took first and second place, followed, more predictably, by Italy, Great Britain, and Belgium. The most stable polities were, not surprisingly, Switzerland, the United States, Sweden, and Austria.

Between the indicators of citizen unruliness, there was a much

Table 10.2. *Relative ungovernability in the advanced industrial societies of Western Europe and North America*

	I. Unruliness: citizen-initiated protest/resistance[a]				II. Unstableness: political-institutional turbulence/change[b]			
	1. Collective protest (1958–67)	2. Internal war (1958–67)	3. Strike volume (1968–72)	4. Combined rank order	1. Number of changes in PM & major ministries (1960–74)	2. Decrease in governing margin (1965–75)	3. Change in party fractionalization (1966–75)	4. Combined rank order
Austria (A)	8	9	13	10	9	12	(10)	(12.5)
Belgium (B)	5	3	8	6	7.5	5	7	5
Canada (CDN)	7	5	3	5	6	14	12	13
Denmark (DK)	9	(13.5)	9	11	5	3	2	2
Finland (FL)	10	10	6	8	2	13	14	9
France (F)	2	2	2	(1.5)	(10.5)	8	(4.5)	7
W. Germany (D)	6	7	12	7	(10.5)	7	3	6
Rep. of Ireland (IRL)	13	8	7	9	13	9	6	8
Italy (I)	4	4	1	3	1	1	(10)	3
Netherlands (NL)	(14.5)	(13.5)	11	14	7.5	15	8	10
Norway (N)	(14.5)	(13.5)	14	15	3	2	1	1
Sweden (S)	11	(13.5)	10	12	15	6	(10)	(12.5)
Switzerland (CH)	12	11	15	13	14	11	13	15
Great Britain (GB)	3	6	5	4	4	4	(4.5)	4
United States (USA)	1	1	4	(1.5)	12	10	15	14

[a](1) "Collective protest (1958–67)": factor scores, the statistical product of a factor analysis of the total frequency of different types of political events from 1958 to 1967 with high loadings for "riots," "antigovernment demonstrations," and "political strikes." (2) "Internal war (1958–67)": factor scores, the statistical product of a factor analysis of the total frequency of different types of political events from 1958 to 1967 with high loadings for "armed attacks," "actual and attempted assassinations of political authorities," and "deaths per million population due to intergroup conflict." (3) "Strike volume (1968–72)": man-days lost in strikes per thousand nonagricultural wage and salaried workers from 1968 to 1972. The specific formula is total strikers ÷ by total workers × the total number of man-days lost ÷ by the number of strikes × the total strikers ÷ by the number of strikes or frequency × duration × size. $w = 0.83$.

[b](1) "Number of changes in prime ministers or presidents and major ministries (1960–74)": the sum total of changes in top executive and in ministers of foreign affairs and finance from 1960 to 1974; (2) "Decrease in governing margin (1965–75)": change in the governing margin (defined as 51 percent minus the proportion of the vote going to the winning party or coalition of parties) in the election closest to 1965 minus the governing margin (as defined in text) in the election closest to 1975; (3) "Change in party fractionalization (1966–75)"; change in the dispersion of voting preferences (according to a formula developed in Douglas Rae's article).

Sources: (a1) Douglas Hibbs, Jr., Mass Political Violence: A Cross-National Causal Analysis (New York: Wiley, 1973). (a2) Data provided in personal correspondence from Douglas A. Hibbs, Jr., initially gathered from ILO, Yearbook (relevant years). For utilization of these data, see Hibbs, "Industrial Conflict in Advanced Industrial Societies," American Political Science Review 70(4) (December 1976): 1033–58 and Hibbs, "Long-Run Trends in Strike Activity in Comparative Perspective," Center for International Studies, MIT (August 1976). (a3) Arthur S. Banks, Cross-Polity Time-Series Data (Cambridge, Mass.: MIT Press, 1971) and The Europa Yearbook. Vol. I (1976). (b1) C. Cook and J. Paxton (eds.), European Political Facts 1918–1973 (New York: St. Martins Press, 1975); scores for Canada and the United States represented all "executive adjustments" from 1960–1967 and have been adjusted for comparability; C. L. Taylor and M. C. Hudson, World Handbook of Political and Social Indicators (New Haven: Yale University Press, 1972). (b2) The Europa Yearbook, Vol. I (1966–76). (b3) Douglas Rae, "A Note on the Fractionalization of Some European Party Systems," Comparative Political Studies 1(October 1968): 413–18, from the election closest to 1966 and that closest to 1975. $w = 0.57$.

higher rank intercorrelation than with the variables selected to measure governmental unstableness. (Kendall's coefficient of concordance equaled 0.83 for the former and 0.57 for the latter.) In fact, the latter variables were so dispersed that one can hardly consider unstableness as a dimension at all. Some countries experienced simultaneously frequent changes at the cabinet level, a major decrease in the margin of victory for the governing party or coalition, and a marked fractionalization of the party system (Italy and Denmark were cases in point), but most countries had no such consistent profile. Consider Finland, with very frequent cabinet turnover but not much change in electoral and party relationships, or West Germany, with relatively low executive turbulence and yet some decrease in the governing margin and increase in party fragmentation.

However tempting and convenient it might be to work with a single ordinal measure of regime governability in highly industrialized, advanced capitalist polities, this would be analytically and descriptively misleading. The two conceptual subdimensions we have identified and measured, citizen unruliness and governmental unstableness, simply are not empirically covariant (the Spearman rho between the two is a completely indeterminant and statistically insignificant 0.00) and Figure 10.2 shows why. When plotted against each other, the scatter is impressive and four "qualitative" clusters emerge. The consistent cases – unruly and unstable, ruly and stable – lie along the positive diagonal. The deviant ones can be found in the opposite corners. The first is a type of "Nordic ungovernability" based on great citizen orderliness and frequent elite turnover; the second is characteristic of the *"monarchies républicaines"* of the United States, France, and, to a lesser extent, Canada, with their greater presidential and ministerial stability and very high levels of mass protest and resistance.[21]

With these rough and nonconcordant indicators in hand, we can now return skeptically to the literature, with its "prototheories" about the ungovernability of contemporary Western Europe and North America, for hypotheses, hints, and hunches about why, when, and where it has tended to occur and its expected results.

The rank-order associations of our two compound indicators with some of the social and economic dysfunctions and misfortunes most frequently mentioned in the literature demonstrate the hidden virtue of a highly relativistic and narrowly specific case study treatment. Conditions that supposedly produce, accompany, or result from rising ungovernability in, say, Great Britain, Italy, or Denmark can be found elsewhere in similar or even greater magnitude without the attendant mass disorder and/or elite turmoil. Inversely, comparable

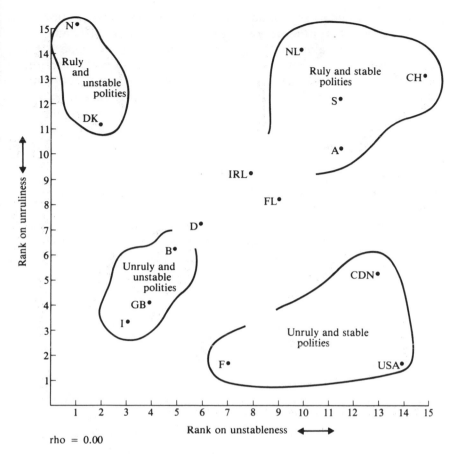

Figure 10.2.   Relation between combined rank orders of unruliness and unstableness. For key to abbreviations, see Figure 10.1.

magnitudes of unruliness and unstableness seem to have been experienced by countries not suffering from the same "postindustrial" ills or "advanced capitalist" contradictions.

For example, higher average annual rates of inflation seem to bear no systematic predictable relation to our first dimension of ungovernability but to be associated significantly with the second. Slow growth, however, has led to neither more citizen unruliness nor governmental unstableness across the fifteen polities of Western Europe and North America, nor has the allegedly "destabilizing" impact of more rapid annual rates of economic growth. Contrary to expectations, increase in the relative importance of employment in the service sector was negatively associated with citizen unruliness and governmental unstableness. Canada was an interesting exception (fifth in unruliness and first in tertiary growth); but elsewhere those advancing most rapidly along such "postindustrial" lines (Sweden, the Netherlands, Denmark, Norway, and Finland) were among the more ruly in their mass politics and social protests. Conservatives who have lamented the rapid expansion of access to higher education may find some comfort in Table 10.3. Its rank-order correlation with both indicators is positive (if, statistically, significant only with respect to governability), that is, the greater the increase in the proportion of the age-eligible population attending higher institutions of learning, the more unruly, unstable, and hence ungovernable was the unit's politics. Both Sweden and Great Britain are exceptions, even though in different directions.

Governmental unstableness, as one can see from Table 10.3, is the least predictable of our two macro-outcomes. In large part, this may be due to the more heterogeneous mix of subcomponents, hence a more arbitrary compound rank ordering. The only "causes-concomitants-consequences" strongly associated with it are inflation and shift in the wage proportion of gross domestic product. The former is directly and significantly predictive of governmental unstableness but not of citizen unruliness. In all Western European and North American economies (except Switzerland), wage shift has been increasing in the recent decade (although evidence on the general pattern of income inequality is much less clear). Countries in which this occurred to the greatest extent, for example, Norway, Italy, Belgium, the United States, and Denmark, whether due to occupational shifts from agricultural or artisanal self-employment or due to negotiated redistribution of benefits from capital to labor, have been relatively unstable in their elite combinations, but not particularly unruly. What is by no means clear, of course, is whether the shift in wages as a percentage of GDP (Gross Domestic Product) is built into the economic structure of advanced capitalism and the accompanying governmental unstableness is a reflection of elite efforts to resist it, or whether the weakening of historical patterns of class alliance opens up bargaining possibilities and encourages co-optive efforts that eventually result in redistributive outcomes.

Those who emphasize intergenerational value change and, particularly, the emergence of "postbourgeois" or "postmaterialist values" in shaping the style, policy demands, or issue content of postindustrial politics[22] will find little solace in Table 10.3. Although the survey data cover only ten countries circa 1970-2, nothing seems less significantly related to the two macro-outcomes. Great Britain, the United States, and Switzerland were recorded as having had the lowest point

Table 10.3. *Causes, concomitants, and consequences of unruliness and unstableness: rank-order coefficients*

		Citizen unruliness	Governmental unstableness
1.	Average annual rate of inflation (14) (1970–75)	0.01	0.45
2.	Average annual rate of economic growth (1969–74)	−0.03	−0.08
3.	Shift in wages as percent of GDP (1965–72)	0.15	0.48
4.	Growth of tertiary sector (13) (1956–73)	−0.48	−0.47
5.	Expansion of university education (15) (1960–71)	0.40	0.03
6.	Differences in intergenerational values (10) (ca., 1970–72)	0.00	−0.28
7.	Increase in government revenue (13) (1956–73)[a]	−0.72	−0.35
8.	Extent of net government borrowing (15) (1970–75)[b]	0.62	0.30
9.	Decrease in reliance on indirect taxes (14) (1956–74)[c]	0.58	0.11

[a] Difference between the total revenue of government at all levels as a percent of GDP in 1956 and 1973.

[b] Overall annual surplus or deficit in government borrowing from 1970 to 1975.

[c] Percentage decrease in the proportion of government revenue derived from indirect taxes and social security contributions from 1956 to 1973. The idea and precedent for using this indicator comes from D. Cameron, op. cit, who refers to prior arguments by Harold Wilensky (*The Welfare State and Equality*) and Aaron Wildavsky (*Budgeting*) to the effect that "the ability of government to enlarge and maintain a highly developed public sector depends, in part, on the availability of such hidden or 'invisible' taxes." (p. 31).

Sources: (1) ILO, *Yearbook 1975* (Geneva, 1976), pp. 747-50; (2) OECD, *Observer* 80(March–April 1976); (3) ILO, *Yearbook 1975*, op. cit., pp. 734-8; (4) David Cameron, "Inequality and the State," paper presented at APSA Annual Meeting, Chicago, September 2-5, 1976, p. 25; supplemented for Austria and Ireland with OECD, *Labour Force Statistics 1956-1966, 1962-1973* (1968, 1975); (5) UNESCO, *Statistical Yearbook 1974* (1976), pp. 135-52; (6); Ronald Inglehart, "The Nature of Value Change in Postindustrial Societies," in *Politics and the Future in Industrial Society*, ed. L. Lindberg; (7) David Cameron, "Inequality and the State: A Political–Economic Comparison," paper presented at APSA Annual Meeting, Chicago (1976). Original source: UN Statistical Office, *Year-book of National Accounts Statistics 1968* (1974). Austria and Ireland were added to Cameron's table, p. 22; (8) OECD, *Revenue Statistics of OECD Member Countries 1966-1975* (1976).

Table 10.4. *Dimensions of governmental fiscal ineffectiveness in the advanced industrial societies of Western Europe and North America*

	Increase in government revenue[a] (1956–73) (rank-order inverted)	Extent of government borrowing[b] (1970–75)	Decrease in reliance on indirect taxes[c] (1956–74)	Combined rank order
Austria	1	10	10	8
Belgium	10	2	6	4
Canada	9	8	2	(6)
Denmark	15	11	1	10
Finland	7	14	4	9
France	3	9	7	(6)
W. Germany	5	6	8	(6)
Ireland, Rep. of	12	3	13	11
Italy	2	1	9	(1.5)
Netherlands	13	7	14	13
Norway	14	12	12	14
Sweden	11	13	15	15
Switzerland	6	15	11	12
Great Britain	8	4	5	3
United States	4	5	3	(1.5)

$w = 0.44$
[a] See Table 10.3, variable 7.
[b] See Table 10.3, variable 8.
[c] See Table 10.3, variable 9.

spreads across cohorts, and Germany, France, and Italy as having had the greatest generational value differences. These normative extremes bear no consistent relation to citizen unruliness or governmental unstableness.

In the last three items in Table 10.3, however, we find some very significant rank-order relationships. Increase in government revenue as a percentage of GDP, the average extent of net government borrowing, and the shift in the pattern of fiscal revenue away from indirect taxes are so closely associated with unruliness and to a lesser extent with unstableness, and somewhat related to each other (a Kendall coefficient of concordance of 0.44), that one is tempted to suggest, despite the caveats already expressed, that we have discovered serendipitously a multivariate set of indicators for *ineffectiveness*. These macroaspects of the political–economic performance of the modern state – all connected with the magnitude and mode of financing its fiscal crisis – are best conceptualized as some of the *characteristics* of the governability–ungovernability syndrome and not main *causes* to explain its relative presence, spurious *concomitants* that accompany its emergence, or clear-cut *consequences* of antecedent mass protest or elite turmoil. Therefore, with some trepidation, given the indirectness with which it measures ineffectiveness and the fact that its internal consistency is none too great, we will include the combined rank order of Table 10.4 with those of unruliness and unstableness among the *explicanda* of ungovernability. In order to avoid any conceptual misunderstanding, however, it will be labeled "fiscal ineffectiveness." Unlike the first two, which were relatively uncorrelated, fiscal ineffectiveness is very positively and strongly associated with the unruliness ranking (0.91) but insignificantly correlated with the unstableness ranking (0.11). If there is a pattern of general ungovernability, it combines citizen obstreperousness and fiscal weakness but not elite turnover or partisan fissiparousness.

Interest promotion and partisan mobilization as possible causes of (un)governability

Having identified, measured, and explored, however tentatively and crudely, three dimensions of (un)governability and a bundle of its most commonly alleged causes, concomitants, and consequences, we can now turn to interest intermediation for a possible rival explanation. Two aspects of the pursuit of self-regarding goals have attracted our attention. One is quantitative: Are the polities of Western Europe and North America less ruly, stable, and effective simply because everyone is finally getting organized? The other is qualitative: Does the form that intermediation has taken historically determine the relative governability of these polities today? The first we have measured by the density of membership in working-class associations; the latter by a rank-ordered indicator of corporatist features in national labor peak associations.

The statistical measures (Spearman's rank-order coefficients) presented in Table 10.5 provide a rather clear answer to both the general question of the importance of interest intermediation for regime governability and the more specific question of which aspect of the pursuit of interests – quantity or quality – is more relevant to understanding macrolevel ruliness, stableness, and effectiveness. The coordinal relationship between the indicator of societal corporatism and that of citizen unruliness (−0.73) is the most significant we have yet observed. The fit is so close that relatively few deviant cases arise to challenge our finding. Switzerland is an exception in one direction

Table 10.5. *Interest intermediation, unruliness, unstableness, and ineffectiveness: rank-order coefficients*

	Citizen unruliness	Governmental unstableness	Fiscal ineffectiveness	N
Density of association membership (ca. 1973–75)	−0.27	0.27	−0.20	(15)
Indicator of societal corporatism (ca. 1970)	−0.73	−0.06	−0.63	(15)

(too ruly for its relatively low corporatism). The correlation with fiscal ineffectiveness (−0.63) is also highly significant. Again, we find it impossible to predict the rank ordering of governmental unstableness. Perhaps this is yet another indication that it is simply not part of the contemporary governability–ungovernability syndrome or that, if it is, our operationalization is defective. Density of membership was not impressively related to any of the three dimensions. What seems to count is not *whether* everyone is getting organized for the pursuit of specialized class and sectoral self-interest but *how* they are doing so.

One is tempted to exclaim "Eureka!" at this point and rest the analysis. Given the likely measurement error and the crudeness of the statistical instrument, it is doubtful that any rank-order correlation between independent variables could top 0.73 without being a tautological or spurious measure of the same underlying phenomenon. We might, therefore, conclude with the counterintuitive finding that (*pace* Madison) corporatism, not pluralism, is the best formula "to break and control the violence of faction" in the post-liberal, advanced-capitalist polity. Rather than proliferating the "number of citizens" and the "sphere of interests," the modern conservative ruler concerned with governability would diminish their number, encourage their centralization and concentration of authority, grant them privileged monopolistic access, and, above all, extend the sphere of governance by licensing or devolving upon them powers to take decisions binding on their members and even on nonmembers. In this way, "responsible," private governments can collaborate in controlling citizen-initiated protest and in ensuring proper fiscal discipline and management. The direct burden on the state is lightened, and the resulting policy outputs are made a good deal less visible. On the other side, the relative autonomy of these associations is respected, so that periodic withdrawals from collusion with those in power is tolerated when the disparity between ruling imperatives, organizational goals, and member interests becomes too great and threatens to provoke direct action by the grass roots or to spill over into the electoral arena. Interest associations, and not just political parties, can take a *cure d'opposition*. [23]

Ruling elites in many of the more troubled Western European and North American polities seem to have arrived at the same conclusion as we have in this chapter: In advanced capitalist, highly industrialized societies, there is a strong positive relationship between a societal corporatist mode of interest intermediation and relative governability (or at least citizen ruliness and fiscal effectiveness). Recent interest in promoting the negotiation of "new social contracts," the establishment of "Economic and Social Councils," the enforcement of compulsory membership schemes, the rationalization and centralization of representational structures, and so forth suggest that the ruling elites are making a concerted effort at implementing that lesson. [24] Their repeated failures at creating such arrangements from above lead to the conclusion that a relatively "benevolent" configuration of outcomes is the largely unintended product of a complex and lengthy historical process, not easily retraced or reproduced under contemporary circumstances.

Much of the resistance to corporatization comes from existing interest associations that prize their organizational autonomy and defend their traditionally pluralistic ways of operating. In fact, previous efforts in imposing a solution from above were accompanied by the severe repression of such associations, especially those representing the working class, and the establishment of a wide range of other authoritarian practices – *vide* Fascist Italy or Franco Spain. Where, however, this mode of interest intermediation evolved gradually and voluntarily within a liberal democratic regime, it depended on concordant and supportive changes in a second realm of formal intermediation between civil society and the state – partisan mobilization.

The most obvious supportive change in the party system was the emergence and eventual participation in power of reformist Social Democratic or Labour parties. [25] Although they did not often stress corporatism at the ideological level – if only because their Catholic or conservative opponents had often preempted the idea – their own internal organizational relationship with the trade-union movement certainly resembled it, and their acceptance of a "responsible" promotion of working-class interests within the framework of capitalism definitely was a prerequisite for its eventual success. The close historical association between Social Democratic party predominance and societal corporatism is still dramatically evident in the contemporarily

Table 10.6. *Partisan intermediation and governability and rank-order correlations*

	Citizen unruliness	Governmental unstableness	Fiscal ineffectiveness	N
Social Democratic performance[a]				
Percent of years during which Social Democrats (and allies) in government (1956–73)	−0.50	−0.03	−0.39	(15)
Average percent of government's electoral base formed by Social Democrats (1956–73)	−0.40	0.29	−0.30	(15)
Social Democratic vote as percent of total vote (ca. 1970)	−0.57	0.21	−0.40	(15)
Structurally determined voting preferences (percent predicted by occupation, religion, and region combined)	−0.69[b]	−0.23	−0.55	(15)

[a] (1) "Years in government (1956–73)" proportion of the years (disaggregated into quarters) during which Social Democratic parties participated in government. (2) "Average Electoral Base of Government (1956–73)": proportion of the electoral base in percent of the vote in preceding election of the party or parties in government that was obtained by Social Democratic parties in election closest to 1970.
[b] Percentage of variation explained (by automatic interaction detection analysis) in survey reported voting behavior by occupation, religion, and region. The Swiss figure is based on a different predictive technique.
Sources: (a1) D. Cameron, op. cit., p. 12. Also Douglas Hibbs, Jr., "Economic Interest and the Politics of Macro-Economic Policy," *American Political Science Review* 71(4) (1977): 1467–87, for the initial use of this indicator. (a2) *The Europa Yearbook*, vols. I and II (1976). (b) Richard Rose (ed.), *Electoral Behavior* (New York: Free Press, 1974), p. 17; Henry Kerr, Jr., "Switzerland: Social Cleavages and Partisan Conflict," Sage Publications, Comparative Political Sociology Series, No. 06-002 (1974), p. 8.

high rank correlation between the two. Whichever indicators of Social Democratic strength one uses (years in government, importance for the electoral basis of the governing coalition, or merely percentage of the total vote), the relationships are all very significant (0.55, 0.71, 0.70). In the last case, Social Democratic vote and societal corporatism, the only noticeably deviant case is Great Britain – fifth in the former and fourteenth in the latter – but then one could question whether the Labour Party is really the full equivalent of continental and Scandinavian social democracy.

Table 10.6 shows that the performance of Social Democratic parties is, indeed, highly and positively correlated with both citizen ruliness and fiscal effectiveness (again governmental stableness falls out of the analysis). The proportion of total vote going to such parties is usually the best predictor of a relatively governable outcome, followed very closely by their longevity in power during the period 1956 to 1973. Their electoral contribution to the governing coalition seems a less secure guarantee of ruliness and effectiveness but is *positively* linked to higher levels of elite turnover – illustrating perhaps their recent decline in hegemony and/or the growing bargaining strength of minor coalition partners in countries such as Norway and Denmark.

The final line in Table 10.6, however, suggests another dimension of partisan mobilization that may be of even greater importance than Social Democratic predominance. Thanks to extensive survey-research in all fifteen countries, one can roughly estimate the predictability of individual voting preferences from knowledge of that individual's occupation, religion, and regional location. The aggregate predictive capacity of these three potential cleavage dimensions varies enormously, from approximately 50 percent in the cases of the Netherlands and Austria (and perhaps higher for Switzerland) to as low as 3 percent for Ireland, 12 percent for Great Britain, and 13 percent for the United States. Needless to say, the relative contribution of occupation, religion, and region is hardly constant (religion is most important in the Netherlands, Austria, and Belgium, even in West Germany and France; occupation structures preferences more in Sweden, Finland, Norway, and Denmark; nowhere is region the predominant factor), but what seems to be most significantly associated with "governable" macro-outcomes is the predictability produced by some combination of all three – the extent to which the voter's individual partisan choice is firmly "locked into" the basic elements of differentiation in the society, regardless of which of those elements is performing the task.

These additional findings strengthen considerably the credibility of our earlier hypothesis that the relative governability of Western European and North American polities is more affected by the qualitative nature of their systems of intermediation than by the quantitative magnitude of the economic and social problems they face. The mode of organization of and control over function- and issue-specific interests emerges as most significant, but its role is contingent on two major coordinant developments in the mode of partisan articulation: its relative domination by Social Democratic-type parties and its predictable rootedness in the cleavage structure of the society. It is, of course, not clear from these cross-sectionally associated outcomes whether, as Stein Rokkan has suggested, the functional "second tier" of corporatist intermediation was created out of an elite *reaction against* the emergence of Social Democracy in the "primary tier" of territorial representation,[26] or whether it emerged as a direct *product* of the efforts of Social Democrats at integrating themselves within the structures of the capitalist economy and liberal polity.[27]

Running Kendall partial rank correlations, which can statistically hold social corporatism, Social Democratic voting, and/or predictability of individual electoral choice constant, only demonstrates that none of the three direct ordinal relationships can be reduced to zero. All retain some strength in predicting both the unruliness and ineffectiveness outcomes, although the effect of the predictability of voting patterns independent of the stronger societal corporatism/governability relation is markedly greater. Controlling for the proportional size of the Social Democratic vote only reduces the rank correlation of corporatism with unruliness, for example, from −0.73 to −0.61, whereas general voting predictability brings it down to −0.50.

Finally, we can try to ferret out the combined or interactive effect of interest intermediation and partisan mobilization on governability (or, better, on unruliness and ineffectiveness, because our indicator of unstableness has yet to be significantly "explained"). To do this, we simply have combined the rank order of societal corporatism with that of Social Democratic voting and with that of voting predictability to produce two new compound rank orders. The fact that both variables of partisan mobilization are closely correlated with corporatism (0.70 and 0.71, respectively) means that their inclusion barely alters the corporatist ranking, but does so in a slightly different manner. Only West Germany (third in Social Democratic voting and eighth in corporatism), Great Britain (fifth and fourteenth), and the United States (fifteenth and eleventh) change more than two combined ranks. However, the combination of corporatism and predictability of voting choice occasions more shifting about: Switzerland moves from ninth rank to fifth; the Netherlands from sixth to third; Ireland from eleventh to ninth; whereas Denmark goes from fourth to 7.5; Italy from fourteenth to 11.5; Germany, from eighth to tenth; and the United States from eleventh to thirteenth.

Table 10.7 demonstrates that "adding" the ranking on Social Democracy to that on societal corporatism does not improve upon the "simple" negative correlations of corporatism with unruliness and ineffectiveness; it even lowers the degree of rank covariance slightly (from −0.73 and −0.63 to −0.72 and −0.60). However, the rank combination of a structurally rooted (pillarized?) electorate and a highly centralized, monopolistic set of interest associations reproduces to an extraordinary extent the ordinal indicators of both governability dimensions (−0.88 and −0.75, respectively). Although it would take a great deal of detailed historical evidence to prove it, one

Table 10.7. *The effect of combining interest intermediation and partisan intermediation on unruliness, unstableness, and ineffectiveness*

	Citizen unruliness	Governmental unstableness	Fiscal ineffectiveness	N
Interest intermediation alone				
Societal corporatism	−0.73	−0.06	−0.63	(15)
Partisan intermedia-tion alone				
Social Democratic vote	−0.57	0.21	−0.40	(15)
Predictability of voting patterns	−0.69	−0.23	−0.55	(15)
Combined effects				
Societal corporatism and Social Demo-cratic vote	−0.72	0.12	−0.60	(15)
Societal corporatism and predictability of voting patterns	−0.88	−0.18	−0.75	(15)

may speculate that the effect of the emergence of a strong Social Democratic electorate is to encourage the corporatization of interest intermediation structures; this in turn facilitates more ruly mass citizen behavior and more orderly state fiscal arrangements in the contemporary period. In those deviant cases where the rise in proportional Social Democratic electoral strength has not been so closely associated with societal corporatism (e.g., Great Britain, Italy, and, to a lesser degree, West Germany), less governable outcomes have ensued. In the inverse cases, however, where corporatism developed relatively more than social democracy (e.g., Switzerland, Denmark, Ireland, and especially Finland), the outcomes have been markedly more ruly and effective.

Societal corporatism and the "locking in" of voter preferences to the cleavage structure do not appear to be parts of a tightly related historical process. It could be argued that they represent independent efforts to organize networks of intermediation between civil society and the state – the one focusing on functional, especially occupational and sectoral interests; the other appealing more to territorial, religious. and cultural interests, with class as the crucial area for their competition and/or cooperation. When, however, they combine through highly predictable patterns of party identification and highly specialized patterns of monopolistic representation and social control, the relative ruliness and effectiveness of the outcome is impressive. This speculative finding seems diametrically contrary to pluralist orthodoxy, which identifies "political stability" (the lexical forerunner of "governability") with moderate, broadly aggregative, sociologically diverse, and weakly structured political parties, and with voluntaristic, multiple, overlapping, and autonomous interest associations. From our data manipulations, this emerges almost as a formula for trouble in the highly industrialized, advanced-capitalist, post-liberal polities of Western Europe and North America.

Instead of a conclusion

The foregoing empirically grounded conclusions about the relevance of intermediation processes, especially societal corporatism, for contemporary governability seem compelling. They may even lead some to the comforting thought that the problems, dilemmas, and contradictions of the status quo do not have to be resolved. It might seem that ruling elites have only to tinker with their systems of partisan and interest intermediation to dissipate their current troubles. If this should be the lesson they draw (and there is considerable evidence many have), they are destined to be disappointed. Not only are such institutional networks the product of very lengthy and complex historical forces but they are also subject to strong emergent organizational properties that guide their development and insulate them from ameliorative meddlings from above. Previous attempts at molding interest and partisan intermediation systems to "fit" the needs of the mode of political domination and the exigencies of economic exploitation have had to involve much more than mere tinkering. Even where societies have protractedly suffered through the repression necessary to impose such comprehensive state corporatist "solutions," dominant classes have only managed to buy time and accumulate tensions, as in contemporary Spain and Portugal.

However compelling, the conclusions reached in this chapter are time contingent. They refer to a rather narrow period, roughly the 1960s through the early 1970s. There is no a priori reason to expect that simply because the corporatist mode of organizing interest intermediation has succeeded for a while in structuring, containing, inhibiting, and controlling conflicts among classes, sectors, and professions in such a way as to make polities less unruly and more effective, it will continue to do so in the future. Precisely because of its "novelty" (and the unobtrusiveness with which it has crept into political practice), we may not as yet have experienced the full impact or comprehended the full extent of its dilemmas and contradictions.

Those polities that did acquire highly centralized, monopolistic interest associations and well-structured, "pillared" political parties and which, therefore, were better able to negotiate voluntaristically and to enforce effectively a series of collaborative policy arrangements and crisis-induced pacts are, indeed, beginning to show strains. That delicate combination of ruling imperatives, organizational goals, and member interests that lies at the heart of the corporatist effort has been called increasingly into question. The decline of public, that is, system-wide, deliberative processes, the segmentation of policy into discrete functional compartments, and the inequity produced by mutually supportive deals among organizationally privileged minorities have led to a revived concern with "the public interest." The legitimacy of leaders protected within highly oligarchic and professionalized interest associations from direct contact with and accountability to members has diminished, as has the willingness of members to comply with the constraints of private governments. The overaggregation of interests through peak associations has left un- or underrepresented certain emergent, more specialized groups, just as their close collusion with power has made the exclusion of diffuse, dispersed, underorganized categories more obvious and less bearable. The demand for personal authenticity and democratic participation on the part of individuals has grown at the expense of mere role satisfaction and vicariously obtained advantage. New "style and quality" issues have emerged, cutting across established functional hierarchies and resulting in numerous single-issue movements and spontaneous protest actions. Awareness that inflation is the real hiding hand equilibrating outcomes and invisibly determining the distribution of benefits has upset many a carefully negotiated social contract or sectoral arrangement. All this points to an uncertain future for today's "corporatist successes."

The sources of contradiction/dilemma inherent in this scheme are multiple and of unequal importance. Generically, they can be reduced to four types, depending on (1) whether the institutional locus of emerging difficulty comes from within the universe of interest associations or from other organizations, such as political parties and social movements, and (2) whether the substantive issues at stake involve an exacerbation or rupture within existing problem content, or a shift in the definition of actor interest to some new domain of concern. Table 10.8 displays this property space and suggests the anticipated modal types of response.

For most convinced liberals or pluralists, the principal difficulty of societal corporatism lies in the internal political process of interest associations. Their stress on professionalized representation by experts, long-term calculations of interest, high-level aggregation of

Table 10.8. *Sources of contradiction in societal corporatist arrangements and types of response*

Institutional locus of contradiction	Substantive locus of contradiction	
	Existing issue content	Changing issue content
Within interest associations	"Rank and file revolts"	"Status or situs organization"
Within other modes of intermediation	"Class mobilization"	"Single-issue movements"

demands, and official recognition of status, on the one hand, and their practices of oligarchic co-optation, centralized organization, bureaucratized exchanges, and interdependence with public authority, on the other, make these associations vulnerable to member dissatisfaction. The most common type of challenge, according to this perspective, comes from "rank-and-file revolts": wildcat strikes, internal factionalism, organizational splits, "voting with one's feet," ideological gambits, accusations of traitorous behavior, and so on – all in the name of authenticity in representation and democracy in procedure.[28]

Without denying this latent threat or the occasional presence of some of these phenomena in even the most established and accomplished of societal corporatist arrangements, such revolts are not, in my view, capable of countermanding the trend. They may cause collaborative associations to take a *cure d'opposition* by withdrawing from corporatist practices for a period of time; they may even compel some associations to engage in imprudent tactics of confrontation and intransigence – especially where the revolt is backed by accountability to some extra-associational political process, such as *Mitbestimmung* or *élections sociales* – but normally these revolts are easy to encapsulate or even exploit for corporatist ends. It is not just that association leaders have at their disposition that arsenal of incumbency resources that Michels and his successors have so extensively documented but that this pluralist view ignores the extent to which the modern interest association has become more and more a service agency and less and less a focus of political aspiration or personal identity. The member pays a fee for services performed (and increasingly does so involuntarily) and demands in return some measure of efficiency and effectiveness in their performance. To the extent that he or she aspires to fellowship, authenticity, participation, self-expression, and so forth, the political party or social movement offers a much more attractive outlet for such passions and moral imperatives.

It is this tendency for the contradictions of corporatism to spill over into wider arenas of public choice and forms of political mobilization – while remaining basically within the nexus of class, sectoral, and professional interests – that is stressed by Marxist critics of the trend. Because societal corporatism is but a superstructural rearrangement of institutions that cannot dissolve the class-based, structural contradictions of capitalism (not to mention accomplish the lesser task of resolving sectoral clashes and professional disputes), they argue it must ultimately fail. It may succeed in the short run in making ad hoc adjustments and generating crisis-induced palliatives, but these are bound to accumulate, to produce further policy irrationalities, and to establish greater rigidities in the system. These may even contribute to the system's demise. Although the proponents of this view of corporatism often point to the same "rank-and-file" events as the pluralists, they stress the extent to which these go beyond the limited agenda of specialized interests, personal moral sentiments, and/or formal democratic aspirations, and serve to mobilize a broad class consciousness and activity across a wider variety of intermediary institutions: political parties, social movements, intellectual currents, and so forth.

Although this approach to the contradictions of corporatism is more sensitive to the changing nature of modern interest associations, it frequently overestimates the evidence for class mobilization and underestimates the barriers to it, thus indulging in a great deal of *ex ante* wishful thinking and *ex post* retractions. If the institutions and practices of societal corporatism, by and large forged during the post-World War II boom years, manage to survive the present general crisis of capitalism (and even to do so at less cost to subordinate classes in terms of job security, real wages, and social benefits), then some revision of the class-mobilization scenario of its demise will definitely be in order.

A third source of contradiction and type of response suggests that corporatism will be threatened by the emergence of new substantive interests or by a shift in the salience of older, previously subordinate, interests. These should provide the basis for a new wave of aggressive associability that will seek access to the established corporatist arrangement. According to this perspective, societal corporatism has succeeded so far largely because it has been partial. It has involved primarily or exclusively those interests generated by the economic division of labor in society – classes, sectors, and professions for short. This has permitted these better-organized, collaborative actors to pass on the costs of their mutually self-serving agreements to the un- or underorganized. If the latter interests, for example, tenants, renters, pensioners, pedestrians, taxpayers, foreigners, workers, automobile drivers, students, sufferers from pollution, payers of insurance premiums, television watchers, welfare recipients, hospital patients, all "policy takers" (to use an appropriate phrase from Claus Offe's chapter) were to create singular, monopolistic, hierarchically structured, officially sanctioned associations, previous externalities would become internalized within the system of organized interest politics and make decisions vastly more difficult. Also, some of the new or more recently salient criteria of differentiation/exploitation – ethnic identity, regional location, religion, sex, age, language, and so on – might cut across existing functional categories or, where they did not, infuse them with renewed passion or ideological fervor. Either shift could seriously jeopardize the stable organizational base, the long-term interest definition, and the predictable contractual capacity of corporatist intermediaries.

The problem with this scenario is that in order for dispersed "entitled" interests, oriented almost exclusively around the provision of public goods, to obtain sufficient resources and access, they must depend on the sponsorship and connivance of public authorities. Their corporatization is less likely to be "societal" than "state" in inspiration, and this raises the question of *why* those in formal power would take such an initiative or *whether* they would be permitted to do so by vested established interests already sharing the benefits of privileged access. In the event that the source of new interest or salience lies in the "cultural division of labor,"[29] the resultant need to mobilize identities around broad ideological goals should make corporatization insufficient. Mere specialized participation in a complex set of policy compromises and services is no adequate substitute for having one's own state or dominating the whole political process.

This brings us to the fourth type of contradiction in which those new status, style, and identity issues cannot be contained within the bounds of "mere" interest intermediation and spill over into other forms of collective political activity. These range from public interest lobbies to spontaneous protests, "green" parties, and successionist movements. Their broader goals, greater intensities, unconventional tactics, and crosscutting differentiations would both weaken existing corporatist associations and shift the attention of the entire political process away from the issues and tactics the latter are most capable of handling. Whether this would be sufficient to dissolve existing corporatist arrangements or to arrest further movement in that direction depends ultimately on if the emergent cultural identities, status sensitivities, situs calculations, territorial loyalties, and/or qualitative demands prove to be permanent. Are they capable of displacing over a protracted period the "functional" cleavages inherent in capitalist property relations and the industrial division of labor? Some may turn out to be ephemeral, especially in conditions of renewed scarcity. Others may be successfully accommodated through symbolic concessions, territorial readjustments, partisan restructuring, and so forth. If so, the apparent shifts in content, despite their raucousness and occasional attention-gathering capability, are not likely to be successful in countervailing the trend toward societal corporatism. At most, they might delay its emergence for a while, or keep it confined to a narrower range of policy arenas.[30]

All the sources of contradiction discussed briefly here originate within civil society, that is, in the economic, social, and cultural division of labor. An alternative possibility, not usually entertained by students of corporatism, is that problems might arise from within the political order itself, which could limit the spread or encourage the dissolution of such arrangements. Instead of just facilitating the management of the state, they could eventually threaten the status and resources of public authorities and party politicians and introduce additional rigidities and irrationalities into public policy making. State bureaucrats might find that devolution of authority to corporatist intermediaries deprives them of their unique status and of important instruments for resolving broader public issues and intersectoral conflicts. Professional politicians are likely to resist the progressive short-circuiting of party channels, territorial constituencies, and legislative processes. To the extent these dilemmas become important, the result is less likely to be renewed militancy, ideological mobilization, or new collective struggles than a legalistic reform effort to preserve the "sanctity" and "distinctiveness" of state/public institutions and to regulate the activities and resources of interest associations.[31]

All these potential sources of difficulty for the future of societal corporatism, and for the relative governability that has accompanied it, can be discerned, to differing degrees, in the contemporary politics of advanced industrial/capitalist societies. Corporatism's very success at keeping political life ruly and effective has been purchased at the price of organizational sclerosis, rigidification of differentials, perpetuation of inequalities, and, most of all, disregard for the individualistic norms of citizen participation and accountability characteristic of a liberal democratic order. How long this form of corporatism can continue in its pragmatic manner to produce such negative behavioral effects and to ignore such fundamental normative aspirations, without resort to coercion, is questionable. Just as it has proved hard to "tone down" established pluralist structures unsuccessful in dealing with existing problems, so it may be difficult to "tune up" previously successful corporatist ones to meet emerging issues.

Acknowledgment

Funding for this research has been provided by the Social Science Divisional Research Fund of the University of Chicago and by the National Science Foundation (Grant No. Soc77-14164 A01). An earlier version was discussed within the framework of the SSRC-ACLS, Joint Committee on Western Europe, and I am particularly grateful to my colleagues on that committee for their suggestions and criticisms. It was also presented at the Conference on "Overloaded Government," European University Institute, Florence (December 1976) and at the panel on "Interest Intermediation" of the APSA Convention, Washington, D.C. (September 1977).

Notes

1 For an excellent, if rather nostalgic and petulant, critique of modern political science for having replaced the more exalted vision of affective "community" with a prosaic, limited vision of instrumental "partnership," see Clarke E. Cochran, "The Politics of Interest: Philosophy and the Limitations of a Science of Politics," *American Journal of Political Science* 25 (4) (1973): 745–66.

2 *Recasting Bourgeois Europe* (Princeton, N.J.: Princeton University Press, 1975), especially pp. 3–15.

3 The preceding passage is excerpted from my "Modes of Interest Intermediation and Models of Societal Change in Western Europe," *Comparative Political Studies* 10 (1) (1977): 15–6.

4 Cf. Mancur Olson, Jr., *The Logic of Collective Action* (New York: Schocken, 1971); James Q. Wilson, *Political Organizations* (New York: Basic Books, 1973); Ian Smith, "Communities, Associations, and the Supply of Collective Goods, *American Journal of Sociology* 82(2)(1976):291–308 for a discussion of the problem of voluntary associability in a liberal society.

5 These definitions were advanced and explored in Philippe C. Schmitter, "Still the Century of Corporatism?" *Review of Politics* 36(1)(1974):85–131. The distinction between a corporatism that comes predominantly from below (societal) and which comes imposed from above (state) was already recognized in the interwar period. Cf. Mihaïl Manoïlesco, *Le Siècle du corporatisme*, rev. ed. (Paris: Alcan, 1936) and Jean Malherbe, *Le Corporatisme d'association en Suisse* (Lausanne: Jordan fils, 1940). More recently, Gerhard Lehmbruch has advocated the term, "liberal corporatism," instead of "societal corporatism," to stress both the voluntaristic nature of the emergent arrangement and the simultaneous presence of an open, competitive party system into which may flow the unresolved issues of concerted policy making. Cf. his "Liberal Corporatism and Party Government," *Comparative Political Studies* 10(1)(April 1977):91–126.

6 These are the fifteen largest and most developed Western European and North American members of the OECD, that is, the sample excludes Greece, Iceland, Luxembourg, Portugal, Spain, and Turkey. Elsewhere, I have discussed the case of Japan: "Interest Intermediation and Regime Governability: A Japanese Epilogue," unpub-

lished paper presented at the SSRC Japan Committee, Workshop on Japanese Interest Groups, New York, May 13-4, 1978.

7 Bruce Headey, "Trade Unions and National Wage Policies," *Journal of Politics* 32(2) (1970):406-39.

8 The literature on corporatism in advanced industrial/capitalist societies has grown enormously in recent years. A compilation of most of the more important theoretical pieces will be appearing shortly in P. Schmitter and G. Lehmbruch (eds.), *Trends Toward Corporatist Intermediation* (London: Sage Publications). For a critical summary of this literature and its dissection into divergent "schools," see Leo Panitch, "Recent Theorizations of Corporatism: Reflections on a Growth Industry," paper presented at ISA World Congress, Panel on Interest Intermediation and Corporatism, Uppsala, August 14-9, 1978, and Kevin Bonnett, "Corporatist Developments in Advanced Capitalist Society: Competing Theoretical Perspectives," paper presented at the SSRC (Great Britain) Conference on Institutionalisation, University of Sussex, September 8-11, 1978.

9 For a brief discussion of the extraordinary ideological diversity of those who have historically and contemporarily advocated something called or resembling corporatism, see P. Schmitter, "Still the Century of Corporatism?" pp. 87-9.

10 In this volume, the chapter that most clearly and consistently employs this usage is Claus Offe's (Chapter 5), where "publicly attributed status" not just to exist but to participate in policy making is regarded as the hallmark of corporatism. See also Gerhard Lehmbruch, "Liberal Corporatism and Party Government," op. cit., for a similar usage.

11 The original source of this distinction between "consultation" and "negotiation" is Harry Eckstein, *Pressure Group Politics* (Stanford: Stanford University Press, 1960), pp. 22-5.

12 In my own work I have chosen to distinguish the two uses of corporatism by reserving the term itself to the process of interest intermediation and by using the concept "concertation" to refer to changes in policy making of the type previously outlined.

13 Except for those, of course, who define it in terms of a specific ideology, particular political culture, or distinctive mode of economic management.

14 This is one of the themes in P. Schmitter, "Interest Intermediation and Regime Governability: A Japanese Epilogue," op. cit. T. J. Pempel and Keiichi Tsunekawa have also insisted on this in their "Interest Intermediation and Economic Development: The Japanese Experience," paper presented at the ISA World Congress, Panel on Interest Intermediation and Corporatism, Uppsala, August 14-9, 1978.

15 This is one of the tentative observations of my current research on "Historical Change, Interest Intermediation and the Governability of Advanced Industrial/ Capitalist Polities," NSF Grant No. Soc 77-14164.

16 *Schweizer Monatshefte* (July 1975):274-98.

17 Richard Rose and B. Guy Peters, "Can Government Go Bankrupt? A Preliminary Inquiry into Political Overload," paper presented at the European University Institute, Colloquium on Overloaded Government, Florence, Dec. 13-7, 1976. An earlier version of this appeared as Richard Rose, "Overloaded Government: The Problem Outlined," *European Studies Newsletter*, 5(3)(1975):13-8. In the same vein, see Anthony King. "Overload: Problems of Governing in the 1970s, *Political Studies* 23 (1975):162-74 and Samuel Brittan, "The Economic Contradictions of Democracy," *British Journal of Political Science* 5 (1975):129-59.

18 Actually, the American literature either tends to stress or is criticized for ignoring yet a fourth dimension: *unlawfulness* or efforts by high-level corporate power holders, public or private, to escape legal and constitutional constraints in their pursuit of advantage and survival. Euro-centric treatments may occasionally mention leadership incompetence, but rarely dishonesty or illegality as part of the ungovernability syndrome.

19 See Table 10.2 for sources of the raw data.

20 The most problematic in this regard would seem to be the indicators of unruliness, because they are based on even-scored data that have proven to be very temporally erratic. Also the data we have used for collective protest and internal war refer to 1958–67, ending precisely at the moment arguments about ungovernability begin.

The "compound" rank ordering on unruliness correlates significantly with other indicators of citizen inspired resistance to power and authority: for example, 0.78 with Ted Gurr's indicator of "Total Magnitude of Civil Strife (1961–5)"; 0.82 with Ivo K. and Rosalind L. Feierabend's indicator of "Political Instability (1955–61)," and 0.86 with their indicator of "Political Violence (1948–61)."

In a recent paper, William J. Linehan has pointed out that per capit-ized indicators of political instability or violence often reveal quite different patterns of association from those measuring total magnitudes. The Gurr indicator previously mentioned did, however, control for population size and remained highly correlated with our factor scores based on total magnitudes. Using the same raw events from the Yale Data Handbook II, weighting both riots and deaths by a multiple of three, adding in the data from protests and armed attacks, then dividing the total by the unit's population in millions, we can generate two alternative indicators for per capita "collective protest" and "internal war" (1958–67). The first correlates 0.58 with the factor score for "collective protest," not too bad considering the latter contains a high loading for "political strikes" which were not included in the *Second Yale Data Handbook*. The second correlates 0.78 with the "internal war" score, despite the fact that it too contains a data series (assassinations) not included in our weighted per capit-ized measure.

The gist of these manipulations seems to be that the rank orderings on citizen unruliness are, indeed, relatively reliable and temporally stable.

References are: Ted R. Gurr, *Polimetrics: An Introduction to Quantitative Macropolitics* (Englewood Cliffs, N.J.: Prentice-Hall, 1972); Ivo K. and Rosalind L. Feierabend, "Aggressive Behaviors Within Politics, 1948–62: A Cross-National Study," in *Macro-Quantitative Analysis*, eds. J. V. Gillespie and B. A. Nesvold (Beverly Hills: Sage Publications, 1971), pp. 141–66; Betty A. Nesvold, "Scalogram Analysis of Political Violence," in ibid., pp. 167–86; William J. Linehan, "Models for the Measurement of Political Instability," *Political Methodology* 3(4) (Fall 1976); and C. L. Taylor and M. C. Hudson, *World Handbook of Social and Political Indicators* (New Haven: Yale University Press, 1972).

21 Cf. Maurice Duverger, *La Monarchie républicaine* (Paris: Robert Laffont, 1974).

22 Ronald Inglehart, "The Silent Revolution in Europe," *American Political Science Review* 65(4)(1971):991–1017.

23 The instability of such corporatist arrangements is stressed in Birgitta Nedelmann and Kurt G. Meier, "Theories of Contemporary Corporatism: Static or Dynamic," *Comparative Political Studies* 10(1)(April 1975):39–60. Also, the article by Gerhard Lehmbruch in the same special issue entitled "Liberal Corporatism and Party Government," pp. 91–126, deals with voluntary, tactical *cures d'opposition* taken by corporatist actors.

24 For a discussion of recent corporatist proposals in Great Britain, see James Douglas, "Review Article: The Overloaded Crown," *British Journal of Political Science* 6(1976): 498–500; R. E. Pahl and J. T. Winkler, "The Coming Corporatism," *Challenge* (March–April 1975):28–35; and G. Ionescu, *Centripetal Politics: Government and the New Centres of Power* (London: Hart-Davis, MacGibbon, 1975). For earlier periods: L. P. Carpenter, "Corporatism in Britain, 1930–1945," *Journal of Contemporary History* 11(1976):3–25 and Nigel Harris, *Competition and the Corporate Society* (London: Methuen, 1972).

One might contrast these efforts to the proposals for a new law on associations (*Verbändegesetz*) in the Federal Republic of Germany, some versions of which are designed to "roll back" or confine corporatist trends. Gunther Teubner, "Zu den Regelungsproblemen der Verbände," *Juristenzeitung* 33(17)(1978):545–8 and U. von Alemann and R. Heinze (eds), *Verbände und Staat: Korporative Tendenzen der Verbandskontrolle* (Opladen: Westdeutscher Verlag, forthcoming).

25 Leo Panitch is largely responsible for my seeing the "Social Democratic connection." "The Development of Corporatism in Liberal Democracies," *Comparative Political Studies* 10(1)(1977):61–90.

26 *Citizens, Elections, Parties* (New York: David McKay, 1970), pp. 40–3.

27 Something like this seems to be implied by Leo Panitch, op. cit.

28 The chapter by Charles Sabel in this volume is a good example of this sort of liberal-pluralist critique of corporatism.

29 Michael Hechter, "Group Formation and the Cultural Divisions of Labor," *American Journal of Sociology* (forthcoming).

30 Cf. a recent essay by Robert Salisbury, where the continued strength of constituency is regarded as a fundamental element inhibiting the emergence of societal corporatism in the United States – along with other factors. "On Centrifugal Tendencies in Interest Systems: The Case of the United States," paper presented at the ISA World Congress, Panel on Interest Intermediation and Corporatism, Uppsala, August 14–9, 1978.

31 Here the recent discussion of a *Verbändegesetz* in Western Germany is a case in point. See the sources cited in note 24.

11

May 1968 and the Hot Autumn of 1969: the responses of two ruling classes

MICHELE SALVATI

Introduction

In May 1968 France was shocked by a wave of social protests without precedent in the postwar period, as widespread student disturbances sparked a workers' revolt that was to paralyze production for almost a month. In Italy the movement spread less dramatically and the first explosion of student protests (1967–8) did not coincide with those of the workers (1969–70). Nonetheless, the Hot Autumn of 1969 in Italy, like May 1968 in France, was much more than the ritual intensification of industrial conflict that accompanies an important contract renewal. It was a mass movement that extended beyond those directly involved in contract renewals, with considerably broader and less defined demands than those expressed by the unions.

Faced by an intense and unforeseen challenge in such a sensitive area for managing the economy, French and Italian authorities reacted in profoundly different ways, and the subsequent economic developments in the two countries were very different as well. From 1968 until 1974, when the oil crisis forced France to adopt sharply restrictive measures, the French economy saw one of the longest and most intense expansive periods in its history. Only the boom of 1959–64 is comparable, although the French boom of 1968–74 was exceptional in Europe at that time. Investments, industrial output, and productivity rose steadily, undisturbed by the brief worldwide recession in 1971, which touched all the other European economies. Inflation, which had been relatively high in the late 1960s, fell below the European average in the early 1970s, despite increasing employment, economic activity, and profits. In Italy at the same time, all these economic indicators went in nearly the opposite direction; industrial output and productivity stagnated in the early 1970s. The brief and violent boom of 1973–4, which accompanied an international upswing, brought a burst of inflation that put Italy, along with the United Kingdom, in the least enviable position on the European economic league tables.

A systematic explanation of the factors that determine two specific, concrete historical experiences is overambitious: The common indicators of economic performance are the final expression of extremely complex and interactive social phenomena. Even if we limit our interpretive aims to what economists call the "short run," Kindleberger's observations in his comparative study of English and French economic development from 1850–1950 apply: "The partial character of our theories, and their qualitative nature, prevent us from saying how much wider markets should be to compensate for a loss of social cohesion, or how far the existence of the Ecole Polytechnique compensates for the thinness of French coal seams."[1] We are still dealing, however, with a promising line of questioning, even if we manage only to delimit the importance of governments' economic policies, large interest groups' strategies, and the collective movements' different orientations and developments. This may serve to identify characteristics of the political and social systems that are associated with the implementation of an "effective" short-run economic policy, as normally defined by economic authorities.

The relationship between the structure of the political system, organized interests, and the conditions for an effective economic policy is today the focus of renewed theoretical interest. Even among economists, at least those with concrete experience in economic policy, interest in the political and social preconditions for an effective short-run economic policy has been growing in recent years, as faith in ever more sophisticated fiscal and monetary engineering diminishes.[2] Among sociologists and political scientists, discussions on emergent neo-corporative tendencies in some European countries have been explicitly tied to the problem of short-run control of the economy, with conditions of full employment and with strong unions.[3]

Naturally, the study of two countries in a given historical moment limits any general conclusions. France, since the institutional reform of 1958, has had a stable conservative government, periodically and sometimes violently challenged by a radical opposition, but always victorious in decisive confrontations. Italy is less exceptional with respect to the dominant tendencies in Europe, with growing participation in government by parties associated with the labor movement and by unions in defining economic policy, although these tendencies have been and still are widely opposed. It is useful, however, to reconsider some of the recent discussions on the relationship between political systems and economic policy in light of these two important experiences, which have not usually been considered by those scholars who have emphasized the prevalence of neo-corporatism in Europe in the sixties and seventies.

The economy and economic policy

A detailed account of the economic policy measures taken in the two countries and of the responses of the two economies has already been given elsewhere.[4] Here we will simply review a few basic facts, which we will need in posing our main questions.

Italy and France: some differences

When the great waves of strikes and labor conflict broke in May 1968 and Autumn 1969, both economies were in a phase of cyclical recovery. The upswing after the "grey years" of the mid-sixties had just begun in France: The low point of industrial employment had been reached in 1967. In Italy, recovery from the brief recession of 1964 had been under way far longer: The trough in industrial employment had come in the winter 1965–6, and in 1969 it approached levels of the previous peak year, 1963. In neither country, however, did the labor market seem particularly tense. From a narrowly economic point of view, as in many other aspects, the conflict and wage "explosions" of May–June 1968 and of fall 1969 were quite unexpected.

French and Italian policy makers reacted very differently to these unanticipated events. In Italy they further tightened the monetary reins that they had begun pulling in mid-1969; moreover, a deflationary fiscal package was enacted in August 1970, despite signs of falling investment. In France, on the other hand, the authorities acted immediately to defend economic activity and profits, which had been sorely tested by the interruptions of production in May and by the Grenelle wage increase in June. Credit for firms was expanded and fiscal policy was promptly redirected to favor profits and investments.

Because of these measures and the responses of the two economies, Italian and French authorities faced completely different situations following the "explosions" of May and the Autumn. With the decline in investment, activity was stagnant in Italy, whereas the current account surplus in the balance of payments offset the speculative outflow of capital and relieved pressure on the lira. With a stable exchange rate, declining activity, and sharply increasing unit costs, business profits suffered their sharpest and longest squeeze of the whole postwar period. Monetary policy was soon relaxed in the second semester of 1970 and the state budget was more expansive in 1971 and 1972; but the stagnation of investment and the disappointing performance of exports restrained activity and profits until the second half of 1972.

In the French case, generous credit and fiscal concessions to the industrial sector, a climate of business confidence after the June elections, and an upsurge of demand after May induced a considerable increase in production. This, in turn, was favored by a surprisingly rapid – at least compared with Italy – return to normalcy in industrial relations. Despite the sharp rise in money wages after the Grenelle negotiations, labor productivity immediately returned to its high levels of 1967, thus containing the growth of unit costs. Increased prices did the rest, so that by late 1968 industrial profit margins were not much lower than they had been before May; with the strong growth of economic activity, a profitable business climate was restored.

The French authorities' major problem was a balance of payments deficit, arising in part from high levels of activity and greater price increases than in competing countries, in part from the relative undervaluation of the German mark.[5] We cannot go into the full story here, except to say that in his last year as president, de Gaulle always tried (even at the cost of sharp policy reversals) to reconcile fast growth of output and investments and a stable international and internal value of the franc. When restrictive measures were required, they were never severe enough to shake business confidence or to impair investment. This testifies to both the relative mildness of the measures and the vigor of French entrepreneurs' "animal spirits."

We cannot discuss here how far de Gaulle's objectives could have been realized in the difficult conditions of mid-1969; Pompidou abandoned the old international parity of the franc in August 1969 and performed a rare successful devaluation maneuver, turning the economy toward very fast growth, led by investment and exports. Understandably, the devaluation boosted internal inflation, but unlike the Italian experience in the spring of 1973, the increase was relatively modest. Also in contrast with the Italian situation, no new wave of wage increases broke loose with devaluation, although industrial conflict did intensify during the final trimester of 1969. The powerful growth of productivity kept wage increases from setting off a rapid wage–price spiral. Moreover, prices were rising sharply among France's principal trading partners so the differential in rates of inflation did not increase but declined, a surprise for a country that had just devalued its currency.

A final aspect of French economic policy worth mentioning is the relative "withdrawal" of the state from the economy, in terms of the share of resources absorbed by the public sector and employed for public consumption, investment, and income redistribution. This contrasts sharply not only with the Italian experience but also with that of most European countries. This measure was solicited primarily by business interests, who for years had denounced "intolerably high fiscal pressure." Government revenues fell from 22 percent of the gross domestic product in 1969 to 19.8 percent in 1973. Public spending contracted proportionally, allowing a balanced budget for four years in a row (1970–3), which in France had its only precedent in the period after Poincaré's stabilization, 1926–9.

Why?

It is now time to define our dependent variables and to establish the plausibility of the arguments we will adopt to explain them. Bringing in the different structures of the two political systems, the different traditions and orientations of organized interest groups, and the different nature of the collective movements would not make much sense if the events we have described could be explained by strictly economic variables.

Economic policy. Obviously this is not the case for economic policy decisions, whose rationale lies outside the strict confines of economics. The principal decisions in Italy and France were different enough to point to rather different political orientations and social pressures in the two countries. We have already hinted at the uncertainties in French economic policy and the genuine break in its general direction after the resignation of de Gaulle. But one basic goal was always maintained: *the defense of economic activity and investment.*

The international strength of the franc had an almost mythic importance in de Gaulle's eyes. The general also abhorred domestic inflation as much as the petit bourgeois groups that supported him did; he saw it as a symptom of disorder and loss of state control over society.[6] The difficulties in defending the franc and fighting inflation that arose from government's attempts to maintain activity and profitability after May demonstrate the higher priority of development and investment.[7] The June elections and the success of the conservative front, although essential to the reestablishment of business confidence, would not have been enough to sustain activity and investments had the authorities tightened credit or sharply restricted demand. De Gaulle never agreed to sacrifice industrial growth for the sake of the franc and price stability, although the high level of economic activity made it ever harder to defend the French currency. The franc and de Gaulle fell together.

The Italian authorities' deflationary position did not mean they were indifferent to growth. Under certain conditions – excess demand, and high sensitivity of wages (and more generally, sensitivity of the balance of power in industrial relations) to variations in effective demand – deflationary measures could have rapidly reestablished monetary and balance of payments equilibrium. This would have allowed a relaunching of economic activity and investment on "a firmer base," as they say in such cases. In 1963 these circumstances were present, although the maneuver had been costly in terms of investment. In 1969, in any case, such a situation did not recur; there was no excess demand and it is very doubtful that a *moderate* deflation could have altered the balance of power in the labor market and in industrial relations. At the same time, it was reasonably sure to have a negative influence on investment, especially because no obvious political sign, such as the June elections in France, had restored business confidence. *Prima facie,* the measures of 1969–70 seemed to indicate that investment was overridden by other priorities in economic policy; or, more plausibly, that no coherent set of priorities could emerge from political pressures that were more contradictory in Italy than in France.

Moreover, far from "retreating" to favor accumulation and exports by "productive" sectors, the Italian state increased its intervention in the economy considerably, almost entirely to satisfy a long-repressed demand for transfers and public consumption.[8] As in the United Kingdom, a political conflict over resource allocation developed between "nonproductive" (i. e., public) and "productive" (i. e., private) sectors, whereas in France the productive sector, essentially controlled by private capital, had always been given precedence.

The response of the economy. The "textbook maneuver" of Pompidou–Giscard would not have turned out the way the textbooks predicted had international and internal conditions not been particularly favorable. After the Italian Hot Autumn, a slowdown in world trade made a strategy of export-led recovery, which both countries sought, more difficult than after the French May. The international context was also more inflationary, and therefore the control of domestic inflation was harder for Italian authorities.

In understanding the different outcomes of the two economic policies, however, differing internal conditions are much more important. *If the response of investments, of labor productivity, of export compe-*

titiveness, and of money wages had not been so "favorable" in the French case – for example, if these variables had developed as they did in Italy – *no measures of economic policy could have sustained such steady development with acceptable levels of inflation.* Together with the economic policy, the response of these variables lies behind the success of the French economy between 1968 and the oil crisis.

1. Economists would readily accept that more favorable credit conditions, higher economic activity, more incisive measures of fiscal and commercial policy, and higher profits are important in explaining the greater development of industrial investment in France than in Italy. A case may also be made that the electoral results of June 1968, the climate of *enrichissez-vous* during Pompidou's presidency, and the reciprocal trust and understanding that government and business had developed in the experience of planning amplified the influence of the economic variables we have just mentioned and boosted business confidence. Investments are one of the most elusive and volatile variables of economic analysis; even though we cannot assess the influence of the political situation with great precision, this does not mean we should discount its relevance.

2. Attempts at explaining wage explosions like those of May 1968 and the Hot Autumn in terms of the customary variables cited to determine wages have generally been abandoned.[9] But problems also remain for any strictly economic analysis of the following years, especially if we want to compare the two national experiences. As fast as they may have grown, French wages remained within limits that never required measures to arrest development. As we have already pointed out, this happened while employment and immigration were high and growing, the labor market as a whole had become a stable seller's market, firms' profits and ability to pay were very high, and monetary and credit policy was expansive. With clearly less favorable circumstances in the market and in economic policy, and despite weaker cost of living pressure, the Italian unions managed to impose higher wage increases than the French, even before the acceleration of the inflationary spiral of 1973; from that point on, the two experiences are not even comparable. It would be very difficult to understand these two different outcomes without studying the segmentation of labor markets, the institutions and procedures of industrial relations, the different kinds and intensities of the collective movements, and the different union policies in the two countries.

3. Long-run economic factors account in part for French productivity and exports, which were exceptionally high in comparison with the Italian experience after the Hot Autumn. The rate of investment in industry had been higher in France than in Italy in the mid-

1960s, and French policy favoring modernization of the productive structure was more explicit and vigorous. Because the degree of integration of France's industrial structure in the European and world economies was the lowest of the large European economies, France probably retained a potential for growth through a greater international division of labor, which Italy had already exploited.

However important these structural economic factors, in the period we are examining short-run phenomena tied to economic policy decisions and the behavior of the great collective actors in the system predominate. One obvious reason for the stagnation of productivity in Italy was the low level of economic activity in a situation in which firms had to hoard labor. Each time demand rose significantly, in 1973, for example, the development of productivity in Italy was also extremely rapid; therefore the different economic policies pursued by the two countries – the one aimed at sustaining activity, the other incapable of stirring it up again – are central in explaining the course of productivity during these years.

In addition to the different levels of activity, we should also consider the different levels of industrial conflict in the two countries. Between 1969 and 1973 there was a real revolution in authority relations within the factory in Italy; for the first time the union set down roots in the workplace. Decisions about the organization of work (internal mobility, hours, and work rhythms), which had been made unilaterally by management in the past, were now contested and negotiated. This revolution certainly had a profound influence on labor productivity. None of this occurred in France after May; after the first flush of the movement faded, management regained its sovereign position in the factory.

4. Striking stagnation of Italian exports between 1969 and 1975 and the declining Italian share of the world's manufactured exports led to various questions, in particular, whether the phenomenon had deep structural causes lying in the geographical and technological composition of exports.[10] In light of available data, the most plausible answer is that the 1969–75 difficulties came in large part from short-run causes: limited supply due to industrial relations disturbances, unfavorable relative costs and prices, and scarce incentives to export, given the reduced profit margins on foreign sales before the devaluation. This was just the opposite of what happened in France, where the 1969 devaluation gave an exceptional stimulus to exports.

A final comment. The French government's economic policy, with its calculated risks in the inflationary conditions around 1970; the readiness of entrepreneurs to exploit every opportunity for growth; the (relatively) moderate response of labor, which was compatible with the principal objectives of government strategy – these (and their corresponding opposites in Italy) are the fundamental dependent variables in our exercise. A satisfactory explanation for the very different measures of policy and patterns of growth in Italy and France cannot be found in economics alone: This is what we have tried to argue, however impressionistically, in the preceding discussions. In the next two sections we will put other relevant variables into the ring: above all, differing degrees of government autonomy in dealing with interest groups and the strength and strategies of the most important groups in the two countries.

Here we should point out that, although these are important variables, they hardly exhaust the field of influences on the events we have described. On the contrary, we have had to omit or give inadequate mention to other very pertinent influences. For example, to understand the origins of labor's responses, which were so different in the two countries, detailed analysis of the differing structures of the labor markets would be indispensable. When they are highly segmented, and when there are such important currents of internal and foreign migration, overall figures on employment and unemployment can be deceptive. The institutions and the processes of industrial relations deserve considerably more attention than the few hints we provide here. And finally, the events with which our parallel histories begin, the great collective movements at the end of the 1960s, are left in the background.

Before May and before Autumn

Around the mid-1960s a tendency toward the participation in governmental responsibility of parties associated with the labor movement appeared throughout West Europe. Various factors pushed in this direction: détente, the strong position of the working class in the labor market, the breakdown of the immediate postwar ideologies of "reconstruction" and of individual mobility. In both France and Italy, however, participation in government by the parties of the Left was rendered rather more difficult by the predominance on the Left of Communist parties. In both countries the Socialists were a minority in the labor movement. Furthermore, in Italy the Nenni Socialists, unlike their French brethren, were closely linked to the Communist party.

Extending the government's parliamentary support to the Left, however, was a problem only in Italy, where the slow but continuous displacement of the electorate in that direction rendered center coalitions vulnerable and compelled a widening of the majority. In France the problem had already been resolved by the institutional reforms and the charisma of de Gaulle – not to mention the divisions within the Left – which helped shelter the French political system from the dominant tendencies in Europe in the 1960s and 1970s. A brief look at the Center-Left in Italy and the Gaullist system in France is indispensable for understanding the different reactions of the Italian and French political classes to May and Autumn and the different behavior of the principal actors in the political system – the parties and large interest groups.

Before the Autumn

The Center-Left was an effective response to the problem that the moderate political elites faced in the early 1960s: how to extend and consolidate the parliamentary majority without including the Communists. Extension to the Right was precluded by the nature of the parties on that end of the political spectrum, the Fascists and the Monarchists. Extension to the Left proceeded by separating the Socialists from the Communists, something that the Socialists themselves had begun in the mid-1950s, with the encouragement of part of the Christian Democratic party (DC). This was not, however, a simple and painless, purely parliamentary operation.

The Center-Left.   The Center-Left aroused enormous worries from the start among moderate social strata of business and the petite bourgeoisie.[11] For many years this political formula had to face the hostility of these social classes, which were not reconciled by the isolation of the Communists in a sterile opposition; the Center-Left's program directly threatened their interests.

The Center-Left was not even a real attempt to integrate socially those classes whose political participation was expressed through the left parties. First, the immediate political purpose of the coalition, the exclusion of the Communists, not only assured the Communist hostility toward the government but also that of much of the union movement, despite the growing autonomy of the CGIL (Confederazione Generale Italiana del Lavoro). The PCI's (Partito Comunista Italiano) hostility certainly did not encourage a neutral or tolerant union position toward the government's economic policy. There were also good reasons for this hostility, independent of ideological and organizational loyalties: the effects of economic policy of the 1960s on the unions and anti-union discrimination of many firms.

Most important, however, was the government's incapacity to effect its much-publicized program for significantly improving the living conditions of the lowest classes, the predominant electoral support of the parties of the Left: large transfers of income to families, better social services, development of the Mezzogiorno and limitation of migration, and so forth. The Socialist party might well have been in less difficulty in 1968–9 (and therefore the Center-Left might have survived longer) if it could have shown its electorate a record of successes.

Why the Center-Left proved incapable of reforms can only be determined through an analysis of the system of power constructed by the Christian Democrats, the dominant party in the coalition. Much has been written on this,[12] and here we will limit ourselves to a few observations.

Interest groups and political leadership. Every mass party receives support from classes and social groups with partially divergent interests. Often these interests are highly organized and can exercise an effective veto over measures that threaten them. An analysis that points to these characteristics to explain a mass party's incapacity for governing can only establish differences of degree and not of kind among parties. What can be said is that the interests within the Christian Democrats, who had ruled uninterrupted since the end of the war, were: first, very divergent and, above all, hardly congenial toward interventions favoring the working class, or the "modern" sector of the economy in general, over the interests of traditional sectors. In fact, these "traditional" middle classes, in agriculture, commerce, and artisanry, still retain a disproportionate weight in the "Christian Democratic system." Next, interests were very organized and organically linked with groups and currents within the Christian Democratic party. Organization of interests had often been promoted by the governing party itself for anti-Communist purposes, and a tangled web of local clientelistic relations underpinned the national organization. Finally, interests were hardly ordered or, rather, were organized in a flexible hierarchy, dependent on the nature of the problem at hand and on the shifting balance of power among different groups.

These characteristics of the Christian Democratic system – the disproportionate presence and veto power of the middle classes[13] – partially explain the inability of the principal moderate party of the moderate coalition to pursue a program of government for both economic reform favoring employees and support for accumulation and industrial modernization. The relations between the Christian Democrats and large private capital were also important.

The "farsighted" design for social integration of the classes tied to the parties of the Left (the strong version of the Center-Left) found large capital hostile and weak within the Christian Democratic party. In the entire history of Italian industrial development, capitalist interests never managed to build an autonomous base of support to achieve ideological hegemony over the moderate social bloc. Capitalists were also weak within the Christian Democratic system; even when the prevailing political orientation of the Christian Democrats had been closest to the interests of large private capital, for example, in the 1950s, industrial interests never clearly prevailed over other interests in the moderate bloc. In this light the contrast with the Japanese Liberal Democratic Party is instructive. Finally, very few large Italian capitalists supported the strategy of social integration in the programs of the Center-Left. It was to take the violent shock of the Hot Autumn, the union conquest of power by force, before a reformist current acquired a majority within the major business association, the Confindustria.

On one side, the history of relations between private capitalism and political power in the 1960s is a story of intense sectoral exchanges, leading to the formation of a vast area of "state-assisted capitalism," through the policy of industrial incentives favoring the Mezzogiorno.[14] On the other side, which particularly interests us here, it is a story of conflicts, of incomprehension, and often of exclusion from the real centers of political strategy making. The employers' association vehemently opposed the Center-Left, betting heavily on a losing horse, the tiny Liberal party, in the political elections of 1964. The nationalization of electricity and destruction of the most powerful private financial concentration generated a profound and enduring split between the government and the Confindustria, the business confederation. Even before the advent of the Center-Left, the continual extension of the public sector of the economy had stimulated periodic conflicts between the government and large private capital. The Confindustria obviously could not endorse a strategy entailing the expropriation of a significant portion of the industrial system, which the DC also pursued in order to have a source of resources independent of large capital. With the Center-Left, this strategy was reinforced by the participation in government of the Socialists, who favored nationalizations and were hostile to large capital for ideological reasons; the business confederation thus had plenty of reason to worry.

It was partially a consequence of these new sources of conflict and partially a spontaneous development in the Christian Democratic system of government that in the 1960s no steps were taken toward closer contact between industry and the government in determining the general lines of economic policy. The intense sectoral exchanges we have mentioned were between single centers of power, normally controlled by the Christian Democrats (public banks, the fund for the Mezzogiorno, etc.) and single capitalists. It is commonly held that these served more to "pollute" the market conduct of the firms involved in the exchanges than to sensitize politicians and public administrators to the difficulties and the general problems of industry. The national centers of economic planning – the Ministry of the Budget and the Office for Planning – were in the hands of the Socialists, which by itself explains the entrepreneurs' lack of inclination to support their work. No steps were taken to improve the scant competence of the economic branches of public administration,[15] to overcome the mental and technical gulf between the public and private sectors, or to encourage the exchange of personnel between government and industry.

Industry's rejection of the Center-Left and the refusal of most of the business world to recognize the symptoms of a shift of power in society and adapt to it – above all, in industrial relations – was one important reason for the failure of the "strong version" of the Center-Left. At the same time, this stance determined the (relative) isolation of the business association and of large private capital, its (relative) loss of contact with the political world and its difficulty in influencing the general lines of economic policy.

The unions. What occurred in the 1960s was the "weak" version of the Center-Left; reforms were not made, and the control of wages and pace of work were left to the market and to a system of industrial relations substantially unchanged since the 1950s. In the face of a deflationary economic policy and industry discrimination, the unions – despite their ideological and organizational divisions – found themselves together on many traditional union issues: wages, employment, working conditions, and union rights in the factory. With the recovery of economic activity in the late 1960s there developed an intense and undifferentiated demand for participation. This included workers coming from nonindustrial backgrounds, thrown en masse by widespread migration into a social environment without the structures to receive them. All the tensions accumulating on social grounds were ready to unload in the factory, and the union became the instrument for expression of a diffused discontent, expressed by a relatively homogeneous sector of the working class, previously un-unionized, unskilled workers.

The homogenity and the intensity of this "demand" were important factors in the unions' unity of action during the Hot Autumn. But there were also convergent tendencies on the "supply" side.[16] In fact, the Center-Left had an important, although indirect, influence on the principal Italian union, the CGIL, which was composed of a Communist majority and a Socialist minority. The leadership of the union was forced to put its own autonomy from the political parties to the test in those years in order to maintain its organizational unity and the effectiveness of its own activity. With the PCI in the opposition and the PSI (Partito Socialista Italiano) in the government, a new fracture in the union movement would have been inevitable if a partly autonomous view of political alignments had not prevailed among both the leadership and the rank and file.

This necessity for autonomy was born, above all, out of the experience of the 1950s in which the "conveyer belt" approach had brought disastrous results: The distinction of duties – unionist rather than politician – was even maintained within the Communist component of the CGIL, with much resistance, but on the whole with greater vigor than in France. The CISL (Confederazione Italiana dei Sindacati Libri) developed similarly. Born in 1948 from a schism in the CGIL as a direct consequence of the Cold War and the fall of the coalition government, the CISL had by the 1960s been transformed (to varying degrees in different areas in different branches of industry) from the "union wing" of the Christian Democratic party into an organization that was ever more attentive to workers' concrete problems and relatively free of ideological superstructure. Some sectors of CISL (notably the Metalworkers' Union) were the most combative and "anticapitalistic" groups in the 1969 battles.

Before May

The passing of the Algerian crisis, the electorate's general loss of faith in the institutions of the Fourth Republic, and de Gaulle's personal charisma all gave the new political elite that took power in 1958 a capacity for control without parallel in other democratic political systems.[17] The concentration of power in the presidency was based on the (relatively) scant importance of political exchange with other centers of power, parties, and interest groups in the decision-making process. De Gaulle always stated his conditions very clearly: It is only possible to govern if you have ample room for maneuvering with respect to the sectoral interests expressed through both parties and interest groups. Wide electoral support – periodically reaffirmed through referenda – is indispensable for the ruling group to emerge with sufficient authority and to pursue the characteristic "national" objectives of Gaullist policy. When this support declined – in April 1969 – de Gaulle's resignation followed as a necessary consequence.

De Gaulle's system.   As the Christian Democrats' political predominance was slowly weakening in Italy during the 1960s, the Gaullists' authority continued to grow. The right wing and the MRP (Mouvement Républicain Populaire) saw their own electorates dissolve and end up in the Gaullist camp. The SFIO (Section Française de l'Internationale Ouvrière) went into profound crisis, unable to find a credible line of opposition. The PCI, exploiting the disappointments of the Center-Left, continued to expand its prestige and electoral strength, but the PCF (Parti Communiste Français) was unable to enlarge its traditional electorate. Also, unlike the Christian Democrats, the UDR (Union des Démocrates pour la République) was hardly an ideal vehicle for channeling sectoral and territorial demands to the executive; the high turnover of parliamentary personnel and the institutional reforms of 1958 and 1962 blocked the principal parliamentary and party channels for transmission and left the executive exceptionally unhampered in its activities.

Finally, the institutional modification of 1958 resolved the tension of the Third and Fourth republics between Parliament and parties, and the bureaucracy. An efficient and homogeneous bureacracy with a strong *esprit de corps* and its own definition of the national interest meshed perfectly with a political authority that shared a rather similar definition and that had sufficient power to free it from the parliamentary and party pressures.[18]

Political orientation and interest groups.   De Gaulle's fundamental political objective is well known: a strong France, with its own role to play in the international field, resisting the bipolar game of the two superpowers. The consequences of this objective are also well known: In the area of industry, which interests us most, the principal consequence was a policy aimed at accelerating the modernization and concentration of industry. The explicit objective of the Fifth Plan (1966–70) was the creation, through mergers, of a few large groups of international stature in the most important sectors, not only to meet international competition but also to keep industries vital for France's political independence from falling under foreign control.[19]

In France this project of industrial modernization, the accelerated schedules in which de Gaulle intended to realize it, and the *dirigiste* instruments that he intended to adopt clashed – as they would have in Italy – with powerful and organized interests. The allocations of resources, time, and instruments were in sharp contrast to the interests of employees and their unions, of the independent *petite bourgeoisie*, and of small firms. Some aspects of the program of modernization and, above all, the instruments adopted to realize it, also clashed with the interests of large private capital.

Suzanne Berger, in Chapter 3 of this volume, has already indicated how the Gaullist system managed to deny the demands of traditional commerce and in a very short time profoundly transformed a sector that in Italy has so far held off all modernization. For agriculture, the other politically crucial "traditional" sector, the same basic consideration came into play. The breakdown of the mechanisms of demand that had operated during the Fourth Republic – de Gaulle's authority and that of the executive succeeded in blocking the emerging protests in the weakest sectors of the agricultural world until the end of the decade, at which time they underwent profound internal transformations. In contrast to its commercial policy, the government accompanied and stimulated the process of modernization of agricultural structures through a policy of active intervention, with considerable organizational and financial resources, generally keeping ahead of the directives of Common Market agricultural policy. Effective measures were taken to renew agricultural proprietorship, providing pensions for the old and financial accommodations for the young.[20] These measures, together with EEC (European Economic Community) policy and French agriculture's comparative advantage, caused substantial development of production and exports and helped limit the grievances that rapid modernization often brings.

De Gaulle's program of modernization and industrial reinforcement corresponded rather more closely with the interests of large capital. Not without some reason, the PCF and many scholars close to the party dismissed the Gaullist economic policy as a pure expression of those interests: as "Capitalisme Monopoliste d'Etat" or in slightly more subtle form, distinguished between une classe hégémonique and une classe régnante.[21] The political trade-off, however, was more complex, and the areas of conflict between Gaullism and large capital should not be underestimated.

On the positive side for private capital, the powerful social control that the government could exercise, and its favorable attitude toward management in industrial relations isolated the unions in all relevant decisions. The distribution of spending toward investments (and a distribution of income favoring profits) were encouraged. Finally, a section of private capital had the possibility for close contact with the bureaucracy and the political world. These informal relations played an important part in the process of economic planning.[22]

On the negative side, the state interfered with the market in ways that many entrepreneurs, even those most favored by the interventionist policies, considered excessive. Businessmen also resented de

Gaulle's disregard of their concrete problems and interests, when these diverged from his plans: "*La politique français ne se fait pas à la corbeille.*" In particular, much of the business world did not share de Gaulle's international objectives. The restriction of the circulation of capital was considered a limitation on the freedom of the firm, with no corresponding positive entry. "Prestige spending," as military and Third World aid spending were called, choked the state budget and retarded the infrastructural development – roads, telecommunications – that industry needed. The monetary war with the United States only distorted economic policy and brought the risk of retaliation.[23]

The sum of these credits and deficits was ultimately positive. De Gaulle's world was not the best of all possible worlds for industry (Pompidou would later guarantee an even better one), but it was good enough to avoid serious tensions between the business world and political power until 1968. Gaullist dirigisme might have generated bothersome interference with business choices, but this was not comparable to the threats to private industry that the extension of the public sector posed in Italy. The Gaullist plan and industrial policy might have favored economically erroneous initiatives, as seen in hindsight; but they also favored a continual transmission of influence between industry and the bureaucracy, an effective exchange of expertise and a further approach of two mentalities that had been rather close from the start. The Italian plan – a pale imitation of the French – was in the hands of politicians whom industry disliked profoundly. What kind of industrial and territorial policy was made had the effects we previously described.

The unions. The Gaullists' relations with the unions were at least as eccentric, in contemporary European experience, as their relations with business interests. In the other industrialized countries of Western Europe, governments sought and often obtained dialogue with the unions; they attempted to involve labor in economic policy making. In return they granted significant concessions in order to limit or at least foresee the evolution of wages and wage conflict. In France the plan was supposed to provide an arena in which the unions could make their voice heard, but the executive was quite impermeable to their demands and based incomes policy on simple power relations, actively intervening to limit the advance of wages.[24] The French unions, weak in membership and lacking ties or influence with the governing parties, did not exercise any direct influence on Gaullist policy. De Gaulle's hostility to every form of autonomous aggregation of interests, his intent to subordinate those that existed to the "common good," and the Gaullist projects' greater conformity to the interests of management rendered relations with the unions rather sporadic and quite tense when they did occur. In 1966 there was a clear rupture when the unions rejected the basic options of the Fifth Plan.

The weakness of the French unions can only be explained through a historical analysis.[25] Organizational weakness, centralization, politicization, and scarce presence and activity in the workplace were all part of a single gestalt, rather similar to that of the Italian unions; particularly with the obvious parallels between the CGIL and CGT (Confédération Générale du Travail) and the CISL and CFDT (Confédération Française Démocratique du Travail), the principal union confederations in each country.

There were, however, two differences that were to be significant in May: one has to do with the different historical traditions of French and Italian unionism. The CGT and CFDT are "old" unions that renewed their divisive polemics from the Third Republic in the Fourth. The CISL instead was born from the schism, in the course of the cold war, of a unitary confederation that emerged from the immediate postwar period. The conflict was extremely violent but the search for lost unity remained a more or less genuine goal within both of the branches that emerged from the schism. A substantial share of the Socialist component of the labor movement remained within the CGIL, whereas the CGT was almost monolithically Communist.

The relationship between the PCI and the CGIL had many of the same characteristics as the relationship between the PCF and the CGT; the precise distinction between "economic action" by the union and "political action" by the party subjected both to the parties' direction. Union action was directed to the ends of the overall advancement of the Communist movement. Likewise, there was also an unjustified (from the "unionist" point of view) preference for large demonstrations to support party political initiatives. But in Italy these appeared in less extreme forms, due to the different development of Italian and French communism. With all its shortcomings, the debate within the CGIL at the end of the 1950s and the critical reexamination of the union's miserable results in the period when the "conveyor belt" had functioned most rigidly led to far more intense stock-taking than the CGT had ever contemplated.[26]

The second set of differences is more recent. We have already noted how the political situation of the Center-Left promoted the independence of the union from the party for the CGIL because the members of the confederation belonged to two different parties, one in government, the other in the opposition. In France, instead, the strength and cohesion of Gaullism seemed to accentuate the politicization of the unions, which could not define a strategy of change without including profound political shifts. The need for the unions to define themselves in relation to politics brought out the very different views of the CGT and the CFDT. As in Italy, organizational weakness and subjection to a program that did not take union demands into account periodically brought the need for unity to light, but the 1966 "pact of unity of action" between the CGT and the CFDT was rather more fragile than the unitary processes that were developing then within Italian unionism.

After May and after the Autumn

After May

This period of French political history can be divided into two distinct subperiods: from May 1968 until the summer of 1969, with the election of Pompidou and the subsequent devaluation of the currency, and from the summer of 1969 until Pompidou's death and the first signs of the depression of 1975. The unexpected social explosion and its aftermath in the first period were followed by a readjustment within the French political system, in particular, within the dominant bloc. The result of this readjustment was the abandonment of historical Gaullism in favor of a more "liberal" system of legitimation.

In contrast to the intensity of the period that closed the Gaullist decade, the years of Pompidou's presidency – at least until 1972 – passed without any major shocks. Although in Italy governmental crises followed one upon another and the presidential elections of 1971 offered a new occasion for uncertainty, the political–institutional situation in France until 1972 was static. The government was unassailable and there were no elections to provoke open clashes among the components of the majority. Next, constant growth of real income allowed the satisfaction of various social groups' demands without reducing industrial profit margins. Unlike the Gaullists' economic policy of state intervention for political priorities that often differed from those of industrial groups, policy under Pompidou was intended to favor the spontaneous course of the market according to entrepreneurs' preferences. The exaltation of free enterprise, the social benefits of profits, and the utility of a prosperous economy in solving all other problems were frequent motifs in public speeches: a clear break from the "primacy of politics" that de Gaulle had imposed and enforced.

In what sense did the first of the two phases prepare the way for the second? How could as intense a political crisis as what we have described – the end of a regime – have coincided with such an "effective" economic policy?

An attempt at corporatism on the old model.   The strong recovery of production that followed May gave birth to a widespread euphoria in the business world. Encouraged by government on one side and by the union movements' apparent loss of initiative on the other (although the fear of a new explosion always remained), firms rapidly recovered healthy margins of profit. The expectation of a prolonged period of growth spread, and a perceptible growth of money wages was seen as the price for the restoration of a system of industrial relations with less risk of explosion. The majority of entrepreneurs did not perceive the Grenelle concessions as a defeat nor as a historical setback, such as that suffered at Matignon in 1936. Whereas the industrialists' association had gone through a profound crisis after Matignon, this time the prevailing opinion was that they had landed on their feet.

This business euphoria, initially reinforced by the strong affinity of outlook between the prime minister and the world of business and finance, immediately ran up against the rather different political designs of the president, who had assumed total control of the executive after Pompidou's resignation. The explosion of May had not taught de Gaulle that it was time to leave a wider area for special interests and organized political forces in the determination of the government's course and that it was time to abandon economic–political projects incompatible with France's international position. The general's economic–political projects remained unchanged. The breakdown in May was seen as a symptom of the state's loss of control over society, which was to be counteracted by reinforcing the direct ties between interests and the state. The state itself would have to institutionalize and discipline these ties, blocking those autonomous forms of organization that, in Gaullist thinking, only led to the transmission of sectoral demands and ungovernability.

It is difficult not to interpret projects like those for the reform of the Senate or for worker participation in management in terms of a model of traditional corporatism. According to the first project, the senate would have lost its character as a legislative chamber to become the expression of professional and local interests, a sort of chamber of the corporations, with the implicit mandate to manage an authoritarian incomes policy. The second project, beyond constraining firms' freedom of decision making, would have raised considerable obstacles for organizing workers on a union basis. The combined opposition of the unions and, above all, of business was very violent and forced the government to abandon the workers' participation design in November 1968.[27] The collapse of the design for reforming the Senate, on which de Gaulle had called the referendum, was the direct cause of his resignation in April 1969.

The end of historical Gaullism came, however, under the shelter of an electoral outcome that was broadly reassuring for the conservatives; the stability of the system was not in question, nor was the security of their predominance over the government. The parties of the Left were still suffering from the shock of electoral defeat, and the unions showed their scarce importance with the general strike of March 1969. The institutional dikes erected by Gaullism held solid; at the end of the revolutionary wave, the state moved on, only brushed by the workers' and students' demands. The opposition was bourgeois, and the crisis was an internal crisis of the dominant bloc. This guaranteed continuity, so that business' confidence was never lessened. Sustained by the growth of consumption, and never braked by incisive credit or fiscal measures, the investment boom was to be interrupted only by the world crisis of 1975.

Enrichissez-vous. Pompidou inherited an overwhelming parliamentary majority from historical Gaullism and reoriented it toward somewhat different goals than those of the general. The implicit demand for order that was expressed in the political elections of June 1968 was met with greater flexibility toward the demands of organized interests. But a significant part of the Gaullist baggage was unloaded; the stability of the franc was no longer dogma (the new government's first step was to devaluate); the systematic opposition to the international monetary system disappeared; some "grand projects" were shelved; and participation – in its double form, in firms and in institutions – was abandoned. The push to modernize the industrial plant, however, was not abandoned. "The acquisition of economic power... without which independence, prestige, and the hope of progress are nothing but passing clouds," was of the first importance for Pompidou, although with an appreciable difference in emphasis from de Gaulle's vision.

The economic strategy was simple. The expansionary orientation that led to the abandonment of the fixed exchange allowed a rapid growth of income. This in its turn allowed a larger margin for satisfying the demand of various interests, a margin that was further increased by the steady reduction of fiscal pressure. With a growing pie, it was possible to make some pieces larger without taking from others.[28]

Workers' interests were also favored in the medium run, with full employment and growing real wages. Above all, though, business interests were favored. A macroeconomic policy that managed in the turbulent international conditions of the early 1970s to sustain high profitability and a high level of investment was practically unique among the large capitalist countries. Moreover, this was effected in the context of growing liberalization of the economy and of greater state sensitivity to the demands of industrial interests. Planning became more flexible and respectful of the interests of French firms that were accelerating their integration in the international market and were thus subjected to growing external constraints.

CNPF (Confédération Nationale du Patronat Français) itself, previously more a gathering of powerful sectoral federations than a center for the elaboration of a coherent strategic line for French business,[29] felt the effects of this change in climate. The crisis of May had posed the urgent problem of creating a centralized body capable of bargaining authoritatively with the government and the unions. The reform of November 1969 served to give more authority and more autonomy to the central bodies relative to the individual federations. In the face of greater activity on the union front, and with a government position that was less *dirigiste* and less hostile to autonomous aggregations of interests, the need for a stronger coordination of mangement's policy was not long in being felt.

The unions. The expansionist environment of the early 1970s made it possible to grant workers a continual increment in real income and helped contain the unions. The alliance between entrepreneurs and government, the obstacles to union action on the political market, and, finally, the weakness and conflicts between the union headquarters all coincided to make this containment possible.

The concessions of Grenelle were only a pale reflection of the earthquake that had shaken Gaullism, and the electoral defeat was critical in curbing workers' expectations and factory agitation. The unions saw their membership grow, and in the course of 1969–70 there was an increase in action over contracts, especially at the level of the individual firms. But management paid close attention to controlling these developments:

It remains to be seen whether it will be possible to organize negotiation *tous azimuts* so that it will not degenerate into disorder or escalate. The Italian system offers us an instructive example . . . we certainly can have discussions at the firm level, at the professional level, and at the interprofessional level, on the condition, above all, that the same things are not discussed twice . . . the first accord must not serve as a trampoline to the others.[30]

These conditions were substantially respected in practice. The relatively "traditional" nature of union demands[31] stood in contrast to the profound changes being made in Italy, as did the unions' difficulty in negotiating over working conditions. The strong growth of productivity after May was due in large part to profound restructuring within firms, accentuating worker mobility, and intensifying work rhythms, the very processes under negotiation and challenge by the Italian unions.

If one important aspect of the different course of contractual negotiations in the two countries lies in the different "demand" that the two labor movements had to satisfy, another part lies on the "supply" side, in particular, in the disunity of the two most important French union confederations.

The worsening political relations between the CGT and the CFDT were felt even at the factory level, where they quarreled over which forms of struggle to pursue. With the electoral needs of the Left in mind, the CGT pushed for more centralized mass demonstrations, although resolutely opposing every illegal form of conflict. The CFDT was more active in conflicts in individual firms, where its base – mostly young and recently unionized workers – was frequently involved in incidents that were not strictly legal. Thus, although in Italy rank-and-file initiatives were channeled through unitary bodies (the factory councils), French militants in the different oganizations continued to follow differing and often opposite courses. The hostility between the two confederations lasted through 1969 and most of 1970, with the CFDT signing many important contracts that the CGT rejected. Although a new unity pact was signed (December 1, 1970), its fortunes were rather variable. The bottleneck of the CGT's political dependency on the PCF has never been eliminated. Thus there have been periodical ruptures and reconciliations, as a closed ideological debate on the nature and scope of socialism continues.[32] The debate hardly promotes effective "anticapitalist" action.

Regarding the political market, in Italy the unions were important pressure groups within the governing parties. And with their greater strength won in the area of industrial relations, they became very actively involved in politics and exerted considerable influence on government decision making. None of this occurred in France, where the unions' estrangement from the centers of decision remained substantially unchanged. The role of unions in the plan is an example of this estrangement. The CFDT, which "officially" joined the Socialist camp at its Thirty-fifth Congress (1970), proposed the long-term objective of *autogestion*. Although the closer ties to the Socialist party never came close to the "team playing" of the CGT and PCF, its growing ideological estrangement from the government led the CFDT to withdraw from work on the Fourth Plan, which it attacked as an embellishment of choices that large capital had already made. The CGT did participate, but with a role of formal and purely ideological opposition. It attacked the principles on which the major decisions were based – the market economy, the role of profit – just as the PCF did. But the CGT lacked the power – and possibly the desire – to enter into debate over the substantive merit of the decisions and to influence them.

After the Autumn

The power system the Christian Democrats created in the postwar period was based on a relative underrepresentation of working-class demands and institutions (the parties of the Left and the unions), with a relatively greater access to state resources for other groups and classes, through clientelistic relations. This underrepresentation did not differ significantly from the French situation, except that it occurred in the context of a coalition government with Socialist participation. In particular, the principal union organizations were tied to parties in the government, playing an important role in the interest systems that determined the parties' political lines. The executive was extremely sensitive to pressures from the governing parties, whereas in France it was effectively isolated by the institutional reform of 1958. Development and modernization of industry were not a top priority in determining economic policy, as they were in France. Finally, the public administration was deeply entangled in the clientelistic practices of the governing parties, and its competence and effectiveness were lower than those of the French.

In these conditions, the unforeseen and significant rise in "demand for representation" by previously underrepresented groups transmitted unmanageable impulses through the parties and unions to the government, especially in economic policy. The Italian political system, unlike that of the French, was highly elastic and susceptible (at least in the short run) to shifts in the balance of power among large interest groups and more generally, to changes in the "social climate." In any case, it was altogether incapable of disciplining demands from society in accordance with a constant pattern of economic policy objectives when their intensity and composition were noticeably altered.

Parties, interest groups, and economic policy.   The behavior of the PSI is very important for understanding the activities of the government in the years we are considering. The disappointment of the expectations for reform raised by the Center-Left damaged the party's image, and the subordinate role it gained in the Christian Democratic clientelist system could not compensate for the loss of credibility it suffered. The PSI was squeezed between the Christian Democrats, who held back a large share of public resources and obstructed the reform process, and the Communists, who never lost a chance to point out the inconsistencies and the failures of the Center-Left.

The spontaneous surge of a social movement on the Left, on the one hand, and the failed merger with the Social Democratic party and electoral defeat in 1968, on the other, influenced the party's policy profoundly, raising the price the PSI demanded for further participation in the Center-Left. The increases in government public spending (particularly in health and social security) and the openly favorable position toward the unions can be interpreted in this light. After years of inactivity, with an implicit incomes policy determined by the market, to oppose the collective movement and to support containment of labor pressure would have been suicidal given the PSI's constituency and its ties to the unions.

The DC could not have, nor did it wish to, take a hard line. First of all, the Center-Left was still the most stable political formation that electoral results allowed and the only valid barricade – barring *coup d'état* – against the PCI's growing electoral power. Furthermore, even within the DC the effects of the new social climate were being felt. The most important conductor of these effects was the Catholic union, the CISL, of which a large part was involved in steadily growing unity of action with the Socialist–Communist union.

The Christian Democratic power system, unlike the Gaullist regime, could not oppose the unions frontally: In 1969 the Christian Democrats designated as minister of labor an ex-unionist of the CISL who was fond of referring to himself as minister of laborers, not the minister of labor. And in 1975, in a far more serious economic situation, it seems that Aldo Moro, then prime minister, laconically replied to the president of Confindustria, who had come for suggestions regarding a plan for wage indexing that was extremely favorable to workers: "You must judge for yourselves."[33]

Leaving aside such episodes, in looking back over the Christian Democrats' position on the economy, we see a flexible policy toward wage pressures and toward union and PSI initiatives in public spending emerge and, at the same time, a strenuous defense of the interest groups traditionally tied to its power system.[34] The necessary consequence of this position was a powerful inflationary dynamic, immediately followed by severe deflationary measures when inflation threatened to become socially disturbing. The interests of industry were objectively, if unintentionally, sacrificed by this erratic policy.

The business front was weak and disunited, and it failed to come up with any clear alternative. Along with the public sector, an important part of large private industry fell within the orbit of the Christian Democratic power system, and one could hardly expect any contributions from this quarter for an economic policy to sustain intensive accumulation in the private sector. The public sector and those sectors receiving direct incentives from industrial policy partly lived on other resources than those furnished by the market, and these resources were not cut off in the period under consideration.

Confindustria found itself in a grave ideological and organizational crisis. Toward the end of the 1960s important capitalist groups had already recognized their mistake in opposing the Center-Left, but Confindustria's initiatives to modify this direction were very hesitant and matured rather late, with Agnelli's presidency in 1974.[35] This was too late to influence the response in economic policy to the Hot Autumn.

The unions.   Union policy in Italy during this period has been extensively treated elsewhere.[36] In the face of the collective movement's intensity, unity, and durability, the unions' objective was to consolidate, institutionalize, and extend the favorable balance of power it had brought about in the factory. The historical weaknesses of Italian unionism had been little presence in the workplace, lack of management recognition for union representation at the shop level, and ideological divisions among the (principal) union organizations. These divisions did not disappear but were greatly attenuated under the pressures of the common objectives that came from the strengthening of the union organization. The other weaknesses were largely eliminated; the union was firmly rooted in the factory and was recognized by management, whereas the organizational forms that had spontaneously emerged during the struggles were disciplined, stabilized, and incorporated (with difficulty, but generally successfully) in the organizational structure of the union.

This process could hardly have been contained within limits allowing the pursuit of an "effective" economic policy. Great wage pressures and the breakdown of the rules of the game governing power relations within the factory were not compatible with an expansionist and noninflationary policy. In fact, both goals had to be abandoned and simultaneous recession and inflation ensued. On the other hand, the union could never have realized its longstanding goal of organizing and being recognized in the workplace if it had not allowed the movement to express its potential, selecting thousands of local leaders through the struggles. It would have won nothing had it put on the brakes instead of taking the wheel.

It was not long before the union had turned around to act on the political market in continuous and extended relations with the government on the general themes of economic policy. The social power it had won, the government's limited capacity for initiative or leadership, the pressure of the Communist party, and the impossibility of making further gains through struggles in the factory made this switch inevitable. However, these efforts on the political market were never made at the expense of initiatives at the base. It was here that the top priority for union activity lay and here it stayed until the steady worsening of the economic crisis and Communist participation in the governing majority changed the leadership's strategy substantially. Until the mid-1970s there was much discussion on the political market but very few transactions. The unions did not intend to "sell" union moderation, nor did the Christian Democrats intend to concede their political exclusion of the largest party of the Left.

The history of the first attempt at "bargained corporatism" in Italy began immediately after the end of the period under review. It was, however, a very hesitant and contradictory attempt; the exclusion of the Communist party was diminished but not eliminated. Important barriers remained, despite the party's commitment to assuring the government's stability and the CGIL's commitment to controlling wage demands. The persistence of this partial exclusion makes it difficult to predict the future of "neo-corporatist" developments in the political system.

Was a different economic policy possible?   It was very difficult to conduct an "effective" economic policy under the conditions that we have described. In the face of such a violent shock to the social system, the political leadership would have had, finally, to make some hard decisions and to support some coherent, however partisan, design for economic policy. Without this, no monetary or fiscal engineering, however sophisticated, could have maintained simultaneous economic growth and moderate inflation. This support was given in France by the June elections, and French economic policy and its success can only be understood by taking into account the radical reversal of the political climate this event signaled. In Italy there was no similarly clear political sign, nor was one possible.

The Bank of Italy, by itself, could not substitute for political authority. The moderate credit restrictions of 1969–70 can only partially be blamed for the decline in investment from 1970 to 1972, nor can the inopportune fiscal package of August 1970 be blamed. The credit restrictions were simply measures through which the Bank pursued its top priorities, defense of the internal and external value of the currency. The fiscal package was probably based on a mistaken evaluation of the conditions of economic activity. Both, however, were much less harsh than would have been necessary to give a clear sign of the government's intentions. Suppressing the movement through a deflationary strategy would have required an even tougher policy than in the winter of 1963, because union pressure was far more intense. But such a strategy could obviously have been adopted only by political authorities, which we have seen was impossible. It would hardly have been justified by economic conditions, and its political meaning would have been quite transparent.

An economic policy like that of the French, which sought to reconcile a priority for industrial growth with an acceptable inflation rate, would have been even less plausible in Italy. In the aftermath of the Hot Autumn, the principal governing forces did not even consider the political act of devaluation, given its obvious redistributive consequences. For a devaluation and expansion of activity to have coincided with an acceptable inflation rate, major changes in the balance of power in society would have been necessary. The collective movement would have had to be defeated and management's authority in the factory reinstated. This would have required political action of a sort impossible in the Italian democratic context (leaving aside some sinister maneuvers in 1969–70).

Devaluation finally came after two years of stagflation, when it was impossible to avoid; thus it was forced on the political system as an "external" and necessary development. Business and the unions were at last given the economic recovery they wanted, athough it was a speculative boom of a sort they had hardly sought. In negotiating some of the most important contract renewals of 1972–3, the unions showed little sign of moderation, and in the following spring they were awarded large wage increases. The blockage of irreconcilable demands was exploded by the rapid devaluation of the currency and growing inflation.

Conclusion

So far we have sought to account for the surprising differences between French and Italian economic policies and their successes from the late 1960s to the early 1970s with noneconomic variables. In this light we have considered the dynamics of the two collective movements, the structures of the political systems, and the role of interest groups, especially unions, in each country. To conclude, we would like to raise three issues that connect these events more directly to the debate in this volume.

The first theme is related to an important common characteristic of the two political systems, the presence of a strong Communist party and its predominance in the union movement. In both countries this was the greatest obstacle to bringing union leadership into economic policy making. An important precondition for the social arrangements known as "social," "bargained," or "liberal" corporatism appears to be that large interest groups internalize the limits that economic policy (and politics *tout court*) must respect in modern capitalism. Moreover, the other actors in the game must recognize this "internalization" as an accomplished fact. Widespread social acceptance, the absence of political exclusions, and a more equitable distribution of resources are the counterpart to this internalization. Conflict of course remains, but only over negotiable ends and for redistributive proposals. A moderate pressure for marginal changes in the rules of the game can also exist. But demands cannot be pushed to the point where party or interest group acceptance of the social and political system can be open to question.

In the early 1960s it was unclear just how far the Italian and French Communist parties, and their associated unions, had "internalized the limits of the system." In each case the ruling classes of the two countries had no intention of testing this internalization if they could avoid it; existing political arrangements were satisfactory. In the more precarious Italian case it had been necessary to extend governmental participation to one of the labor movement parties. But at the same time, the larger party was still excluded and there was no possibility or capacity for a bold move to integrate the classes and groups identified with the organizations of the Left. The French situation was more stable and "effective": Here the conditions existed for a long-term exclusion from economic policy making of the unions (and the parties on the Left).

When consensus and mediation are not politically necessary, and the number of major collective actors (and of divergent interests) who influence decision making can be reduced without grave consequences, decision making is likely to be quite "effective." It should work at least as well, perhaps better, than situations in which institutional actors (insofar as they have internalized the rules of the game) participate in "contractual corporatism," as in Austria or Sweden.

Our next theme regards the relationship between entrepreneurial interests and macroeconomic policy making. One preliminary point must be raised: it is not easy to determine whose interests are favored by particular macroeconomic policies, an important difference from more specific, microeconomic interventions, which normally allow us to distinguish precisely the interests advanced or hurt. It is true that the French government's expansionary policy favored investment and profits, but it also favored employment and, in the medium run, the growth of real wages. One the other hand, an analogous argument could be applied in reverse to a deflationary policy, as we have already mentioned, regarding Italian policies in 1963–4 and 1969–70. Going behind imputations of "objective" interest and evaluating management associations' and major capitalist groups' explicit positions on important measures of macroeconomic policy is often not much help in resolving these difficulties. De Gaulle's decision in November 1968 to maintain the foreign value of the franc had a positive reception from official spokesmen of business, as did the Italian authorities' deflationary policies in 1970.[37]

Whatever the ambiguity about the interests "objectively" favored or injured by macroeconomic measures, the circumstances and manner in which these measures are taken clarify government's orientations considerably. High economic activity and full employment, in the short run, can also be reached through massive increases in public consumption and transfers, with redistribution of income in favor of wage earners. But several factors can temper full employment to favor industrial interests: government freedom from union and left-wing party pressures; income distribution favoring profits without stimulating excessive inflation; containment of public spending for transfers and consumption; and pursuit of an intensive program of investment and economic modernization. Likewise, deflationary measures, although they are always an evil for business and for workers, are the lesser evil for business interests if they succeed in suppressing excess demand or "excessive" union power. In this case as well, the circumstances and the manner of such operations help us decipher their political significance.

A second observation may be advanced to corroborate an argument that Offe makes in Chapter 5 of this volume that formal organization is far more important for labor than for capital. The different orientations of economic policy making in Italy and France are not reflected in any great difference in the role or weight of business associations in the two political systems. In this chapter we have emphasized the Confindustria's difficulties at the threshold of the Hot Autumn and the reorganization and revival of the CNPF after May. But however important these differences, they are far too small to have had a noticeable impact on economic policy. Moreover, they partly depend on the political orientation of the governments: They are influenced by government policy making more than they influence it.

The influence of business on government need not pass through formal organization – and may well circumvent it. Direct and immediate pressures on specific measures, exercised at the summits of government and public administration by representatives of the business and financial worlds, can hardly be reconstructed and documented except in a historical setting. But the long-term influences that lead (or do not lead) the world of business and the summits of government and public administration to share the same language and basic attitudes may be more important. These influences have deep historical roots, and in this chapter we have briefly mentioned the circumstances that favored them (in France) and obstructed them (in Italy). Such exchange, interpenetration, and mutual adaptation between economic and political–administrative elites is a complex process, with notably different outcomes for national styles of economic policy.

The French political system's special capacity for guaranteeing favorable conditions for "effective" economic policy was based on particular historical circumstances, whose influence was already beginning to run out in the period under review. The passage from de Gaulle's charisma to Pompidou's secular power did not alter the overall effectiveness of government decision making; the "surplus of authority" that de Gaulle had collected made for a smooth transition. The succession did carry a major risk, however: that the partisan biases of the government were too clearly exposed and that the government was identified with the government of big business.

De Gaulle had reacted to the social crisis in May by accentuating his posture of being "above taking sides" and by turning to an explicit traditional corporatist solution. The nation, *étatisme*, direct appeals to the people, hostility toward autonomous interest groups, and the attempt to challenge them with state-organized interest representation are all ingredients of traditional state corporatism. The general's final projects, his version of industrial democracy, and his Senate reform were aimed in this direction. With Pompidou many of these plans were discarded, and in the short run this may have contributed to the revival of business initiative and favored the government's economic policy. But the bias of the governing elites showed through with dangerous clarity.

In the immediate aftermath of de Gaulle's fall this did not lead to any reorganization of interest groups or parties that would modify the dominant orientation of economic policy, although there have been significant preliminary shifts. In any case, the parliamentary strength of the moderate coalition gave the government ample room for maneuver. But these advantages will be hard to perpetuate. Increasing activism among interest groups and behavior that is less compatible with the aims of economic policy are no longer unthinkable. Neither is an electoral defeat of the moderate coalition.

The political history of the last twenty years, however, would make it very traumatic for the parties of the Left to succeed the Center-Right government. In France, in contrast to Italy, there has been no progressive convergence of various party positions and no "internalization" of the rules of the game. The Communist party's progress toward a party model "like any other" has been halted, and the *programme commun* was hardly a basis for any corporatist consensus. In the latter half of the seventies, the French economy, in comparison with France's neighbors, was much less successful than in the first part of the decade. In all likelihood, the search for the reasons of this worsened comparative performance would carry us again beyond economic factors to those we have just outlined: the erosion of de Gaulle's authoritarian legacy and the French elite's inability to find an equally "effective" substitute for it.

Acknowledgment

In writing this chapter I have been considerably helped by A. Gigliobianco whose research assistance has come rather close to coauthorship. I would also like to thank Suzanne Berger and Charles Sabel for their invaluable advice.

Notes

1 Charles Kindleberger, *Economic Growth in France and Britain, 1850–1959* (Cambridge, Mass.: Harvard University Press, 1964), p. 324.

2 As R. Keohane, "Neo-orthodox Economics, Inflation and the State: Political Implications of the McCracken Report," *World Politics* 21(1) (October 1978): 108–128 observes, one of the OECD's most influential documents on economic policy (*Towards Full Employment and Price Stability*, Paris: OECD, June 1977) makes extensive, although not explicit, use of political and social variables in analyzing the recent economic situation and in justifying proposals for intervention.

3 Very close to our view is the analysis of corporatism which can be found in C. Crouch, "The State, Capital and Liberal Democracy," in *State and Economy in Contemporary Capitalism*, ed. C. Crouch, (London: Croom Helm, 1979).

4 For example, in the *Country Surveys* of the OECD. See also M. Salvati, *Lo sviluppo economico italiano: Analisi di una crisi* (Bologna: Il Mulino, 1975) for Italy, and J. Mistral, "Vingt ans de redéploiement du commerce extérieur," *Economie et Statistique* 71 (October 1975): 23–40, for France.

5 A good analysis of the franc-mark "see-saw" can be found in Susan Strange, "Monetary Relations," in *International Economic Relations of the Western World, 1959–1971*, Vol. II, ed. A. Shonfield (London: Oxford University Press, 1976).

6 Here de Gaulle can speak for himself: "The currency (is) the basis for economic value and the terms of credit, whose stability guarantees and attracts savings, encourages the spirit of enterprise, contributes to social peace and brings international prominence, but its weakening unlooses inflation and waste, smothers development, provokes disorder, and endangers independence."

"I gave France a model franc, whose parity did not change as long as I was there." *Mémoires d'Espoir,* Vol. I, (Paris: Plon, 1970), pp. 142, 144.

7 The volume that Gilbert Pilleul has recently edited (*L'"'Entourage"' et de Gaulle,* Paris: Plon, 1979) sheds some light on the attitudes of de Gaulle and his advisers on the devaluation of the franc. J. M. Jeanneney recalls that a couple of days before the declaration of November 28, 1968, de Gaulle apparently agreed that devaluation was necessary: although reluctant, he openly confessed his incompetence in economic matters and was ready to accept the majority opinion among his advisers. The experts who opposed devaluation (the same Jeanneney, Roger Goetze, Alain Prate, and Raymond Barre) managed to convince him at the very last moment that it was possible to maintain parity for the franc without impairing economic development. The two points we have made in the text are confirmed by this story. On the one hand, the primacy of the goal of economic growth: Had it been unanimously presented as a necessary means for reaching that goal, de Gaulle would have swallowed the devaluation. On the other hand, the strong relevance of the parity goal: De Gaulle was satisfied by the minority opinion that growth and parity of the franc were not incompatible.

8 A political analysis of these, and of the deficit of the Italian public administration can be found in M. Salvati, "The Italian Inflation," mimeo. Paper presented to a conference on *The Politics and Sociology of Global Inflation and Recession* (Washington, D.C.: The Brookings Institution, December 10–13, 1978).

9 For a brief discussion of the state of studies in Italy see F. Modigliani and E. Tarantelli, "Forze di mercato, azione sindacale e la curva di Phillips in Italia," *Moneta e credito* (April–June, 1976): pp. 3–35. For France see D. Mitchell, "Incomes Policy and the Labor Market in France," *Industrial and Labor Relations Review* (25: 3) (April 1972): 315–335.

10 A review of the discussion and a balanced analysis of the principal tendencies of Italian international commerce is found in F. Onida, "La collocazione dell'Italia nel commercio internazionale," *Giornale degli economisti e annali di economia,* 36 (new series): 11/12 (November–December, 1977): 663–717.

11 The history of the Center-Left is told in great detail by G. Tamburrano, *Storia e cronaca del centro-sinistra* (Milan: Feltrinelli, 1973).

12 A good review of the studies on the Christian Democrats can be drawn from G. F. Pasquino, "Recenti trasformazioni nel sistema di potere della Democrazia Cristiana," in *La crisi italiana,* Vol. II eds., L. Graziano and S. Tarrow, (Turin: Einaudi, 1978). The point of view mentioned in the text is very close to Pasquino's and to that of G. Amato, *Economia, politica ed istituzioni in Italia* (Bologna: Il Mulino, 1976).

13 For an analysis of the influence and the role of traditional interest groups in the Christian Democratic power system, see S. Berger, "Uso politico e sopravvivenza dei ceti in declino," in *Il caso italiano,* eds. F. L. Cavazza and S. R. Graubard, (Milan: Garzanti, 1974).

14 The scarce literature on this subject is reviewed in A. Martinelli, "Borghesia industriale e potere politico," in *La politica nell' Italia che cambia,* eds. A. Martinelli and G. F. Pasquino, (Milan: Feltrinelli, 1978), which furnishes an interpretation similar to that which follows. For a journalistic account of "assisted capitalism" see E. Scalfari and G. Turani, *Razza padrona* (Milan: Feltrinelli, 1974).

15 The best works on the Italian public administration are those of S. Cassese. See, for example, the introduction to *L'Amministrazione pubblica in Italia*, ed. S. Cassese (Bologna: Il Mulino, 1974), and S. Cassese, *Questione amministrativa e questione meridionale* (Milan: Giuffré, 1977).

16 On Italian unionism, see Volume XVI of the Annals of the G. G. Feltrinelli Institute, *Problemi del movimento sindacale in Italia* (Milan: Feltrinelli, 1976). The introduction by A. Accornero and the third section are particularly relevant.

17 See Jack Hayward, *The One and Indivisible French Republic* (London: Weidenfeld and Nicholson, 1973).

18 This is Pierre Birnbaum's thesis, *Les Sommets de l'état* (Paris: Seuil, 1977), pp. 64–6.

19 On the aims of the plan see, for example, Y. Ullmo, *La Planification en France* (Paris: Dalloz, 1974). A "pure Gaullist" exposition of the motivations for the economic policy is found in A. Prate, *Les Batailles économiques du général de Gaulle* (Paris: Plon, 1978).

20 On French agricultural policy see *Vingt ans d'agriculture française, 1948–1968*, special issue of *La Revue française d'économie et sociologie rurale*, (79–80) (1969).

21 The first theory (the official PCF position) is presented in Henri Claude, *Gaullisme et grand capital* (Paris: Ed. sociales, 1960). For the second see, Nicos Poulantzas, *Pouvoir politique et classes sociales* (Paris: Maspero, 1968).

22 See, for example, Andrew Shonfield, *Modern Capitalism*(London: Oxford University Press, 1969), p. 137. There is a review of the criticisms of excessive discrimination deriving from "soft" planning in Vera Lutz, *Central Planning for the Market Economy* (London: Longmans, 1969), p. 46.

23 Ambroise Roux (vice-president of the CNPF) in "Les Charges qui pèsent sur l'industrie," *Le Monde*, May 6 and 13, 1969, lists the demands of big business. The Pompidou–Chaban–Giscard Administration was to satisfy many of these requests.

24 In the public sector wages were subject to ceilings set by the so-called "Toutée" procedure. In the private sector, to give one example, Prime Minister Debré recommended to the CNPF in 1961 that salary increases not surpass 4 per cent. Management found this too restrictive.

25 The classic text is J. D. Reynaud, *Les Syndicats en France* (Paris: Seuil, 1975).

26 Increases in CGT autonomy from the PCF did not proceed from the concerns of unionists. Rather, the PCF itself recognized the "political" value of the "economic" struggle. "The new division of labor did acknowledge that the PCF could not hope to control the labor market throught the CGT in a narrowly political way. But PCF and CGT actions in their respective spheres were meant to be complementary." George Ross, "Party and Mass Organization: The Changing Relationship of PCF and CGT." in *Communism in Italy and France*, eds. D. L. M. Blackmer and S. Tarrow, (Princeton, N.J.: Princeton University Press, 1975), p. 539.

27 Speculation on the franc, fed by lack of confidence in the government's policy, probably contributed to this decision. The Gaullist L. Vallon (*Notre République* [November 22, 1968]) sees a direct connection between speculation on the franc and the Gaullist project for participation.

28 Even the surplus in the trade balance was held within tight limits (1 percent of the GNP).

29 See Bernard Brizay, *Le Patronat* (Paris: Seuil, 1975), Chaps 2 and 3; and the views in Claude Alphandery, *Pour nationaliser l'état* (Paris: Seuil, 1968).

30 Jacques Ceyrac (vice-president of the CNPF) interview given to *Dirigeant*, 23 (June–July, 1971): 20–21.

31 See J. D. Reynaud, P. Maclouf, J. Dassa, and S. Dassa, "Les Evénéments de mai–juin 1968 et le système français de relations professionelles," *Sociologie du travail*, 13: 1 (1971): 73–97.

32 On the repercussions in unions of the conflict within the Left, see J. Poperen, *L'Unité de la gauche* (Paris: Fayard, 1975), pp. 150–220; also, Edmond Maire and Jacques Juillard, *La CFDT d'aujourd'hui* (Paris: Seuil, 1975), Chap. 5.

33 Personal communication to the author by a high functionary in the *Confindustria*.

34 See M. Salvati, "The Italian Inflation," *op. cit.*

35 A chronicle of these initiatives can be found in D. Speroni, *Il romanzo della Confindustria* (Milano: Surgarco, 1976).

36 The most important research is that organized by A. Pizzorno and published in six volumes between 1974 and 1978. The last volume contains the summary essays: A. Pizzorno, E. Reyneri, M. Regini, I. Regalia, *Lotte operaie e sindacato: il ciclo 1968–1972 in Italia* (Bologna: Il Mulino, 1978). For the testimony of one of the protagonists in that cycle of conflict, Bruno Trentin, then secretary of the CGIL Metalworkers' Federation see B. Trentin, *Da sfruttati a produttori* (Bari: De Donato, 1977). In English, of the research group previously mentioned, see I. Regalia, M. Regini, and E. Reyneri, "Labour Conflicts and Industrial Relations in Italy, 1968–1975," in *The Resurgence of Class Conflict in Europe*, eds., C. Crouch and A. Pizzorno, (London: Macmillan, 1978).

37 The restrictive policies of Italian authorities between summer 1969 and summer 1970 and de Gaulle's open refusal of a devaluation strategy in November 1968 did not provoke any negative reactions from the Italian and French business associations. The main polemical targets in that period were, for the Italian association, the "illegal" actions of the unions and the government's weakness in opposing them; for the French association, "les charges qui pèsent sur l'industrie." In its official statements, the CNPF consistently opposed devaluation. At the general assembly of June 17, 1969, Ambroise Roux declared that "devaluation is inadequate as a monetary measure, since reserves are still sufficient, and it is unnecessary as an economic measure," adding: "The duty of the government is not to devalue the franc; on the contrary it is solemnly to promise the nation that the parity of the franc will remain unchanged." When the devaluation was already a *fait accompli*, the CNPF was to show "surprise" and state that "devaluation, by itself, will not solve the basic problems which constrain the economic, social and psychological equilibrium of the country and the growth of the economy." [See *Patronat français*, 298 (August–September 1969): 3.] Given the advantages that devaluation would have brought to French large industry, it is difficult to avoid the impression of a verbal "façade."

12

A century of politics and interests in Spain

JUAN J. LINZ

Spain in the last one hundred years has been governed by five different political regimes: a liberal oligarchic constitutional monarchy, a military dictatorship attempting to institutionalize itself, a short-lived democratic republic, an authoritarian regime of Franco for almost forty years, and now a democracy which is in process of consolidation.

Over this century Spanish society and economy have undergone a slow but more recently a rapid economic and social change. In the nineteenth century Spain was an agricultural country, with 72 percent of the male labor force in agriculture. The economy was largely a subsistence rather than a market economy. Modern commercial, and industrial capitalism developed only in a few centers in the periphery, particularly in Catalonia and somewhat later in the Basque country, the mining enclave of Asturias, and some commercial agriculture areas.[1] The nation's capital was the political-administrative and, to a large extent, educational and cultural center, but even though it played a central role in the financial system until recent decades, it was not an industrial city.[2] Foreign capital played a very important role in the expansion of the railroads and in the exploitation of mining resources. Whereas in 1930 only 10 percent of the population in the United Kingdom depended on agriculture, 22 percent in Germany, and 27 percent in France, it was still 50.2 percent in Spain. Spain would not be an industrial country until the sixties, although some parts of the nation were heavily industrialized long before. Neither the economy nor society, however, was as dependent on agriculture as was Eastern Europe, and therefore the economic and social interest conflicts have had more in common with what would become the "Europe of the Nine" than with the agrarian East. Even when the development of democratic institutions in contrast to liberal institu-

365

tions has been slow and painful, the importance of a Western urban social structure, of professional and bureaucratic middle classes, and of commercial activity, and an incipient industrialization have provided a very different context for the articulation of economic and social interests.[3] In many respects, Italy provides the most valid comparison, although the Spanish economic, social, and geographic dualism is less accentuated than that between the north and the Mezzogiorno. In Spain the state developed before the age of nationalism and since the turn of the century found itself increasingly challenged by emerging peripheral nationalisms – first in Catalonia and later in the Basque country.[4] The multilingual and multicultural character of Spain and the peripheral nationalisms against the state provide a context that cannot be ignored in the study of the evolution of the interest conflicts and that has no equivalent in Italy, Portugal, or Greece.

Although it lagged in economic development, Spanish society had undergone radical changes on the road to modernity. Feudalism had been weakened by a powerful monarchy, and the Napoleonic invasion made possible the political revolution that had dismantled the estate system earlier than in other European societies, deprived the nobility of seignorial rights, made military careers accessible to commoners up to the highest levels, and established freedom of commerce and occupation by doing away with guild privileges that still existed.[5] The sale of mortmain of the church and public bodies had created a new landowning bourgeoisie, whereas aristocratic and bourgeois latifundia owners enjoyed a privileged position in relation to farm laborers and tenants.[6] Much of the countryside was populated by independent medium and small peasants. The political turmoil, the civil and colonial wars, the expansion of the bureaucracy, and the emergence of the political class provided unusual opportunities for social mobility in spite of economic backwardness. Political instability contributed to the delegitimation of traditional institutions. We should not forget that Spain proclaimed itself a republic almost at the same time that Germany and Italy unified under their monarchy. Despite a certain isolation from Europe reflected in the lack of active involvement in the power conflicts leading to World War I and its nonparticipation in World War II, Spain was open to ideological influences from abroad. All the constitutional texts or their preambles refer to European or American models. The great ideological and social conflicts, many of the legislative innovations, sometimes in a delayed and distorted form, reflect the patterns developed in other European countries.[7]

Of the distinctive characteristics of interest politics in Spain, perhaps the most noteworthy is that politics takes precedence over interests. Partisan cleavages are more important than interest conflicts. The articulation of interests on a permanent and continuous basis is therefore delayed and in part unsuccessful. This does not mean that interest, economic, and social groups do not exercise a decisive influence on the policy-making process but that their institutionalization and legitimation is less successful than in other countries. Perhaps the organization and legitimation of interests requires prolonged periods of political stability; they may to some extent be incompatible with intense conflicts. The struggle between an early liberalism and absolutism after the 1812 constitution, the Carlist civil war in the thirties, the conflict between *Progresistas* and *Moderados*, between republicans and monarchists, between unitary and federalist republicans, clericals and anticlericals, Socialists and anarchists, Socialists and syndicalists and within the Socialist party in the thirties, and the peripheral nationalisms and the centralist state all aroused passions, popular mobilizations, and violence, which left little room for the defense of more concrete and narrow interests, for bargaining, and for the creation of stable organizations. This does not mean that behind the ideological conflicts there were no real social and economic interests or different ways to defend those interests.

Leadership was recruited and legitimated by achievements ranging from military success to oratorical and demagogic capacity rather than by continuous representation of social or economic constituencies in the day-by-day policy-making process. Political alignments very often crosscut interest groups, with political considerations taking precedence over economic interests. This resulted in shifting and sometimes paradoxical and covert alliances, particularly in the three-cornered conflicts among the central government, the peripheral nationalisms, and the labor movement. The salience of the religious conflict gave politics an ideological dimension that heightened and cut across class conflicts and distracted attention from other possible alliances. The growth of the middle class, whose status and income was more dependent on the state than on the economy, contributed to the importance of ideological rather than interest politics, as did the relatively greater role of professionals and civil servants in the political elite than of businessmen.

The army, serving as an arbiter in conflicts, as an institution with independent prestige and power, as an interest group defending its own status, as a potential ally for social and economic interests, and as a defender of national unity, also played a role that in more stable politics would be left to interest groups.[8] The role of the army in industrial conflicts is especially significant in this regard. Sometimes it repressed strikes and revolutionary movements, other times it forced employers to give in to the demands of workers for the sake of public order and political stability.[9]

The political class controlling the state under the different regimes, as we shall see, was relatively independent of civil society. The control of the state apparatus, the manipulations of elections, the granting of privileges, and the control of violence often rendered the political class relatively autonomous and independent of interests or at least able to discriminate among them. Sectors of society that became conscious of how their interests were being neglected turned not against other sectors but against the state and its representatives: the politicians, the bureaucrats, and the agents of public order. This is not only the case of the anarcho-syndicalist labor movement but also, in certain situations, of the peripheral bourgeoisie in Catalonia and of broad segments of the agricultural and commercial middle classes alienated from the parliamentary regime earlier this century.

The salience of ideological conflicts, of the clerical–anticlerical cleavage, and of peripheral nationalisms, contributed to the fragmentation of interest alignments and organizations, to the importance of regional and local differences, and ultimately to the weakness of nationwide interest organizations. This fragmentation also allowed the government to play on the regional or local level with one or another group, making concerted action difficult in terms of class alignments or broad movements for political reform based on dissatisfied sectors of the society.

Class conflicts, particularly in the three most industrialized regions – Catalonia, the Basque country and Asturias, and sporadically in the countryside, particularly the Guadalquivir valley and, after 1931, in latifundia Spain – were the basis for militant labor organizations that on occasion turned to revolutionary action.[10] The bitterness of class conflict that ultimately led to semirevolutionary general strikes, local or regional insurrections, the October revolution in 1934, and ultimately the Civil War should not hide the fact that over most of the period under consideration the labor movement was weak by comparison with other countries. Spanish labor lacked numbers, organizational and economic resources for strikes, success at the polls, and capacity for nationwide coordinated revolutionary activities. The violent confrontation with employers and authorities reflected in part that weakness and periods of high mobilization and intense conflict were succeeded by others of disintegration and defeatism, which cannot be explained exclusively by repression by the government. The history of Spanish labor in a comparative European perspective needs to be written, and therefore explanations should be taken with caution.[11]

One decisive factor, obviously, was the existence of a massive re-
serve army of unemployed or underemployed workers, the basic underdevelopment and poverty of the country. This gave employers a
capacity to resist; many were rigid in defense of their often quite
fragile position. The government or its local representative, the prefect, and sometimes the highest military authority, intervened as ar-
bitrators, imposing their decision on the parties in conflict. Even with
trade union freedom, collective bargaining was only slowly and imperfectly institutionalized.[12] Recurrent economic crises exacerbated
those conflicts. To this we have to add the division of the Spanish
labor movement between Socialists and syndicalists and their two
rival federations – the Unión General de Trabajadores (UGT) and the
Confederación Nacional del Trabajo (CNT), with their regional im-
plantation and occasional competition within a city or trade.[13] The
ethnic division between mostly immigrant workers and the Basque
working class, reflected in the existence of a separate Basque trade
union movement, the Solidaridad de Obreros Vascos (SOV), founded
in 1911, and the presence of a weak but hated Christian trade union
movement, were further sources of fragmentation that made the institutionalization of conflict resolution mechanisms more difficult
than in countries with a unified labor or Socialist trade union movement or than in countries where the Christian trade unions had their
own areas of strength and were recognized as legitimate by the Socialists.

The corruption of the electoral process contributed to the alienation
of part of labor from the struggle for political participation and its opt-
ing for nonvoting in bourgeois parliamentary elections. The labor movement, after its flares of hope for revolutionary breakthroughs and its
occasional victories were spent, was ultimately dependent on the
goodwill of the government and authorities. Even the gains of labor
in the first two years of the Second Republic were due more to the
presence of Largo Caballero in the ministry of labor and to two more
Socialists in the government than to its bargaining power. The importance of the business cycle; the political crises, linked, for example,
with the Moroccan War; the sympathy of the authorities for the
mobilization of labor, and the occasional gains from employers also
account for the instability of organizations and large fluctuations in
membership of trade unions.[14]

In a number of countries with large Catholic populations, the
Church contributed much to spawn or sponsor organizations that
articulated social and economic interests.[15] In Spain, despite or
perhaps because of the intensity of the clerical–anticlerical conflict,
the Catholic subculture did not promote the creation of such organizations as it did in the Netherlands, Switzerland, Belgium, Austria,

Germany, and Italy. One factor must have been the absence of a clerical or Christian Democratic party. Only in 1920 did small groups of Social Christians attempt to form a Christian Democratic party. Shortly afterward the dictatorship of Primo de Rivera cut that development short. The great Catholic party of the thirties, the CEDA (Confederación Española de Derechas Autónomas) led by Gil Robles was too defensively clerical and conservative to play the same role as the Christian Democratic parties in other parts of Europe.[16] The progressive tendencies within Catholicism arrived too late to reach the industrial working classes and the farm laborers, who had already been secularized or at least committed to anticlerical positions.[17] Only among the medium and small peasantry of north-central Spain was the Church able to create a large organization, the Confederación Nacional Católica Agraria, which in the thirties would support CEDA and play an important role in the Catholic response to the anticlerical policies of the republic.[18]

It is not easy to account for the comparative weakness and lateness of the mobilization of the laity by the church. Dependence on the state, on the one side, and fear of upsetting the compromise achieved with the constitutional monarchy by allowing the mobilization of the antiliberal Catholic laity derived from Carlism, on the other, must be taken into account. The church enjoyed an established status in the 1876 constitution that on occasion was threatened by the mildly anticlerical traditions of the Liberals at the parliamentary level and by antisystem forces outside. Reliance on the state was reinforced by economic dependence, because after the sale of mortmain in the 1851 Concordate, the church needed the state for financial support. The right of presentation of nominees for the bishoprics, a historical legacy of the Spanish crown, made the careers of ecclesiastics dependent on the government and supported the policy of *ralliement* to the restored monarchy after almost a century of conflict. Early attempts of lay Catholic mobilization showed the importance of Carlist or Integrist sentiment among the most religious, particularly in the Basque country and Navarra, which would have led the hierarchy into conflict with the state. Later, the importance of regional nationalist sentiment among some of the most devout sectors in Spanish society would have been another source of conflict. In view of this, the creation of Catholic Action took place later in Spain than in other European countries.[19] There were early attempts to create a Catholic labor movement, but the role played by aristocratic and bourgeois supporters, and the consequent conflict between those who wanted fundamentally pious and charitable circles of workers favoring class cooperation and those favoring real unions, limited the success of these organizations. Official Catholicism of the Spanish state before 1931 made other forms of Catholic mobilization less necessary than in Protestant or more secularized societies. A decisive choice was made by the modernizers of Spanish Catholicism, particularly some Jesuits, by creating a small and elitist Catholic organization, the Acción Católica Nacional de Propagandistas (ACN de P), which has played a decisive role in Spanish politics during the republic and under the Franco regime. The ACN de P directed its attention to the elites of Spanish society, high civil servants, professionals, and academics rather than to a broad mass membership organization. The lay leadership of Spanish Catholicism and politics was recruited from this small group under the influence of Jesuits. This development must have delayed creation of the broadly based Catholic Action organizations that later developed functional organizations under Catholic sponsorship and inspiration and that have become independent interest groups in recent years.

Despite these differences, many of the factors that led to the organization and mobilization of interests in other countries have also been central in Spain. Certainly, labor conflict has been decisive in the emergence of employers' organizations – La Patronal – as well as in the struggle between free trade and protection, which lies at the origin of the most important regional industrial interest groups.[20] As in other countries, the need for regulation of the market, the desire to establish monopolistic practices, especially in times of crisis, the occasional need for the organization of export activities, and the need to respond to government intervention, particularly taxation, have led to the creation of interest groups. Within that common European pattern, the Spanish case presents some differences that can be understood better by a reference to the political and social contexts created by the different regimes in the period under consideration. It is to this aspect that we now turn.

The restauración: interest groups in an oligarchic, liberal, constitutional monarchy

The political system established in 1875 and reflected in the 1876 constitution provided almost fifty years of relative political stability, a wide range of political freedom, the emergence of an organized and increasingly tolerated and recognized labor movement, a serious effort to return the armed forces to their proper task, efforts to curtail the most extreme clerical ambitions, and an important record of legislation in all fields. The more apparent failures of the regime – loss of the colonies, war in Morocco, peripheral nationalisms, terrorism, labor violence, and ups and downs in many of its policies, aforementioned – created a recurrent climate of crisis, resulting in losses of effectiveness and legitimacy, which in 1923 led the way to a military takeover without resistance and with considerable support from large segments of the population.

The turn of the century was also a period in which the interest articulation found a legal framework;[21] made its first, rather unsuccessful, attempts to organize its potential constituencies; and moved between opposition to the system and collaboration with the politicians to achieve considerable gains. With the exception of the close link between Catalan business and the Lliga Regionalista (the party fighting for Catalan autonomy) and that of the Unión General de Trabajadores (UGT) with the Partido Socialista Obrero Español (PSOE), the interest groups were tied more to individual politicians than with either of the two system parties, Conservatives and Liberals.[22] Among the private interest groups, some of the most influential were regional, particularly in Catalonia and the Basque country rather than in the nation as a whole, reflecting great differences in industrialization and economic development.[23]

In a largely agrarian and underdeveloped society, organized interest groups were less important than the personal and family links between the political class and large landowners, bankers, railroad magnates, and many new industrialists. Their number and the concentration of wealth made organized interest groups less necessary than in other societies with a larger bourgeoisie. On the other hand, regional differences, particularly in the Basque country, ideological leanings such as republicanism, and ties with intellectual groups made some leading people in the economic development political outsiders. Public institutions for interest representation such as the Cámaras de Comercio, Industria y Navegación, the Cámaras Agrarias, the professional Colegios, and some early vehicles for interest representation and mediation of labor conflicts, such as the Instituto de Reformas Sociales (1903) (which provided an opportunity to the moderate segment of the Socialist Labor movement to represent workers), emerged in this period.[24] At the same time, there appeared a professional civil service in the tradition of the French *grand corps*, which in time would become one of the most effective forces in the policy-making process and in the defense of their own interests.[25] Legally and institutionally many of these bodies of interest representation have an excessively state-controlled character and only occasionally become the center of a more dynamic and aggressive representation of interests rather than bodies cooperating with the administration.

The defeat of Spain in the Spanish-American War (1898) made intellectuals deeply aware of the backwardness of the country and the need to modernize, and of the failure of the political class – parties, falsified elections, and Parliament. The protest found different channels; one was the call for mobilization of the "real" country identified with a wide range of interests: farmers, taxpayers, small businessmen, the "neutral masses." Under the leadership of Joaquín Costa, a self-educated polymath, together with Basilio Paraíso, the president of the chamber of commerce, the National League of Producers was formed in 1899 and then in 1900 the Unión Nacional[26] was established. The movement had elements of modern articulation of specific interests – "Poujadism" – and its ideology has been characterized as proto-Fascist. It ended closer to a shopkeepers' tax protest than to a broad *classes moyennes* movement and could not become a party nor help reform existing ones, even when some of its leaders joined the parties. The movement, however, led to a greater awareness of economic interests and the need for organizations, although it ultimately failed in its purpose to regenerate politics and the country. First the conservative leader Maura and later the dictator Primo de Rivera tried to capitalize on this diffuse sentiment, which was particularly strong in the provincial and agrarian regions of the Castillian-speaking interior, without deep class cleavages. The Catalan bourgeoisie, with its own interest organizations, party, and nationalist sentiment against centralism, remained outside and the sectors that responded to this sentiment would always feel uneasy about Catalan selfishness and the industrial oligarchies of the periphery. Later the CEDA, Falangism–Francoism, and now the UCD, represent those sectors. However, the hope for lively interest articulation of the middle classes, both of the countryside and city, has remained largely frustrated, reactive rather than innovative.

This is a period of parliamentary politics in which the leading personalities, consisting mostly of lawyers with oratorical abilities and inside knowledge of the machinery of the state and administration, governed with considerable independence from real constituencies and interests, thanks to their control over the electoral machinery. However, the system, designed by Antonio Cánovas with the cooperation of Práxedes Sagasta and modeled after the British two-party system, began to disintegrate after the disappearance of those two leaders and proved unable to structure the conflicts of civil society or to mobilize genuine electoral support. Ultimately weak and delegitimized, "parliamentary" government was pushed aside by the dictatorship. It is far from easy to account for the ultimate failure of this two-party system. To ascribe this failure to clientelistic and

largely corrupt electoral processes is really only to describe the phenomenon.[27] To attribute it to the tensions and discontents created by
deep crises such as the defeat of 1898, the Semana Trágica and its
aftermath in Barcelona, the Moroccan War, the crisis generated by
World War I and its subsequent economic difficulties and
semirevolutionary climate, the difficulties of handling emerging
peripheral nationalisms bears more weight but does not account for
the lack of internal change in the parties. One decisive factor must
have been the early introduction, by European standards, of universal suffrage in 1890 in a fundamentally agrarian society with a poor,
largely illiterate electorate, which was largely unaware of its interests
and therefore willing to give its votes to local notables or their representatives, or to tolerate with more or less grumbling the outright
manipulation, even falsification, of the electoral returns. The electorate of the cities and the rapidly industrializing areas did not carry
enough weight.

The Catalan bourgeosie turned to a regionalist autonomist and
partly nationalist opposition to the central political class rather than to
change within the party system.[28] In an overwhelming rural country
with many provincial capitals where middle-class elites not connected
with commerce and industry played an influential role, where
ideological differences divided those middle classes, and where family tradition divided the elites, the parties could not become identified
with fundamental social economic interests. Whereas in the United
Kingdom (overstating the case) the Conservatives identified with
a landed interest and the Liberals identified with emerging industrial
interests and increasingly served as a channel for some moderate
demands of the working class, and electoral politics forced the Conservatives to create an incipient organization to mobilize voters, in
Spain such a development could not take place. The sale of mortmain
had created a new bourgeois landowning class whose interest was
not in conflict with the aristocratic latifundia owners. These agrarian
elites very often lived in the cities; had close ties with professionals,
the administration, and even the military and the emerging industrialists; and rather than competing for power shared it and alternated
through the *turno pacífico* between political leaders. When one government faced failure it left power to another to "make" an election
and a new temporary majority in parliament. The raging debate between free trade and protectionism was only imperfectly articulated
through the parties, and representatives of regions with distinctive
economic interests could be elected independently of the position of
their party.[29] On the other hand, the Bilbao industrialists could

change party and still be reelected in response to government policies favoring or not favoring their interests.[30]

The pressure groups emerging in this period indirectly contributed to this development not by identifying themselves with either party but by maintaining an independence very often mixed with criticism of the failures of the parliamentary system and the political class. The same holds for the emergent ferment of intellectual criticism of the system by groups such as the Institución Libre de Enseñanza (1876), which put its hopes on an educational and cultural revival in society and studiously avoided direct involvement in partisan politics, although its link with the Liberals is obvious in the names of its patrons. This is also true for the great meeting of intellectuals initiated by Ortega y Gasset with the Liga de Educación Política in 1914, which could be considered a "public interest" group.

The nonpartisan character of much interest politics, combined with the lack of real mass mobilization, which is inevitable given the numerical weakness of the modern sectors of capitalist bourgeois society (except in Catalonia), prevents the kind of linkage between interests and parties that we find in other European constitutional monarchies in the same period. Nothing in Spain compares to the linkage between the Bund der Landwirte (1892) and the Conservatives in Germany or that between the industrialists and the National Liberale. Another likely factor was that the individual voter, particularly in the rural areas, had more direct ties with local notables or powerful representatives of the state – who controlled or influenced daily life through taxes, court cases, exemptions from military service, patronage in the bureaucracy – than he did with those exercising economic power. Landlords and employers thus lacked a solid basis of votes such as those of the east Elbian Junkers. The political class could win elections without effectively assuming the representation of economic interests by using the state apparatus and the favors it could grant its clientelistic network. Those who needed to defend their interests could always, in exchange for their influence on the voters, reach an understanding at the local level with the politicians without having to create nationwide organizations to bargain with the politicians. The uneven economic development between a few highly industrialized areas and extensive areas of subsistence noncommercial agriculture, and between latifundia and peasant Spain, the fragmentation of modern industrial interests due to their localization and the identification of the Catalan bourgeosie after 1900 with a regional autonomist movement, the dominant role of a financial capitalist oligarchy rather than the purely entrepreneurial industrial bourgeosie, and even the presence of foreign economic interests in sectors like mining must have contributed to that lack of articulation of interest group conflicts through the party system. Interests were represented through the party by politicians who were very often lawyers of railroad, mining, and industrial companies and who had close affiliations with the capitalist bourgeoisie, whose landed interests tied them to the agrarian economy. However successful the representation of interests in this mode, it did not produce clear alignments. The fact that Spain remained neutral in World War I prevented the strengthening of interest groups and integration of the labor movement which in many countries accompanied war economy planning and patriotic exultation. Even so, the economic crisis produced by the war led to some interventionist policies and the creation of a ministry of supplies, which affected business interests.

Any analysis of interest articulation around the turn of the century would be incomplete if it neglected the role of the press in Madrid, Barcelona, and even provincial capitals and smaller towns. At the time it was easy to create a newspaper, and leading journalists exercised considerable political influence with their campaigns and many gained seats in parliament. Particular newspapers became the most effective voice for economic interests, particularly in the debates on free trade and protection, as well as the basic source for information on economic matters, contributing to organizing the market and making and unmaking the political careers of leading figures. The same applies to some scientific and/or technical journals, such as the Revista Minera (1850–1914), which is closely linked with the economic development of the particular branch, and to a number of economic journals of information and those advocating protection. It is indicative of the role of the press that many newspapers called themselves *El Mercantil*.[31]

Another institution of the nineteenth century that played a role in the articulation of interests is the cultural association, such as the Barcelonise Ateneu Català founded in 1836. This association had sections devoted to agriculture, commerce, and industry and contrasted in its apoliticism with the homonymous institution founded in Madrid in 1820, which was so closely linked with the history of liberalism and later with the opposition to the dictatorship of Primo de Rivera. In many provincial cities and even in the larger agrotowns and villages, *atenos, liceos, casinos, and sociedades recreativas* became the meeting place of local notables, landowners, merchants, and industrialists. In an underdeveloped society where a small number of men engaged in such activities, communication between them and the representatives of the national elite involved in decision making was often better achieved in such settings than through formally organized interest groups. Even the names of some of the nineteenth century clubs reflected the interest in economic matters. One example is the Sociedad Sevillana de Emulación y Fomento, which was founded in 1843. The last word refers to what we today could call development, which was also the name of the ministry in charge of public works, agriculture, commerce, and industry. In Sevilla in the nineteenth century a number of such casinos linked with different social and economic groups were established.

One of them, the Real Círculo de Labradores y Propietarios (the royal circle of farmers and owners), founded in 1859, has survived to this day as a meeting place of the landowning elite of Sevilla and Andalucia.[32] As a matter of fact, its statutes stipulate that military officers, graduates of academies, and higher civil servants with university degrees could become visiting members, thus bringing aristocratic and bourgeois large landowners into contact with the elite. The death and decadence of this type of institution probably resulted from the dictatorship and the republic, and the weak role its officers play today in the Andalucian local elite indicates how some of their functions were progressively taken over by more formal organizations and political groups.[33]

The early localized, but visible, mobilization of working-class and farm discontent produced a highly class-conscious, ideological, moralistic, and weak labor movement with bursts of activity, occasional enthusiastic hopes of revolution, trade union reformist bargaining, and extremely slow electoral progress. The Spanish working class, divided after 1910 between those committed to the socialist UGT and to a lesser extent the PSOE, under the charismatic leadership of Pablo Iglesias and the anarchosyndicalist Confederación Nacional del Trabajo (CNT), with its antiparliamentary commitment, remained isolated and ineffective. It could not establish the link that trade unions in other European countries had with the Left liberal parties. Because of its small membership, economic dependence, and low level of education, the Spanish trade union movement was weaker organizationally and electorally than the Italian trade union and Socialist movement (even before the extension of suffrage in 1913) in the north.

Perhaps the keys to this period are the persistence of a political class largely through the electoral mechanisms of *caciquismo*, its capacity to govern with a minimum of flexibility using the legislative process, and an increasingly effective administration that did not, however, speak for the real country – the *país real*. Ultimately those interests depended on the politicians to achieve their goals or were condemned to opposition to the system, such as the labor movement.

The dictatorship: attempts to co-opt social corporatism, incentives to interest articulation, and failure to institutionalize a corporative regime

In September 1923, the military governor of Barcelona, Primo de Rivera, staged a bloodless coup, which initially established a purely military directory.[34] Later, the dictatorship faced a political vacuum that it tried to fill with the civil–military directory, co-opting civil servants and professionals to initiate a period of development made possible by prosperity. Some success did not, however, hide the incapacity to achieve political institutionalization. The Unión Patriótica conceived as a civil movement rather than as a real political party could not serve as a support to the regime and had little in common with a modern mass party like the Partito Nazionale Fascista (PNF) in Italy. As a halfway out, the dictator convened a consultative Asamblea Nacional to which he invited the representatives of interest groups from the official chambers and professional *colegios*, academies, and universities, as well as private interest group representatives, the administration and regime officials, and those elected by the largely lifeless Unión Patriótica.[35] In this corporativist attempt, Primo de Rivera tried to enlist the UGT and, through it, the Socialist party. The more political wing of the party, committed to democracy and potentially to republicanism, refused this co-optation to the Asamblea, but trade union leaders, more interested in the defense of workers than in political principles, cooperated with the regime by sitting in the Consejo de Estado in the person of Largo Caballero and in the labor management boards – the *Comités Paritarios* – established by the labor minister Eduardo Aunós in 1926–28. It is significant that the powerful leader of the coal miner union, Llaneza, met with the dictator during this period.[36] Some of the Social Catholics also were co-opted in the regime. The *Dictadura* policies are closer to what Philippe Schmitter calls social corporatism than to the state corporatism of Mussolini and Salazar. The possible influence of the Italian corporatist Fascist model is highly debatable; but Primo de Rivera never saw himself as a Spanish Mussolini. He attempted neither a real mass mobilization nor a totalitarian state that would break totally with liberal constitutional and democratic traditions.

The institutional impasse of the dictatorship, combined with the growing opposition of intellectuals and students, the demands of the old political class to return to constitutional government, the discontent in the army, and finally, the impact of the world economic crisis, undermined the Primo de Rivera alternative and led to his resignation and exile. The dictatorship had destroyed the political system of the constitutional monarchy but proved unable to create new institutions in spite of its achievements in many fields. Eventually, the monarchy had to turn over power to the opposition, swelled by accumulated discontents, which had little experience in government and few ties to the many conservative sectors of society.

The Primo de Rivera period is of great importance in our analysis of interest group politics, for by displacing the political system of the Restauración and by committing itself to the participation in power of "real" society (and therefore economic interests, including labor), it contributed decisively to the increasing articulation of a wide variety of interests. The fact that this coincided with a period of economic development and the beginnings of regulatory activity also contributed to this process. Social corporatism received a boost during this period and many of the organizations created then are still active. The principle of representation of interests in a variety of public regulatory and advisory bodies was institutionalized and the labor arbitration bodies were, with fundamental modifications, taken over by the republic and the Socialist leadership. This indirectly limited pressures on employers and workers to bargain collectively rather than rely on binding authoritative decisions. At the same time, the muting of class conflict on a national scale and the encouragement of reformist trade unionism did not force employers to develop a nationwide organization; regional, local, and sectoral economic interest groups remained outside larger representative bodies. The rapid economic development of a few successful enterprises within a protected market facilitated monopolistic tendencies. Private law corporations acted as lobbies and market regulators while narrow but effective interest groups emerged in steel, paper, cement, sugar, cotton, canning, and so forth. In many cases the interest groups can hardly be distinguished from cartel-like monopolistic groups and organizations that served the few dominant firms.

The policies of the Primo de Rivera regime are an interesting example of state-guided but not planned development policies of an authoritarian regime in a semideveloped capitalist society. The dictatorship attempted to coordinate the myriad interest groups, ranging from fairly large federations, such as the Fomento del Trabajo, to organizations dominated by a few enterprises; local groups, such as the *appellation controlée* of wines; public bodies, such as the official chambers of commerce; and totally private groups by giving them representation in the Consejo de la Economía Nacional and in the Asamblea Nacional Consultiva. After creation of the national economic council in 1924, each year new groups were granted representation. The debates in those bodies reflect their incapacity to articulate general policies and the constant demands for protection, subsidies, limits on the opening of new firms, official credit – a variety of disaggregated policy demands.[37] Another characteristic feature of the period is the creation of a large number of regulatory boards and commissions, which consisted of representatives of the administration; those of all the interested parties. The civil servants representing the administration on those boards devoted only limited time to that task (as Calvo Sotelo, the finance minister at the time, admitted), initiating a practice that would continue to the present. Membership in many of these bodies was obligatory for all the producers, and the dues exacted often took the form of a fixed percentage of production, in fact, a tax that was neither recorded nor controlled by the budget. The primary purpose was to limit production in order to keep prices up; a policy that ultimately affected competitiveness in many sectors and that substituted a policy of price supports for policies directed toward an expansion of the internal market. During this period a policy of intervention in wheat, wine, oil, rice, and meat markets, among others, was instituted. The dictatorship enormously expanded policies that had been initiated in the years after World War I and that were reflected in a decree enacted two months after the *coup d'état*, reorganizing the Committee on Commercial Treaties by giving representation to the most important industrial and agrarian interest groups as well as to the UGT and the Catholic trade union.

Another example of this policy is the creation of the Confederaciones Hidrográficas, which Velarde compares to the TVA (Tennessee Valley Authority) in the United States. All the affected parties were represented in an assembly: the communities in the river basin, the users of water from irrigation dams and canals, the producers of electricity, the users of electricity, the provincial administrations, the chambers of commerce and agriculture, and the representatives of the ministries, under the chairmanship of a president and with the assistance of the technical director and legal adviser appointed by the Ministry of Public Works. In the case of the Ebro Valley, this assembly had 121 members and a governing junta of twenty-seven members representing those interests. This institution, like others created by the regime, still survives and plays an important role in forming policy on public works and use of water resources.

There is a fundamental difference between the corporatism of

Primo de Rivera, which built on existing interest groups independent of their political orientation or on ad hoc creation, and the corporatism of the Law de Unidad Sindical of 1940 and the Ley de Cortes of 1943, which created a corporative structure *ex novo* by outlawing and absorbing existing groups and creating by law a limited number of functionally differentiated and hierarchically ordered constituent units. In these, only institutions of public law were given representation. In many ways the dictatorship's system of interest group representation is a halfway house between pluralism and corporatism. And in particular, the recognition of the UGT meant that no interclass peak associations of employers and workers were attempted.

The corporatist policies of the regime were not the result of ambitious ideological formulations like those elaborated in Italy. They were neither the result of a long historical tradition nor a cultural pattern. If there was any intellectual root to Primo de Rivera's design it was regenerationist thought – its critique of corrupted parliamentarism and its call to take account of the "real" rather than the "legal" country. In practice, the groups called to participate had emerged in the early decades of the century, partly in response to the postwar economic crisis and to specific situations not dissimilar to those leading to their creation in other countries. Their ad hoc character, their narrowness and number, did not make them an instrument of a rational economic policy.

The years of peace and order imposed by the dictatorship must have created a legacy of latent sympathy for authoritarian rule among conservative interests that would make their adaptation to the Franco regime easier. The Primo de Rivera period was in a sense a more liberal and humane, but politically ineffective, version of the harsh regime that Franco would establish after the sudden and passionate mobilization of all the discontents and cleavages of Spanish society in the thirties. The dictatorship provided an embryonic model of an active state with an emphasis on public works, the *estado de obras*, heralded by the ideologists of the developmental phase of the Franco regime. In this period, too, the public sector of the economy emerged with the founding of the petroleum sales monopoly, CAMPSA – under the initiative of Calvo Sotelo – and the image of technocratic ministers, recruited from the prestigious professional corps, gained appeal.

The idea that the state through its bureaucracy should play a growing role in the development of the country by creating financial institutions to assist the municipalities, agriculture, and the export sector has its origin in the Primo de Rivera regime. Although political regionalization is rejected, a policy of administrative decentralization is instituted, with the creation of local bodies to regulate and administer harbors, water rights and irrigation, social welfare funds, and so on under the leadership of government-appointed officials (generally civil servants). This became a permanent feature of Spanish administration. In summary, although the Primo de Rivera regime failed totally in creating a political system, it initiated many of the corporatist tendencies that persist to this day. In addition, the role of the state in many of those bodies has offered opportunities for patronage and clientelism that have assured their survival under changing regimes.

The republic: *politique d'abord.* Interest politics in the shadow of class, religious, and regional conflicts

The republic proclaimed in 1931 represents a radical discontinuity on the conservative Right, in that few of the notables of the political parties of the restoration returned to Parliament. In their place a new generation of politicians appeared, many of whom had been recruited from the Catholic forces that had been revitalized in reaction to the anticlerical policies of the new regime.[38] The new bourgeois Left-Republican Socialist coalition initiated major new policies: a reform of the army, some anticlerical laws, an expansion of education, a half-hearted agrarian reform, and a successful institutionalization of regional autonomy. It also gave labor an opportunity to mobilize behind the great trade union federations, and allowed Socialists to penetrate the masses of farm laborers and initiate an expansion of labor legislation and gains for the trade unions and their members. These labor policies satisfied neither the anarcho-syndicalist activists, whose new hopes of revolution sparked local uprisings and violence, nor the large and militant CNT, which was unwilling to leave the field for the government-supported UGT.

The real change in the interest group politics of the period is the emergence of a powerful labor movement with masses of new recruits. This movement had little experience in collective bargaining and was divided and ambivalent as to whether to follow a strategy of institutionalization of labor conflicts with reliance on government support and political action through electoral mechanisms or, rather, to rely on mass mobilization in the hope of revolutionary outcomes. This activation of labor forced employers to organize more effectively, and the latent threat of socialization and workers control led to the emergence of a national organization of employers' groups, the Unión Económica Nacional, which remained rather inactive in the republic.[39] The changes in rural labor relations and the agrarian reform threatening the latifundia owners and its potential application (due to technical errors in the law) to more affluent peasant owners in north-central Spain mobilized rural interests against the reform proposal.[40] The ill-advised import of wheat, combined with an unexpectedly abundant harvest helped to arouse the wheat-growing countryside of dry Spain and particularly the Castilian peasantry, already agitated over the antireligious policies of the republic. In Catalonia the wine-growing tenant farmers organized in the Unión de Rabassaires, which was closely linked with the Left Catalanist nationalists of Esquerra and created a powerful pressure group that forced the regional parliament to pass legislation to which the old landowners' interest group, Instituto Agrícola de San Isidro (founded 1851) responded by encouraging the central government to question the constitutionality of that law.[41] The impact of the depression contributed to the mobilization of demands by a wide range of interest groups – from the professionals who wanted to exclude foreigners from working in Spain, to orange growers who were concerned with the impact of British imperial protection on their crop, to coal miners who were faced with foreign imports, and so forth. Ever-widening conservative discontent over the policies of the first *bienio* of Socialists and Republicans and the breakdown of their coalition over the demands of socialist labor, combined with an electoral law that gave great advantage to coalitions, contributed in 1933 to the victory of a more conservative Radical party and a new mass party of the clerical right – the CEDA – under the leadership of Gil Robles. The growing strength of Basque nationalism led to the founding of interest groups such as the Solidaridad de Obreros Vascos (Basque Workers Solidarity) (1911) in the trade union field, the Eusko Nekazarien Bazkuna (1933) to organize farmers, and the Agrupación Vasca de Acción Social Cristiana (AVASC), in which businessmen played a dominant role. This last group combined a Christian-social ideological orientation with nationalism and was linked to the Partido Nacionalista Vasco (PNV).[42]

There were important ties between the parties and the interest groups, particularly in the case of the Lliga in Catalonia and the right-wing Renovación Española with Bilbao big business and the landlords. However, politics ultimately was the arena of politicians who were mobilizing the population on broad ideological and symbolic issues, such as defense of religion, national unity, the family, and property. Interest politics became salient in a number of crises, but was rapidly transformed into broader conflicts. Thus the Ley de Cultivos in Catalonia became a conflict between Catalan autonomy and nationalism and the central government, when it had started as a conflict between the Catalan left and the Catalan landowners who were encouraging the rightist central government to question the constitutionality of the law. For example, a change in the wine tax in the Basque country, benefiting winegrowers with surpluses in other parts of Spain, contributed to the Basque municipalities' opposing the central government and allowing the Socialist leader Prieto to encourage a shift of Basque nationalism from the Right to the Center-Left. The serious crisis in coal mining in 1934 became fuel for a revolutionary attempt of the Socialist party in coalition with other Left bourgeois forces to stem the entry of the CEDA into the government, and was perceived by the Left as a threat comparable to that of Dolfuss in Austria in February 1934. The October 1934 revolutionary attempt was in a sense a preemptive revolution against what seemed to be a counterrevolution and transformed a possible fight among interests into a more total confrontation of ideas of policy and society. The relative calm of 1935, after the defeat of the revolution, is perhaps the period in which the interest groups were most effective in torpedoing the initiatives of some cabinet ministers, who were trying to cope with depression and social problems. At this time, the links between interest groups and parliamentarians of the parties of the majority became most important in blocking any constructive government policy and in condemning the new majority to sterility.

Interest politics may be more central to the period of the "black *bienio*" than much of historiography reports, but ultimately the defeat was due to conflict over political principles and the play between political leaders often moved by petty jealousies, mutual distrust, and longstanding enmities. It is significant that the outstanding study of Spanish interest groups' politics in this period by Manuel Ramírez[43] is to a large extent a study of the political process and the elites rather than of the organizations and their internal politics. The Socialist party, closely linked with the UGT, underwent a deep internal crisis, being torn between the maximalist wing, led by Largo Caballero, and the reformist pragmatic politician Indalecio Prieto. This conflict became decisive after the February 1936 election. There is no evidence that the trade unions lined up on one side while the party and its leadership held to another, or of particular trade union federations holding consistent positions throughout the period. The Asturias miners, for example, who had been the most enthusiastic supporters of a revolutionary line before October 1934, disassociated themselves from the maximalist position after the bloody defeat. Similarly, it is not easy to see a distinct social basis in the movement toward moderation of the so-called *treintistas* who wanted to move the CNT from its radical course toward more trade-union-like tactics and to disassociate it from the terrorist organization – the Federación Anarquista Ibérica (FAI) – which had penetrated it since the twenties.[44]

In this and other cases, political ideological climates at the local and regional level are important, for they cut across social and economic cleavages and groupings. The map of politicosocial violence after 1936 shows regional patterns that do not correspond neatly to well-defined differences in socioeconomic structure. The relative peace in Catalonia contrasts with the radicalization in Madrid, central Spain, and even Old Castile, in spite of the affiliation with the CNT in Catalonia and the Socialists in other regions. In fact, political factors, such as the competition between the two trade union federations, the presence of Communists and Falangists, and local problems, seem to provide a better explanation of the tension leading to the total polarization in the society than the initiative of organized interest groups or even socioeconomic factors.

The intensity of class conflict and the ideology of the labor movement probably had another consequence: There were few, if any, traces of conflict between the interest groups of medium or small-sized industrialists or shopkeepers and medium-sized owner-farmers and banks, big businesses, or big landlords. The class conflict ultimately aligned most of their interest groups, the various employers' organizations, and the chambers of commerce with the more economically powerful sectors of big business. This is one of the alignments that changed after Franco, with the emergence of interest groups of medium and small business. In the thirties there was middle-class resentment on status and cultural lines, but there was little middle-class politics in the sense of powerful *classes moyennes* interest groups and lobbies as in other West European countries. In some cases, impoverished small commerce, shopkeepers, and artisans, particularly where they had a working-class clientele, identified with the PSOE and affiliated with the UGT or even the syndicalist CNT. The more conservative and religious sectors of this class turned to the CEDA. The authoritarian and even pseudo-Fascist tendencies in that party, among other factors, however, limited the appeal of the newly founded Fascist groups. Ultimately, those sectors in other societies put their hope in Fascism when threatened by the Left; in Spain they put their trust in military intervention.

In summary, the republic was a period of social and political mobilization reflected in mass membership in political organizations, in the activism of minorities, and in the violence of local and fringe groups for political purposes. The integration of real socioeconomic interests in effective membership organizations for the day-by-day pressures and bargaining, as well as bidding for support of parties, was a secondary phenomenon. The fractioned party system cannot be understood in terms of links with interest groups in the same way that the Weimar party system can be at least partly interpreted. The broad coalitions required by the electoral law and the polarization of society appealed to the electorate by offering existential alternatives rather than using the influence of intermediary groups. The intense polarization of society penetrated arenas that might have been apolitical or professional. Elections for office in professional *colegios*, student and youth organizations, and probably private groups, such as recreational associations, became politicized.[45] As a symbol of that politicization I can remember from my childhood that the customers of the local bus lines from El Pardo to Madrid in the spring of 1936 tended to choose one or the other service based on political lines. Perhaps the full development of interest group politics requires either a stable democracy capable of avoiding the polarization and centrifugal tendencies of extreme multipartism or the depoliticization of a nontotalitarian authoritarian regime. Spain in the mid-thirties, with the sudden mobilization of all the cleavage lines of a society offered by a new democratic and ideological context, and by demagogic responses, and with the ineptitude of the government, was not the arena for stable institutionalized membership interest group politics. Trade unions, which in the twenties and at the advent of the republic were moving in the same direction as other European labor organizations, in Spain, became instruments in the struggle for power and in the mobilization of class conflict. Those sectors of Spanish society that were reluctant to enter into the confrontation, particularly in the regional peripheries, increasingly felt threatened, alienated, and forced to take sides.

Aside from a few isolated individual initiatives and the failed hopes put in political leaders like Azaña, no one person articulated a broad movement of citizens or interest groups to restrain the conflict and reequilibrate the political system. Ortega y Gasset's early call in 1933 to that effect went unheeded.[46]

The Franco regime: from military uprising, through arrested totalitarianism, to organic statist authoritarianism[47]

On July 17–18 the army took the initiative of a *pronunciamiento* with the support of the extreme Right and the sympathy of conservative sectors of society. It encountered the effective resistance of some forces loyal to the government, above all, the militant working class. This led to a civil war lasting for almost three years. The core of the resistance of the republican government was the working-class militia, recruited among the militant Left and trade unions, which quickly initiated a profound social revolution and took control in many parts of the country where it socialized production. The military, particularly where class conflict had been most bitter, enjoyed the active support of bourgeois and landowning interests. There was no time for interest politics in the ensuing struggle; working-class organizations were rapidly and brutally destroyed and repressed, as were on the other side all the organizations perceived as conservative or identified with the church. The new military authority assumed the "full representation of the collective interest" and in the September 13, 1936, proclamation outlawed political and interest group activity and gave power to local commanders. This clearly favored the conservative interests, although there were isolated manifestations of military populism. Political forces that were in the minority before the civil war and had few links with real socioeconomic interests, such as the small Fascist Falange Española de las JONS and the militant Carlists, began to play a more important role than the less militant conservative groups that had dominated the Right. Some Fascists saw this as the moment to organize the popular classes in their national-syndicalist structure, but the military and Conservatives did not favor such attempts. The political enthusiasm of militias and party members of extremist groups and the military officers proved insufficient for managing the problems of a modern state. The military Junta de Defensa had to be supplemented by a Junta Técnica del Estado, which served to some extent as a civilian cabinet and began regulating the economy with technocratic criteria.

In addition to a disproportionate representation of the military officers and higher civil servants in the junta, there were those who had already played a role in the Primo de Rivera regime and a significant number of people who had important connections with the financial and industrial oligarchy, as well as some large landowners. The relative importance of these two last groups in the Francoist elite was reduced with the greater institutionalization of the regime at the end of the civil war and the entry of old and new Falangists into the cabinet in the first period of Franco's regime. A new political class, recruited from the "political families" that had supported the uprising, came into being: Falangists, traditionalists, monarchists, and Catholics, all co-opted by appointment by Franco.[48]

The new men, particularly the Falangists, were neither by age nor regional origin nor social origin linked with the organized interests of business. They hoped to create a corporative system to integrate the defeated working class, disciplining it and at the same time giving it more symbolic than real participation in the new state. They sought to integrate the professional, technical, and middle classes and the employers into the "service of a national economy," a single large organization politically controlled by party men. The execution of this grand design, which inspired the Ley de Unidad Sindical of 1940, was "sidetracked" by the resistance of powerful interests to such a Gleichschaltung along German or Italian lines. The free professions and their *colegios profesionales* were exempted, the Cámaras de Comercio managed to survive, although weakened and co-opted by government.[49] However, the powerful Catholic rural organization was, despite its resistance, finally incorporated under special conditions. Segments of the business community managed to save from absorption the powerful and effective interest groups legally constituted as commercial corporations. Some of the regional business groups linked with the financial industrial oligarchy, such as the Fomento del Trabajo, the Liga Vizcaína, and the Liga Guipuzcoana de Productores, survived but kept a low profile throughout the regime. As the official *sindicatos* structure developed in the mid-forties, some specialized groups were incorporated into the large national *sindicatos*, retaining, however, considerable autonomy and continuity. Of the seventy-one organizations that formed part of the Unión Nacional Económica, in the thirties, twenty-six survived, two with a change of name but not of function and two as official bodies. Of thirty-six with headquarters in Madrid, twenty had disappeared. Of the twenty-one in Barcelona only six survived in the late fifties, and four of the eight located in the Basque country survived.[50] Although the law for syndical unity controlled the creation of interest groups by allowing the syndical organization to veto any group that represented class or professional interests, a few managed to emerge by finding sponsors in ministries unsympathetic to the Falangist aspirations to hegemony. Others circumvented the law by creating commercial law organizations in which a small group of enterprises with considerable economic power participated. While *Gleichschaltung*, favoring corporatist organizations controlled largely by the Falangists, was not fully successful, even organizations like the *cámaras* and *colegios* were subordinated to national control, and for a long time their officers were government appointments and not chosen through elections. These appointees had a background in the profession or in the business community, but their selection responded to political criteria and clientelistic ties with the new political class. The smaller businessmen in the less industrialized regions found in the *sindicatos* the possibility to make themselves heard, whereas the large entrepreneurs in the advanced industrial regions, with their contacts with top-level national elites and their independent, specialized interest groups, had less need for and less confidence in the *sindicatos*.[51]

The labor charter Fuero del Trabajo (1938) stated that the national syndicalist organization of the state would be "inspired by the principles of unity, totality, and hierarchy." All elements of the economy were to be organized in *sindicatos verticales* by branches of production or service and hierarchically ordered under the direction of the state; the organization was to be "an instrument to service the state, through which it would realize its economic policy." The hierarchies of the *sindicatos* were necessarily to be recruited from militants of FET y de las JONS. The *sindicatos* "would be concerned with problems of production and propose solutions in the national interest." Although the *sindicatos* structure was supposed to incorporate the working class into the regime, it was unable to do so. In contrast to the Nazis, who had a certain working-class following – an incipient trade-union organization in the National-Sozialistische Betriebszellen-Organisation (NSBO) before 1933 – and the Italian Fascists, who could build on trade unions they had created or taken over before the March on Rome, the small pre-civil war Falange had never been able to develop its Central Obrera Nacional Sindicalista (CONS).

A decisive event in the development of the Franco regime was the control of the Ministry of Labor in 1941–57, by a powerful personality, the Falangist José Antonio Girón, while the *sindicatos* had a less forceful leadership. The regulation of labor relations by decree remained fundamentally in the hands of the Ministry of Labor. In addition, Girón expanded the social security system and created a national health service. The result was that the welfare state activities were based on citizenship rather than on membership or participation in the *sindicatos*, thus depriving these organizations of the mechanism of legitimation and source of clientelistic loyalties. In this respect they were in a very different position from that of the Deutsche Arbeitsfront (DAF), or even the Mexican Partido Revolucionario Institucional (PRI). The leadership of *sindicatos* was a preserve of Falangists, although with time, professionals recruited into their bureaucracy began to look for projects that were sometimes in favor of the workers, and sometimes related to local economic development studies, statistics, and marketing, all useful to businessmen. The representation allotted to *sindicatos* in the Cortes in 1943 gave officials a new status and influence, but it also became necessary to consider making representatives of employers, technicians, and workers more "representative" through a complex system of multistage elections. At the same time, the *sindicatos'* tax on all wages and salaries – the *cuota sindical* – provided the organization with a solid financial basis.[52]

The mid-fifties was a crucial period for the regime. The first labor strikes took place, and with them a wage hike which, when accompanied by inflation, a serious crisis in the balance of payments, and international pressure, led to the stabilization program.[53] This shift was endorsed by a new cabinet appointed in 1957, in which a new group – the technocrats of the Opus Dei – assumed control of economic policy, introducing liberal measures that ended the previously autarchic economic development policies. In this context the 1958 law on collective bargaining was enacted.[54] It has often been argued that this law, with its de facto break with the verticalism of the *sindicatos* structure, responded to the needs of a neo-capitalist system for greater flexibility in labor relations. However, a 1960 survey showed that large numbers of employers did not favor collective bargaining, but preferred the old system of the *reglamentaciones* by the Ministry of Labor, which raises doubts about this functionalist-Marxist interpretation.

Perhaps a diffusion of institutions from advanced industrial countries and the need to adapt to the principles of the ILO (into which Spain had been admitted) may have played an equally important or more important role. The prospect of having a part in collective bargaining, and the continuity in the *sindicatos* secretariat of José Solís, a dynamic and crafty politician who also occupied the general secretariat of the party, helped give new vitality to the old structure. The Consejos de Empresa, a works-council type of organization, was created in the early fifties to represent the personnel and was elected by it. The increased freedom granted in the 1963 syndical elections and the decision by the Communists and the new Catholic activists to participate in the official structures rather than boycotting them, as the underground labor movements had in the past, initiated a complex and contradictory period of change in Spanish labor relations. Growing prosperity, migration to Europe, and full employment would also make labor protest more viable. The literature has emphasized this aspect but has tended to ignore another that accompanied it: a more dynamic economy's need for the services normally provided by economic interest groups – from collecting statistics and information to facilitating export operations, lobbying, and contacts with foreign counterparts. Some of the *secciones económicas* of *sindicatos* must have played a role in the period of indicative planning, but this aspect remains to be studied.

Economic and subsequent social change made the organized representation of interests increasingly necessary, but it also required legal changes and new government policies. These were introduced not so much to meet new needs but as the product of ideological commitments, the diffusion of institutions from other societies, and the initiative of influential higher civil servants and professors. In the world of interest representation, as in the political system, there was a limited pluralism, one that excluded any autonomous organization of the working class and limited even conservative forces. Some critics of the expression *limited pluralism* (coined to compare the situation with the totalitarian ideal type) have pointed out that it would be equally adequate to speak of a *unitary pluralism*. Interest politics did not disappear but was subordinated to Franco's ultimate power. These developments leave open the question of the extent to which the surviving groups and the new *sindicatos* structure and its leadership became identified with the interests they were supposed to regulate and represent and the extent to which they used their power for their own benefit or to pursue their own goals. Only analysis of concrete decision making processes and specific policies could answer these questions. Our impression is that *sindicatos nacionales* with formally identical functions developed very differently from the forties to the end of the regime. Some of them remained ineffective bureaucratic patronage organizations, others became technocratic instruments by performing some of the functions of real interest groups, such as gathering information; helping the business community, particularly smaller business and exporters; and serving as a channel for demands before the state bureaucracy and later before the committees of Cortes – the legislature created in 1943 where they would be represented. In some instances they became organizations closely connected to the informal leaders of the business community and were at their service. Our research on the Spanish business elites in 1960–1 provides evidence for all these patterns.[55]

On the other hand, there is no doubt that the new political elite used its power and influence to gain access to positions of economic power or privilege by occupying seats on the board of directors of the newly created enterprises of the public sector under the holding of the Instituto Nacional de Industria (INI)[56] and the boards of the public banks and private businesses, particularly the large corporations and increasingly the banks. Except for the INI enterprises, the new political elite's presence on the boards of directors did not give them control over these firms, but, rather, gave the old business elite access to the new power holders. Interests were not without influence; in fact, they could achieve, in some cases, outrageously privileged positions, but the system did not provide for their autonomous collective organizations and representation. This, as our interviews with top business leaders in 1960–1 revealed, made concerted action difficult and limited collective resistance to the decisions of the authorities. It allowed those with direct access to people in power a privileged position that they did not always share with their fellow industrialists and that gave them enormous opportunities to increase their personal, as well as their enterprises' wealth and influence.

State corporatism as an instrument of planning by a powerful state and corporatism as an instrument for the collective representation of interests attempting to control the state and create a self-managed economy in the hand of the economic leaders were both condemned to fail. The reality was a complex network of influences and mutual favors, in which economic rationality and consistent policy formulation were often impossible, and in which business won privileges at the cost of a considerable degree of collective impotence in relationship to those holding political power, for example, the ministries and the bureaucracy.

The Franco regime in no sense constitutes a viable example of institutionalization of the corporatist ideology reflected in doctrinal statements, legislation, formal institutions, and some academic commentaries on those instutions. The constitutional position of the corporative system (for instance, its share in the Cortes) should not obscure the fact that the corporative sector in that chamber shared its power with the appointees Franco recruited among the notables of the regime: politicians and military personnel, civil servants, and local elites of the regime. In the Cortes the corporative representatives did not play a role proportional to their representation.[57]

Particularly after 1945 the regime recruited some of its personnel from the Catholic sector, mostly men from the ACN de P (civil servants, professors, and free professionals), who had limited links with economic interests. Later, coinciding with a shift in economic policy in 1957, another Catholic organization, the Opus Dei, became a nursery of elites.[58] After the successful economic stabilization plan (1959), this group used its political power during the subsequent boom to create a large number of enterprises and banks that its members staffed and that provided influence and opportunities for that elite, which also occupied key positions in the public sector and the economically powerful savings banks. Both the ACN de P and the Opus Dei can be considered interest groups in that they were organizations defending the interests of the church. This was clearly the case of the ACN de P, closely linked with the hierarchy and serving its interests, but it was perhaps less so for the Opus Dei. In many respects these religious groups are more ideological-political groups than instruments of the representation of social interests, however, even those of the Catholic community.

The access of the political elites, the military, bureaucrats, Falangists, Catholics, and Opus Dei to positions of economic power in the public sector, and increasingly in the private sector, poses the interesting and difficult question of the extent to which political power can be transformed into economic power rather than the reverse. In an authoritarian regime that can reward its friends and punish those unwilling to cooperate with it, where public criticism is impossible, such a process might well be inevitable. It also poses the question of the extent to which new economic power holders became integrated and co-opted into the existing economic power structure and therefore served as a channel of access, thus making the organization of interest groups on a broader base less likely and to some extent less necessary for the most powerful groups and firms in the economy. An adequate answer to these two questions would greatly increase our understanding of interest group politics under the Franco regime.

The transformation and crisis of an authoritarian regime: interest groups as an arena for politics

The forty years of the Franco regime cannot be treated as a unitary phenomenon. Even though many of the basic laws enacted in the most Fascist and repressive post–civil war period remained in the books, and sometimes were even further developed, the political reality changed. Some of these changes resulted from the international context that delegitimized the regime after the defeat of the Axis powers and forced it to make concessions to international pressures, and to adapt its practice and occasionally its laws to gain a minimum of acceptability internationally; others resulted from the rapid economic and social change of the sixties and seventies, from generational turnover, or from changes in some key institutions, particularly in the Catholic church after Vatican II.[59]

The more liberal press laws of 1966 are the symbol of a new period of liberalization of the regime. It is a period in which a wide range of pseudo-semilegal, and even illegal, oppositions became visible and contributed to a climate of opinion that became decisive after Franco's death.[60] The regime attempted half-heartedly to respond to those changes and to those in the Church after Vatican II. So the Fuero del Trabajo was amended in 1966 and article 222 of the Criminal Code was changed to authorize (with some ambivalent language) economic strikes.

The debates internal to the regime about the liberalization and democratization of the party – the *Movimiento* – have been discussed at length elsewhere as has the creation of associations not of the *Movimiento* but under its protection, which represented a variety of interests, and engaged the "doves" and "hawks" of the regime in lively and sometimes bitter debates.[61] Interest groups, such as a group studying problems connected with entry into the Common Market under the leadership of Gil Robles Sr., became a focus of political activity. There was even an ill-fated effort to create political clubs along French lines. The late Franco period, with growing prosperity, urbanization, and limited liberalization, was characterized by the emergence of a larger number of voluntary associations,[62] some of which, like the neighborhood associations, were to be taken over by the Left, in particular, the Communists. They naturally have proliferated with democracy: feminist groups, gay liberation groups, common prisoners, consumer organizations, and so on. A few of these have fought successful battles against the administration, the national telephone company, and others. However, they, too, have been weakened by political fragmentation and ideological radicalization. In the process of politicization, issues that normally concern interest groups are instrumentalized politically, and to some extent the articulation and aggregation of interest is distorted.

In the labor field, the illegal organizations of the working class – the *Comisiones Obreras* – initially obtained the support of the workers on the basis of specific "bread and butter" grievances. On that basis they, with more or less repression, and within or outside the institutions of the *sindicatos* structure – particularly through the *jurados de empresa*, which they had infiltrated – were able to appear publicly as spokesmen for the work force.[63] The types of issues that provoked strikes during this period and the geographical distribution of the types of issues varied over time. Thus from 1963 to 1967 economic demands were predominant – 44.2 percent of the 1,676 industrial conflicts were economic demands, followed by 15.2 percent of claims related to collective bargaining and 4.0 percent of solidarity issues, which were relatively rare. From 1967 on, the situation changed – solidarity issues reached 45.4 percent of 7,694 cases, demands related to collective bargaining increased to 20.1 percent, and economic demands dropped to 25.6 percent.[64] Politically oriented demands for free and democratic unions and for the right to strike appeared.

On the business side, changes were more limited and seemed to respond to new labor pressures. Contrary to some interpretations, I see little evidence that business groups played an active role in favor of or against the political transformation in this period and even less evidence of structural alignments for or against change. Certainly there were contacts between opposition leaders and some business leaders who, however, felt that they did not want to compromise their interests by coming into conflict with the state. It was within the interest groups, more specifically, the *sindicatos* structure – the Sindicato Español Universitario (the official student organization), the professional *colegios*,[65] and prominently the Catholic Action organizations – that with liberalization and greater opportunities for democratic participation, the opposition found new arenas. In this respect, the internal transformation of interest groups and associational life in the last years of the Franco regime provided an alternative that compensated for the lack of any opportunity for vocal or organized opposition at the local or national political levels.

The history of this process still remains to be written. There is a wealth of information on the history of the illegal labor movement, the birth and rebirth of trade unions in the last years of the Franco regime, and some useful accounts of the student movement. But unfortunately, we have no equivalent study of the growth and role of the opposition within the professional *colegios*, nor an adequate account of the internal development within the Catholic lay associations, in particular, those close to the working class. The very special status that the Concordate accorded the church-sponsored organizations that limited the direct intervention of the state in their internal affairs, except by exercising pressures on the hierarchy and through the bishops, accounts for the importance that developments in those organizations had for the growth of opposition and the emergence of new generations of anti-regime leaders. The social pluralism that the state and initially the party had tried to control, therefore, played a fundamental role in the process of disintegration of an authoritarian regime, which in this respect had sources of instability not found in totalitarian systems.

Belated attempts to organize the more democratically elected segment in the Cortes by giving 108 seats to the representatives directly elected by the heads of households, and the even more half-hearted attempt to create authorized and controlled "political associations" in the place of real parties, were condemned to total failure.[66] They were, however, an implicit admission that corporative representation – "organic democracy" – could not serve to articulate the cleavages of modern society. There can be little question that the verbal commitments to change made by some regime leaders contributed to a climate of opinion clearly reflected in public opinion surveys of the period in which a large number of Spaniards expressed their preference for democratic representation, direct election of officials and representatives, political parties, and even ideological tendencies parallel to those of other European countries.[67] Pseudo-and semi-freedom of the last years of the regime was the womb in which democracy was born, although the pressure of the more active anti-

regime forces of the illegal opposition, including the terrorist assassi-
nation of Admiral Carrero Blanco and the shock of Franco's death,
would be necessary for the birth of democracy.

Democracy through *reforma* under the threat of *ruptura* and the emergence of pluralistic interest group politics

When Franco died in November 1975 the complex institutional structure he had created was in crisis, but no one knew how a new democratic regime would be instituted. There were those who hoped for a
clear break with the past – the *ruptura* – with a provisional government formed by the opposition, while on the other side there were
those hoping to assure the continuity of the regime in one way or
another under the new monarch. Neither was strong enough, and
under the leadership of King Juan Carlos, particularly after the appointment of Adolfo Suárez as prime minister in June 1976, the complex process of the *reforma* was initiated. The dismantling of the regime from above (specifically by the law for political reform enacted
according to the Franco Constitution, which opened the way to free
elections to what was to be a constituent Cortes) and the slow incorporation of the opposition into the process in 1977, including the
legalization of the Communist party and recognition of trade union
freedom (the phase called *ruptura pactada*), were the steps that led to
democracy.[68]

The change of regime represented a radical discontinuity in the
structure of interest representation and the emergence of a pluralistic,
highly fragmented, politicized, and relatively weak system of organizations, which was still in flux in 1980.

One of the most interesting questions about interest representation
in the post-Franco era is why the unitary structures of the trade
unions, the agricultural organizations, and the employers' federations within *sindicatos* were dismantled and a highly pluralistic and
competitive system of organizations emerged – in many cases closely
linked with political parties, in particular, the Left. Without doubt,
some of the illegal organizations, those controlled by the Communists, such as the Comisiones Obreras, favored the maintenance of
unitary organizations, hoping to control them as the Portuguese
Communists had done with the Intersindical in 1974–5. This desire for
unity, combined very often with a desire for apolitical, that is,
nonparty-linked, organizations, was widespread. One important factor was the slow, piecemeal, and inconclusive way in which the government proceeded to dismantle the official structure, retaining the
administration of its properties in a receivership for future disposal,

and the step-by-step legalization of the illegal trade unions and organizations (more specifically, the initial tolerance for the UGT and the much later recognition of the CCOO and other trade unions of the extreme Left). Another factor that contributed to dismantling the old system was the ideological cleavage between the different organizations, which prevented any concerted effort to take over a single organization. There was no opportunity to use the "internal democratization" to establish a hegemonic control over trade unions and other corporative organizations of the regime, as was largely the case in Portugal. The result has been a system of trade unions and interest groups that are highly fractioned along political lines. The main trade unions recognized since May 1977 are: the Confederación Sindical de Comisiones Obreras (CCOO), linked with the Communist party (PCE); the Unión General de Trabajadores (UGT), linked with the Socialist party (PSOE); the Unión Sindical Obrera (USO); the Confederación de Sindicatos Unitarios de Trabajadores (CSUT), linked with the Partido del Trabajo de España (PTE), and the Sindicato Unitario (SU), linked with the Organización Revolucionaria de Trabajadores (ORT) (after the fusion of the PTE and ORT, these two federations are also in the process of unification); the old syndicalist Confederación Nacional del Trabajo (CNT); the three regional federations: the Solidaridad de Trabajadores Vascos (ELA–STV) (which has split), the weak Solidaritat d'Obrers de Cataluyna (SOC), and the Confederación Canaria de Trabajadores (CCT), linked with Canary Islands nationalism, to which one would have to add the small radical Basque separatist Langille Abertzale Batzrdeak (LAB) (Comisiones Obreras Patriotas); and minor organizations in Galicia.[69] The system that has emerged is full of ambiguities compounded by the ambivalences of the UCD government as the result of the *reforma* process and the fear of political polarization. In the absence of a clear institutional and legal framework, and in the presence of multiple and competing organizations, the government hesitates to recognize these unions as representative and vacillates between allowing all organizations to participate as equals, irrespective of their strength, or giving them representation according to their electoral strength (because membership is unascertainable). The desire for consensus with the parties of the Left, particularly the PSOE, and the fear of pushing the PCE toward radical opposition, permits the organizations linked with them to veto other groups – the "independents" that are labeled "yellow," government supported, or, worse, linked with the Francoist past, even if their seats were obtained through elections. In such a context any decision to incorporate interest groups in peak negotiations easily leads to accusations of favoritism or discrimination.

In spite of competition among unions, they have shown considerable capacity to cooperate, particularly in collective bargaining with employers. The two major organizations, the CCOO and the UGT, have collaborated in a wage and price stabilization policy agreed on by all major parties in the Moncloa Pact of 1977. The Spanish labor movement will not undergo the painful process that led in Italy and France to the withdrawal of the Socialists and the Catholics from the Communist-dominated general confederation of labor and other joint organizations, a process now underway in Portugal. It is debatable if the initial competition will not lead to greater cooperation than the ill feelings created by the resistance to an effort of hegemony within a unitary organization.

Another question that is difficult to answer with the available evidence is why, in spite of considerable support in public opinion, the presence of many active Catholics in the underground, and the role played by Catholic Action organizations in the last years of the Franco regime, no Christian Democratic network of interest groups has emerged. It is significant that many of the leaders emerging from the Catholic organizations, such as the Jesuit-sponsored Vanguardias Obreras, should have opted for the creation of secular and often extreme Left organizations with no reference to Catholic social doctrine nor ties to the Church. The ideological climate after Vatican II; the deep internal divisions within the Church; the desire of the hierarchy to stay out of politics, with all its risks, to neutralize, perhaps, the hostility that identification with the Franco regime in the past aroused; and the organizational and electoral failure of Christian Democratic candidates in the 1977 legislative elections are among the many factors accounting for this development that distinguishes Spain from other Western European countries that have extensive networks or organizations anchored in a Catholic subculture. These developments undoubtedly represent a considerable source of weakness for the Center-Right governing party, the Unión de Centro Democrático (UCD), which is sociologically quite similar to Christian Democratic parties. The weakness of its articulation with interest groups not only of the working class but also of the peasantry, and even with employers organizations, makes it much more difficult to transform the UCD into a mass membership organization. It also diminishes the UCD's potential left-oriented and populist character and accounts to some extent for its electoral weakness compared to similar parties in Western Europe.

The influence of the different Leftist parties and ideological cleavages were responsible for the division of the labor movement, but there is no clear evidence of party influence on the appearance of different employers' associations in the course of 1976–7. Initially, three different organizations of national scope, the Agrupación Empresarial Independiente, the Confederación General Española de Empresarios, and the Confederación Empresarial Española, were founded. In June 1977 they had agreed to constitute the Confederación Española de Organizaciones Empresariales (CEOE), the most important Spanish employers' association. But a conflict between the perceived interests of small and medium enterprises and those of large ones that had already manifested itself under the aegis of the *sindicatos* in the first National Assembly of the Small and Medium Enterprise and the creation of a Junta Intersindical Central de la Pequeña y Mediana Empresa in 1963 has become a major cleavage line and has led to the creation of two national organizations – the Federación Independiente de la Pequeña y Mediana Empresa, in December 1977, and the Confederación de la Pequeña y Mediana Empresa. The latter has been accused of links with Leftist parties. Apparently the Catalan business class most closely identified with the Fomento del Trabajo has been integrated into national organizations, whereas the Basque entrepreneurs, particularly the medium and small ones, are identified with two regional associations and are almost equally divided over whether their association is of the "Basque country" or of Euzkadi, thus reflecting the internal Basque division between more or less nationalist positions.[70]

The heterogeneity of economic and social interests, the variety of crops, the national and regional and even local cleavage lines, and the political ideological divisions have led to a fragmentation of the organizations of the Spanish peasantry. In the April 1978 elections to the Cámaras Agrarias in many municipalities there were only single lists of candidates, whereas in many others there were no candidacies: 2,811 of the 7,713 for which we have information. The Left was able to present candidates in 15 percent of those municipalities, the Socialists in 7 percent, the Center in 19 percent, and the Right in 11 percent. The independents ran in 33 percent of the municipalities and in 22 percent there were only independents. If we look at the competitiveness of the elections we find that in 82 percent, that is, in 6,350 municipalities, there were either no candidacies, only independents running, or in 23 percent of the cases only one list running, whereas in 16 percent there were two lists, and in 3 percent, three lists competing for the vote of the farmers. The level of participation was generally low; only in four of the regions was the turnout over 50 percent in more than half of the municipalities – Old Castile, New Castile, Extremadura, and Aragón – whereas in a number of regions the participation was over 50 percent in less than one-fifth of the municipalities, including highly developed agricultural regions, such as the País Valenciano. Neither the very critical attitudes toward the previous leadership of the Cámaras Agrarias nor the extended and sometimes violent protests of the farmers (occupying the roads with their tractors) led to a massive participation in these first democratic elections.[71]

Otherwise the interest representation system, except for public bodies like the *cámaras* and *colegios*, whose status is anchored in the legal system, is the same or more fragmented than ever. The forced unity under the Franco regime has created an enormous desire for autonomy, and success of the parties in sponsoring affiliated organizations on one side and the desire for independence from parties on the other has led to the multiplication of groups.

Given the available data, the impossibility of checking the membership claims by the different organizations, and insufficient information about dues-paying members of those organizations, it is difficult to determine to what extent they have been able to mobilize their potential constituencies. There are, however, indications of much apathy, considerable delays in collection of dues, and, in the case of agrarian interest representation, a low level of participation in elections to agrarian chambers. Also, there are some indications that the initial surge of interest has waned, which is not surprising in light of other indicators of political apathy, such as the drop in participation in the 1978 constitutional referendum, the legislative elections of 1979, and especially the municipal elections of 1979, as well as the drop in newspaper readership and the apparently very low rate of affiliation to political parties. The explanation of this relatively low participation and involvement, particularly of the less political and ideological sectors of the population, and the reluctance of many who stayed aloof of the Franco regime to participate actively in the new democracy, parties, local government and interest groups, is not easy to explain.

Undoubtedly, the *reforma* rather than the *ruptura* process did not create a vacuum to be filled by an upsurge of mobilization, nor did it allow the opposition to take over and attract those persons into the new system. The fact that many institutions under the UCD remained largely in the hands of the same people as before did not encourage them. In this, Spain was different from Portugal after 1974. Initially, the doubts about how far the change would go and the fear of involution discouraged many, and in the meantime the leadership groups consolidated and did not welcome latecomers.

In a more totalitarian regime like that of Fascist Italy, the affiliation to the Fascist party and organizations had considerable advantages and might have created a predisposition to have a membership card – the *tessera* – of a party when democracy came, perhaps in the expectation of the patronage advantages offered. This had not been the case in Spain under the authoritarian regime, for neither the official party nor many of the sponsored organizations required any participation and had only limited rewards to offer. Finally, the economic weakness of the new organizations means that they offer few services to their members and are forced to charge for those services they offer, such as legal advice, whereas at least for some time the official organizations continued providing some free services.

The trade unions rightly complain that the government has not offered a satisfactory solution to the allocation of the property of the *sindicatos* organization and those that had been confiscated from the pre-war organizations to the new trade unions. The tradition of an automatic checkoff of membership dues to corporative organizations has probably made it more difficult to collect membership dues; therefore it is not surprising that some voices among the unions have demanded that the old *cuota sindical* should be reestablished and redistributed among the unions.

The fact that political reform, the legalization of political parties, the calling of free legislative elections, and the creation of a legal framework for the democratic process took precedence over liberalization and democratization in the field of interest representation, elections for representative bodies of workers and peasants, and calling the parties to negotiate and agree on the Moncloa pacts rather than the employers' and workers' organizations have given a more visible, legitimate, and influential role to the parties in the management of conflicts than they have to the interest groups.[72]

There has been no process parallel to that in Germany after World War II in which the numerically weaker social groups agreed to form powerful organizations of the peasants, the artisans – the Handwork – and the middle classes, thus overcoming the fragmentation along ideological religious and sectoral lines that characterized the German interest group system of the Weimar Republic. Only among employers are there indications that the regional cleavages that were so important in the development of Spanish business interest representation in the first decades of the century have now lost some of their salience.

One interesting consequence of forty years of corporatist ideology has been that no one has attempted to create any national chamber in which economic and professional interests would be represented. Only in the first phase of the transition, when there was an effort to cover up the liquidation of the institutions of the Franco regime and to find some way out of the dissolution of the semicorporatist Cortes, was the idea broached, and in the initial projects of syndical reform such a possibility was discussed. The leader of the Partido Socialista Popular (PSP), Enrique Tierno, in a lecture at the Club Siglo XXI, suggested still a three chamber system, but such proposals did not come up in the constitution-making process, perhaps because it would have further complicated the bicameral system in which the senate was to serve as representation of Spanish regions. At present, there is no body of this type in sight even with advisory functions. The discredit of corporatism had gone so far that even an institution-alization of social corporatism seems unwarranted. In this, 1978 is parallel to 1931.[73]

It is too early to make predictions about the future of interest politics in Spain. Who will turn out stronger in the competition between CCOO and the UGT? Will the unions to the left of the CCOO make gains in the course of an economic crisis in which the two great confederations have to moderate demands for the sake of democratic stability? Will the UCD give support to some type of labor organization? Some articles in the Estatuto del Trabajador – now under discussion – might affect these developments deeply, for example, by undercutting a possible growth of the Confederación General de Cuadros modeled after the Franch Confédération Générale des Cadres. Will there be a more unified and strong organization of farmers that is politically conservative but radical in the defense of the farmers' interests? Is the division in the employers' organizations permanent? Are the parties to continue preempting the place of interest groups in top-level negotiations on wage and price policies, or will they devolve to the nationwide interest groups? How able will the groups be to build up their constituencies and finances without direct or indirect government help?

It remains to be seen if the entry of Spain into the Common Market in the mid-eighties will encourage the growth and strengthening of interest groups. What will be the relationship between the peak as-sociations and their constituent members, and between the national union federations and the plant-level workers' representatives, par-ticularly in view of some tendencies toward direct assembly democ-racy? To what extent will organizations with long-term divergent ideological commitments collaborate pragmatically at the national, sectional, local, or plant level? How will the relation between parties and interest groups, in particular between the PSOE and the UGT, and the PCE and CCOO, develop? It is too early even to speculate on these questions, but Spanish society and democracy will be very dif-ferent depending on the answers.

Conclusion

Our journey through five periods of Spanish history shows some of the difficulties for the articulation of interest politics and organized interest groups in a politically unstable society. The Restauración period shows that (even with considerable freedom) uneven development, the importance of clientelistic politics, radicalization of labor as a consequence of underdevelopment, and the weakness of national integration slowed the development of interest politics as known in other European countries. The dictatorship of Primo de Rivera represented an interesting attempt, and the failure of such an attempt, to incorporate existing groups, even the Socialist trade unions, into a corporativist framework. Spain was by then too far advanced politically and ideologically for an inclusionary corporatist model and the situation did not warrant, nor was the dictator ready for, a repressive exclusionary policy.[74] The regime was not prepared to shift from an incipient "social corporatism" to the "state corporatism" of more self-conscious authoritarian regimes.

The short-lived republic (1931–6), with more open social conflict in a period of economic difficulties, an open support for labor (in the first period), and a competitive party system, led to more lively interest organization, membership, mobilization, and pressure politics, similar to other democracies. However, the intensity of social and ideological conflicts, expressed through the parties and ultimately mobilization for revolution and counterrevolution, overshadowed interest politics.

The authoritarian regime first excluded by force and later limited the articulation of many interests, particularly labor. It failed in building an effective state corporatism as a basis for citizen participation and subordinated (but could not eliminate) real interest representation to those in control of the state, the bureaucracy, and a new political class. The Franco regime clearly fits Stepan's model of "exclusionary" state corporatism, and the "inclusionary" attempts based on Fascist ideological commitments and their populist components were doomed to failure for structural reasons (the level of polarization and previous party and trade-union development, the limited resource capability of the economy before the sixties, and the elite's lack of ideological unity), even when the expansion in the sixties and the growth of the welfare state offered opportunities that were not fully used. The ultimate illegitimacy of an authoritarian regime born in a civil war and the aegis of Fascism, both internally and internationally, forced it to use repressive and exclusionary policies. That illegitimacy in the context of Western Europe, the social and economic changes, and the succession of generations, has led to a crisis situation that transformed many of the existing and newly emerging interest groups into arenas from where the regime can be questioned and the transition to democracy can be initiated. Once repression became too costly and the risks of toleration of political and social pluralism appeared to be lower, Franco's death precipitated a return to a pluralist model. With the advent of freedom to organize, the apparent imposed unity of the corporative structure disintegrated, and a process of intense politization, creation, and reorganization of interest groups was initiated. However, the particular circumstances of the transition, *reforma* rather than *ruptura*, the habits of dependence on the state, the politico-ideological fragmentation, and the dominant role assigned to political parties all have limited (until now) the emergence of a strong system of interest groups capable of assuming the role they are expected to play in a stable democratic polity.

Acknowledgment

This chapter has been made possible by a grant from the German Marshall Fund of the United States, which is gratefully acknowledged.

Notes

1 Economic history has been a growing field and contains many references to our topic. See Jaime Vicens Vives, with the collaboration of J. Nada, *An Economic History of Spain*, trans. F. M. López Morillas (Princeton, N. J.: Princeton University Press, 1969); Nicolás Sánchez Albornoz, *España hace un siglo: una economía dual* (Barcelona: Península, 1968); Gabriel Tortella Casares, *Los orígenes del capitalismo en España. Banca, Industria y Ferrocarriles en el siglo XIX* (Madrid: Tecnos, 1873). In addition, there are regional and sectorial studies for references – see the works cited.

2 This is one of the main themes of Juan J. Linz and Amando de Miguel "Within Nation Differences and Comparisons: The Eight Spains," in *Comparing Nations*, eds. Richard L. Merritt and Stein Rokkan (New Haven: Yale University Press, 1966), pp. 267–319. In 1910 31 percent of the active population in the province of Barcelona was in industry, compared to 12 percent in Madrid, whereas administration and professional activities represented 7 and 15.8 percent, respectively.

3 For the political and social change in the nineteenth century, see Raymond Carr, *Spain 1808–1939* (Oxford: Clarendon, 1966); Miguel Artola, *La burguesía revolucionaria (1808–1869)* (Madrid: Alianza Editorial, 1973); Miguel Martínez Cuadrado, *La burguesía conservadora (1874–1931)* (Madrid: Alianza Editorial, 1973); Miguel Artola, *Antiguo Régimen y revolución liberal* (Barcelona: Ariel, 1978). For an illuminating analysis of social classes in the nineteenth century, see José María Jover, *Política, diplomacia y humanismo popular* (Madrid: Turner, 1976).

4 Juan J. Linz, "Early State-Building and Late Peripheral Nationalisms against the State," in *Building States and Nations: Models, Analyses, and Data across Three Worlds*, eds. S. N. Eisenstadt and S. Rokkan, Vol. II, eds. S. N. Eisenstadt and S. Rokkan (Beverly Hills: Sage Publications, 1973), pp. 32–112.

5 The freedom for industrial and commercial activities was decreed in 1813, and after some setbacks was definitively established in 1836.

6 An example of the recent monographic research by Spanish scholars is Miguel Artola et al., *El latifundio. Propiedad y explotación, ss. XVII–XX* (Madrid: Servicio de Publicaciones Agrarias, Ministerio de Agricultura, 1978). In English, Edward Malefakis,

Agrarian Reform and Peasant Revolution in Spain. Origins of the Civil War (New Haven: Yale University Press, 1970) and "Peasants, Politics, and Civil War in Spain, 1931–1939," *Modern European Social History,* ed. Robert Bezucha (Lexington, Mass.: D. C. Heath, 1972), pp. 192–227, show the diversity of agrarian social and economic structures.

7 Juan J. Linz, *Tradición y modernización en España* (Granada: Universidad de Granada, 1977) calls attention to these diachronic dimensions of nineteenth-century development.

8 On the role of the army, see Stanley G. Payne, *Politics and the Military in Modern Spain* (Stanford: Stanford University Press, 1967); Carolyn Boyd, *Pretorial Politics in Liberal Spain,* (Durham: North Carolina University Press, forthcoming).

9 Juan Pablo Fusi, *Política obrera en el País Vasco, 1880–1923* (Madrid: Turner, 1965) provides several examples such as the Pacto Loma in 1890, p. 93, or the intervention of General Zappino in 1903, p. 241. The military intervention in Catalan social conflicts is well known (see the works of Romero Maura, Cuadrat, Connelly Ullman, Meaker, which we refer to later).

10 See Malefakis, op. cit.; Manuel Tuñón de Lara, *Luchas obreras y campesinas en la Andalucía del siglo XX. Jaén (1917–1920), Sevilla (1930–1932)* (Madrid: Siglo XXI de España, 1978; and the classic work of Juan Díaz del Moral, *Historia de las agitaciones campesinas andaluzas – Córdoba* (Madrid: Revista de Derecho Privado, 1929). See also Manuel Pérez Yruela, *La Conflictividad campesina en la provincia de Córdoba 1931–1936* (Madrid: Servicio de Publicaciones Agrarias, Ministerio de Agricultura, 1979).

11 There are excellent general histories of the Spanish labor movement and an increasing number of regional and local monographs as well as studies of the different union movements. For an overview in English see Stanley G. Payne, *The Spanish Revolution* (New York: Norton, 1970), and Gerald H. Meaker, *The Revolutionary Left in Spain, 1914–1923* (Stanford, Calif.: Stanford University Press, 1974). In Spanish, Manuel Tuñón de Lara, *El movimiento obrero en la historia de España* (Madrid: Taurus, 1972), Xavier Cuadrat, *Socialismo y anarquismo en Cataluña (1899–1911). Los orígenes de la C.N.T.* (Madrid: Ediciones de la Revista de Trabajo, 1976), Amaro del Rosal Díaz, *Historia de la U.G.T. de España (1901–1939),* 2 vols. (Barcelona: Grijalbo, 1977), José Peirats, *La C.N.T. en la revolución española* (Buenos Aires: Ediciones CNT, 1955). As examples of regional monographs we cite: Emili Giralt, Albert Balcells, Josep Termes, *Els moviments socials a Catalunya, País Valencià i les illes* (Barcelona: Lavínia, 1966), Joaquín Romero Maura, *La Rosa de Fuego, Republicanos y anarquistas: La política de los obreros barceloneses entre el desastre colonial y la Semana Trágica, 1899–1909* (Barcelona: Grijalbo, 1975), David Ruiz González, *El movimiento obrero en Asturias: De la industrialización a la Segunda República* (Oviedo: Amigos de Asturias, 1968), and the outstanding work by Juan Pablo Fusi, op. cit. See also Antonio Ma. Calero Amor, *Historia del movimiento obrero en Granada (1909–1923)* (Madrid: Tecnos, 1973). This is not the place to refer to the numerous studies of nineteenth-century labor protest and anarchism.

12 For the legal treatment of labor organizations and strikes, and the parliamentary debates on the issue, see Manuel R. Alarcón Caracuel, *El derecho de Asociación Obrera en España (1839–1900)* (Madrid: Ediciones de la Revista de Trabajo, 1975).

13 On the split in the twentieth century, see the outstanding analysis by Cuadrat, op. cit. and the analysis of ideological tendencies by Meaker, op. cit., who also deals extensively with the socialism–communism split and the forming of the Communist party by dissidents from socialism and anarcho-syndicalism.

14 The UGT had 89,601 members in 1917, 150,000 in 1918, and 240,113 in 1921, a figure that dropped only slightly in the twenties to rise in 1931 to 958,176 and to 1,041,539 in 1932. The Italian Confederazione Generale del Lavoro experienced a similar sudden rise almost a decade earlier: In 1919 it had 249,059 members, which rose to 1,159,062 in that

same year and to 2,150,000 in 1920. The difference at the end of World War I cannot be explained by differences in industrialization, level of education, or even degree of freedom and democratization (universal male suffrage was introduced in Spain in 1890 and in Italy in 1913). One factor was the early capacity of the Italian labor movement to penetrate the countryside, whereas the UGT and the PSOE had to wait until 1931. The electoral weakness of the PSOE is even more striking. In 1918 it presented thirty-seven candidates to the lower house and elected six, thanks to 138,880 votes, whereas the Italian Socialists had 137 deputies (after the split of the PCI), thanks to 1,834,792 votes (32.4 percent). The PSOE at the time had fewer municipal council members than the Italian party deputies! These differences cannot be explained by the larger population of Italy. They cannot be ignored when we compare the early strength of the Confindustria (the Italian business federation) with the late appearance of an equivalent Spanish organization.

15 For the history of the church and its ideological positions see José Manuel Cuenca, *Estudios sobre la iglesia española del XIX* (Madrid: Rialp, 1973) and the same author, *Sociología de una élite de poder de España e Hispanoamérica contemporáneas: la jerarquía eclesiástica (1789–1965)* (Córdoba: Escudero, 1976); José Antonio Portero, *Púlpito e ideología en la España del siglo XIX* (Zaragoza: Libros Pórtico, 1978); Domingo Benavides Gómez, *Democracia y cristianismo en la España de la Restauración, 1875–1931* (Madrid: Editora Nacional, 1978).

16 José R. Montero, *La CEDA. El catolicismo social y político en la II República*, 2 vols. (Madrid: Ediciones Revista de Trabajo, 1977). See vol. II, pp. 541–89 on the relations to interest groups, particularly the Confederación Nacional Católico-Agraria (CNC-A) and the Confederación Española de Sindicatos Obreros (CESO).

17 On Christian trade unionism, see Antonio Elorza, "El sindicalismo católico en la Segunda República. La C.E.S.O. (1935–1938) "in *La utopía anarquista bajo la Segunda República* (Madrid: Ayuso, 1973), pp. 295–350, Juan N. García-Nieto Paris, S. J., *El sindicalismo cristiano en España, Notas sobre su origen y evolución hasta 1936* (Bilbao: Instituto de Estudios Económico-Sociales, Universidad de Deusto, 1960); Juan José Castillo, *El sindicalismo amarillo en España* (Madrid: Edicusa, 1977).

18 Juan José Castillo, *Propietarios muy pobres: Sobre la subordinación política del pequeño campesino (La Confederación Nacional Católico-Agraria 1917–1942)* (Madrid: Servicio de Publicaciones Agrarias, Ministerio de Agricultura, 1979), and Josefina Cuesta Bustillo, *Sindicalismo católico agrario en España (1917–1919)* (Madrid: Narcea, 1978).

19 On the history of Catholic Action, see Zacarías de Vizcarra, *Curso de Acción Católica* (Madrid: Gráficas Benzal, 1953); and for Catholic organizations see *Anuario Social de España 1929*, ed. Juan Soler de Morell, S. J. (Madrid: Fomento Social, 1930).

20 Manuel Pugés, *Cómo triunfó el proteccionismo en España (La formación de la política arancelaria española)* (Barcelona: Juventud, 1931); Guillermo Graell, *Historia del Fomento del Trabajo Nacional* (Barcelona: Imprenta de la Viuda de Luis Tasso, 1911, and A. A. Elorza, "Sobre el proteccionismo Catalán," *Anuario de Historia Económica y Social* (1968): 528–66. On the conditions on which both industrial and agricultural protectionism were introduced (1891) after a period of moderate free trade since 1869, see José Varela Ortega, *Los amigos políticos. Partidos, elecciones y caciquismo en la Restauración (1875–1900)* (Madrid: Alianza Editorial, 1977), pp. 204–215, 242–247. He argues that the conditions were quite different from the iron and rye coalition described by Gerschenkron for Imperial Germany, even though Ramos Oliveira suggested the existence of a similar pact between the Catalan textile interests and the wheat growers. Varela underlines the lack of correspondence between the position of the parties and the interest alignments, particularly before 1888, and the persistent lack of congruence between the economic interests of the district and the position on the tariff issue of its elected representatives. There is a difference between Manuel Tuñón de Lara, *Estudios sobre el siglo XIX español*

(Madrid: Siglo veintiuno de España, 1972), Chap. 4: "La burguesía y la formación del bloque de poder oligárquico 1875–1914", pp. 155–238, and Varela Ortega in the interpretation of the relationship of politicians and interests, the former emphasizing their ties and dependence or identification, Varela noting the lack of congruence and the independent electoral basis created by clientelistic *caciquismo* that made it possible.

21 For a detailed history of the right of association and the debates surrounding the enactments of constitutions and laws and their political background, see Blanca Olias de Lima Gete, *La libertad de asociación en España (1868–1974)* (Madrid: Instituto de Estudios Administrativos, 1977). During the liberal periods of the ninenteenth century a wide range of associations existed, but only with the 1868 revolution was the right of association established without restriction (except leaving the sanction of those associations that were immoral or against the security of the state to the courts). In the seventies the outlawing of the International became a hotly debated issue. The 1887 law came to regulate this right, requiring the submission of documents for the founding of associations and a chance to suspend it with approval by the courts, which interpreted the law restrictively against anarchist and collectivist labor organizations. In 1909 an article of the criminal code, sanctioning the "coalitions of workers," was abrogated and in 1916 the need for negotiation in labor conflicts in public services was recognized. The efforts of the anticlericals to limit the establishment of new religious orders led (1901–1919) to a lively debate, as did the right of the members of the judiciary, the military, and the civil servants to form associations. In 1922 there was an attempt to regulate trade union organization in Barcelona in the context of the bloody social conflicts there. After a restrictive period under the dictatorship, the republic reestablished freedom except for limitations in the Decree for the Defense of the Republic (1931), which not only excluded those threatening the peace but also any defense of the monarchy, whereas trade union freedom was formally recognized for employed persons but not for mixed organizations of employees and employers. In 1934 the youthful violence linked with Fascism led to legislation forbidding anyone under 16 to belong to political associations.

22 On Spanish parties the fundamental work is Miguel Artola, *Partidos y programas políticos. 1808–1936* (Madrid: Aguilar, Tomo I: *Los partidos políticos*, 1974, Tomo II: *Manifiestos y programas políticos*, 1975). In English, see Juan J. Linz, "The Party System of Spain: Past and Future," in *Party Systems and Voter Alignments*, eds. S. M. Lipset and S. Rokkan (New York, Free Press, 1967), pp. 197–282.

23 On Catalan interest groups in addition to Graell, op. cit., see Jaime Vicens y Vives and Montserrat Llorens, *Industrials i polítics del segle XIX* (Barcelona: Teide, 1958), pp. 132–6. For a "study group" founded in 1930, the Unió Catalana d'estudís politics i economico-socials, linked with the Lliga, see the biography of its founder by J. A. Parpal and J. M. Liadó, *Ferrán Valls i Taberner* (Esplugues de Llobregat: Ariel, 1970), pp. 161–74.

24 The best source on the Cámaras, Colegios, and so on, are the collections of legislation such as León Medina and Manuel Marañón, *Leyes Administrativas de España* (Madrid: Reus, 1957); and legal encyclopedias such as *Enciclopedia Jurídica Española* (Barcelona: Francisco Seix, 1911–23), different editions, which include historical essays on those institutions.

25 There is a history of the bureaucracy in the nineteenth century, Carlos Carrasco Canals, *La burocracia en la España del siglo XIX* (Madrid: Instituto de Estudios de Administración Local, 1975), but no monographic history of the growth and structure of the bureaucracy in the twentieth century, particularly the cuerpos. Interesting materials can be found in "Sociología de la Administración Pública española," *Anales de Moral Social y Económica*, Vol. 17 (Madrid: Centro de Estudios Sociales de la Santa Cruz del Valle de los Caídos, 1978), and for the contemporary period see Miguel Beltrán, *La élite burocrática española* (Madrid: Fundación Juan March/Ariel, 1977).

26 *Regeneracionismo* denotes a broad movement of opinion, associations, and institutions inspired by intellectuals in response to the crisis of 1898. Ricardo Macías Picavea, *El problema nacional* (Madrid: Librería de Victoriano Suárez, 1899), goes furthest in the critique of parliamentarism and parties to advocate instead an active role of a wide range of interest groups. Juan José Gil Cremades, *El reformismo español. Krausismo, escuela histórica, neotomismo* (Esplugues de Llobregat: Ariel, 1969), offers a review of these currents of thought. On the leadership of the Unión Nacional and the organizations represented in it, see Tuñón de Lara, *Estudios sobre el siglo XIX español*, op. cit. p. 236. The error of the *regeneracionistas* was that they intended to separate the economy from politics, and intellectual and educational reform from politics. They created "apolitical" interest groups that were largely ineffective in reaching their potential constituencies, and which on account of their political neutrality had to open their doors to the *caciques* they attempted to fight by not linking with the parties or entering the political battle. The politicians could retain the clientelistic bases that elected them and demand the apoliticism of the interest groups.

27 *Caciquismo* since the famous inquiry of Costa has concerned political and social historians. Recently, monographic studies based on archival research have been published: José Varela Ortega, *Los amigos políticos. Partidos, elecciones y caciquismo en la Restauración (1875-1900)* (Madrid: Alianza Editorial, 1977); and Javier Tussell Gómez, *Oligarquía y caciquismo en Andalucía, 1890-1923* (CUPSA, 1977).

28 Isidre Molas, *Lliga Catalana. Un estudi d'estasiologia* (Barcelona: Edicions 62, 1972) is an outstanding monograph not only on the great party of the Catalan bourgeoisie and its organization but also on the regional party system. Chapter 29 deals specifically with the relations between the Lliga and pressure groups (Vol. 2, pp. 221–8).

29 Varela Ortega, op. cit., Chap. 3, pp. 204–15, 242–7.

30 Fusi, op. cit., and Javier de Ybarra, *Política nacional en Vizcaya* (Madrid: Instituto de Estudios Políticos, 1947).

31 Manuel Tuñón de Lara, Antonio Elorza, and Manuel Pérez Ledesma eds., *Prensa y sociedad en España 1820-1936* (Madrid: Edicusa, 1975).

32 Antonio Miguel Bernal and Jacques Labroix, "Aspects de la sociabilité andalouse. Les associations sevillanes (XIX ^{e}-XXe S.)" *Mélanges de la Casa de Velázquez*, Paris, 1975), Chap. XI, pp. 435–507.

33 Juan J. Linz, *Estudio socioeconómico de Andalucía*, Vol. II, *Factores humanos, elites locales y cambio social en la Andalucía rural* (Madrid: Institute de Desarrollo Económico, 1970).

34 There is no comprehensive study of the dictatorship nor scholarly biography of Primo de Rivera. The best monographic study is James H. Rial, "Revolution from Above: Dictatorship in Spain, 1923-1930," unpublished PhD dissertation in history, Northwestern University. An informative propagandistic book is José Pemartín, *Los valores históricos en la Dictadura española* (Madrid: Publicaciones de la Junta de Propaganda Patriótica y Cuidadana, 1929). The basic legal text and constitutional projects can be found in Ramón Sáinz de Varanda, ed. *Colección de Leyes Fundamentales* (Zaragoza: Acribia, 1957), pp. 500–615.

35 On the Asamblea Nacional, see Sáinz de Varanda, op. cit., pp. 536–44, and for biographies, see Publicaciones Patrióticas, *La Asamblea Nacional. Biografías y retratos de los 400 asambleistas y numerosos datos del mayor interés* (Madrid: Publicaciones Patrióticas, 1927).

36 On the relationship between labor and the regime see David Ruiz, *El movimiento obrero en Asturias. De la industrialización a la Segunda República* (Oviedo: Amigos de Asturias, 1968), pp. 183–204. On the other side, the repression of the CNT weakened its purely syndicalist potential and strengthened the anarchist tendencies. See Antonio

Elorza, "El anarcosindicalismo español bajo la Dictadura (1923–1930). La génesis de la Federación Anarquista Ibérica (I)," *Revista de Trabajo* 39–40 (1972): 123–218 and (III) (Nota preliminar), *Revista de Trabajo* 46 (1974): 163–72.

37 Juan Velarde Fuertes, *Política económica de la Dictadura* (Madrid: Guadiana, 1968). Basic information, particularly on the support for different interests can be found in José G. Ceballos Teresí, *Historia Económica, Financiera y Política*, op. cit. Vol. 5 (1922–26) and Vol. 6 (1926–9). The attempts to regulate labor relations are discussed by Eduardo Aunós, *La política social de la Dictadura*, Discurso leído . . . Real Academia de Ciencias Morales y Políticas, Madrid, 1944. See also Simone Comes, *L'Organisation corporative de l'industrie en Espagne* (Paris: Librairie de Jurisprudence Ancienne et Moderne Edouard Duchemin, 1937).

38 The literature on the republic is large and often highly partisan. Among the major works in English are Gabriel Jackson, *The Spanish Republic and the Civil War, 1931–1939* (Princeton, N. J.: Princeton University Press, 1965) and Hugh Thomas, *The Spanish Civil War* (New York: Harper Row, 1977). The most comprehensive and documented work in Spanish is Ricardo de La Cierva, *Historia de la Guerra Civil española, antecedentes: monarquía y república 1898–1936* (Madrid: San Martín, 1969). From a different perspective, see Ramón Tamames, *La república: la era de Franco*, 6th ed. (Madrid: Alianza Editorial, 1977); and Manuel Tuñón de Lara, *La II República*, 2 vols. (Madrid: Siglo XXI, 1972). Manuel Ramírez, *Las reformas de la II República* (Madrid: Tucar, 1977); the volume edited by him *Estudios sobre la II República española* (Madrid: Tecnos, 1975); and *Los grupos de presión en la Segunda República española* (Madrid: Tecnos, 1969) are major contributions of political science that are most directly relevant to our topic. Santiago Varela, *Partidos y parlamento en la II República española* (Madrid: Fundación Juan March/ Ariel, 1978) contains, in addition to an analysis of the party system and the legislature, studies of the religious and agrarian questions with insights into the role of interest groups. On the party system see also Artola, 1975, Linz, 1969, Payne, op. cit. and Malefakis, op. cit. Juan J. Linz, "From Great Hopes to Civil War: The Breakdown of Democracy in Spain," in *The Breakdown of Democratic Regimes*, eds. J. J. Linz and Alfred Stepan (Baltimore: The Johns Hopkins University Press, 1978), pp. 142–215 has further bibliographic references.

39 José G. Ceballos Teresí, *Historia económica . . .* , op. cit., Vol. 8 deals extensively with economic policies, the response of interest groups to them in the year 1931, and the representation of those groups in an *asamblea económica nacional* (pp. 499–502) and the founding of the Unión Nacional Económica in December 1931, the first nationwide employers federation.

40 In addition to public bodies to represent agrarian interest, such as the Cámaras Agrarias (regulated by a law of 1890), the Comunidades de Labradores, with rural police powers (created by law in 1898), there were numerous private groups: the Asociación de Agricultores de España (founded 1912 with 226 associations and 668,333 members in 1934); the Asociación General de Ganaderos (1854) of the cattle growers (which traces its origins to the Mesta, the great organization of sheep growers founded in the Middle Ages); specialized groups of olive, orange, sugar beet and wine growers as well as exporters; in addition to the Instituto Agrícola Catalán de San Isidro. In 1933, as a result of the strength acquired by the Federación de Trabajadores de la Tierra (of the UGT) and the policies of the Socialist labor ministry, an agrarian employers organization, Confederación Española Patronal Agrícola, was founded. We have already mentioned the Confederación Nacional Católico-Agraria (CNC-A, also abbreviated as CONCA). The landowners were affiliated with the Agrupación de Propietarios de Fincas Rústicas. These different organizations intervene in the debate on the agrarian reform and attempt through their ties with legislators to influence policy. In September

1934 they constituted a coordinating committee: Comité de Enlace de Entidades Agropecuarias de España; previously they had joined the Unión Nacional Económica. Unfortunately, with the exception of J. J. Castillo, *Propietarios muy pobres*, op. cit. on the CNC-A and a history of interest group politics of the cork growers and industry (R. Medir Jofra, *Historia del gremio corchero*, Madrid: Alhambra, 1953), we have no adequate monographs on these groups, some of which were very effective.

41 On the Unión de Rabassaires and the Institut Agrícola Català de Sant Isidre of the landowners, respectively linked with the Esquerra and the Lliga, whose actions follow a pattern much closer to the European model of relationships among interest groups, parties, public opinion, parliament, see Albert Balcells, *El problema agrari a Catalunya (1890–1936). La qüestió rabassaire* (Barcelona: Nova Terra, 1968) and *Crisis económica y agitación social en Cataluña (1930–1936)* (Esplugues de Llobregat, Barcelona: Ariel, 1971); Jesús Pabón, *Cambó. Parte segunda: 1930–1947* (Barcelona: Alpha, 1969), pp. 339–60; and the memoirs of the lawyer who argued the case before the constitutional court, Amadeu Hurtado, *Quaranta anys d'advocat: Historia del meu temps* (Esplugues de Llobregat, Barcelona: Ariel, 1967), Chap. 10, pp. 256–98.

42 See Antonio Elorza, *Ideologías del nacionalismo vasco, 1876–1937* (San Sebastián: L. Haranburu, 1978), pp. 201–32.

43 Manuel Ramírez Jiménez, *Los grupos de presión en la Segunda República Española* (Madrid: Tecnos, 1969) studies the whole range of interest groups, their relation to the parties and elites, and their response to the reform policies of the regime. See also Jiménez's essay, "La agregación de intereses en la II República: partidos y grupos," in *Estudios sobre la II República Española*, ed. Manuel Ramírez Jiménez, (Madrid: Tecnos, 1975), pp. 27–46. An invaluable mine of information is Mariano González-Rothvoss ed., *Anuario español de política social, 1934–1935* (Madrid: Rivadeneyra, 1934), see Chapter 4, pp. 107–11 for a list of groups. This work contains data on their representation on corporative bodies, legal texts, bibliographic references to official publications, the composition of the *jurados mixtos* (worker and employer arbitration committees) including names, and transcribes the *bases de trabajo* (collective agreements), and so on. Any social historian would do well using this source. Leandro Benavides, *La política económica en la II República* (Madrid: Guadiana, 1972) describes the impact of the depression and the pressure group activities.

44 José Peirats, op. cit., and Antonio Elorza, "La utopía anarquista...," op. cit.

45 A good indicator of the fragmentation and politicization of the society can be found in the youth and student organizations, see Ramón Casteras Archidona, *Diccionario de organizaciones políticas juveniles durante la Segunda República* (La Laguna: Departamento de Historia Contemporánea, 1974).

46 J. J. Linz, "From Great Hopes...," op. cit.

47 The author has attempted to define the distinctive characteristics of the regime in "An Authoritarian Regime: The Case of Spain," in *Mass Politics. Studies in Political Sociology*, eds. Erik Allardt and Stein Rokkan, (New York; Free Press, 1979), pp. 251–83, 374–81. The more totalitarian tendencies in the early days of the regime, at the time of the Axis hegemony (but also the countervailing tendencies) are discussed in my essay "From Falange to Movimiento-Organización: The Spanish Single Party and the Franco Regime, 1936–1968" in *Authoritarian Politics in Modern Societies. The Dynamics of Established One Party Systems*, eds. Samuel P. Huntington and Clement H. Moore, (New York: Basic Books, 1970), pp. 128–201, which also discusses in detail the unviable attempts at liberalization and democratization in the sixties, including references to the literature on the *sindicatos* organization. The characterization of this period as an authoritarian regime has stimulated a discussion reflected in the contributions of Martínez Alier; Oltra and De Miguel; Sevilla Guzmán, Giner, and Pérez Yruela; and Borja

in a special issue of *Papers* (El régimen franquista), 8 (Barcelona: Península, 1978), which also includes a bibliography. For a review of the debate, see José Félix Tezanos, "Notas para una interpretación sociológica del franquismo," *Sistema* 23 (1978): 47–103. See also Guy Hermet, "Dictature bourgeoise et modernisation conservatrice. Problèmes methodologiques de l'analyse des situations authoritaires," *Revue Française de Science Politique* 6 (1975): 1029–61; *La Politique dans l'Espagne franquiste* (Paris: A. Colin, 1971); and *L'Espagne de Franco* (Paris: A. Colin, 1974). Klaus von Beyme, *Vom Faschismus zur Entwicklungsdiktatur Machtelite und Opposition in Spanien* (München: Piper, 1971). Kenneth Medhurst, *Government in Spain: The Executive at Work* (Oxford: Pergamon Press, 1973).

48 On the elite see Amando De Miguel, *Sociología del franquismo. Análisis ideológico de los Ministros del Régimen* (Barcelona: Euros, 1975) and Carles Viver Pi-Sunyer, *El personal político de Franco (1936–1945)* (Barcelona: Vicens Vives, 1978). DATA S. A., "Quién es quién en las Cortes," *Cuadernos para el Diálogo, Suplementos* 7 (1969). Juan J. Linz, "Continuidad y discontinuidad en la élite política española. De la Restauración al Régimen actual," in *Libro Homenaje al Prof. Carlos Ollero* (Madrid: Gráficas Carlavilla, 1973) pp. 362–423.

49 For the early period of the sindicatos the most revealing source is Antonio Bouthelier, *Legislación sindical española* (Madrid: Instituto de Estudios Políticos, 1945), 2 vols. For an account of the process of *Gleichschaltung*, of even a conservative Catholic organization, see J. J. Castillo, *Propietarios . . .* , op. cit., pp. 393–444.

50 On business interest groups: institutions like Cámaras de Comercio, Industria y Navegación, and the Sindicatos; old and new private organizations around 1960, their effectiveness, and the attitudes of businessmen toward them and participation in them, see Juan J. Linz and Amando de Miguel, *Los empresarios ante el poder público* (Madrid: Instituto de Estudios Políticos, 1966), based on interviews with a sample of entrepreneurs (overrepresenting the larger ones). The study includes a bibliography of articles resulting from that research.

51 This is one of the findings of our research. In addition, it should be stressed that no analysis of the articulation of interest in Spain can ignore the monopolistic elements in the economy ranging from the legally established monopolies to those in which the control and/or ownership by oligopolistic groups combined with tariff protection and legal difficulties for entry of new firms assured the domination of the market. The economic power concentration in cases like electricity, cement, and paper, was reinforced by joint marketing and lobbying private groups. The role of the banks, particularly industrial investment banks, in the initiation and control of many key enterprises through interlocking directorates is a highly polemic question and more evidence is needed on the practices followed and their consequences. Undoubtedly, this pattern of industrial organization assured many of the functions that otherwise would have fallen on formally organized and broader organized groups. See Ramón Tamames, *La lucha contra los monopolios* (Madrid: Tecnos, 1961); Fermín de la Sierra, *La concentración económica en las industrias básicas españolas* (Madrid: 1953); Carlos Muñoz Linares, *El monopolio de la industria eléctrica*, (Madrid: Aguilar, 1954); Delegación Nacional de Provincias de FET y de las JONS, *Notas sobre la política económica española* (Madrid: Publicaciones de la Delegación . . . , 1954) contains essays by leading economists on monopolistic tendencies; Juan Muñoz, *El poder de la banca en España* (Algorta: Zero, 1969).

52 On the *sindicatos* structure at the height of organizational expansion and influence, and the attempts to transform them, see Carlos Iglesias Selgas, *Los sindicatos en España* (Madrid: Ediciones del Movimiento, 1965) and *Comentarios a la Ley Sindical* (Madrid: Cabal, 1971), two works by one of the *sindicatos* leaders.

53 On the economic policy, see Manuel Jesús González, *La economía política del franquismo (1940-1970). Dirigismo, mercado y planificación* (Madrid: Tecnos, 1979) and Charles W. Anderson, *The Political Economy of Modern Spain. Policy-Making in an Authoritarian System* (Madison: University of Wisconsin Press, 1970).

54 For an excellent discussion of labor relations since 1958, see Jon Amsden, *Collective Bargaining and Class Conflict in Spain* (London: Weidenfeld and Nicolson, 1972) and Fred Witney, *Labour Policy and Practices in Spain* (New York: Praeger, 1965). See also International Labour Organization, (ILO), *Report of the Study Group to Examine the Labour and Trade Union Situation in Spain* (Geneva, 1969).

On the attitude of businessmen toward labor regulation versus collective bargaining see Juan J. Linz and Amando de Miguel, "El empresario ante los problemas laborales," *Revista de Política Social* 60 (1963): 5-107 and "La representación sindical vista por los empresarios," *Fomento Social* 78 (1965): 115-147 for their opinions on the representatives of the workers in the enterprise.

55 J. J. Linz and A. de Miguel, *Los empresarios . . .* , op. cit., Chap. 6 deals extensively with formal and informal leadership in the industrial community, noting the disjunction between officeholding in formal organizations, or public office, and informal leadership. Both were correlated with size but informal leadership, combined or not with formal positions, was found more often in the largest enterprises. Leadership was related to the awareness of policies, contact with interest groups, perception of their effectiveness and active defense of interests. Informal leadership appeared more related to efficacy than to officeholding.

56 Pedro Schwartz and Manuel-Jesús González, *Una historia del Instituto Nacional de Industria (1941-1976)* (Madrid: Tecnos, 1978).

57 Corporatism in Ibero-American societies has recently led to a lively polemic, particularly between Philippe Schmitter and Howard J. Wiarda. See P. Schmitter, "Still the Century of Corporatism?" in *The New Corporatism: Social Political Structures in the Iberian World,* eds. F. B. Pike and T. Strich (Notre Dame, Ind.: Notre Dame University Press, 1974) and Schmitter, *Corporatism and Public Policy in Authoritarian Portugal* (Beverly Hills: Sage, 1975); H. J. Wiarda, "Corporatism and Development in the Iberic-Latin World: Persistent Strains and New Variations," in eds. F. B. Pike and T. Strich, op. cit., pp. 3-33; F. B. Pike, "The New Corporatism in Franco's Spain and Some Latin American Perspectives" in the same work, pp. 171-210. For a balanced view see Alfred Stepan, *The State and Society. Peru in Comparative Perspective* (Princeton, N. J.: Princeton University Press, 1978), Chap. 2, pp. 46-72. On the Cortes in English with bibliographic references to the Spanish literature, see Juan J. Linz, "Legislatures in Organic Statist-Authoritorian Regimes - The Case of Spain" in *Legislatures in Development: Dynamics of Change in New and Old States,* eds. Joel Smith and Lloyd D. Musolf (Durham, N.C.: Duke University Press, 1979), pp. 88-124.

58 On the ACN de P, A. Saez Alba, *La Asociación Católica Nacional de Propagandistas y el caso del Correo de Andalucía* (Paris: Ruedo Ibérico, 1974); José R. Montero, "El Boletín de la Asociación Católica Nacional de Propagandistas (1939-1945)," in *Las fuentes ideológicas de un régimen, (España 1939-1945),* eds. Manuel Ramírez et al. (Zaragoza: Pórtico, 1978). For its ideology see Fernando Martín-Sánchez Juliá, *Ideas claras, Reflexiones de un español actual* (Madrid: Gráficas Nebrija, 1959). The author was one of the grey eminences of the regime. On the Opus Dei see Daniel Artigues, *El Opus Dei en España, 1928-1962* (Paris: Rudeo Ibérica, 1971) and Jesús Ynfante, *La prodigiosa aventura del Opus Dei, Génesis y desarrollo de la Santa Mafia* (Paris: Ruedo Ibérico, 1970) from a critical perspective. From the Opus point of view see Francisco Martineli, ed. *Cristianos corrientes, textos sobre el Opus Dei* (Madrid: Rialp, 1970).

59 On the growing conflict between church and state see Norman Cooper, "The

Church from Crusade to Christianity," in *Spain in Crisis. The Evolution and Decline of the Franco Régime*, ed. Paul Preston (Hassocks; Sussex: Harvester, 1976), pp. 48–81, and Cooper, *Catholicism and the Franco Regime* (Contemporary European Studies, 3) (Beverly Hills: Sage, 1975), and Guy Hermet "Les fonctions politiques des organisations religieuses dans les régimes à pluralisme limité," in *Revue Française de Science Politique* 23 (1973): 439–72.

60 Juan J. Linz, "Opposition to and under an Authoritarian Regime: The Case of Spain," in *Regimes and Oppositions*, ed. Robert A. Dahl (New Haven: Yale University Press, 1973), pp. 171–259 and bibliography cited.

61 For a detailed account of the debates on the liberalization of the *Movimiento*, see Linz, "From Falange to Movimiento-Organización . . . ," op. cit.

62 J. J. Linz, "La realidad asociativa de los españoles" in *Sociología española de los años setenta*, ed. Confederación Española de Cajas de Ahorros (Madrid: Confederación Española de Cajas de Ahorros, 1971), pp. 307–48, reports on the number of voluntary associations of all kinds in the sixties and the growth in numbers. A sociological analysis shows the relationship to economic development and other social correlates such as regional cultural patterns. Also Manuel Bonachela Mesas, *Para una crítica de las asociaciones voluntarias en Ciencia Política*, unpublished PhD thesis, Universidad de Granada, 1975.

63 The best source on the emergence and development of the illegal labor movement and the present trade unions is Fernando Almendros Morcillo, E. Jiménez-Asenjo, F. Pérez Amorós, and E. Rojo Torrecilla, *El sindicalismo de clase en España (1939–1977)* (Barcelona: Península, 1978). See also Marco Calamai, *Storia del movimento operaio spagnolo dal 1960 al 1975* (Bari: De Donato, 1975) with an introduction by Nicolás Sartorius of the CCOO. The publisher Advance/Mañana of Barcelona published in 1976 the following short volumes by leaders of the unions: Julián Ariza, *Comisiones Obreras;* José Maria Zufiaur, *Unión Sindical Obrera;* Colective Sindicalista de la UGT, *Unión General de Trabajadores.* On labor conflict in this period, see José Félix Tezanos, "Los conflictos laborales en España," *Revista Española de la Opinión Pública* 38 (1974): 93–110. Ministerio de Trabajo, *Informe sobre conflictos colectivos de trabajo, 1971* (Madrid: Ministerio de Trabajo, 1973) is for 1972 and 1973.

64 See the outstanding sociological analysis by José Maravall, *Dictatorship and Political Dissent. Workers and Students in Franco's Spain* (London: Tavistock, 1978), pp. 37–8, based on interviews with militants, and *El desarrollo económico y la clase obrera* (Barcelona: Ariel, 1970).

On the Communist line and their conception of the Comisiones Obreras as a new type of labor movement, their crisis, and the debates about their transformation into a trade union, see Eusebio Mujal-León, *Spanish Communism and the Post-Franco Era*, unpublished PhD dissertation in Political Science, MIT, 1979.

65 A survey showing the attitude of professionals about the political role to be played by their colegio is Jaime Martín Moreno and Amando De Miguel, *Los arquitectos en España. Estudio sociológico de la profesión* (Madrid: Hermandad Nacional de Previsión Social de Arquitectos Superiores 1976), pp. 80–95. On the changing position of the professionals and their colegios, see Daniel Lacalle, *Profesionales en el Estado Español. Situaciones objetivas y formas de organización* (Madrid: Ediciones de la Torre, 1976). For references to the sociological literature on the professions and their politics, see José Félix Tezanos, *Estructura de clases y conflictos de poder en la España postfranquista* (Madrid: Edicusa, 1978), Chap. 10, pp. 333–51.

66 José Amodia. "El asociacionismo político en España: aborto inevitable," *Iberian Studies* III, (1) (1974): 9–15.

67 In addition to some of the sources already cited, see Linz, "Opposition in and

under an Authoritarian Regime . . . ," op. cit., with bibliographic references not repeated here, and Xavier Tusell, *La oposición democrática al franquismo, 1939–1962* (Barcelona: Planeta, 1977). On the changed climate of opinion that made possible the greater participation in and politization of a wide range of organizations and that in part was a result of it, see Antonio López Pina and Eduardo L. Aranguren, *La cultura política de la España de Franco* (Madrid: Taurus, 1976); Rafael López Pintor and Ricardo Buceta, *Los españoles de los años 70, una visión sociológica* (Madrid: Tecnos, 1975); and the chapter by M. Gómez-Reino, F. A. Orizo and D. Vila, and DATA, "Sociología política" in Fundación FOESSA, *Estudios sociológicos sobre la situación social de España 1975* (Madrid: Euramérica, 1976), pp. 1145–319.

68 The transition to democracy is still too near for a scholarly study. There are, however, important contributions to it: Jorge de Esteban and Luis López Guerra, *De la Dictadura a la Democracia (Diario político de un período constituyente)* (Madrid: Sección de Publicaciones, Facultad de Derecho, Universidad Complutense); Pablo Lucas Verdú, *La Octava Ley Fundamental. Crítica jurídico-política de la Reforma Suárez* (Madrid: Tecnos, 1976) with forward by Enrique Tierno; Lothas Maier, *Spaniens Weg zur Demokratie* (Meisenheim am Glan: Anton Hain, 1977); and the collection of papers in the volume edited by Giuseppe de Vergottini, *Una costituzione democratica per la Spagna* (Milano: Franco Angeli, 1978); Juan J. Linz, "Spain and Portugal: Critical Choices," in *Western Europe: The Trials of Partnership*, ed. David S. Landes, (Lexington, Mass.: Lexington Books, 1977), pp. 237–96; two overall surveys are Raymond Carr and Juan Pablo Fusi, *Spain: Dictatorship to Democracy* (London: George Allen & Unwin, 1979) and John F. Coverdale, *The Political Transformation of Spain after Franco* (New York; Praeger, 1979). Since the constitution of 1978 represents the end of the transition and the policy of consensus as well as the basic framework for future interest policies, the reader is referred to a commentary by a professor and UCD M. P., Oscar Alzaga, *La Constitución española de 1978* (Madrid: Foro, 1978).

69 In January–March 1978 elections to the Comités de Empresa gave 35.8 percent of the seats to CCOO, 22.7 percent to UGT (even when the estimates range from 38 to 44 percent for CCOO and 27 to 31 percent for UGT, once those with no information on affiliation are allocated). The reporting of the returns presents many difficulties for a sociological analysis. See Robert Fishman, "An Analysis of the 1978 Trade Union Elections," (Unpublished paper, 1979), and J. M. Maravall, "The Socialist Alternative. The Politics and the Electoral Support of the PSOE," in Howard Penniman, *Spain at the Polls* (Washington: American Enterprise Institute, forthcoming). For the correlations between trade-union vote and party vote (at the provincial level) see Juan J. Linz, "Il sistema partitico spagnolo," in *Rivista Italiana di Scienza Politica* 3 (1978) 364–414. On the political attitudes of workers, employees, and technicians and their response to the Pactos de la Moncloa, see Víctor M. Pérez Díaz, "Orientaciones políticas de los obreros españoles hoy," *Sistema* 29–30 (May 1979); 159–79. One of the great discontinuities with the past in the trade-union field is the weakness of the CNT. A special issue of *Cuadernos de Ruedo Ibérico: CNT: Ser o no ser. La crisis de 1976–1979* (Paris, 1979) contains interesting essays on the recent history of this once powerful trade-union federation.

70 On the new organizations of business, farmers, professionals, and so on we could refer the reader only to their publications (few) and newspapers and magazine articles. A paper presented by Roberto Martínez at the International Institute of Management, Workshop on Employers Associations as Organizations (Berlin, 1979), "The Structure and Operations of Employers Associations in Spain," is a useful account.

71 Unpublished report by DATA, Madrid.

72 On the party system see Linz, "Il sistema partitico spanolo," op. cit. Francisco Alvira et al., *Partidos políticos e ideologías* (Madrid: Centro de Investigaciones

Sociológicas, 1978); and Raúl Morodo et al., *Los partidos políticos en España* (Barcelona: Labor, 1979).

73 The 1931 constitution makers coming also after a period of state corporatism, in spite of the influence on that fundamental code of the Weimar experience, did not incorporate an institution such as the Reichswirtschaftsrat, nor did the ideas debated among German Socialists in the early twenties find an echo. Only two PSOE leaders and intellectuals, Julián Besteiro, reflecting Krausists and Fabian thought, and Fernando de los Ríos advocated an "industrial parliament," but the party and the constituents rejected the idea. See Mariano García Canales, *La teoría de la representación en la España del siglo XX (De la crisis de la Restauración a 1936)* (Murcia: Publicaciones del Departamento de Derecho Político, 1977), pp. 249–66. Chapter 2 is also an excellent exposition of the corporatist ideas and plans of the Primo de Rivera period, pp. 115–68.

74 We use these terms in the sense of Alfred Stepan, *The State and Society,* op. cit., Chap. 3., pp. 73–113.

Index

417